Comm
PERSONAL

Ralph Langer's novel, *Personal Verdict,* is an absorbing tale set in the days of the Civil Rights Movement. The work is a first novel for Langer, a longtime journalist and witness to the milieu he recreates. Like the best journalists, he's also a good storyteller—a writer who peoples his drama with credible and convincing characters and events that engage the reader's heart and mind.

--Paula LaRocque, author of the acclaimed *Book on Writing: The Ultimate Guide to Writing Well* and a debut novel, *Chalk Line,* to be published by Marion Street Mysteries in September 2011.

***

Personal Verdict is great story-telling. It's about justice and it will be with you long after you've wrestled with the ending.

--Joann Byrd, retired newspaper editor, ex-Washington Post Ombudsman and author of *Calamity.*

***

Set during one of the pivotal times in this country's battle for civil rights, *Personal Verdict* is the compelling story of one idealistic journalist who confronts racism, hatred and his own concept of justice. The plot moves quickly, with a mystery unfolding that is brutal and believable.

--Nancy Erickson, recovering newspaper editor and acclaimed cook.

***

Ralph Langer's *Personal Verdict* recounts the story of how the education of a young college student who grew up in the rural North moves from a Michigan campus to a tangle of mysterious and dangerous lessons in the rural South. The work is a thrilling civil rights odyssey.

--Paul R. LaRocque, writer, editor, and author of *Heads You Win* and *The Concise Guide to Copy Editing.*

Personal Verdict

A Civil Rights Novel

For Barry

Ralph Langer

Ralph Langer

authorHOUSE®

AuthorHouse™
1663 Liberty Drive
Bloomington, IN 47403
www.authorhouse.com
Phone: 1-800-839-8640

This is a work of fiction. Characters, places, organizations, businesses and incidents depicted are from the author's imagination and any similarities to actual persons or events is entirely coincidental.

© 2011 Ralph Langer. All rights reserved.

No part of this book may be reproduced, stored in a retrieval system, or transmitted by any means without the written permission of the author.

First published by AuthorHouse 5/9/2011

ISBN: 978-1-4567-6696-2 (sc)
ISBN: 978-1-4567-6694-8 (hc)
ISBN: 978-1-4567-6695-5 (e)

Library of Congress Control Number: 2011907445

Printed in the United States of America

Any people depicted in stock imagery provided by Thinkstock are models, and such images are being used for illustrative purposes only.
Certain stock imagery © Thinkstock.

This book is printed on acid-free paper.

Because of the dynamic nature of the Internet, any web addresses or links contained in this book may have changed since publication and may no longer be valid. The views expressed in this work are solely those of the author and do not necessarily reflect the views of the publisher, and the publisher hereby disclaims any responsibility for them.

1. *Civil rights, Civil Rights Movement*
2. *Michigan, University of Michigan, Ann Arbor, Michigan'*
3. *Mississippi, Jackson, Mississippi, Vicksburg, Mississippi, Meridian, Mississippi*
4. *Alabama, Birmingham, Alabama*
5. *Rosa Parks, bus boycott*
6. *Emmett Till*

In Loving Memory of Terri Beth Langer Abbey

Acknowledgments

I'm grateful to friends and family members who read various versions of this book and provided helpful guidance and support.

In particular, Joann Byrd, Paula and Paul LaRocque, and Nancy Erickson, all offered broad insights and detailed comments that were invaluable.

I'm also grateful to Gail and Don Chapman, John H. Davidson, Judy Stratton, Barbara Pogue, Jeanne Metzger, Garrett Abbey, Ann Johnston and Phil Langer.

And most of all, I'm grateful to my wife, Kathy, for continued support during the writing process, and for repeated readings and significant observations and suggestions that greatly improved the final result.

Any errors are entirely my responsibility.

PROLOGUE

Two middle-aged white men held the Negro teenager, wrenching his arms behind his back as if to rip them from his body. A white youth's fist deformed the right cheek of the helpless captive, pain and shock starkly visible on the black youth's face. Three blurry white faces in the background of the black-and-white newspaper photo seared 12-year-old Jeff Martindale's consciousness; vicious hatred distorting the faces, eyes squinting, screaming mouths gaping.

Several weeks later, racial violence erupted again as six teenagers invaded a Virginia restaurant. A television camera captured the drama as two black youths, two white girls and two black girls, sat at the lunch counter. The tallest black girl asked a thin-faced waitress for a menu. Without looking up from her order pad clutched tightly in both hands, she said, "I can't. Y'all have to leave."

"We just want lunch," a black youth said.

"I can't serve you. Y'all gotta leave. We don't serve nigras," still not looking up, staring at the back of the pad where the words she spoke had been written for her.

"I'm white," one of the girls said. "I want six sandwiches."

The waitress momentarily looked confused then said, "We don't serve mixed groups."

The six sat, staring straight ahead, playing their roles while the waitress played hers. The young men wore suits and ties, the girls dressed as if for church. They joined hands and bowed heads in barely audible prayer.

A mob ranging from young white men to housewives gathered outside, only a few feet through the window from the praying young people. Yells penetrated the restaurant, but the bowed heads did not flinch. The mob screamed taunts at 25 or 30 blacks, adults and children, watching from across the street.

"Come heah and watch your nigger friends starve to death," one white teenager shouted above the din, thumbing over his shoulder to the six unfed young people, stoically waiting for a meal they all knew was impossible on this day.

"Hey niggers, hey niggers, hey niggers" and the two groups suddenly rushed into the street, yelling and shouting, whites waving steel pipes and baseball bats that materialized from nowhere. Images wobbled as the cameraman dashed from the restaurant into the street chaos; people scattering in all directions, shouts without words.

The camera focused on a black youth squared off with a white boy of about the same age in a parody of an old-time boxing match, fists up guarding faces--one black, one white--each with one foot forward, head bobbing. Someone in the crowd threw a heavy rock, striking the black teen's forehead, dropping him to the concrete as if he'd been shot. The other youth kicked the fallen boy precisely in the groin. And then in the head, before walking away as if he'd merely punted a discarded can from the sidewalk.

CHAPTER ONE

A geology text slammed on the desk startling Don, slumped on the easy chair, legs extended with feet resting on the adjacent bed, a blue calculus book on his lap.

"Sorry," Jeff said, rising from his chair. "If I read one more page explaining silt deposit patterns in rivers I may need hospitalization."

"You scare me like that again and you'll definitely need hospitalization," Don said.

"Let's get outta here," Jeff said, glancing at his watch. "7:35 on a Friday night and we deserve a break."

"Movie?" Don asked, stubbing out his cigarette and standing, tucking his shirt into his chinos. "Ol' German for pickles and a Reuben?"

"A guy in my soc class mentioned a party over on Frost. Wanna wander by? If it's too awful we can move to the Old German or the Pretzel Bell."

"Saddle up."

It was one of many casual, ad-hoc evening gatherings in neighborhoods near the University of Michigan's sprawling campus; places to be instead of writing papers, or exploring lonely, depressingly quiet library stacks or slogging through piles of assigned reading.

Jeff and Don took the three steps to the porch of a large, dark-gray house, every breath visible in Ann Arbor's early March cold, a light snow dusting sidewalks. Don knocked. They toted matching grocery bags, each holding a six-pack of "Fire-Brewed Stroh's."

"Let's compare notes in a half-hour to see if we're staying," Jeff said.

"If some cute little thing takes an interest in my romantic well-being, I'll see you when I see you," Don said with a slight smirk.

"Yeah, that may happen sometime…in your dreams."

"I'm always optimistic."

The door opened. "Hi, I'm Mark. Come in."

Neither Jeff nor Don knew Mark but that wasn't unusual or important.

The lighting was dim, the air smoky, the Brubeck soft. Jeff headed for the kitchen visible down the hall. He glanced left through a wide, arched opening where voices drifted from a nearly dark living room. He sensed Don wasn't behind him. Glancing over his shoulder he saw Don's right arm braced against the wall as he leaned into a short, dark-haired girl in beige slacks and a blue sweater.

Jeff edged through the crowded kitchen to the refrigerator, finding it crammed with assorted beer bottles. He pried the cap from a Stroh's and the bottle sighed with relief, the yeasty odor teasing his nose as the beer bathed his tongue. He used a long swallow to survey people in the jammed room and seeing no familiar faces, turned to the small opening, a second route into the living room illuminated only by light spilling through the two entrances and a dim table lamp in the back. He leaned against the door-less frame and took another long swallow, waiting for his eyes to adjust to the gloom. Unidentifiable objects gradually became people covering the floor, two sofas and all four chairs, three holding two forms each. He saw faces without features, most aimed at a large, dark figure to his right, who was like a boulder in the middle of a river creating a vee of current, always pointing upstream toward the large, dark rock.

He eased into the room, pressing his back against the wall and sliding to the floor. Another sip and he could see better, but with few colors or details, mostly blacks and grays.

The Rock wore dark pants and a sweater that looked as if someone had left football shoulder pads in it. He sat on the floor, back propped against an upholstered chair that held an attractive girl with long dark hair. She slumped sideways in the chair, back against one soft arm, legs over the other, feet dangling between the chair and a sofa.

"Are you really self-sufficient?" the Rock was asking, his tone gentle while tossing a question to the room. "Are you capable of understanding your life, handling your problems by yourself? Can you help me with mine? What are we doing on this planet anyway?"

Looks older. Must be a professor firing questions like that. He's black.

The man was looking at and challenging someone to Jeff's left but his voice remained soft, though the words were pointed and direct, his eyes sweeping the room as if he expected everyone to answer. No one did.

"I think," he added, filling the silence, "everyone has some kind of religious belief even if he or she doesn't consciously know it."

He paused, apparently hoping again for an answer but getting a very long half-minute of silence.

"I don't," finally came from a barely visible girl on the far sofa, staring at the Rock.

"Why not?" he asked, voice even softer now.

"I just don't," she said.

"Well, he said, "Are we nothing but a handful of random seeds blown by the wind to fall willy-nilly on various kinds of soil to germinate or die depending on the fortunes of climate? And where'd the seeds come from?"

"I really don't know," the girl said, straightening on the sofa but still a shadowy presence. "I need something more than negative elimination of possibilities. I need something positive, something concrete."

"Proof?" the Rock asked quickly, leaning a bit toward her. "A sign? A voice? A burning bush? Michigan winning the Rose Bowl every year? You say you 'need' which is, in a way, an answer," he added gently, eyes probing the room again. "We all need and most of us search. Probably all of us search. What's wrong with that? I think it's wrong to reject without a good search."

Jeff raised the bottle to his lips, but the beer was lukewarm and he put it on the floor. This person, whoever he was, compelled attention, demanded it, but in a soft voice. Jeff watched the interplay, remaining on the fringes, suiting his accustomed role as an observer. He drew up one leg, leaning forward, embracing the knee with both arms, following the winding conversation path, captivated by watching the man engage people who had coalesced into a group instead of just assorted random individuals migrating to the same living room on a Friday night.

The man shot questions, lobbed comments through the smoky air, sparking and responding to the group, keeping the ball moving around the room like a basketball drill.

A real Socratic dialogue. Bet his classes are great.

"Governor Faubus is pitiful but genuinely dangerous," the black man was saying. "He's held the same views for so long, and so successfully, that he can't change even if he wanted to. He's a demagogue. That got him to power and that's how he'll stay there."

He put his right hand on the carpet, leaning forward.

"It's too bad strong moral leadership didn't develop in the South when it might have moderated rather than reinforced racist attitudes and barriers. But we must realize Faubus, and others like him, personify the real, almost genetic fears in the minds and hearts of many whites…and not only in the South." Then, so softly Jeff almost didn't hear it, "Even the hearts and minds of church-going folks."

A husky feminine voice from a dim form sitting against the far wall broke the pause. "Do you think violence is sometimes needed to help change the system and end discrimination?"

"If you're asking if I believe in violence as a means to an end, no, I don't," the Rock said. "Violence has taken too many lives. Too much blood has already stained our country."

"I mean," the girl said, rising to her knees, back straight, "do you think violence is *ever* justified as part of the civil rights fight? Should violence ever be part of the struggle to create justice and freedom for Negroes?"

Jeff recognized her from staff meetings at the Michigan Daily.

Susan…Susan something.

"I believe in Gandhi's philosophy," the Rock said after a slight hesitation. "If violence by one side isn't justified how can it be ok when done by the other?" He paused and then added: "But I can't truthfully say I won't respond violently to a life-threatening attack on my family, or on me, or on *any* human being. In fact I'm sure I would. Peacefully seeking a worthwhile goal through peaceful means doesn't mean one has to offer himself as a human sacrifice to some hate-filled, bigoted son-of-a-bitch."

His face lost animation, mouth tightly closed in contrast to the frequent smiles he flashed to the group. The smile abruptly returned and he focused on Susan Something.

"I didn't want to say that, and I apologize for the language, but, Lord, I couldn't *not* say it. It's true. I don't know what I'll do when my personal challenge comes. We don't know what we're capable of until our moment confronts us. But I know nothing that tells me God wants me to forfeit my life to a hater, to someone who considers me less than an animal. But I also know we're not going to win this fight by knocking heads together, although I could probably hold my own there." Another brief smile. "I believe we must push relentlessly for what's right—what's supposedly guaranteed to every person in this country—and hope that mostly life and limb can be protected. But we all know that won't entirely happen. Some people are going to be hurt. Some will die. Many already have."

"When will it be over?" Susan Something asked.

"I don't know. It'll probably never be fully over, but I know what the score will be when there's some kind of victory. It'll be when people find a more rational method of deciding whom to dislike than just skin color or religion or the origin of someone's ancestors. We need a more discriminating form of discrimination."

He put a hand on the chair's arm and pushed himself off the carpet, picking his way through the crowded floor to the kitchen. As he passed Jeff he said, "You seem to be an intense listener."

Jeff was startled that the man had noticed him against the wall. Jumping up, he said: "I was admiring your ability to make people think."

"Thanks. Beer?"

"Yeah, this one's warm and flat," thrusting out a hand. "I'm Jeff Martindale."

"Isiah Booker," his hand making Jeff feel petite. "Come on, Jeff, I'll buy."

Booker took two bottles from the refrigerator, opened one and handed it to Jeff. Jeff took a drink and said impulsively, "A phrase kept running through my mind as you provoked people in there. You really are a fisher of men, as I believe the biblical reference goes." He stopped, embarrassed and fearful that he sounded naïve, not sure if "fisher of men" was actually in the Bible.

"Thanks," Booker said, "that's one of my favorite phrases. I've occasionally used it to justify sneaking my fly rod out to the car and skipping a study period in theology school."

"You're studying to be a minister? I thought you might be a professor who probably used to play football."

"Close. I'm already an ordained Baptist minister and I did play halfback at Temple until the knee went. I'm working on a doctorate. I teach one course a semester and hope to finish in a couple of years. You?

"I'm a journalism student. I'll be a sophomore in the fall if the grade gods smile."

"I've seen your byline in the Daily," Booker said. "Didn't you do a piece last week on the visiting Saudi Arabian professor lecturing on Islam?"

"Yeah, that was a difficult one to put..."

"Excuse me," a duck-tailed young man shouldered past Jeff, peering up at Booker, who put out his hand. After the briefest of hesitations, the man shook it and said, "I'm wondering, how do we know God intends for us all to live together, work together, marry each other? Didn't God create the different races in different places, intending for each to stay where they belong?"

Booker was expressionless in face and voice. "How do we know what God intended? How could we...."

Jeff moved away, turning back toward the living room to see Susan Something a few feet away, walking toward him, looking up and talking to a very tall, sandy-haired youth in a button-down blue dress shirt with rolled up sleeves who was scanning the room, looking everywhere but at her.

CHAPTER TWO

Susan looked at Jeff and held his gaze as she and the extraordinarily tall youth reached the kitchen. Jeff saw a scraggly, barely visible moustache below his long, straight nose.

Basketball player?

"Hi. I'm Jeff Martindale," offering his hand to her. She took it into a firm, warm grasp.

"Susan Adams," she said. "I've seen you at the Daily."

"Yeah, you're on the editorial page."

"Yep," she smiled. "I'm chock full of opinions."

She seemed short next to the tall moustache but at close range Jeff realized she was about five-eight. Her rich chestnut hair was shoulder-length and framed an attractive, friendly face with lively chocolate eyes.

"I was intrigued by your conversation with Rev. Booker," Jeff said. "You know him?"

"No. I'd heard of him but just met him tonight. He makes you think, doesn't he?"

"Yeah, except for his smile and gentle voice you'd think you were in one of those law school classes where everything you say is challenged."

"You in law school?"

"No

"I'm aiming at it," she said. "I've got another three years first but," she hesitated, noticing that the tall guy was still standing at her side, looking annoyed.

"I'm sorry," she said. "Jeff, this is Derrick Miller."

"Hi," the two young men said simultaneously, thrusting right hands forward, Jeff at six-feet-plus looking up Derrick.

"See you later," Derrick said, not quite under his breath, leaning close to Susan's ear before turning back into the living room, massaging the faint moustache with two fingers.

"Your boyfriend seems peeved," Jeff said.

"He's not a boyfriend," waving a dismissive hand. "He's a celebrity. Basketball forward. I'm too busy for boyfriends, even if his interest actually extended beyond tonight or at most early next week. He'll make another few casts in there and find another fish. He needs one lower on the food chain."

"Nice moustache," hoping the smirk stayed inside his cheeks.

"Isn't it just sad?" she said, looking at him with a bemused smile. "I assume you're talking about Derrick and not me."

Jeff grinned and said: "We're thinking of walking over to the Pretzel Bell for pizza or a sandwich or something," Jeff said, improvising. "Would you like to join us?"

"Well, ah, sure. Who's 'we'?"

"My roommate and maybe a friend of his. That's him in the blue sweater over there; Don Chapman," Jeff said, pointing with his chin. "I'll see if he's ready."

She nodded and he zigzagged down the hall where Don was talking with a willowy blonde.

"I'm headed for the Bell," Jeff said. "You?"

"Naw. I'm fine. I think we're going to Rachel's sorority house."

"Good. That's what I hoped."

He ignored Don's questioning look and hurried back to Susan who had been watching him.

"They may join us later."

They zipped coats as they stepped into Michigan's frosty, late-winter air. The flakes were larger now, floating gently in the windless night, creating halos around streetlights, the accumulating snow turning the grass into a white shag carpet.

The restaurant was crowded with pizza and garlic aromas plus clumps of people waiting for seats. A beckoning arm waved from a booth in the back and Jeff saw Matt from his geography class. Jeff and Susan pushed through the crowd to the booth, Jeff not recognizing the girl opposite Matt.

Matt started introductions: "Jane, this is Jeff Martindale…"

"Susan," Jane interrupted. "I thought you were going to a party."

"I did, but we were hungry and…"

"Obviously you two know each other," Matt said, looking at Susan before turning back to Jane. Do you know Jeff too?"

"No, sorry," Jane said, smiling.

"Ok then, as I was saying, Jane this is Jeff Martindale."

"Hi," Jeff said, shaking Jane's hand and introducing Susan to Matt, then turning to Susan, "and how do you two know each other?"

"We're roommates at the DZ house," Susan grinned.

Matt said, "I'd invite you to join us but we're about to leave," glancing at Jane.

"How bout we sit with you for a couple of minutes, then when you leave we'll have your booth?" Jeff said.

"Great idea. Sit. Stay."

After Matt and Jane left, Jeff's mind failed him. He wondered what to say next. This had the feel of a date except the person across the table was a stranger.

After a waitress took their order, Jeff said "Where's your hometown?" carefully aligning the salt and pepper shakers on the table, hoping the question was at least a notch above "do you come here often?" or "what's your sign?" but knowing it wasn't.

"Small town, upstate New York. You?" a smile flickering.

"Small town, upstate Michigan."

"Ok, which one?"

"You tell me yours and I'll tell you mine" he countered, adding the napkin holder to the salt and pepper lineup.

"Glen Falls, about 60 miles from Albany."

"Angel Harbor," he said. "Pretty far north on Lake Michigan although not the Upper Peninsula. About thirty miles from Traverse City.'

"Got it. Upper left corner of the Michigan mitten," she said, pointing at her hand.

"Yeah. Not a bad place but pretty quiet. Ann Arbor's a lot more stimulating, always something going on, somebody reasonably famous coming through, all these people from all over. I really like it."

Babbling

"Me, too," she said. "Beats Glen Falls. Except for my mom including me in all of her volunteer causes, it's pretty quiet there. Mostly I spent a lot of time with my mom's grownup friends." She brushed her hair back over her shoulders, glancing briefly at the crowded room. She looked back at Jeff. "Have you taken Rev. Booker's sociology course?"

"No, but I'd like to now that I've seen him in action. I'd even get up early without complaining. What's the class about?"

"Race relations and American culture. I checked it in the catalog last semester and it's the history, philosophy and effects of racial conflict. I've heard he's a terrific prof. Keeps everybody awake."

"I could probably count it toward my soc minor."

The pizza arrived with wondrous vapors of tomato sauce and cheese.

"Why don't we sign up for next semester," she said, surprising both of them, reaching for a pizza slice, her eyes focused on it as if the transfer to her plate was as complicated as heart surgery.

"Sure," he said instantly, strangely excited at her suggestion.

Later, as they left the restaurant, he was amazed at how good he felt after an hour with this interesting and attractive woman he barely knew. Walking through the deepening snow to the Delta Zeta house, the slowly falling flakes drew the night closely around them as if in a holiday snow globe. Car headlights, streetlights and windows glowed indistinctly through the snow, feeding his inner warmth.

"It's magical," he heard himself say.

Susan looked at him for a long moment as they walked, then at the winter scene. "Yes, it's wonderful isn't it? Like walking in a Christmas card."

At her front door he hesitated, again unsure of what to do or say. After an awkward pause he said, “I really enjoyed talking with you. I’m sure I’ll see you around the Daily office. Maybe we could slip out to the Coffee Hut or a movie sometime.”

He saw the barest beginning of her smile.

“That’d be nice,” she said. “Let’s do that.”

“Ok,” he said, with too much enthusiasm. “Good night.”

He turned toward the street, walking rapidly as if he had somewhere important to go and needed to be there right away.

CHAPTER THREE

Susan smiled, watching him striding purposefully, disappearing into swirling snowflakes falling as if from a heavenly flour sifter. He vanished completely through a hole in the wall of snow. She pulled open the heavy wood door and went in, brushing snow from her long hair with both hands, still smiling. The lanky, boyish Jeff intrigued her but she wasn't sure why.

Did I actually invite him to take a class with me within an hour of meeting him?

She was seldom uncertain, not after growing up with the strong, supportive mother who relentlessly encouraged young Susan to be fiercely independent and to know positively that she could accomplish anything she set as a goal.

She opened the door to her room and found Jane in bed, already in pajamas, leaning on two pillows behind her head, reading a textbook.

"You didn't have a date when you left here," Jane teased, grinning and resting the book on her stomach. "So what happened? Tell me everything."

"No date," Susan said, hanging up her coat. "We bumped into each other while I was trying to ditch Derrick who was hanging around, using me as cover while looking for other prey. We talked a bit and decided to escape to the Bell for pizza. His roommate and a friend were going to join us but they didn't show up."

"Uh huh," Jane said. "You're probably the only one who thought they were coming. Sounds like a setup to me."

"I don't think so. Glad we ran into you and Matt. That back on?" stifling a yawn.

"Not really. Just fun. This Jeff guy seems the serious type. But kinda cute. You like him?"

"Yeah. He's interesting. Maybe. Maybe I do. I think I do."

***

"Hey," Don called from his desk as Jeff came through the door, "who was that? I've never seen her before but you left together. And you definitely didn't want me tagging along. What happened?"

"Pizza happened," Jeff said, his grin giving him away, clearly sparked by more than pizza. "She's Susan Adams. You've probably read some of her stuff on the Daily editorial page. I've seen her around the paper but we never met. She's pretty interesting…and…uh…."

"She's interestingly pretty too," Don filled in. "I assume you noticed that."

"Sure. Of course. And, she's got a lot going on *inside* her head. Her mom's some sorta activist in upstate New York and she and Susan have been involved in several causes and she's thinking about law school and we may take a class together next semester and…"

"Whoa, whoa," Don said, holding up both hands and staring at Jeff with amazement. "All this happened in a couple of hours? We've been best friends since third grade but I've never seen you so lit up over someone. You're giddy about this Susan. You need a cold shower."

CHAPTER FOUR

"Got a great feature idea," Jeff announced, walking up to Larry Williamson, campus editor of *The Michigan Daily.* Williamson didn't look up from his small desk in the middle of the newsroom, stabbing pencil changes onto a story about an anthropology professor's trip to Chile.

Jeff put both hands on desk's edge, leaning forward, seeking eye contact.

"I met this guy at a party Friday. He's an ordained minister, played halfback at Temple till he hurt his knee. He's here for doctoral studies. Very charismatic, had everyone's attention Friday night, a big guy, interesting." Jeff ran out of impressions and facts.

"Interesting? Hmmmm," the stocky editor grunted, still not looking up, enthusiastically jabbing with his pencil. "What's the interesting part? Why would anyone want to read about him?"

"Well, he's older, probably around 30. His story's got to be interesting; he's a former football player, black, a minister, a popular prof here while working on his PhD."

"He's black?" Williamson said, finally looking up. "Whata ya mean he had everyone's attention? How? About what? He some kind of show-off?"

"About religion, about civil rights, about attitudes toward violence. It's impossible to look away when he's talking; he just captures you?"

"If you think you can *capture* that on paper, give it a shot."

***

Isiah Booker and a half-empty coffee cup occupied a booth in the Student Union when Jeff arrived. "Good to see you again," Booker said. "You want to do a story about me," mostly a question. "Why? What about?" tipping the cup to his lips.

"I was intrigued with some things you said and the little bit of your history I've heard," Jeff said. "How bout I ask you some questions and we see where it goes?"

"I'll try. I've never been interviewed outside a locker room."

"Ok, I can see just looking at you why you became a halfback," Jeff said, putting his notebook on the table, "but what made you become a minister?"

"That was my goal by the time I was nine. My family was deeply churched; you know, sometimes twice on Sundays. Daddy and Mama believed a strong faith meant practicing what you believed seven days a week. I saw them do it and realized I was being called."

"By God?"

"Yeah, although we didn't have a 'conversation' or anything like that. It was just in me and I felt it and I knew."

"What happened after you *knew*," Jeff held up two fingers on each hand, wiggling quotes and instantly regretting it.

"Nothing super dramatic. I was a normal kid in a normal, mostly Negro, blue-collar Philadelphia neighborhood. I didn't suddenly grow a halo or anything," smiling and rotating the cup in jerky little motions on the table with his fingers. "I played sports, got pretty good grades, fell in love a couple of times, first time in fourth grade. Sometimes I thought my parents were too strict. I didn't like a few of my teachers, worked summer jobs to get money toward college. The usual stuff."

"And football?"

"Thought I had a calling there, too. The basics came fairly naturally but I worked hard too. Daddy always said, "Do the best you can at everything you do. Don't waste your life doing stuff half –ass. Don't *be* a half-ass.' He hated half-asses. Even though he died when I was eighteen, I've never forgotten it. Football paid most of my college costs. I could tell God was watching out for me," a big smile, Jeff unsure if he meant it literally.

"But you hurt your knee?"

"Yeah, it was pretty bad," stroking his right leg. "Just twisted out from under me in practice my junior year; not even in a game. Finished me as a player."

"But you graduated and got ordained?"

"Yeah. I was an intern and helper in a tiny church in the Upper Peninsula one summer after my football career was over. After graduating I spent most of a year pastoring a small church near Mount Pleasant. Went there as a youth minister and when the regular guy unexpectedly left I held the fort until a replacement came about six months later. And last summer was mostly in Mississippi trying to register black voters."

"And now Ann Arbor for your doctorate?"

"That's the plan."

"What's next?"

"Not sure. I may go back to Philadelphia, near Mama and my sister," he added. "Or I might find a church in the South where I can serve God and a community."

"Why in the South? You're from Philadelphia. Are you thinking of getting more involved in the Civil Rights Movement? Did your summer in Mississippi spark that?"

"I think that may be where the need is greatest," Isiah said. "The fight for civil rights is expanding. And heating up. This is another battle for the soul of America; and it's as difficult and historic as the Civil War. It's way past time to correct an original sin by the Founding Fathers. One was that women couldn't vote because they were inferior. The other one was that black people could legally be slaves. In practical terms, most of us aren't full citizens to this day. We can't legislate to change people's hearts, but we absolutely must be a country where everyone can *exercise* equal rights, such as voting. And sitting anywhere we please on public buses. Or eating in any restaurant when we're hungry. Or using any public restroom when we need to. This is the time to finally get this done. If we can't, America, even with all its high-minded beliefs about itself, is nothing but a fraud on the world. That's what we're struggling to fix. I'm considering working fulltime for the NAACP or CORE or SNICK. Maybe that's where my efforts would be most effective."

"Are you volunteering with any of those groups now?"

"The NAACP because they have an office on campus. If you want to see it sometime, I'll give you the tour. But all of this is too long a story and probably more than you or anyone else would ever want to hear."

"No. It isn't. I want to know more. I'd appreciate a visit to the NAACP office," Jeff said. "This is an interesting story. I think my editor will like it."

"I don't know about that but if you want to check with your editor and chat more later, we can reschedule. I'm teaching a class in 20 minutes."

"Want to dust off your fishing gear?" Jeff asked, as they walked to the door. "If you can get away some weekend, I'll show you my favorite river. It has some decent rainbows plus great scenery," exuberant now.

"That's tempting. Didn't you used to peddle apples in the Garden of Eden?" Isiah smiling his full-voltage version.

"I'll call you in a day or so for the rest of the interview," Jeff said as they walked briskly into the crisp, sunny morning.

CHAPTER FIVE

"Hi, Susan, it's Jeff Martindale, we met last week."

"Sure. Hi, Jeff. Thanks for helping me escape the scraggly moustache," her intriguing voice husky even through the phone.

"I was glad to help," he said, grinning to himself. "I was wondering if…uh, you'd be interested in a movie Saturday night. Uh, *"West Side Story"* is opening and I hear it's really good and I could pick you up about 6:30 and…."

Cripes, put a cork in it already.

***

After popcorn and Junior Mints, Susan and Jeff left the theater slipping on gloves and walking briskly on the sidewalk flanked with dingy, four-day-old snow piles. Every exhale materialized in the cold air, punctuating their discussion of ethnic New York gangs becoming *"Romeo and Juliet"* wrapped in Broadway show tunes.

In two blocks, at the Go Blue Café, menus were studied intently, Jeff again feeling awkward, as if dancing to undanceable music.

"Ok," he grinned, after they'd ordered, "Tell me your life story beginning with being born in that log cabin in Illinois. Or was that Lincoln?"

"Is Glen Falls, New York close enough?" she smiled, picking up the spirit of his light tone. "The highlights only. Actually the biggest event of my life was my father dying of leukemia when I was eight. So my mom has been the major influence on me. And she's great. She's a compulsive volunteer and she's always treated me like a grown-up.

"She was one of the first people active in feminist causes, even before "feminist" was a word everyone knows. She raised money for leukemia research after watching my dad drift farther and farther away over four tough years. She's volunteered at the Humane Society and worked in Democratic Party politics in Glen Falls.

"My least-favorite cause was when she tried vegetarianism for nearly a year when I was 12. I finally complained strongly enough about needing an occasional hotdog or hamburger, and that faded away. You noticed my cheeseburger order," she grinned.

"I didn't notice you looking guilty about it," he said.

"Not a bit. My dad was the beneficiary of a trust fund from the mid-sized commercial printing business his family owned in Glen Falls," she said, turning serious again. "His grandfather started the business that specialized in brochures and booklets for tourist destinations up and down the East Coast. My dad left my mom and me comfortable, although certainly not wealthy. He was a serious man who had been trained since childhood to run the family firm. He enjoyed it and was content for Judith, my mom, to juggle her various causes and he never complained when she was engrossed in meetings or bringing home another homeless dog or cat. Once we took care of a goat for two weeks.

"After he died, she immersed herself in even more projects," Susan continued, head-flipping her long hair over her shoulder. "I think she hoped she wouldn't miss him quite as much if she had less time to think about her loss. All through my childhood she took me to meetings, fund raisers and hands-on activities from hosing out cages at the animal shelter to folding fliers, sealing them in envelopes and rubbing stamps over wet sponges to support a seemingly endless parade of groups from the NAACP to equal rights for women and several diseases.

"Whether it was heredity or the hectic activist environment that she exposed me to, I became interested in many of her causes. That's why I want a law degree; I'll probably end up a low-paid lawyer for a bunch of non-profits," she smiled. "I'm on a soc and pre-law degree plan. Working on the Daily keeps me involved in what's happening in the world."

Jeff saw a flicker of embarrassment cross her face and she laughed briefly, looking at him and quickly away and back again.

"Well, that was pretty serious," she said. "And long. Enough of my story, what's yours?" scooping up the cheeseburger in both hands.

"How about saving that tale for another time?" he said. "Is that intriguing enough to entice you into doing this again? Although I need to warn you, my version is pretty dull compared to yours," glancing hopefully at her, then carefully selecting the precise French fry he wanted.

"Sure," she said, pulling paper from a straw and dropping it into her Pepsi. "I'd like that."

Jeff leaned back, swiping his mouth with a paper napkin. "Are you still thinking about Prof. Booker's class next semester?" hoping to confirm that her astonishing invitation to take the class together was still open. He had replayed over and over in his memory her tantalizing idea, hoping that it came from interest in him but afraid she was just a spontaneous person, swept up in a moment.

"Sure. Sounds more interesting than any other elective I've looked at. You still interested?"

"Very much," he said, answering her direct question plus the one he hoped she was asking. "Definitely," he added. "Let's do it," hoping to close the deal.

She watched his eyes a tiny fraction of a second longer than necessary. Or did she? And for the second time in less than a week he was overwhelmed by a feeling so wonderful that he couldn't describe it, even to himself.

Am I interpreting this right? Is something happening? Or is it just me?

CHAPTER SIX

Bull Bryant was a mean son-of-a-bitch. Everyone thought so. Some of his friends said it to his face, always smiling, sometimes substituting "tough" for "mean." Bull considered it a compliment.

Growing up in the early 1900s in rural Mississippi, you were tough and resourceful or you were a victim. Being mean was optional. Born Albert Hiram Bryant in 1902, he hated his first name and after age nine virtually no one ever called him anything except "Bull," not even his parents or teachers, although later a few adults, strangers or Negroes, called him "Mr. Bryant." He was Bull Bryant and he loved it from the moment he heard it the first time.

Young Albert was an aggressive and rough fourth-grader who nearly every day found an excuse to push or shove some smaller kid, trying to provoke retaliation, either physical or verbal, so he could pound the kid with his fists until he got surrender from the victim or interference from a teacher. Either way he was happy.

One spring day after school, Albert and Ronnie, a fellow fourth-grader, trudged barefoot across the school yard, turning on the red dirt road toward the unpainted Bryant family cabin over a mile away. Suddenly Albert was knocked to his hands and knees, books flying from his hands. Then a foot kicked him in the butt, driving his face into the dirt.

Albert jumped up, turning to see who had struck him, when he was shoved in the chest by a grinning sixth-grader. Stumbling backward but not falling, Albert regained his balance and amazed the bigger and older boy by screaming and charging, right shoulder lowered, catching him in the belly, knocking him to the dirt. Albert jumped astride the fallen attacker's chest, his arms wind-milling wildly but some of his blows smashing the bully's nose and mouth, drawing blood. The older boy struggled to free himself but the fury of Albert's retaliation overwhelmed him and the unrelenting fists of the smaller boy struck again and again and again.

A teacher saddling his horse to return home, ran across the school yard, yelling and pulling the screaming Albert upright, fists still flying, rage unslacked.

"You should be ashamed of yourself," the misunderstanding teacher shouted at Albert over his shoulder, escorting the bloody and crying bully toward the school.

"You really whipped his ass!" Ronnie shouted at Albert who, though breathing heavily and with fists still clenched, was eerily calm watching the retreating teacher trying to comfort the battered attacker. "You were wild!"

Albert raised his fists to chest level, savoring the look of blood on his hands, immune to the pain. He watched Ronnie retrieve the fallen books. "I never saw anythin like that," Ronnie said, brushing dirt off the books, handing them to Albert. "You charged him like Mr. Sander's bull. You made him cry and he was bleeding all over his face. Jesus. That was somethin'. Holy shit. Way to go, Bull."

The newly christened Bull Bryant turned, walking toward home, exhilaration in every cell of his body, a slight smile flickering on his lips. As long as he lived, he never forgot that day.

CHAPTER SEVEN

Young Eddie Bryant grew up awed by, and a little scared of, the man he called "Daddy" but who was "Bull" to everyone else.

Daddy always knew what to do and exactly how he wanted it done. Even in elementary school, little Eddie felt his father's over-shadowing presence looming even when Bull wasn't actually there. Bull was the driving force, the thunder and the lightning, the dominant star in the galaxy of grownups Eddie knew, including teachers and Rev. Bob, plus people who came into the hardware store where Eddie hung around on Saturday's and most afternoons. He was always "Bull's boy," never Eddie or even Little Bull. When people saw Eddie they seldom used his name. They mentioned Bull. Only the youngster's best friends since First Grade, Roy and Roll, called him Eddie.

Bull wasn't abusive to his son. In fact, he doted on him, bringing home new bicycles from the store as Eddie grew into the next size. Bull was obviously proud of Eddie as he excelled in boyhood sports, particularly when he got to high school and was starting left guard as a freshman, benefiting from maturing earlier than most of his peers.

"Bull's kid sure gets after it, don't he?" was heard in the bleachers.

"Bull's boy takes after his Ol' man out there," one fan said.

It was like that at the store, too. Starting in Junior High, Eddie helped Bull on Saturdays and during the summer, carrying out trash, sweeping the wood floors, later assisting Bull taking inventory, restocking bins, putting the lawn mowers and wheelbarrows on the sidewalk in front of the store in the mornings and returning them at closing.

But later, after high school, when he worked fulltime in the family store, he was always Bull's defacto assistant, doing what Bull told him to do and in the ways Bull taught him; never a partner in attitude or fact, even into his early twenties when he was sometimes angry that Bull still dealt with him the way he had years earlier, when he was only a boy.

Then suddenly one warm summer day, Bull was gone, dead from the stroke that dropped him to the floor in Paint Supplies as if he'd been hit in the back of the head with a sack of cement.

Bull was gone but hardly without a trace. It was as if Eddie had lived his entire life inside a tornado and suddenly the wind stopped. It was violently quiet. A dozen times a day he found himself uncertain about what to do as he struggled to adjust, keeping the store running and comforting his stunned mother whose own tornado was also suddenly gone.

But soon he realized that now being "Bull's boy" was a godsend, and when people began referring to him as "Ed" it meant they saw him as heir to the relationship they had with Bull. It helped that the son had the barrel-chested physical presence of his father, and that everyone already knew him.

In a few months he was confident enough to make a few changes to the business and was enjoying the role he realized everyone expected from him. He became a leader and he liked it. Customers expected him to answer their questions; Rev. Bob and others asked him for opinions and advice on the church budget. His mother consulted him before buying a new car or painting her house.

The one person who had influenced everything he did and how he did it was gone. Ed became himself, who, it turned out, was more like his father than he could have ever imagined. When he saw that others expected him to be assertive and opinionated, he accepted it, grew into it and then reveled in it. He grew from assertive to domineering in public and at home without an ounce of awareness.

Eventually he began meeting his dead father in the bathroom mirror each morning. It hit him that he even looked like "Bull," the man who founded both *Bryant Hardware & Sporting Goods* and the Dixon County Ku Klux Klan.

CHAPTER EIGHT

Two weeks after Jeff interviewed Isiah, he loaded his blue Plymouth with fishing and camping gear. As he coasted to the curb in front of Isiah's address, the minister instantly walked from the front door of the old frame house where he had a two-room apartment. Jeff waved across the car's roof.

"Hey, all set?"

"I've been ready since you mentioned this," Isiah said, arms loaded with gear. "Apparently the weather gods have blessed us," scanning the sky. "Hey, thanks for the nice story about me a couple of weeks ago. I had to get extra copies for relatives. Mama loved it."

As they headed for the highway Jeff said: "I found this place accidentally. Several years ago I fished a short stretch of the Muskegon River where it runs through a county park. Later I took a backpack and fished upstream for an entire day. The fishing got better the farther I went. By early evening I found a nook in the pine trees and draped a light tarp over a few low limbs for an overnight shelter."

"Pretty primitive," Isiah said.

"Yeah, that wasn't the most fun part," Jeff said, "but it was a great weekend. That piece of river probably gets fished only a few times a year."

Two hours later, Jeff steered from a narrow county road into a small gravel parking lot. The late-morning sun reflected twinkling highlights off the river only a few yards away, visible intermittently through bushes, oaks, elms, maples and pines bordering the stream.

They shouldered packs and angled through thick, shoulder-high bushes near the river. In a few hundred yards they abruptly stepped through a screen of short pines into the darkened forest where tree canopies interlocked overhead in a natural cathedral. They strolled on a soft brown carpet of compressed leaves blended in spots with cushioned layers of pine needles among tall, unorganized trees. The river bounced nearby over and around rocks, more heard than seen. They walked without talking, immersed in the park-like surroundings.

Suddenly a whitetail doe exploded from a small copse of maples ten yards to their right, bolting away in high bouncing leaps, disappearing into the trees.

"That got my heart going," Isiah said, quietly, one hand patting his chest.

They emerged from the enveloping forest into a sparsely treed area, expanses of blue sky overhead and paused at the crest of a gentle hill sloping toward the river. In ten minutes they reached the gravel bank.

"This is it," Jeff said, kneeling to slip off his pack and untie the tent rolled tightly across the top. Isiah remained near the river, feet planted, eyes sweeping the panorama before breaking his spell. Within minutes they had two small tents set up.

Jeff pulled two wax-paper-wrapped ham and cheese sandwiches from his pack and gave one to Isiah.

"What's the plan for meeting with some trout?" Isiah asked, already shrugging into his green fishing vest. "Can we fish together, at least to start? I can use some help finding the good spots."

They pulled on hip boots, strung fly rods and trudged upstream, staying far enough from the river to avoid spooking any lurking fish. In a few minutes Jeff angled back toward the river, walking quietly. "There's a trout in this pool that I've seen three times and hooked once but he's never glimpsed me or my net," he whispered. "I'm going to be impolite and go first."

He moved quietly to the river's edge and made two short false casts before dropping the fly upstream into a small riffle feeding the head of the pool which began above them and ran about 30 feet before shallowing into another riffle. The fly floated past them to the foot of the pool.

"Whew," Jeff said. "I couldn't handle it if I got a strike on the first cast. I always like to get the first one over with. Now the odds get better and I don't have to hold my breath."

He made a dozen casts, fishing various parts of the pool but nothing happened. Then a large trout lunged at something on the surface just as Jeff cast his line which fell directly on the spreading circles marking the fish's attack a split second earlier.

"That ends that for awhile," Jeff said, reeling in his line, walking toward Isiah. "I probably scared him out of his spots. Let's try the next hole and you can show me how it's done in Pennsylvania."

Isiah hooked and landed two small trout from the next hole and Jeff duplicated this in the third.

In an amazingly short time it was mid-afternoon and they were both hungry again. At a sandy area slightly above the river, Jeff slipped off his vest and produced, with the exaggerated flourish of a magician, a bag of crackers, a small block of cheddar, two hard-boiled eggs and two apples.

After the snack Jeff stretched out on the sand, warmed by the sun, feet pointing at the nearby river. Hands beneath his head, he watched a hawk skywriting circles. The flying hunter made large, then smaller and smaller circles, dropping lower before soaring up again.

Jeff jerked awake, arms asleep and tingling, trapped behind his head. He heard the river running just beyond his boot soles. He sat up, eyes blinking, Isiah asleep five yards away. Jeff stood, rubbing feeling back into his arms, glanced at his watch and realized he'd been asleep for nearly an hour. He selected a small pebble from between his feet and tossed it underhand near Isiah where it bounced into his ribs.

Isiah didn't move and Jeff looked down for another pebble when Isiah spoke.

"Fishing is hard work." He opened his eyes and sat up, yawning. "I got pretty relaxed."

"You mean unconscious," Jeff said.

"Yeah, for a while," Isiah said. "This is great. I love everything about rivers, the sounds they make moving over rocks, the light flickering off riffles. Everything, including the old saying that you never step in the same one twice."

The rest of the afternoon flowed quickly past. As the sky began hinting at dusk, Jeff was bent over ducking low branches trying to reach one final pool. Squeezing through the brush, he found Isiah already drifting a fly.

"I'm heading to camp to get supper started," Jeff called, deciding not to try for the next stretch of water.

A few minutes later a small trout took Isiah's fly. He released it before scrambling through bushes to the faint path along the bank, walking slowly and contently toward camp, snippets of the day flickering through his mind, dusk wrapping the trees in its folds and draining color from the day, painting with a dark gray brush.

He passed the hole where Jeff had earlier startled the giant, elusive trout and thought for a moment before flipping his line across and upstream. Almost immediately the water bulged under the fly. He instinctively swooped the rod straight up and only then felt the weight and power of the unseen fish as it dived quickly into the deepest part of the dark-green pool, slashing right and then left, Isiah's line cutting through the water faster than he could react. He held the rod tip high, desperately trying to keep tension on the line.

I've got Jeff's trout.

He was torn between yanking hard enough to break off the fish or attempting to land the trout for a brief but close look at the magnificent creature; the two of them linked through the pulsing fly rod and a spider-web-thin, two-pound leader.

The trout strained and Isiah allowed line to slip through his fingers. The fish torpedoed the length of the pool, turned and shot downstream again. And again. Isiah stripped in line, trying to avoid slack. Abruptly the fish stopped. Isiah tightened the line and began a gentle tug-of-war, trying to turn the trout's head toward him. In the growing darkness he couldn't see the fish clearly even as it broke the surface, rolling once before jumping free above the water, flashing the reflection of the last rays of sunlight. Isiah's heart pounded and he whooshed out a lung-full of air.

He felt the trout tiring and soon he was leading the resisting fish slowly toward the waiting net. Two short dashes caused Isiah to release line but the fish was beaten. Finally it was within reach and Isiah had the net ready to scoop. Instead, he dropped the net, reached with his left hand while holding the fly rod high with his right. His hand found the leader, followed it down, grasping the fly and pulling gently upward for a quick glance at the monster trout. He gave a downward tug, freeing the fish which momentarily held its position, slowly fanning his fins, unaware of its freedom. Isiah saw the long outline of the trout, barely a shadow in the dusk-darkened water. The current swept the fish downstream and, although tired, it rolled on the surface, flipped once and disappeared downstream to deeper water.

Isiah stumbled and lurched to the bank, sinking to the ground, feeling the cool gravel through his jeans above the hip boots, rapidly breathing in noisy pulses, filling his chest with blessedly cool night air.

A few minutes later Isiah materialized into the area lighted by the campfire's dancing flames, momentarily startling Jeff.

"Oh, there you are. I didn't hear you coming."

"And I'm kinda hard to see in this light," Isiah said, squatting by the fire, absorbing the warmth and enjoying his secret. What's the fire for? I thought the little stove was our link to civilization."

"Yeah, but I'd rather cook on an open fire if I can. 'Besides, a fire is comforting at night."

"Definitely. When night lurks, mankind yearns for fire. Probably true since the beginning of time."

Jeff held up an aluminum cup in an unspoken question and filled it with coffee when Isiah nodded.

Isiah backed as close to the fire as he could, heating and drying his damp jeans. Then he sat on a log and pulled off his boots, stretching his legs toward the fire, feeling warmth toasting his wool socks, wiggling his toes and knowing the snapping flames would soon make it too hot to be this close.

Cooking smells enriched the night air, already spiced by scents of pine trees and campfire smoke and freshly cleaned trout. Scooping browned potatoes and corn niblets onto aluminum plates, Jeff refilled the pan with light-pink trout fillets. He glanced across the fire at Isiah who was silently hypnotized by the flames.

"Come and get it," Jeff's voice cheery, holding up a crowded plate of fillets, potatoes and corn. The food instantly made the aluminum plates hot to the touch. Isiah returned to his log and Jeff sank into a semi-comfortable seat on the sand. The rest of the fillets were fried and devoured; the corn and potatoes also vanished. Isiah gathered the plates, frying pan and pot and took them to the river, filling them with water and balancing them on rocks pushed close to the fire. Returning to his log, he looked at Jeff.

"Thanks for bringing me here. I feel ten years younger."

"I don't want to feel that young," Jeff laughed. "I'd only be nine years old."

"Ha," Isiah grinned. "Youth is wonderful. I'm 31 going on 55. By tomorrow I should be back to a mildly elderly 34."

They watched smoke drifting and swirling like a mystery before disappearing into the night sky.

CHAPTER NINE

Three days later a mishmash of unmatched tables sprawled randomly in the huge room, as if waiting to host a church dinner, but instead of food they supported piles of papers. Four people, three black, one white, shuffled stacks from table to table.

Jeff and Isiah paused at a waist-high counter just inside the door; the faded green linoleum counter top was bare except for a small poster propped in a corner.

The National Association for the Advancement of Colored People
Ann Arbor Office

At least fifty feet long and nearly as wide, the room looked like the retired classroom that it was, including the faintly musty odor. A black youth in the back looked up, spotted Isiah, waved enthusiastically and smiled broadly while striding quickly to the newcomers.

"Rev. Booker. I told you I'd be back."

"I believed it," Isiah grinned back, vigorously shaking the youth's hand. "I brought a friend to see what's happening around here."

"I wish more was happening," the tall, thin young man said.

Isiah interrupted. "This is Jeff Martindale. He works on the Daily." He nodded to Jeff and said, "And Vernon Jones here is a sociology student with a minor in N-double-A-CP. I have to get back for a meeting. Vern, how about giving Jeff the two-bit tour?"

Vernon turned to the nearest table, pointing to three stacks of papers, each a different color. "These are promos for our next speaker in two weeks. We'll post them on every bulletin board in every dorm, every Greek house. We'll put 'em on telephone poles and in every campus business that'll let us. We need an army of volunteers to do all that but, unfortunately, instead of an army we barely have a squad and all of them have classes to study for and most of 'em have part-time jobs for actual cash. The pay here isn't much…if you consider zero 'not much.'"

They moved to the next table, laden with boxes of envelopes and larger boxes of pre-printed letters.

"These are donation solicitations waiting to be stuffed, sealed, stamped and mailed," Vernon said.

Then Jeff saw Susan in a back hallway, walking and talking with a slender young black woman. As the pair got to the big room, Susan looked up and spotted Jeff, waved, said something to the other woman and they headed for Jeff and Vernon.

"Monica, this is my friend Jeff Martindale. Jeff, Monica Peters."

"Got a new recruit?" Susan asked Vernon.

"Or are you pitching him for a big contribution?" Monica asked, provoking laughs from all four.

"Just explaining some of the stuff we do here," Vernon said, looking at Jeff. "And hoping he'll want to help the cause."

"Exactly what is the cause? What are the goals?" Jeff asked, turning serious but looking more at Susan than Vernon.

"Promote the brotherhood of all mankind," Vernon said. "How's that for a big thought?" smiling broadly. "There's lots more detail but that's the distilled version. I'll be glad to expand some other time, but now I need to get to my paying job at the bookstore."

"Me, too," Monica said. "I've got three wonderful hours of spooning almost-food in the cafeteria."

Jeff looked at Susan. "Got time for a java break?"

"I was surprised to see you there," Jeff said as they balanced steaming cups while sliding into a window table at Go Blue Cafe. "You volunteering regularly?"

"When I have time and particularly if something special's going on and they need help," she said. "But frankly, I wonder if we're doing much good here. We're pretty far from where the real action is and we're mostly preaching to the proverbial choir…or singing songs they already know. It's a gut cause for me but at this rate I don't expect it'll be solved in my lifetime."

"Then why do it? Is it because of what you told me about your mom including you in her volunteer causes?"

"Partly, I guess. Volunteering's definitely in my genes. But this is one I've always felt strongly about. We only had 13 NAACP members in Glen Falls, and five of them were white including my mother and me. I got quite an education from the black members and occasional outside speakers. It took me awhile to wrap my mind around the stories of spirit-crushing discrimination blacks face every day, even in Glen Falls. And the stories from the South made my heart ache; the separate schools and cruel segregation signs everywhere hammering home the message that black people are sub-human and so disgusting that they can't even get water from public drinking fountains."

Jeff couldn't take his eyes from her face, feeling her emotion and seeing her eyes moistening, but barely hearing her words, entranced just to be with her, sitting this close. She glanced toward the window, then down at the coffee and brought her cup to her lips, only her large brown eyes visible, but still hypnotizing him.

"You sound as if you were a super-serious teenager," Jeff said. "Didn't you play with dolls or girlfriends your own age?"

She laughed. "I skipped several teenage phases while hanging out mostly with my mother's friends. I sorta metamorphosed from girl to woman way ahead of most of my peers. I certainly preferred the adults surrounding my mother to endless, loopy conversations with most of the girls I knew who were consumed by life-and-death topics ranging from boys in general to specific boys or dating and relationships and mascara and "how do I look?" she said, brushing her chestnut hair back over her shoulder with both hands.

"The immature guys my age, and even older, disappointed me over and over in high school. I never dated any of them more than twice. None had the slightest interest in causes I was immersed in. These guys—just boys really-- were incapable of discussing anything beyond sports and parties.

"I preferred the deep discussions that engaged my mother and her cohorts over the shallowness of my classmates, male or female. At first, when I was with my mother and her activist friends, I just listened, trying to develop my own thoughts. She encouraged me to participate and soon, probably about age 13, I was reading everything I could find on things they talked about and I gradually joined the conversations. My mom's friends accepted me and encouraged me. I became comfortable there," she said before glancing away, clasping her hands in her lap.

"It thrilled my mother to see this," she said. "She encouraged me in every way possible, telling me how proud she was that I was earning the respect of her friends. She and I carried signs walking side-by-side at an anti-segregation rally when I was 16.

"Which is a long way of explaining why I may never have been an actual teenager," laughing self-consciously, then smiling and looking at him. She brought her cup to her lips but instantly put it down, the cold liquid making her wrinkle her nose.

What a cute nose!

CHAPTER TEN

Late one afternoon three weeks later, after investing many hours in the sprawling, semi-organized NAACP office, Jeff and Vernon filled paper cups with the remaining stale sludge from the ancient coffee maker in a small conference room.

"So this is what liquid shit looks like," Vernon said, sipping the over-cooked brew.

"Vern, I wanna do something real," Jeff said, sitting on a battered green folding chair, elbows on a rickety table. "I can't stand much more of this crap…and I mean paper shuffling, not this alleged coffee."

"I'm surprised you've lasted this long," Vern said, standing at the end of the table, sipping. "What do you want to do?"

"I'm not sure. What else is there to do? I need something more substantial or…." He paused realizing he'd almost said "…or I want out," and suspected Vern had completed the sentence.

"I wish I could be more encouraging," Vern said. "You've discovered we're pretty much a busywork outpost. The sit-ins and the marches aren't happening around here although some of us have or will be in some of those. And we *do* provide massive opportunities for endless bullshitting sessions exploring political ideas and assorted universal and religious truths."

Jeff forced a grin but it vanished instantly. "Yeah, those are wonderful benefits," he said, his voice rising. "But I can't just sit on my butt moving paper from one table to another and not seeing any results. No victories, no defeats. Hell, we don't even have anyone mad at us." He stopped, flushed by his outburst, looking away from Vern.

"Maybe I'll arrange for someone to beat you up a little or burn a cross on your lawn," Vern said, putting his cup on the table.

"That might help," Jeff said, "but I want to *do* something, not just *talk* about maybe doing something, sometime, somehow about injustice. I want to get on with it. As someone, possibly Lincoln, once said, 'the world will little note nor long remember what we beat our gums about here, but it'll pay attention if we do something." A pause, "Or something like that," pursing his lips and shaking his head.

"Jeff Martindale for president," a soft, husky voice came from behind him. "Anyone who can whip off speeches like that without even the back of an envelope to write on deserves our vote."

"Hi, Susan," Vern said.

"Ah, yes, John Wilkes Booth, I presume," Jeff said, turning to look at her and realizing his tone was too serious and his comment silly.

Vern intercepted her reply. "Susan, I think you'd better prepare a transfusion for Mr. Martindale since he's growing weary and faint of heart. I think shock treatment is in order."

Jeff was unamused by Vern's apparent brushing off the dark frustration fueling his mood. "I need more," Jeff said.

"How about a double Coke on the rocks?" Susan looking directly into his eyes.

He was unequipped to deal with her directness but he tried to match it.

"Shameless hussy. The things you'll do for free refreshments."

She spun around, tossing her hair and her reply over her shoulder. "We'll make it Dutch treat some other time, Abe."

Jeff jumped to his feet, knocking the metal chair noisily to the floor, picking it up and hurrying after her, stung by her reaction to his clumsiness.

"Susan," he called to her retreating back. "Susan. Wait."

But she didn't stop, walking rapidly down the hall, through the door and down the steps. When he caught up and touched her shoulder, she paused but shook off his hand.

"I'm sorry," he said to her still-angry profile. "I didn't mean it that way." Then, encouraged by her lack of outright rejection, "I'm just discouraged and frustrated. Sorry I was such a jerk."

"I'm sorry, too," she said turning to face him, "I overreacted," she said softly, covering his awkwardness.

Slightly relieved, Jeff said, "Come on, it's almost dinnertime. Let's get something to eat."

"Ah," she said, hesitating, "where?"

"Follow me."

To her surprise he began walking away from campus.

"You know some secret French café this way?" she said, hurrying to catch up.

"Nope. The anti-French café. The Old German restaurant. They have great knockwurst and sauerkraut and cabbage rolls and unusual sandwiches. I need something different."

"Are you having problems with Vern?" Susan asked. "What did he mean you need a transfusion?"

"I need more action, more results," Jeff said. "I'm bored and frustrated sitting around doing busywork and listening to endless chit-chat and bull sessions about equality and brotherhood, etcetera, etcetera until it's coming out of my ears."

"First time I've ever heard anyone admit they were full of etcetera."

He smiled briefly. "I don't think this so-called movement is *moving* anywhere. And it won't get anywhere without stronger measures than we're using. Hell, if I were the racists, I'd let protestors sing and march until their legs wore off at the knees. I'd let them protest and do sit-ins until they starved to death. We need laws and we need enforcement if we're ever going to change anything."

"Sure," she agreed, hurrying again to catch up with his unconsciously lengthening stride. "But a lot of groundwork has to be laid first."

"It's been laid. It's called the Constitution," Jeff said as they headed for a booth. Neither spoke for a few minutes, taking in the room's Swiss Alps atmosphere, not anxious to re-thread the conversation.

After a waitress took orders, Jeff abruptly pushed on. "Why are you working there? I know you believe in the cause, but what's really being accomplished?"

"Why do you think I'm there?"

"Not sure. Some of the whites are there because they're realizing for the first time in their lives that racism actually exists and that it's grotesque and cruel and completely indefensible; suddenly it's not just a term paper topic. And they feel guilty. It's often the first cause they've truly experienced. They sincerely want to help and this is the only way they know how. They haven't thought much about effectiveness or whether they're causing actual change. They seem to believe if we work hard enough something good will automatically happen."

"Why are you there?" she said.

"Damned if I know. That's my whole point. I thought I'd contribute something toward the larger cause, but it's not happening. We're just spinning our wheels; no traction toward progress. I want some results. I haven't seen squat. Have you? I think nothing's come from the so-called activity except the activity itself. I'm about to bail out. I can think of lots of things I'd rather *do*."

The ferocity of "do" was clear.

"You need a break," she said. "You should join a march or a sit-in somewhere. Get some action. See if that changes anything for you. You need up-close experience. Get the personal feel of the people and the movement. Do some shouting and singing, maybe get spit on or tossed into a nice southern-hospitality jail. You'd see what both sides are doing," she said, her voice underlining 'doing.'"

"Both sides," he snapped. "There's no such thing. Good and evil are not equals."

"Ok, ok," she said, holding up both hands, palms aimed at him. "I still think if you get some firsthand exposure you'll never forget it and you'll probably feel better. Think about it."

Deal," he said, forcing a small smile. "Let's change the subject. Who do you think will win World War Three?"

"This *is* World War Three," she said softly.

CHAPTER ELEVEN

"Ever shoot a gun?" Jeff asked several weeks later, enjoying the surprise splashing over Susan's face.

"No. Why?" she said.

"I'll take that as no," he said. "Women from New York don't have guns? Any friends who are hunters or target shooters?"

"I don't know anyone who has a gun. Certainly not my mother or any of her friends. They don't need guns. Why are you asking?"

"Partly because that's the narrow, anti-gun attitude. It's like saying we don't need rakes or hoes or baseball bats because they can be used to as weapons.

"I, and practically all of my friends, grew up with guns, usually for hunting. It was common, no big deal. We're all comfortable with guns and highly conscious of using them safely. Some of my best memories are of my grandfather teaching me to shoot a 22-rifle that he gave me and I still have. I realize New York, particularly urban New York, is different, but anyway, you want to see if you can kill a pop can just for fun?"

"Uh, maybe. Sure. I'll try."

Saturday morning Jeff parked the Plymouth on a narrow gravel road ending at an abandoned rock quarry north of Ann Arbor. He lifted a green canvas gun case from the trunk and extracted a rifle with a scope plus a cardboard box nearly full of empty soda cans. He also pulled out a pair of gallon jugs of water that he used to fill six cans before lining them up across the path about 30 feet from the car.

"Ok," he said, handing her the rifle. "Just heft it, it's not loaded, just get comfortable."

She put it to her shoulder, then took it down and looked at it, feeling the burnished wood stock. She handed it back to Jeff and watched as he snapped a clip of cartridges into the rifle.

"I'll fire a couple of shots so you can hear the small noise it makes. It's only a 22 and it's really not loud at all, and there's no recoil."

He sat on a grassy patch alongside the path, elbows resting on upraised knees, right cheek pressed against the stock. She winced at the first shot, blinked at the next two, hands tented over both ears, face serious, then uncovered her ears.

"Ok, now watch the can on the far left," he said, squeezing the trigger and the can of water exploded. "Cool huh? Ready?"

"I guess so."

"Sit here," he said, patting a spot on the grass. He positioned her, feet flat, elbows braced on knees and handed her the rifle. "Close your left eye and look through the scope. Put the cross-hairs on a can. Take a deep breath, hold it and when you're lined up, squeeze the trigger as slowly as you can."

She did it so gently that when the gun finally went off she was surprised. The bullet puffed the dirt near a can.

"Great. Try again."

She did and when the water-filled can exploded she saw it clearly in the scope and looked up at him with joy and surprise. "Let me kill another one," she said, already peering into the scope, finger tensing. She missed once before another can exploded.

A half-hour later, Jeff replaced the rifle and mangled cans in the trunk. He pulled a rolled-up towel from behind the spare tire and unwrapped his grandfather's World War One-era revolver and handed it to Susan.

"He put this in a box of things he wanted me to have someday. This was at the bottom and I don't think my grandmother even knew it was there when she gave it to me after he died. It's so old and an unusual caliber, a 32-short, that I don't know if you can buy cartridges for it anymore. I may never fire it again but it came with a box of shells. Maybe I'll fire one shot a year for the rest of my life."

He rewrapped the pistol as if it were made of gold.

As the car moved slowly back on the gravel path, she said: "that was fun. It really was. Thanks. I never thought I'd enjoy it so much."

"And yet you came," he smiled, glancing at her in the passenger seat. "I'm glad you did. It was fun watching you," his eyes locked on the primitive road, the car bouncing. They were both quiet for several minutes until they'd almost reached the paved highway.

"I like being with you," he blurted, his eyes scanning as if expecting to see a water buffalo blocking the road. "I mean, really. I guess…I mean I like you a lot."

"You *guess*?" she said in a mocking tone, watching the side of his face. "Any chance you're sure?"

He slowed to a stop on the one-lane path, turned the key off and shifted to look at her, his cheeks a little pink.

"I'm very sure. I'm just not very good at saying so. I'm *very* sure. I think you're terrific and interesting to be with and…" his eyes glancing left and right like someone afraid of stepping into quicksand.

She startled him by bursting into her musical laughter that he liked so much. "Let me make it a bit easier for you. I like you a lot too, so we're agreed on that. Let's just proceed and see what happens."

He re-started the car and she laughed again, her face bright with amusement.

He turned off the car again and started to turn toward her and she was already leaning toward him, reaching for him, brushing against his hand moving to her shoulder, pulling her into a lingering kiss dramatically more intense than the tentative and brief 'good-night' kisses at her sorority-house door after their serial set of first-date; one-hug-and-a-kiss experiences. After the first movie date and the awkward episode several weeks ago at the NAACP office, they had several encounters that they later agreed were toe-dippings, not-quite dates, inviting each other to campus events, a lecture or a foreign film or "got time for coffee?" on the spur of the moment.

They had been flirting with flirting, feeling the attraction, but wary.

Now, she leaned back slightly, opening her eyes, touching the sides of his face with her fingers, both of them looking at each other in the intense way lovers do, trying to read each other's thoughts, overwhelmed by the closeness. He cupped her chin and she found his lips with her fingertips, then with her lips, sliding as close to him as she could.

He caught the faint aroma of her shampoo along with a slight hint of something else. He started to smile and she sensed it, leaning back a bit more, squaring her shoulders to the seat, looking straight ahead and then back to him.

"Well, she said, "I think we're proceeding just fine."

He reached for the key. "You want to know something I just learned?"

She studied him.

"The smell of gunpowder in a woman's hair is quite seductive."

CHAPTER TWELVE

Bright sunshine and spring's moist, earthy aroma caressed Jeff's senses as he walked briskly across The Diag, the spoked-wheel of sidewalks organizing the park-like open space in the center of the main campus, surrounded by classroom buildings. He inhaled deeply, refreshing his lungs with pungent, humid air. He spotted Susan watching him from one of many benches scattered throughout the tree-shaded area. She must have seen him coming with his long strides, glancing side to side, looking for her. He planned to sit beside her and marvel at the delightful day and at the closeness of her but she jumped to her feet as he arrived.

"Come on," she said, grabbing his hand, whirling him half-way around. "Let's go somewhere. A drive in the country? We can run through a cornfield or something."

"Simple, simple city girl," Jeff smiled, catching her spirit. "There's no corn this time of year except for that stuff that even now pours from your mouth."

"I feel so good I'll overlook your insults," she said tugging him by the arm down the sidewalk. "Let's toss our books and fly somewhere."

"Why not?" he said, fully in the moment now. "Let's grab sandwiches and sodas and head for the river. It's only two-thirty. We deserve it. We've been working too hard."

"Liar. You haven't done a lick of work in months."

"Unfortunately that's true. You're a bad influence on me; a distraction," he said, taking her hand and swinging it as they walked. "A wonderful distraction," he added, holding her eyes when she looked up at him.

Later, on the riverbank with the Plymouth's floor mats as a pad under a blanket, Jeff sat up and stared across the flowing water dimming into the settling dusk. He inhaled a deep breath of rapidly cooling air spiced with the fragrance of new flowers and damp earth, then ran his hands along the sides of his head, smoothing his hair and looked down at Susan on her side next to him, head propped on one hand.

"I think I'm seeing too much of you," he said softly, glancing briefly at the river, then back to her.

"I have the feeling you were trying to see all of me" she said, the barest trace of a smile toying with her lips, sitting up, hands brushing her hair back and smoothing her blouse.

"Uh, well, exactly. We may need to back off a bit and sort ourselves out."

He looked at her again, both of them searching the other's eyes, her skirt halfway up her thighs.

"It took both of us to return to reality that time," he said quietly, checking again to be sure the river was still there. "Next time maybe one or both of us won't be trying."

She hugged him close, putting her head on his shoulder. He felt her soft breasts surrounding his arm like a blood-pressure cuff, his pounding pulse echoing in his ears.

"The ever-serious Jeff. You're such a straight arrow. I'm not afraid. We're not a couple of kids likely to be overwhelmed by white hot passions," she smiled up at him.

"Says you."

"Relax. I've met some of America's greatest lovers, or so they said. I'll succumb when and where and with whom I choose."

"You really can bust an ego, can't you?" he grinned.

She grabbed his head with both hands and pulled him back to the blanket. The thorough and long kiss rekindled the fiery feelings of a few moments ago. Her fingers dug into the back of his head and neck before finally releasing him.

"How's your ego now? I can almost see it."

"I'm really fine all over."

"Me, too. That should explain that there's no conflict between realism and love."

"That's a strong word," he said, gently holding her chin in his hand, one finger caressing her cheek, their eyes focused on each other.

"One of us had to bring it up sooner or later, or is what I've been feeling a one-way experience?"

"You know it isn't," he said quickly, his finger tracing her lower lip.

Abruptly he rolled to one side, raised to an elbow, resting his head on his hand. He pushed the hair from her face and filled his vision with her eyes, soft and dreamy, desirous and trusting.

"Oh, Susan Adams, I love you. I do. I'm not used to it. I think I'm afraid of what to do about it. But I know I do. I should be able to describe what I feel but…and I know I keep things in my head too much sometimes. And I…"

"It's one of the things I love about you," she whispered. "There's no owner's manual for this. Love, whatever that is exactly, is a growing, changing thing. Let's check back tomorrow and the day after that and again and again after that and just enjoy."

"Ok, but first…"

He pulled her to him, her face above his, mouths exploring, his hands moving to the small of her back, removing the space between them. She moved her head slightly back but still looking deep into his eyes.

"Yikes," he said.

"Yes," she agreed.

CHAPTER THIRTEEN

A few days after the river picnic, Jeff described for Isiah the vivid feelings that engulfed him as a 12-year-old when he first saw photographs and television coverage of racial hate and violence. They sat at a splintered and raggedy wood table outside Rick's Bar-B-Q, hunched over paper plates of ribs slathered with sauce; trying to keep drippings off their clothes.

"The newspaper photo showed a white kid punching a black kid right in the face," Jeff said, wiping his chin with a napkin. "The TV film of the sit-in was like being there. Screaming and swinging bats and pipes. One black kid was hit by a rock and he crashed to the pavement and I thought he was dead. Maybe he was. Then the white kid kicked him in the nuts and head. I had no idea what actual hatred and violence looked like. I see it all this time now, but...how can people be so twisted? Brutalizing people? Why can some racist thug take away rights guaranteed in the Constitution? Why doesn't the federal government put a stop...?"

Isiah cut him off, leaning across the table, whispering, almost hissing.

"Whoa. Man, listen. Hatred's blind. Hate's not logical. Hatred comes from all the other hostilities and fears clogging up people's heads and souls. Hatred makes violence acceptable. War does the same thing," he said, leaning back. "We were *supposed* to hate Germans and Japanese during World War Two. Everyone knew it. It was acceptable. And honored.

The government preached it and handed out medals. And the churches sanctioned it. Everybody agreed," he said.

Jeff started to speak but Isiah jabbed a finger at him and leaned across the table again. "You're part of the problem, you know."

Jeff glanced into Isiah's eyes and then quickly away, stung by Isiah's words, though unsure of their meaning.

"You really are," Isiah said, looking past Jeff. "Your whole exposure to racial hatred is long-distance. You haven't experienced smothering repression or actual brutality. You haven't been exposed to hate every day of your life; or even for one day."

Jeff brought his coffee to his lips, hiding behind the cup.

"I know you feel intensely about this," Isiah continued. "And you really work up a head of steam sometimes, but you're mostly feeling an abstract emotion fueled by second-hand exposure. You haven't absorbed the oppression into your soul. You've got a long way to go before really *knowing.*"

Then, apparently seeing Jeff's stricken face and realizing how harshly critical he sounded, Isiah smiled, further confusing Jeff. He slid his right hand across the table, putting it on Jeff's wrist, squeezing. "I'm sorry for how that sounded. I didn't mean it as criticism. You haven't had the opportunity yet for personal battles. You're more fired up about this than anyone I've ever seen coming from your background. You, and people like you, can be part of the path to progress.

"I love the way you're looking for ways your idealism can cope with brutal things like lynchings or the degradation of an entire race by law. I know you're struggling for a way to change the world to the way you think it should be."

Isiah frowned at his watch and stood up. "We better get going. Professors are standing by to educate us in twenty minutes.

***

The next day, Jeff said, "You were right, Padre," as he and Isiah settled into a cafeteria booth for their almost-daily caffeine and conversation. "I'm embarrassed at my ignorance about lots of stuff and…"

Isiah erased an invisible blackboard with his hand. "And I needed more context," he said. "I struggle myself to understand why some people are afraid of me, and hate me, and hate my mother, at first glance without knowing her at all. In the early days of this country, the so-called melting pot wasn't very accepting of lots of white folks. *'Dogs and Irish Keep Out'* were common signs in Boston and elsewhere. Ditto for Italians and others. Everyone needed at least one ethnic group or nationality or religion to look down on, and it was usually the latest group to arrive. Sometimes it was the same groups that disliked or hated or feared each other when they shared Europe together. They already had names for each other: Hunkie, Wop, Kraut, Polock, Slant-eyes, Wetback, Nigger, Jap. Our 'Little Brown Brothers' of the Philippines still remember the patronizing attitude of many of our soldiers toward those fighting side-by-side with them in World War Two.

"Blacks easily feed the need some folks have to feel superior to *someone.* Black people are easy to spot. We were brought here in chains, treated as sub-humans. Blacks were property, bought and sold, often at auction. Our children were sometimes torn from parents' arms and sold for cash. The system degraded and dehumanized all races and religions, black and white, Asians, Christians and Jews and Muslims; everyone involved, both slaves and owners.

Jeff sensed the anger and frustration in Isiah as his words quickened.

"Sound like ancient history to you?" Isiah asked, fingers caressing his cup's rim. "Not so. State laws have maintained the equivalent of the 'master-slave' relationship. And not just in the South. Oregon's Constitution still says the only blacks who can legally live there are slaves. The 1891 Mississippi Constitution described white superiority as if writing it down made it true. The legal slave-master relationship was abolished by Lincoln but in reality not much changed. Some states, including Kansas and New Mexico, still have laws prohibiting Asians from owning property. Lynching—in effect legally killing blacks—still isn't a federal crime. That leaves many states without laws making murdering blacks any kind of crime. Less serious than jaywalking. Not even a misdemeanor."

"But," Jeff said, "our generation is less blindly prejudiced and bigoted. Overall aren't things better?"

Isiah puffed out his cheeks and sighed. "Maybe a bit better in a few ways," he said. "But it's actually worse in most of the South. The civil rights fight itself is intensifying the underlying fear and hatred in some bigoted whites. Don't forget blacks can still lose jobs or be beaten or killed just for *trying* to register to vote. And no one worries about getting arrested or convicted for terrorizing potential voters…or even for murder. Often the beaters and killers are cops."

He tilted his head back to stare at the ceiling. "Less than a year ago, the Freedom Riders were viciously beaten and jailed just for entering white waiting rooms in bus stations. Overall better? Not hardly," he said, holding a stare, rekindling Jeff's discomfort.

Then he added: "I hope and dream that in my lifetime, young people, when told of how things are now, will be astonished and wonder how the country could have been so stupid. And so cruel. If that doesn't happen, we'll have lived a national disaster in the meantime."

CHAPTER FOURTEEN

The pungent aroma filled the booth and Jeff laughed softly.

"I never thought I'd be eating sauerkraut on a date," he grinned. "This can't be socially acceptable."

"This is getting to be a habit," Susan said, fork-cutting a piece of waffle.

"Whata ya mean? This is the first time I've ordered it; we're not even half-way through the menu here."

"I mean Friday night at the Old German," she said. "You realize we've been here four straight Fridays?"

"We have? You want to break the habit?"

"I was only pointing out how fast time has zipped by and how quickly we've developed a groove," she said.

"A groove? Like a rut?" He faked a sad face.

"You know it's not that."

"Yeah, now clean your plate or there's no dessert," he said.

"Nag, nag, nag."

"Second time this week I've been accused of that," Jeff said. "I may have to change my ways. Or my friends."

"Who else has discovered your true character?"

"The padre accused me of impatience and of continually trying to push our compatriots at the N-Double-A office into doing something beyond scheduling speakers and suffering paper cuts. He's right. Months ago you said you doubted we were accomplishing much."

"I still don't see much progress," she said. "I'm getting more impatient, too, and that's not bad if it keeps us focused on the big picture. But maybe we need to rethink everything. You've made me wonder about it.

She sipped her water. "I agree we need more effective actions and less navel gazing. It's easy to generate energy and enthusiasm just talking about the outrageous and massive injustices, but maybe we're just bleeding off pressure with all our yakkin."

"Right," he said, impaling a slice of wurst on his fork and aiming it at her. "But I'm more pissed off now than I've ever been; much more so than when we came here the first time five months ago. That seems like a year long ago. "

"Actually four months, three weeks and a day," she said, sliding both arms across the table, covering one of his hands with both of hers.

He put his fork down and topped her hand with his, squeezing and releasing.

"I love you," he said. Another squeeze.

"I know. Me, too, you. Good grief, listen to us."

They laughed, still new at this and thrilled with each other.

CHAPTER FIFTEEN

"Hey Jeff," Vernon called, waving from a converging sidewalk on The Diag. "You still want to do something important? What are you doing Spring Break?"

"Going home. Why?"

"How about going to Nashville instead? Monica and I are joining a sit-in." Then, as they merged onto the same sidewalk, "You still want to *do* something? Here's your chance."

"Well, maybe I…that sounds intriguing…I think I can arrange… What're the details? Who all's going?" Jeff said as they stepped onto the grass.

"Just Monica and me at this point. I'm headed to see if Rev. Isiah'll go. He'd be our team leader but we're going either way. A friend of mine at Fisk is setting up a couple sit-ins at Nashville restaurants. He's recruiting some Vanderbilt students. We'll know more in a few days but we'd have to leave a week from Friday and drive straight through. It's close to 550 miles. You in?"

"Yeah," Jeff said, already rehearsing calls to Angel Harbor. And Susan

***

"Let's go to Tennessee over Spring Break and integrate some restaurants."

He saw her eyes widen the instant he said it.

"You and me?" her face sliding into astonishment.

"Yeah," he said, grinning. "Vern and Monica, and maybe the padre, are heading to Nashville to team up with some Fisk and Vanderbilt students for a couple sit-ins. Long drive there, but it's *actual* action. I've already agreed. You in?"

"Oh, yes," she said immediately. "Yes, yes, yes. Give me the details. I am absolutely in." She hesitated, then added: "I've been hoping we could escape somewhere for a weekend," one eyebrow raised.

CHAPTER SIXTEEN

"There's a bar-b-q place," Isiah said, pointing through the windshield. Vernon's ancient, battered black Buick slowed and swung into a busy parking lot surrounding a large ramshackle wood building: Billy Jack's Finest Bar-B-Q.

Vernon and Isiah stepped out of the front doors as Jeff, Susan and Monica climbed stiffly from the back of the long sedan that looked as if it belonged to a funeral director.

"Even if it's only the finest bar-b-q in Kentucky, it'll be wonderful," Isiah said, bringing up the rear as Vernon led the weary quintet trudging across the dusty lot to double screen doors. The cavernous dining room was crowded and noisy as they stepped inside, but it abruptly went completely silent, every face, some in mid-chew, turning toward the newcomers. All the white faces.

Isiah turned silently back through the door and reappeared a moment later.

"Well," he said softly, "we missed a sign by the door. We're in the "Whites Only" section."

They turned to look at each other, forming an impromptu huddle. "Let's go," Vernon said, stepping to the door.

"No," Jeff said, loud enough to be heard half-way across the room. "This is bullshit. Let's sit."

"We've no time for that," Isiah said quietly, putting a hand on Jeff's shoulder, firmly guiding him to the door. Then they were out and headed to the Buick, Susan holding his hand; no one speaking.

Crawling into the backseat Jeff said, "That was an opportunity to make a point. Why didn't we take it?"

"We already have a mission on our plate," Isiah said from the front seat. "And we need to get to Nashville. An impromptu sit-in wouldn't have worked. We had no plan."

Jeff glanced at Susan beside him. She met his eyes and added a microscopic nod. Several hours later the semi-hearse passed the Tennessee State Capitol and in a few blocks, just past the edge of the Fisk University campus, swung into a driveway leading to a white Victorian three-story house with black-trimmed windows, doors and gables. Late afternoon light lengthened shadows, sliding into a dusk scented by unfamiliar flowers. Tall trees further darkened the lawn.

Jeff put his hands on the sedan's roofline as if to tip it over, leaning forward and back, trying to banish weariness from 12 hours of nearly non-stop driving since leaving Ann Arbor in the middle of the night. Vernon and Isiah were already walking up the driveway. The front screen door banged open, ejecting a stream of excited young men and women, all black, greeting them with hugs.

"Everybody inside," a tall youth yelled. "Iced tea, sodas, beer, bathrooms," waving a welcoming arm. The two groups merged through the door, into a large space that could have been a ballroom. Jeff took Susan's hand and they moved to the imposing gray-brick fireplace dominating the room, trying to absorb the disjointed din of everyone talking at once.

"We're the only white people here," he whispered to her. I didn't expect many others but…who's this?"

"It's Robert Lewis," she said. "From Atlanta. I saw his photograph. He was on the Freedom bus rides."

Lewis walked briskly across the room to them, his arm already extended.

"Hi, I'm Robert Lewis. Thank you both for coming. We're gonna relax a bit and get acquainted before our planning meeting," already turning toward the door.

Five young whites, three men and two women, came in, two wearing

Vanderbilt shirts, greeting the Fisk students as old friends. Twenty minutes later, with no visible signal Jeff saw, the minglers began taking seats on the furniture and floor, facing the fireplace where Lewis and Isiah stood talking quietly. Susan and Jeff followed suit. Then, as if he'd just noticed the assembled people, Lewis turned to face them.

"Hi, everyone. We need to get down to serious business. First let me introduce Rev. Isiah Booker of Philadelphia. He's a doctoral student in Ann Arbor."

Isiah introduced Vernon, Monica, Susan and Jeff and made a back-to-you gesture to Lewis.

"Ok, here's the plan," Lewis said. "Tomorrow morning at 10 sharp, after the restaurant's breakfast crowd is mostly gone, the five white Vanderbilt volunteers, plus Jeff and Susan from Michigan, will take seats at the counter if any stools are open. If not, go to booths or tables. No Vanderbilt or Fisk t-shirts or caps. No Michigan clothes either.

"At 10:05, six of us, including me and Rev. Booker, will come in. Those of you at the counter will immediately get up and we'll take your places. All of you move to whatever seats are open. We'll be polite and orderly but we'll be definite. We'll order food.

"We definitely won't get any food and we'll probably get arrested. We won't instigate violence but, if arrested, no one will cooperate. Everyone will go limp and we'll probably be carried or dragged out. When we get to the jail we'll go limp again. We've been practicing going limp," he added, smiling, then laughing with the rest of the Fisk students. "Actually, we're pretty good at limp.

"The rest of you are observers and occupying space to minimize the number of non-protesters in the place. That's it. No matter what happens, do not involve yourselves in any active way. No chanting, no confrontations with the cops. Observe only. Nothing else. Got it?"

Heads nodding around the room.

"Leave your wallets and purses here. Nothing in your pockets, not even lint. All you gals will want to wear jeans or slacks. We'll go over all of this again in the morning. All Fiskers be here and ready to go by 9 a.m. Our Michigan friends are staying here so that'll be easy. The rest of you get to the restaurant on your own and begin infiltrating at 10."

Isiah stepped forward. “God bless and protect us all.”

A Fisk student held up a hand, momentarily inheriting the attention given to Isiah. “Michigan visitors,” she said. “Make yourselves at home. Any bedroom door that’s open is available thanks to Spring Break. Guys can find rooms on the third floor, gals on the second floor.”

Susan looked at Jeff and held her palms up, making a disappointed face.

Donations for pizza and drinks were collected and the evening filled with conversations before disappearing into night and then became the early hours of the next day. The day some of them would try to exercise the simple right to eat at a public restaurant.

They knew they would fail.

CHAPTER SEVENTEEN

The ride to downtown Nashville was a blur, trees and utility poles whizzing past the windows, no one talking. Jeff's mind raced and flitted, flying without a pilot. He sat next to Susan in the backseat but he traveled alone, like the others, each pondering individual thoughts, barely aware of the journey. Jeff found himself quietly humming "Onward Christian soldiers, marching as to war…"

Susan sat silently staring through the side window, her hand on Jeff's knee. She turned to look at him as he hummed.

"Christian' soldiers?" he muttered. "Half the white kids here are Jewish…Christianity has nothing to do with this. If the Christian churches in Nashville started marching and integrating we wouldn't have to drive here from Michigan."

The black hearse slowed rapidly as Vernon pulled to an unoccupied curb. Susan, Monica and Jeff saw a small blue car parked about a block away and recognized two Vanderbilt students, Mike and his friend Amy, both from New York, standing by the car. Mike, short and stocky, looked like a linebacker next to Amy, a pixie with close-cropped black hair and a small, pointy nose.

Isiah half turned in the front passenger seat. "Ok, guys," he said, "this is the real thing. We're less than a block from the Waffle and Sandwich Shop. It'll be on the other side of the street. You two," he said, nodding at Susan and Jeff, "mosey down there and get seats at the counter if any are open, otherwise a booth or a table. Amy and Mike should arrive at the same time. Split up if you have to. We want to occupy as many seats as we can. If you're at the counter, move as soon as Vernon, Monica, Robert and I and the others get there. Questions? Ok. Time to go," staying in his seat as Jeff and Susan started up the street, not talking or looking at each other. The sidewalk was ragged and uneven as they marched.

Feeling oddly detached, Jeff's mind was still racing when he saw the restaurant and they angled across the street, holding hands so tightly his fingers hurt. Mike and Amy came from the opposite direction. Mike held the door as the others filed in, Jeff at the rear. The four open seats at the counter filled so quickly it looked like game of musical chairs. Mike pulled menus from their leaning post against the napkin holder and passed them to Amy, Susan and Jeff. All four studied them as if the secrets of the world were written there; but they saw nothing. Waiting.

Four more white conspirators came in, going to a booth, no one talking, as if they didn't know each other, just happened to arrive simultaneously and from the same direction. A leather-faced waitress with gray hair slightly streaked with brown delivered an order to a table, took orders from the booth conspirators then slipped behind the counter looking expectantly at the newcomers. They were apparently memorizing the menus they held like hymnals in front of them.

"What can I getcha?"

The door opened and Robert Lewis came in, followed by two black Fisk students, one male, one female, and Monica and Vernon plus Isiah. Jeff and the three others rose in unison and moved to an open table near the back, their stools immediately filled by Robert, Isiah, Monica and the female black student. The others took seats at a nearby table. The waitress stood as if flash-frozen, not moving, not lowering her pencil. Not a sound in the room. The four surprises picked up the discarded menus and Lewis waved at the waitress from the other end of the counter.

"Grilled cheese and small Coke please."

"I, uh, can't," she said, looking at him but not moving closer. "We can't help y'all," bewildered, panicky, glancing toward the kitchen. "I'm sorry," she added. "I can't."

"Sure you can," Isiah said, giving her his full smile. "We're just hungry folks. And you're a fellow human being. Make mine a cheeseburger." She glanced at him and turned in a jerky motion, almost running into the kitchen. In a few seconds a short, round white man with hooded eyes came out. His grimy white t-shirt had permanent stains partially covered by an apron. His thin, gray comb-over was in disarray, topping a perspiring forehead, his apple cheeks bright red.

"Ya'all leave right now. We're closed," he said, sweeping the counter with his eyes. He flicked one hand toward the door. "Go. We're closed. We ain't serving."

"We just want lunch," Isiah said. "We won't cause you any trouble. We're hungry and we heard you make great cheeseburgers."

"I told you, we're closed. Everybody out." He returned to the kitchen but they saw a sliver of his bright red face peeking through a gap in the swinging door. Three regular patrons sitting in a booth near the back got up and left, quickly joined by two more. No customers now except protesters. They waited quietly, without moving, for five minutes, then ten. Twelve.

Finally Apple Cheeks burst through the kitchen door waving a huge cleaver in one hand.

"Get the hell outta heah," he screamed, advancing a few steps, almost within reach of the demonstrators at the counter but his eyes going throughout the room. "Goddamn you niggers, get out. Out. Now," moving around the counter, toward the people in the back, slicing the air with cleaver sweeps, headed directly for Jeff and Susan's table. They, plus Amy and Mike, scattered, keeping as far from the cleaver as they could, pouring through the door onto the sidewalk. The fat man turned to the counter and took two quick steps as the stools emptied, Isiah, Robert and the others walking deliberately slowly toward the door and then everyone was outside, "Ah *told* ya niggers and nigger-lovers we was closed," echoing after them as the door slammed. Apple Cheeks turned the deadbolt and flipped the sign hanging by a wire: CLOSED.

The demonstrators buzzed and chattered, keeping an eye on the restaurant door, still wary of the cleaver.

Isiah and Robert moved a few feet from the others, talking quietly but with intensity. Jeff moved close enough to listen.

"Fact is," Isiah was saying, "we were outmaneuvered. We're outside and he's inside and this time it's essentially over. We can march around out here but we don't even have signs."

"We couldn't let anyone get cut," Robert said, his face grim. "Most of us are willing to take a beating if that'll show people what vicious thugs some of their fellow citizens are, but I'm not sure we're ready for slashings. Yet."

"Let's start walking back to the cars," Isiah said. "Keep everyone orderly and dignified. We'll work out a new plan later."

He and Robert went quietly from person to person and soon everyone had regrouped, walking in small clumps.

Four Nashville Police cars appeared and matched the walkers' pace to the cars. The police escort followed them back to campus, like a parade, then parked for several hours along the street in front of the white Victorian.

The day's events were discussed and analyzed endlessly throughout the evening until Robert banged his spoon on a glass, commanding silence.

"Everyone did fine today. It didn't work out the way we planned, but y'all did well. We were disciplined and focused but he out-maneuvered us. Tomorrow morning's plan is the same as today's except Woolworth's restaurant counter is to the left of their door and runs front to back. Other than that, we'll infiltrate starting at 10 and take over the counter five minutes later.

"If any of you have small cameras that can be hidden in a purse or jacket pocket, you can try to take some photos, although that could attract trouble right to you. Any questions or ideas? Good, let's get some rest. Tomorrow's another day we'll all remember forever."

Susan whispered to Jeff: "So far, all I'm remembering is action without results."

CHAPTER EIGHTEEN

The next morning Jeff and Susan escaped the Buick's backseat, along with Mike and Amy, into Nashville's already oppressive humidity. The quartet hiked two blocks and Jeff opened the glass door to Woolworth's. All eight seats at the counter were occupied, five by white students he recognized, the other three by middle-aged white men. The rest of the room was empty except for an elderly couple in a back booth plus two booths each hosting two Vanderbilt students.

He and Susan slid into a booth with Vanderbilt students, all eight eyes focused on the door and the counter; Amy and Mike sat a nearby table.

A frizzy-haired waitress came through a swinging kitchen door grabbing menus from a counter stack; quick stepped to Jeff and the others, pad and pencil poised.

"Drink?"

They all ordered Cokes, just watching the door, not looking at her.

"Ah'll be raht back," she said, disappearing into the kitchen.

Almost simultaneously, Robert Lewis and two black students invaded. Three white students stood up at the counter, their seats immediately filled by newcomers. Then Isiah and Monica invaded. The two remaining white students left their seats at the far end of the counter and moved quickly to tables as Monica and Isiah replaced them.

The three middle-aged white men at the counter stared at the seated blacks, seeming uncertain, glancing at each other. Two of them, in white short-sleeved shirts and ties, got up, one tossing two one-dollar bills on the counter and left, glancing back briefly. The other man, in a dark-green *Sinclair* shirt labeled "Bobby" with dark stains in the armpits, put his hand on his coffee cup but didn't lift it, and glared at the intruders.

Total silence. No one moved. A coffee percolator burped.

Bobby stood, counting change from one hand to the other. He slapped the coins on the counter and left, a quarter rolling to the floor as the door closed.

Miss Frizzy returned and stared at the counter, not looking at the people sitting there. The old couple in the back stood up, then sat down again. Watching.

"We can't serve y'all. Everyone hasta leave." She returned to the kitchen, not waiting for a response, never having looked at any of them.

They all heard the phone being dialed, then her quiet mutterings. They waited.

Robert Lewis said, to no one behind the counter, "We'd like to order lunch, please."

A few minutes later, two black and white Nashville Police Fords rolled up, visible through the windows. Eight uniformed cops jumped out, already holding nightsticks. A brief sidewalk huddle and they were inside, lining up behind the people at the counter.

One, with three gold chevrons on his sleeve, announced: "All of y'all leave. Outside. Right now!" his voice rising to a shout.

No movement anywhere for long seconds. "OUTSIDE NOW! MOVE!"

The silence was broken only by heavily breathing people; none of them moving. Jeff's heart pounded in his ears, a marching band practicing in his head.

The police sergeant hesitated, then, pointing at Lewis at the end of the counter nearest the door, shouted: "You're under arrest. Take him outside." A police van pulled up, backing toward the sidewalk between the two police cars.

Two officers grabbed Lewis by his shoulders but he didn't move. The hands shifted to his armpits, pulling him up. He slumped to the floor. "Drag him out," the sergeant barked. The officers grabbed Lewis by his wrists, pulling his arms over his head and dragged him on his back to the door. Two officers from the police van ran in, one brandishing handcuffs. The cops pulled Lewis to a semi-sitting position, yanked his arms behind him and snapped cuffs on his wrists before slamming him backwards, the back of his head thudding on the tile floor. The four officers half-carried, half-dragged him through the door onto the sidewalk to the open van, scraping him over the bumper and jamming him inside.

"Her next," the sergeant's finger aimed at Monica.

She immediately sat on the floor as two cops reached her. They hesitated, unsure what to do.

"You two," the sergeant shouted, pointing at two more officers. "Grab her feet and wrists." They did and Monica was carried out, suspended like a sagging hammock between four officers. No one spoke.

The cops worked down the counter, clicking cuffs on each person, dragging or carrying them to the police van. Finally only Isiah remained at the counter. His forearms rested on the counter, hands clasped, staring straight ahead. Two cops hesitated behind him, glancing at the sergeant, realizing they probably couldn't lift Isiah from his stool.

"Get up," the sergeant barked, poking his nightstick into Isiah's side. "Let's go. Up," jamming the stick more sharply into his ribs.

"The Lord is my shepherd, I shall not want. He makes me to lie down in green pastures, he leads me beside still waters, he restores my soul, He..."

The nightstick hit high on Isiah's right shoulder, bounced sideways and struck him in the temple, knocking his head to the side. Blood ran down his right cheek as he straightened, hands still together, looking relentlessly ahead.

"He leads me in paths of righteousness for his name's sake. Even though I walk through the valley of the shadow of death, I fear no evil...."

Another blow, this time on the point of his shoulder and uniformed arms pulled him backward, crashing him to the floor. Two officers jerked his arms over his head and cuffed his wrists while and two other cops grabbed his ankles and the quartet lifted him a few inches and lurched toward the door, but one lost his grip and Isiah again smashed to the floor.

The four cops tried again and got him to the police van where they began swinging him from side to side.

"One, two, three, oops," an officer chanted as they simultaneously released his hands and feet, sending him to a hard landing on the vehicle's steel floor. He lay stunned for several seconds, then climbed awkwardly to one knee, his hands cuffed, and struggled upright before sitting heavily on one of the benches lining each side.

Jeff, momentarily shocked into immobility when Isiah was struck, had pulled the small 35mm camera from his windbreaker to his eye. He squeezed off several frames, clearing his throat or coughing slightly to mask the sound of the shutter.

As Isiah was dragged to the van, Jeff stood, trying to photograph his arrest. Susan grabbed his belt, trying to pull him back into the booth.

"Sit down," she whispered sharply. "There's nothing you can do. This is part of the plan."

Jeff pulled away from her, trying to keep Isiah in view and document the police abusing Isiah. Suddenly, in the viewfinder, he saw the police sergeant staring directly at him, looking startled and angry, raising his arm. *Click.* Right thumb winding the film. *Click.* Wind.

"Him," the sergeant shouted, walking at Jeff and pointing. "Arrest him. Arrest everyone. Call another wagon! Move it!" *Click.* "And I want that goddamn camera."

Jeff started to lower the camera but it was smashed back into his face, then yanked forward out of his hands. He felt himself spinning around, facing away from the counter, rough hands grabbing his wrists, handcuffs clicking shut, painfully pinching his skin. Anger, then fury heated his veins. He tried to free his hands, dimly aware of cop and student voices rising and overlapping.

N*on-violence. No resistance. Go limp!*

He slumped to the hard floor, his head grazing the table on the way down. He was on his side, cheek on the floor, his vision limited to a couple of feet of tile, hearing shouts and grunts.

Then he heard Susan's angry voice. "Get away from me, you cracker Nazi."

He twisted, trying to see her just as a cop grabbed her by the hair and yanked her head backward, and another uniform snapped handcuffs on her wrists before shoving her to the floor.

"Cowards!" Jeff yelled. "Get your hands off her, you chicken-shit bastards. She hasn't done anything."

A nightstick cracked painfully against his shinbone and he felt his feet being lifted and his body dragged backwards across the floor, butt and head scraping the sidewalk. He was lifted again, then swung with another 'one, two, three, oops' cheer and tossed into the van. He tried to sit up, banging his back on the bench seat, as another student landed on his legs, spreading pain from head to feet, his face wet with blood.

"Susan," he screamed. "Are you ok? Susan!"

A cacophony of undecipherable voices ricocheted off the metal walls, floor and ceiling, then Susan was shoved into the van and fell against him just before the door slammed shut with a stunning clang and the wagon lurched forward, bodies banging together, then sliding off benches as the vehicle turned violently left, then abruptly right, before straightening, leaving its cargo jumbled on the floor in mass chaos. Voices rose and intertwined in the near-darkness, prisoners calling to friends, trying to locate each other and assess wounds. Suddenly the truck braked hard, sending bodies flying forward out of control, colliding with each other and the hard metal edges of the seats; re-jumbling everyone, before speeding up again.

"Susan," Jeff yelled, seeing the back of her head and part of an arm poking from under a pile of humanity in the right front corner of the truck, three feet from where he lay, her legs pinned by prisoners squirming to sit up, hands still cuffed.

"Susan. Over here," he called again. He saw her head jerk, trying to turn, looking for him, finally rolling onto one shoulder, still mostly hidden under a pile of bodies.

"Hey," she said, finding him from the corner of her eye. "You ok?"

Relief swept over him. Then he saw the blood on her extended arm.

"Your arm's bloody" he yelled over the competing din.

"I'm ok," she said. "Not hurting. Your face..."

The van skidded to a violent stop, again launching everyone to a hard collision with the front wall and rearranging the mound of confused and tangled people. The rear door clanked opened and bright light blinded prisoners as a line of officers began pulling them out, dropping them the last foot or so onto the concrete before dragging them across the rough parking lot, over the door jamb and into the County Jail, where the city cops turned them over to Sheriff's deputies.

"Come on, nigger-lover," a gigantic officer grinned, needing no help to pull Jeff along by his feet, with his head and shoulders scraping on the concrete, heels crashing down when unexpectedly released by Patrolman Goliath, who explored Jeff's arms and armpits with his night stick, then banged into his crotch and along his legs, as if examining an inanimate object.

"Ok, sombitch, on your feet unless you wanna be dragged up two flights of cement stairs. Your choice," grinning happily.

Jeff struggled to his feet, looking for Susan. He saw the black protesters, including Isiah and Lewis, Monica and Vernon, corralled together in a corner of the fenced parking lot. Isiah had a trail of blood running from his right temple, down his cheek and under his chin. Although still cuffed, he seemed to be instructing the others, speaking quietly, looking from face to face.

Jeff glimpsed Susan, Amy and several other white women, disappearing into a stair well, escorted by a heavyset female deputy.

A few minutes later Deputy Goliath herded Jeff and four other white men up the same flight of scarred, gritty stairs to a processing room where the cuffs were removed long enough for fingerprinting, then pinched tightly back on their wrists.

Where'd they take Susan?

The five were asked for identification and having none, were asked for their names and addresses by two officers filling out a form on each person without looking at them. The officers seemed not to care when some of the students gave obviously false names—"Liberty Now"—or "Freeman X. Freeman."

Two deputies ushered the students up another set of pocked cement stairs to a cell-lined hallway and shoved them into a large cell, already occupied by five disheveled white prisoners sitting or reclining on all but one of the six metal cots bolted to the floor and with stained mattresses so thin they could have been blankets.

Drunk tank regulars?

The cuffs were removed again. "Enjoy," a round-faced deputy grinned, slamming the steel door. A missing front tooth made him into a jack-o'-lantern. Then, to the other prisoners: "Here's some nigger-lovers for ya."

"You ok?" Mike asked Jeff. "You've got blood on your face," leaning in, examining Jeff's forehead.

"They shoved my camera into my face," Jeff said. "I'm fine," using two fingers to check his forehead and the back of his skull where it had clipped the table. "I don't think it's bleeding anymore," he said, then noticed the rings of blood, like bracelets, encircling each wrist. "Damn that hurts. You all right?"

"Yeah," Mike said, rubbing his own wrists. "They enjoy putting cuffs on so they pinch, just for fun. This your first arrest?"

"Yeah. Everything I expected and more. I need some aspirin."

"My first arrest was in Birmingham," Mike said. "They hit me all over with their devil sticks. I walked like an old man for days and could barely raise my arms above my shoulders. A doctor told me I'll probably be arthritic before I'm 35. If I live that long."

Mike checked the others for injuries, guiding them to the one unoccupied bed. They clustered there, two sitting on the bed, the others, including Jeff, standing. Mike leaned against the wall, all of them together, barely separated from the other five prisoners who stared at them but were not talking.

Mike was clearly the most experienced now that the senior protest leaders were segregated in black-only cells; the older brother who's been through this before.

Jeff looked at him. "Now what?"

"We'll wait," Mike told the group. "It'll be awhile before we know what the final charges are and what the prosecutor wants to do. Our lawyers are likely working to get us out, but don't count on anything happening quickly. There'll probably be bail and the money has to be raised. They try to hold us as long as they can even if charges are minor or not likely to be pursued. Sometimes they don't actually file charges because they don't want to give us a forum in court. Better to just arrest us, rough us up, keep us in jail as long as possible and let us go. Inconvenient for us, less public notice for them. We could be in here for several days. They consider it punishment for being uppity."

About three hours later, Deputy Jack-o'-lantern reappeared and unlocked the cell. "You five," pointing at the students then hooking his thumb over his shoulder, "Let's go. Move it."

They trooped down the two flights of stairs, finding Monica and Susan already there. Jeff grabbed Susan in a long hug. She touched the dried blood on his face while whispering assurances that she was not badly injured.

Lewis greeted them and introduced Abe Thomas, a short, bulging, balding man with a hound-dog face and a lawyer's briefcase. The long-time volunteer for the Nashville NAACP, said: "Everyone's being released."

"No bail," Lewis added, "everything's over."

The black students clattered into the room, got the same news and everyone moved outside, back into the oppressive humidity and the bright, eye-blinking sun glare of the parking lot where assorted vehicles waited to take them back to the house.

"You niggers and you nigger lovers better get out of our town while the gettin's good," followed them out.

Jeff didn't remember his missing camera until the next day. He never saw it again.

"That's it?" he said to Susan. "They turn us loose without us making any legal point? Or any point at all? That's all there is? Hell, they won. They beat us again."

CHAPTER NINETEEN

"A complete waste of time," Jeff said vehemently, a donut chunk plopping into his coffee.

"You think straining coffee through a donut is a waste of time? What a strange sense of priorities," Isiah laughed across the booth near the back of the Java Joint.

"I'm talking about the trip to Nashville," Jeff said, his glare erasing Isiah's grin. "We accomplished nothing. Nada. We lost ground. A fat slob waving a cleaver chased us out of one segregated restaurant and at the second one we were arrested and harassed, roughed up and turned loose as minor nuisances. Net change, less than zero. Racists two, protesters minus two."

Isiah drained his cup before responding. "We can't know the impact of those two sit-ins. They weren't done in a vacuum. There's an overall national movement and the total effort helps make changes. Integrating restaurants is just the beginning. The sit-ins are symbolic and easily understood. Just folks eating together in the same place. A public place. Someday black people will be part of the public. Imagine that. Some day hardly anyone in the whole country will think it's a big deal for black and white people to sit together at restaurants or in movies or in classrooms or offices. Or walking together down the street in Nashville or Birmingham. Even if they're holding hands. Things *will* change. And, by the way, you're sounding more and more like a cranky old man instead of a college student in the prime of life."

"I'm flailing around, getting nowhere," Jeff said. "I'm not accomplishing anything important. Tilting at windmills would be an improvement."

"Sometimes you sound like a guy with a real obsession," Isiah said. "And while you think about that I'll refresh our caffeine," sliding out of the booth.

When he returned, Jeff plunged in. "I don't think I'm obsessed but even if I am, don't you feel the pressure? The fantastic number of things that need doing and the unending stuff that needs learning and the books I'll never live long enough to read? There's always this nagging feeling about all of the things that aren't getting done."

"Chores? Homework? What?"

"Everything. How will I spend the rest of my life? How can I get prepared? Am I just going to *'be'* or is there something I need to *'do'?*"

"You're searching for ways to put your beliefs into action. It's great that you're thinking like that. You've aged five years since we met but that's fine, you're pondering important questions. Are you zeroing in on any answers?"

"No. I'm more uncertain now than ever. I was baptized as a baby and confirmed as a 12-year-old in a Christian church and I have somewhat religious parents, but I don't know enough about religion to decide anything that important. I don't know enough about anything. I'm not sure I'm religious. Honestly, I don't know what I believe about God. If anything."

"You're describing someone who feels death yapping at his heels twenty-four hours a day," Isiah said. "Do you feel compelled to leave some kind of mark?"

"Doesn't everyone?"

"No."

"Don't you?"

A hesitation. "It's important," Isiah began slowly, looking past Jeff, seemingly talking to himself, "to be prepared to die, to be at peace with yourself and with God. Then, anything you can do to influence history, or mankind or, more likely, a few lives, even one or two lives is wonderful.

But first things first. It's not good enough to be president of the United States and put your mark on history without first having come to grips with yourself and your relationship to God."

"What if you don't believe in God or don't know if you believe or not? I guess if you don't *know* that you do, that's proof that you don't," Jeff said, "What if it takes most of your life to figure out that one critical aspect of your life?"

"I think only a few people early in life come to a comfortable relationship between themselves and God and never look back. Maybe no one does."

"You know what bothers me most about dying?"

Isiah watched him without expression.

"It's such a damn waste. Even if along the way you gain some understanding of life, and hone your talents to their sharpest, then, bang, you're dead. Even worse, death can wipe your slate before you've even written anything on it. A tragedy. We're so temporary."

"I think," Isiah said, "the greatest tragedy is to die without having some understandings about life, at least as much as we're capable of understanding. We're going to get bloodied and bruised but each new piece of scar tissue refines the final product. To die without fulfilling our potential is terrible but it happens for reasons we can't possibly understand. There are all kinds of deaths besides physical; don't forget emotional, moral or spiritual deaths. They're worse. I can see why an apparently premature physical death seems so awful but I'm sure it fits into the divine plan."

"I sometimes have this horrible dream where I'm treading water in a huge vat of alphabet soup. All I have to do to understand life is discover what the pasta letters spelling, but every time I get close to the answer a wave scrambles the letters and I never find the meaning. Every time I get a little optimistic about the human race some damn wave or some incident or some jackass comes along and mixes up the letters. What a way to die, drowned in a giant kettle of soup."

"Wow, what do you suppose that dream means…if anything?" Unsuccessfully suppressing a smile.

"I know what it means," Jeff said, turning serious again. "It's me realizing how insignificant we are and recognizing the futility of our tiny, mostly useless little efforts, to decipher what this world is about before it's all over. Maybe there's nothing to understand. Maybe the soup never spells anything."

"Is that all the credit you give to mankind? And to God? " Isiah asked.

"Sometimes I think man is a great and noble being and then I see some sonuvabitch like George Wallace or Orville Faubus or Richard Shelton or Adolf Hitler and the common denominator plunges to zero. Lots of people impute high motives to mankind because they're afraid to admit we're part of a pretty terrible species."

Isiah's voice was gently reproving. "We can't know what our lives will bring. Hemingway said if we follow any story long enough it ends in death. We can't peek at the last chapter to see how everything turns out. And frankly, I don't want to know how many pages are left," his face serious. "If there's an easy solution you'd have found it by now. The important thing is to try. The fact that you're concerned means you're out of the ordinary."

"Yeah, Padre, but if you get too far from ordinary they lock you in a padded cage."

CHAPTER TWENTY

"Hi, Mom.

"Yeah, sure, I'm still coming home next weekend. I want to bring Rev. Booker from Philadelphia with me. He's an incredibly interesting person and I want you and Dad to meet him. But it'll only be until Saturday evening when we'll head back to Ann Arbor because he has to help with Sunday services at his church. If it's ok, I'll invite him and see some of Angel Harbor."

***

Jeff eased the blue Plymouth into the driveway and Isiah said: "Looks like a good house to be in during a storm."

Jeff nodded, seeing the familiar solid brick house framed by four huge blue spruce trees, smaller shrubs and well-tended flower beds blending the structure into the soil. Even before they exited the car he saw his mother coming from the door. A thin, medium-height woman with dark hair lightly streaked with gray, she embraced Jeff.

"You made good time. I wasn't expecting you for an hour," not explaining why she apparently was scanning the street for their arrival.

"Rev. Booker, we've been looking forward to your visit," she said, offering her hand. "Jeff's told us quite a bit about you."

"Well, I'll take the Fifth Amendment on whatever he's said," Isiah laughed.

She smiled and led them into the kitchen and through an archway to the large living room with four upholstered chairs angled toward a substantial, dark wood coffee table decorated with three white candles in silver holders, a pile of books by the chair nearest the fireplace, a console television with a blind eye staring from the far corner.

"Sit and relax," she said. "Coffee?" slipping out of sight into the kitchen the moment they agreed.

Isiah sank into the chair nearest the fireplace, where three logs were stacked over crumpled newspapers, waiting for a match to birth a fire.

Jeff sat on the sofa. "Tomorrow I'll give you the two-bit tour. We'll go along the lakefront by the small downtown and some other things that won't get your blood pressure soaring but that I'd like you to see."

Mrs. Martindale brought two mugs of coffee on a tray. "I've got to tend dinner," she said, vanishing again.

Jeff felt a flicker of uncertainty, wondering if his mother was uncomfortable, but the moment passed as he heard the garage door going up and, a few moments later, his father strode in. "Rev. Booker, I presume," he said, extending his hand as Jeff and Isiah rose.

"Just Isiah, please," returning the firm handshake.

"We're really glad you could come," James said, settling into a chair. "Did you fudge your arrival time to your mother again?"

Jeff nodded, tossing a quick glance over his shoulder toward the kitchen.

"Jeff says you're partly a doctoral student and partly an assistant minister and partly a civil rights worker," James said, loosening his tie against the white shirt. "Sounds like a busy schedule."

"It's seldom dull," Isiah smiled. "Jeff and I manage to include lots of coffee-soaked conversation as well."

"Hmmm," James said with mock sternness, glancing at Jeff. "I hope your grades are holding up," knowing that they were.

"Sure, I'm getting better organized all the time," Jeff said. "I may be turning into you."

"You two had quite an experience in Nashville," James said. "I'm glad to see in person that neither of you seems seriously hurt. It was scary just hearing Jeff tell about it. And I suspect he might have sugar-coated it a bit," he added, looking at Jeff and then Isiah.

"It wasn't all that bad and it's important work," Jeff said quickly as his mother announced from the doorway:

"This all sounds pretty serious, but dinner's ready."

Jeff rose immediately. "Last one in has to say grace.

Isiah remained standing until Mrs. Martindale was seated. "I guess I was the last one," he said, sitting and bowing his head.

"Heavenly Father, we thank you for this meal and for the hospitality and friendship we share. Help us to know your will and help us make our lives count for good through positive deeds and not for evil through action or inaction. Amen."

***

The next morning Jeff backed from the driveway. "I'm gonna show you my grandparent's fruit farm," he said. "It's about ten miles south. It belongs to someone else now but it was an important place to me as a kid. I spent lots of summers there. I learned to drive on an old orange tractor pulling a trailer toting cherries and peaches from the orchards to the barn. I didn't like trimming grape plants or the mind-numbing tedium of hoeing tomatoes but I realize now how all those experiences shaped me, made me want to find a way to make a living that definitely did not involve dawn-to-dusk, back-breaking, dirty fingernails labor," he said.

Jeff paused the car on the gravel driveway leading to a light gray, two-story farmhouse. A tall, matching gray barn stood 30 yards from the house on a spur of the main driveway. Peach trees lined the left side of the driveway from the road to far past the barn, a cherry orchard on the right.

"That barn's where I nailed handles on the baskets pickers used for peaches and grapes, and where I learned to make welding repairs to the trailer. Over there, past the cherry trees, my grandfather taught me to shoot a BB gun and later his .22 rifle and even an old revolver that looks like something the British used in World War One.

"There used to be a well with a hand pump over there," pointing through the passenger window. "We'd tote buckets of water when I was a boy, before an electric pump brought water into the house. There was a water tank right there, sorta like a big bathtub. He had a sprayer mounted on a trailer and we'd pull up here and mix pesticides and water. I remember the first time, I was probably about ten, he asked me to drive the tractor for spraying. I drove up and down the tree rows while he stood in the trailer and sprayed peach trees. I felt so grown up. I miss him so much. He died when I was 13," his eyes misting, throat pulsing for breath. He put the car in gear to avoid having to speak.

Fifteen minutes later, he pulled in another driveway where a longtime pal, Ron, in a white t-shirt and red shorts, was launching a basketball toward a garage-mounted backboard. He grabbed the rebound and shouted: "Hey, man," as he dribbled toward Jeff exiting the Plymouth. "I didn't know you were home," then his eyes shifted to Isiah climbing from the passenger side.

"This is my friend Isiah Booker. Jeff said. "Isiah's a Baptist minister working on his doctorate," he added as the two shook hands. "Ron's been a friend since third grade, and though you probably can't tell from those two misses as we drove in, he's a scholarship player at Central Michigan. You here for the weekend?"

"Until Sunday afternoon," Ron said, holding the basketball against his left thigh. "Hey, how about a pop? You got time?"

"Sure," Jeff said, "but first I need your john. We've been driving around seeing the sights and I'm about to explode," already heading for the familiar back door.

"I didn't know we had any *sights*," Ron laughed, beckoning to Isiah still standing by the car. "Let's go in where it's cooler."

In the kitchen Isiah looked through large windows, absorbing the neatly mowed backyard, a fringe of shrubs and flowers along the wood fence framing the picture. Jeff reappeared as Ron held the refrigerator door open and gestured to a choice of soft drinks. A half-hour later Jeff drained his Nehi Orange and said, "We better get along. Still a couple of highlights to show you before we have to be back for lunch. Mom's probably already cooking," grinning at Ron who knew Mrs. Martindale's penchant for over-producing food.

As they trooped through the screen door into the yard, Isiah scooped up the basketball discarded by the driveway and took a little jump shot that clanged off the rim toward the fence. As he retrieved the ball, Ron and Jeff continued to the car. Ron flicked a glance toward Isiah.

"You know, he's the only colored guy ever been in our house. Isn't that something?" his face astonished as if a flying saucer had just landed.

CHAPTER TWENTY-ONE

"I'm not sure how it went," Jeff said softly, standing behind Susan, gently massaging her shoulders with both hands as they waited for a table at the "Go Blue."

"I know that's hard to understand but I really couldn't tell," his brow furrowed.

She turned toward him, spreading both hands, palms upward. "Well, what *happened*? Did someone say something awkward or…."

"No. Not really."

"What are you avoiding?" impatience on her face.

"Well, my mom might have been a little uncomfortable but I'm not really sure. I hope Isiah didn't notice. If there was anything to notice. She probably would have been a little different just having someone she'd never met show up for three meals and an overnight stay. I may have been looking too hard and seeing something I was afraid would be there. Or maybe not."

"That's *it?* Aren't you over-reacting? A smidgen paranoid?"

"Possibly," he said. "I hope so. Oh, and my friend Ron—you haven't met him, he goes to Central—said in a stage whisper that Isiah was '… the first *colored guy* to ever be in his family's house. Isiah didn't hear it and it's not a big thing but just the phrase 'colored guy' jarred me; although it didn't used to."

"And your mom, what did she say? Or do?"

"Oh, just seemed pre-occupied with cooking, a little fuss-budgety, not really saying much, not unfriendly but not quite as welcoming as she normally seems."

"Well," Susan said, giving him a brief hug, "maybe it's time for you to introduce me to your folks and then you'll have a comparison," arching her left eyebrow.

* * *

Jeff's call to his mother three days later telling her he wanted to bring Susan to Angel Harbor sparked only questions.

"So is this getting serious? Is anything new? What should I do? What are you going to do while you're here? Dad and I'll look forward to meeting her. What does she eat for breakfast? What should I cook for dinner Friday night?"

***

Mrs. Martindale opened the door just as Jeff knocked.

She's been keeping the driveway under surveillance again.

"Hi, Mom, this is my friend Susan."

My friend? Does that sound right?

Susan quickly extended her hand and Mrs. Martindale took it but gently pulled Susan to her for a brief, barely touching hug.

"We're so glad to finally meet you," she said. "Jeff has told us a little about you, but not nearly enough," smiling but her voice hard to read. "And you're early."

"What a warm and welcoming room," Susan said, staring at the flickering flames in the living room fireplace. "Any chance I can toss a sleeping bag in here and pretend your fireplace is a campfire?" she said, smiling at Mrs. Martindale.

"I don't know why not," Jeff grinned. "It's not exactly a park but…"

"Some tea?" Jeff's mom said. "Or coffee or a soft drink?

"Tea sounds great, Mrs. Martindale," Susan said. "I'll help."

As they turned toward the kitchen they heard the garage door going up.

Dad left work early?

James quickly joined them. "Susan, how nice to meet you," taking her offered hand.

"Dinner'll be ready in about half-an-hour," Mrs. Martindale said, reappearing in the doorway. "Why don't you show Susan the guestroom and she can freshen up."

Jeff carried Susan's small suitcase up the stairs to the guestroom.

"I'm sure my mother has been cooking up dinner since noon," he said. "See you downstairs whenever you're 'freshened up,' whatever that is."

"I hope I don't embarrass myself by spilling something on me or your mom's tablecloth," Susan smiled, stepping to him for a hug and lingering kiss.

"Just don't eat with your fingers and you'll be fine."

***

"Wonderful roast, Mrs. Martindale," Susan said. "I don't get home cooking in Ann Arbor."

"And you need more carrots," James said, reaching for the bowl. "Tell us about your family," he added, sparking a quick eye roll from Jeff.

"Well, my Dad died when I was eight," Susan began.

"Yes, Jeff mentioned that," Mrs. Martindale said. "How awful for a young girl. It must have been difficult growing up."

"It was in some ways. It seems like it's been just my mom and me forever. But she's included me in so many of her activities over the years that now we're almost like sisters. When I'm in Ann Arbor we talk a couple of times a week and we write back and forth often."

"A couple of times a week?" Mrs. Martindale said, glancing with a mock frown at Jeff. "You mentioned being included in your mom's activities; does she work?"

"Oh, yeah" Susan said, laughing and spooning carrots. "She works all the time. She just doesn't get paid." Susan explained her mother's addiction to causes and her dedication to helping and willingness to do almost anything.

"Since I was a little girl she's been taking me to clean cages at the animal shelter or to stuff envelopes at the local NAACP office. When I was 10 she took me to her book club and eventually I became 'one of the girls.' She's treated me like an adult since I was a little person. She's always insisted that I can do anything I set my mind to and all the years of hearing her friends discussing the struggle for women's rights, I'm pretty independent, a lot like my mom."

"What do you mean women's rights," Jeff's mom said. "Don't we already have rights?"

"Well, officially, sure," Susan said after a brief hesitation. "But like the civil rights movement, it's about having rights but sometimes not being able to actually use them because someone else doesn't agree that you have them."

"Mom, remember your mother couldn't vote until she was in her forties. It's like black people in the South now," Jeff said. "Black people have the *right* to vote. But *exercising* that right is often illegally blocked by unconstitutional state laws. And the federal government does nothing about it. Plus, most of the South approves of blocking blacks from voting. They've used beatings and hangings to intimidate and keep political power..." trailing off, realizing that his mother didn't identify with a rambling comparison between women's rights and blacks voting in Alabama.

"Isn't that bound to take time?" she said.

"Why? For equality?" Jeff said instantly. "It's already taken too much time. Why should anyone have to wait for equal treatment?"

Susan covered his hand with hers and said: "This is something Jeff and I discuss all the time. He's frustrated by seeing only a few tiny improvements in black civil rights and I have the same feeling of urgency, but maybe with a smidge less frustration," flashing a smile to Mrs. Martindale. "That's why we went to Tennessee for those sit-ins," she added, alarming Jeff who wanted to avoid that subject.

"We agree on lots of things," Susan added. "We study together and we like most of the same movies and music...but not so much that it's boring," meeting James' bemused eyes, then turning back to Mrs. Martindale with a face so cheerful she might have been at a Disney movie.

"And I bet we're ready to agree," James said, standing with his plate in hand and reaching for Jeff's empty one, "that Elizabeth's banana-crème pie is wonderful and not a smidge boring."

***

The next morning Jeff repeated Isiah's trip to his grandparents' old farm, managing to avoid noticeably choking up although his face revealed the lingering emotions churned by his memories of Grampa Martindale and the bonding of working in the fields and orchards at the old man's side.

Late that afternoon he drove to a small park at the base of one of the nearly twin concrete piers that jutted westerly into Lake Michigan. The piers ran for about 500 feet, ushering the river running between them to a merger with the big lake. At the ends, the darker river water, freed from the constricting concrete structures, expanded right and left, blending and disappearing into the cool blue of the big lake. The northern-most pier was slightly longer, capped at its end by a small lighthouse.

They walked the north pier hand-in-hand, sitting in the shade of the lighthouse, quietly talking, and watching sailboats and power craft bristling with rods and hopeful fishermen traveling the river to and from the lake. Jeff told her a few nostalgic stories of boyhood fishing and cigarettes secretly smoked right where they now sat.

"Bring any girlfriends out here?" Susan asked, teasing, glancing at him.

"Not that I recall," he said. "And if I did it was a long time ago."

"Yeah, that's what I thought," she said.

"Mom and Dad like you," he said. "As we left this morning she put her hand on my arm and whispered: "She's nice, Jeff. And smart."

"Wow, best reviews I've had in a long time," she said.

"For her, those are major compliments. Otherwise she'd just smile, be polite and say nothing."

"I like them, too," she said. "They seem grounded, solid and a bit less frantic than my mom gets sometimes. I'm glad we came."

"Me, too. I've been trying to see them through your eyes and that makes me appreciate them in new ways. And you, too. I can tell they're impressed with the range of stuff you comfortably talk about. And I'm know my bringing you here has them buzzing. I've never brought anyone home before and in high school I'm sure none of my dates made them think seriously about any future I might have with any of them."

"You think they're wondering about that?"

"Sure."

"Are you?" nearly a whisper as she stared at his profile.

"Well," he said, returning her gaze, "if you tell me it hasn't crossed your mind I'll just jump off the end of this pier. Have you? Are we ready to talk about the rest of our lives?"

She put her arm across his shoulders. "Yes," she said, squeezing. "Let's talk about that soon," pulling him to her in a lengthy kiss.

***

After Sunday lunch, as Jeff's dad helped him lift suitcases into the trunk, Jeff saw his mom leaning close to Susan and heard her whisper: "I'm so glad to get to know you, Susan. Your mother must be very proud of you," pulling Susan to her in a lingering hug.

Jeff closed the trunk and his dad took his hand, putting his left hand on Jeff's shoulder and leaned in.

"Is she a keeper, son?"

"Yes," Jeff said immediately. "I think so." And, after hugging his dad, "I really hope so."

CHAPTER TWENTY-TWO

Isiah paced the raised stage; Susan and Jeff sitting side-by-side in the second row of an auditorium-style classroom.

"It was my sophomore year of high school and my friend Jeremy and I were in downtown Philadelphia walking to a pizza place, when we saw four white guys coming toward us about a half-block away. We were side-by-side, close to the street and these guys were looking in shop windows," he said, talking as if to himself.

"About 20 feet from us they veered directly into our path and kept coming; it was obviously deliberate. We kept walking and it became a pedestrian version of "chicken." At the last second, two of them lowered their shoulders, knocking us off the curb into the street. One of them said: 'Outta our way, niggers.'

"I spun around and started for them but Jeremy grabbed my arm so hard I almost fell. 'Keep walking,' he said. 'It's not important. Keep going."

"And we kept walking, even though I was so furious it's a miracle I didn't have a coronary. I'm still angry now, right this minute, just standing here," glowering around the room. "I'm as humiliated now as I was then, and I'm disgusted with myself. I understand 'turn the other cheek' as well as anyone but there are times…And although I'm not sure what I was going to do, I know in my bones Jeremy was *wrong*. It *was* important. It *is* important."

A front-row hand shot up. "What should you have done, Professor Booker? What was the right thing to do?"

"I honestly don't know for sure. I know how I felt and how I feel now. I don't know what's right." He stopped, looking over the heads of his students, the scowl frozen on his face. "Why don't all of you think about it and bring some thoughts for next class," he said, gathering his notes, the first person out the door.

CHAPTER TWENTY-THREE

"What really happened to you in Mississippi?" Susan asked Isiah. "From snippets you've mentioned it was a life-changing experience."

Susan, Isiah and Jeff sat under an umbrella at an outdoor picnic table by a drive-in restaurant, after class.

Isiah lifted his water glass, eyes darting between Jeff and Susan across from him before answering.

"Mississippi changed me a lot. At first I was really excited about being in the field where the action was. I was assigned to a small black church near Jackson. I felt like I was on the frontier, preaching an occasional sermon and helping the pastor develop youth programs. I was supposed to be a role model for kids. You know, former football player, college graduate, doing God's work. And I helped a CORE organizing group boost black voter registration from basically zero to a few.

"I had no car and one day the pastor sent me to help a church across town that was trying to organize teen activities. I got on a bus and dropped money in the box, just like in Philadelphia, and took the first seat, directly behind the driver, wanting to see the city as we traveled. The bus didn't move and the driver, a short, skinny white man about 40, said without even looking at me: 'Get to the back, boy. You ain't allowed up here.'

"For a second I thought no one was permitted to sit right behind the driver just as there are rules against standing in the stairwell. Then I *really* understood. Obviously I'd heard of such customs and laws but hadn't experienced being personally targeted and rudely ordered where to sit because of how I looked. This was long after Rosa Parks refused in 1955 to give her seat in the white section of a bus to a white man, thereby sparking a year-long boycott that desegregated the bus system in Montgomery, Alabama.

"As I moved back, humiliation and anger seared my face like an open oven. The other passengers were staring straight ahead, avoiding even looking at me. I wanted to squash that arrogant little weasel who had such power over me. My harsh reactions startled me, actually scared me."

"Why did you move?" Susan said. "Were you afraid you might attack the driver?"

Isiah paused again, looking across the parking lot. Not blinking. "If I could do it over, if I'd been a little more experienced, I would have stayed in that seat and forced something to happen," his eyes icy, staring at Susan. "I was caught by surprise. I muffed it."

"When I entered theological studies I tried to shed some normal feelings, particularly anger. But the up-close-and-personal reality of being seen as some*thing* that must be controlled and confined behind barricades to somehow protect *real* people from contact with me, was overwhelming. Stray dogs with rabies are treated with more respect than I was."

He shifted sideways, one long, chino-clad leg stretched out on the bench. "Later I wondered if I'd have been so outraged if I'd been humiliated every day since childhood. Probably not. I'd have been used to it by then. How does anyone develop self-pride when the all-powerful system smothers it at birth and denies your human dignity every hour of every day?

"'That just how things are,' people in the local church told me. They weren't shocked by what happened but they were highly worried by my flaming anger. They told me to calm down, keep it in perspective and reminded me that we were working for change. They had long ago accepted that they can't sit wherever there's an open seat and that they must move aside for whites walking a sidewalk and that it's illegal to sell food to black people at public restaurants because they're not considered *people.* And those parishioners lived with the custom requiring them to knock on the *back* door of a white family's house no matter why they're there. They accepted the indignity that they *always* need to know how far they are from a "colored" bathroom.

He rubbed his eye with a fist and sat up. "If it's possible to be simultaneously enraged and depressed, that's what I was. It infected me and kept me feverish all summer. I realized later that this was a key reason they recruited me for Mississippi. I needed to *live* the cruelty. And understand that the attacks never stop coming, every day and every night for your entire life; the assaults never, ever stop. Never," his forehead perspiring and his eyes closed.

"It's easy to understand how someone growing up like that eventually can believe he *belongs* in the back of the bus. To think otherwise makes you so furious that you can sink into the muck of mental illness. Whose mind can live a lifetime of oppression without pathological damage? I've already ridden in the fronts of buses. It's not better than in the back, but by god I deserve enough respect and dignity to sit anywhere I darn-well want," pounding a fist on the table.

Jeff said, "Isn't that why civil rights activists are risking their lives? To fight for voting rights and equal education? To break that cycle of oppression and create empowered black adults?"

"There's so much to fix," Isiah said, his normally powerful body slumped. "Do you know that a black doctor can't belong to the American Medical Association? Doesn't matter if his or her medical degree is from Harvard? Can't even be a member. How's that for humiliation?"

Jeff shook his head, eyes going to Susan, who didn't move.

"Something else that made a big impression while I was in Mississippi was my name," Isiah continued. "In Jackson I saw a store: '*Booker Appliances.*' Since Booker is my family's slave name, probably provided by someone who bought and sold black people, I wondered if any of my relatives had been *owned* by ancestors of the current store owners. That's an amazing thought to ponder. I went inside. All the washers and dryers and refrigerators were white and so were all the employees, from cashier to salesman," a slight smile crinkling his mouth. "It's possible that I'm related by blood to some of the people in that store."

"I have no way of knowing my real name, my African name. I don't even know the country where my relatives were kidnapped and transformed into *property*. Maybe somewhere there's a receipt for the sale of my great-grandparents. Wouldn't that be something to frame and hang on my wall?

"I thought about stuff like that and, frankly, I was pissed off the rest of the summer. I wondered if I was capable of bringing the word of God to people who are humiliated every day.

"When I left Mississippi I knew deep in my soul that much of America is the opposite of what I had believed. I went to help kids develop passion for getting an education and, by voting, to get their constitutionally guaranteed place at the tables where decisions are made. But I'd never fully grasped the extent of segregation, let alone its massively cruel impact. I didn't fully understand the insidious effects of oppressing an entire race for generations. I didn't know in my bones what it was like to live in that system day after day, year after year. I know now.

"The irony," he said, "is that the plantation owners established conditions that fostered exactly what they had claimed as an excuse for slavery in the first place; an uneducated, mostly subservient people whose previous culture was erased.

"The entire southern economic and social system required black slave labor to prosper and to maintain the wealthy, land-owning life where white owners were considered genteel ladies and gentlemen and slaves were animals. They morally justified--to themselves at least--physically enslaving men, women and children. If you were a slave owner you could sell mothers or fathers; even black infants. They were all just cattle. They used chains and whips and guns and laws criminalizing anyone helping slaves escape. They punished whites who had the guts to teach blacks to read or write, add or subtract. Fact is, they were afraid of educated blacks. Many of them still are.

"After the Civil War, when forced to provide schooling, the whole culture continued enslavement by providing unqualified teachers, dilapidated buildings and tattered, outdated and incomplete books discarded earlier by whites. And they enslaved blacks again by denying them their rights to vote. They levied poll taxes and required outrageously unfair tests for black voters. And when all else failed, they enslaved through murders that weren't even against federal law and certainly wouldn't be punished in places like Mississippi or Alabama or Arkansas or Georgia or Texas. Southern juries have never convicted a white man for murdering a black person. Not even when there were dozens of witnesses of both colors."

"I seriously considered quitting my ministerial studies. I thought I'd be living a lie. Could I be a spokesman for a god who seems to have tolerated centuries of this oppression? Or was I supposed to be one of his agents bringing change? I thought about moving to a country where I could be a human instead of a 'nigger' and where I could tell the United States of America to go straight to hell. America is already hell for most people who look like me."

He poked a finger into the congealed cheese sandwich on his plate and grimaced in disgust.

"Are you free Saturday?" he said, looking at Jeff.

"I guess. Why?"

"I want you to meet some people I know in Detroit."

"Sounds mysterious."

"Just keep an open mind."

CHAPTER TWENTY-FOUR

Isiah swooped the car through Detroit's outlying residential ring, through the industrial band, to the inner city abutting downtown's commercial zone with its huge department stores, tiny boutiques, glass and lights and people and cars. Busy on a Saturday morning. In the core inner city, four-story and taller brown and red brick buildings rose next to crumbling sidewalks, looming over narrow streets, blocking the sun most of the day.

Jeff tried to absorb everything, kids playing stickball between parked vehicles, scattering at each passing car, teens and adults clumping with no visible purpose on the sidewalks, watching cars, practicing boxing moves on each other, eyeing young women walking by, staring at Isiah's car cruising slowly.

Isiah was silent but Jeff didn't notice, impressions of his first big-city ghetto cramming his mind with random impressions. Block after block of parked cars randomly constricting traffic. Discarded cans, paper bags and other debris disfiguring the neighborhood's face. Isiah pulled to the curb in front of a building indistinguishable from dozens of others.

"Remember that what you see is pretty much what you'd see if we stopped on any of the other streets."

Easy to believe.

Outside the car, the neighborhood wrapped Jeff in its sounds, smells and sights; trash blown into crannies of the building, against the base of gray concrete stairs, paper cups, newspaper pages, exhausted cans adding stale beer to the fetid aroma of uncollected garbage. No grass. No trees. No police cars. No garbage trucks. No white faces.

Isiah took the six steps in three bounds, pushing through a scarred, battle-weary wood door, Jeff hurrying behind. A quick climb up three unlighted flights and Isiah knocked twice on a flaking green door. Jeff saw identical doors down a long dim hallway with two faint lights barely keeping total darkness at bay.

The door opened tentatively, barely a crack, two safety chains still in place, closer to the floor than normal. No one. Then a small boy peered up at Isiah. The door nearly closed and chains snicked from their keepers and clicked against the door before it swung fully open.

"It's Rev. Booker," the boy screeched. "He's here. It's Rev. Booker."

Isiah glanced briefly at Jeff and stepped into a small living room. Jeff closed the door behind him just as a large black woman filled a doorway in the opposite wall leading to the kitchen. Her flowered housedress hung loosely on her soft, ample body.

"Hello, Reverend," she beamed.

"Hi, Louise. This is Jeff Martindale, a friend from Ann Arbor who's helping me today. Jeff, this is Mrs. Louise Crandall and this is Donnie," formally shaking hands with the boy who had opened the door so noisily but now stood silently beside his mother, tucking a white t-shirt into blue shorts, looking at Jeff as if he had just discovered a giraffe in the room.

"Can I get you some coffee, Mr. Martindale?" the woman asked. "I know Rev. Booker will have some."

When she and Isiah disappeared into the kitchen, Jeff sat on the floor, pretending to examine a battered red-metal toy truck, turning it over in his hand, pushing it back and forth on the linoleum, his eyes not even flickering toward the boy squatting three feet away.

"Donnie," Jeff said, "how does this work?"

The boy stood, slowly closed the distance between them.

"Like this," the boy said, rolling the truck back and forth.

"How old are you, Donnie?"

"Four. And a half," still looking at the truck.

Mrs. Crandall reappeared with coffee in a "Detroit Tigers" cup.

Jeff scrambled to his feet and quickly sat back down, hoping the boy would stay. Donnie got up, vanishing down a hallway, returning quickly with a stuffed bear and a small metal race car, which he handed to Jeff and sat down facing him, cuddling the bear.

They pushed the car back and forth between them. Isiah and Mrs. Crandall sat on the nearby sofa talking as if they were alone.

"Everyone doing ok at school?" he asked.

"Oh, yes, they're fine. I nags and works with them ever night about homework and they seems to do ok. It's awful hard sometimes, with everything that goes on."

"Have you heard from Harold?"

"No. Still nothin. She momentarily bowed her head. "You know how it is. Will you be able to visit Mae while you're here? I know she'd love for you to come by."

"Sure. We're headed there next. I wanted to see how you're doing. I'm still working on the scholarship for Margaret. If she keeps her grades up I think we'll get some help for her to come to Ann Arbor."

"Oh, I hope that can be; but I don't see how it can…even with free schooling, they's everything else…I just don't see how…"

"Don't worry, Louise, we'll work it out, God willing. You tell Margaret I'm counting on her to keep doing so well in school."

"I guess God hassa have a pretty big checkbook."

Isiah laughed. "He not only has that but he has a lot of help. You get her to do her part and we'll work on the rest."

He stood and so did she. He took her hand, "God bless you, Louise. I know it's hard but you're doing just fine. You're a good mother and these kids are going to do just fine too."

Jeff got to his feet, noticing the sudden moistening of the woman's eyes and he looked away. An intruder.

Isiah dropped to one knee and held Donnie's hand in his own two massive hands. "You keep helping your ma."

"Yessir," face adult-serious, solemn, eyes on Isiah.

"Ok, then," Isiah said, starting to get up, pausing to sweep the boy into his arms and standing up. We're all counting on you. We all love you, Donnie." Another squeeze before putting the boy down.

Jeff bent down, shook the boy's hand, smiled and put one hand on the tiny shoulder. "I enjoyed meeting you Donnie. I hope to see you again."

The boy nodded but said nothing.

Isiah opened the door, pausing to hug Mrs. Crandall. "See you soon. You know to call if you need anything."

"Yes. Thank the lord for you, Rev. Booker."

They clattered down the three flights of stairs to the car. Neither spoke as Isiah turned the key and drove slowly down the street. Six blocks later he pulled to the curb, keeping both hands on the wheel, looking at Jeff.

"Mrs. Crandall's daughter is a high school junior and doing very well academically. There's a son in 7th grade. You can't see it all the time, but Mrs. Crandall has early symptoms of muscular dystrophy. She's devoting all her strength toward raising three good and well-educated kids. She's hoping to accomplish that before the M.S. gets too bad. There's no way to know."

Jeff was stunned into silence. Through the windshield he saw more discarded paper, cans and bottles.

Discarded cans. Discarded lives.

Finally Isiah put the car in gear. "One more place to visit. We'll talk later."

CHAPTER TWENTY-FIVE

Nine blocks more and they climbed to the second floor of another dingy building. Isiah knocked at a slightly open door. There was no response although Jeff heard children's voices. Isiah knocked again, louder and when no one came, he pushed the door fully open and called in: "Mrs. Horton? Mae? It's Rev. Booker."

The voices stopped, three small faces materializing in the doorway to an adjoining room.

"Hi," Isiah said. 'I'm here to see you and your mother. Can I come in?"

The children did not respond, two disappearing from the doorway. Isiah beckoned Jeff and they stepped into a small living room as the third little face vanished.

"Wait here," Isiah said, motioning to an old blue upholstered chair to the right of the front door. Isiah headed for the other door and peered into the kitchen. "All right, kids, everyone out here."

Slowly two girls and a boy inched into the room as if to the gallows, eyes shifting from Isiah to Jeff, lingering, and back to Isiah. The oldest girl, nine or ten, headed for the corner of the room farthest from Jeff and the other two quickly followed. They all slumped to the floor like a bedraggled bundle of unwashed laundry.

Isiah squatted to eye-level with the kids.

"Sarah, do you remember me?"

"Yessir."

"Where's your momma?"

"At work," she said, head bowed.

The other two, a girl about six and a boy about four, sat looking at their feet.

"When did she leave?" Isiah was insistent. He cupped Sarah's chin, turning her face up toward him.

"This morning. She'll be back soon, I bet." The girl met Isiah's eyes, looked instantly away.

"What did you kids have for lunch?"

"I ain't made it yet."

Isiah straightened with a quiet sigh. "Come on. Let's get something started." He headed for the kitchen trailed by three ducklings in stair-step order, leaving Jeff on the threadbare chair by the front door. He heard Isiah talking and cupboards opening and closing.

Wondering if he should join them, he surveyed the living room, realizing it was also a bedroom; the couch across from him had obviously been slept on, a bed pillow on the floor and a rumpled quilt drooped onto the worn maroon carpet. Faded flowered wallpaper looked as if someone had opened a heavy book where blooms from long-ago dance corsages had been pressed, colors now dimmed, barely recognizable. In several places, green paint peeked from rips in the wallpaper, looking like leaves and hinting of unknown residents and other colors and other persons from an unknown history of unknown people who had spent a percentage of their lives in this room. Jeff wondered what the other people had been like, what they thought and said and felt in this room and what had happened to them. Did they move into these rooms filled with optimism about a new home? Did they survive the spirit-killing neighborhood? Or were they eventually ground into dust? He realized he had no better clues to the present occupants. No pictures of the missing mother or the apparently non-existent father. The sparse furnishings included the chair he sat in, the rumpled couch-bed and another upholstered chair, dark pink and puffy, like an alcoholic's face, plus two unmatched end tables, one holding a small television set. Jeff shuddered at the sudden vision of living in the bare surroundings.

"Who the hell are you?"

The harsh voice halted Jeff's mental tour of the room and he catapulted to his feet, the front door open next to him framing a woman standing defiantly, hands on hips, purse over one shoulder.

"Uh, I'm Jeff Martindale." Then, realizing how meaningless that was, "I'm with Rev. Booker. He's in the kitchen."

The tall brown woman was thin, a plain green dress visible under a tan raincoat even though it wasn't raining. She looked briefly past Jeff toward the kitchen, back quickly to scan Jeff again, undecided. Isiah's voice came into the room and she went past Jeff without a word, stopping in the doorway, hands on her hips again.

Isiah came into Jeff's vision. "Mae. Hello. I'm helping the youngsters rustle up some grub."

"You don't have to do that," she said, sounding as if she were accusing Isiah of something.

"I know," he said softly. "I wanted to." Then, in the same tone, "these kids are awful young to be alone."

"I know that," she snapped, turning suddenly and returning to the living room where she nearly bumped into the forgotten Jeff still standing in the center of the room. The woman pivoted back to Isiah.

"Who's this?" she demanded. "I come home from work and find my place full of people."

Isiah's voice was conciliatory. "This is Jeff Martindale. He's helping me today. We came, as I always do, to see if there's anything you need or any way I can help you."

"Of course," her voice resigned, barely audible, her body sagging, shrugging the purse from her shoulder. "I'm glad to see you," she said without conviction, staring past Isiah with vague, unfocused eyes. Then, with a slight jerk of her body, "It's not that I don't like seeing you, I do, but it seems everybody comes around and tells me what to do but nobody really can do anything…just lots a telling as if telling can make it so. You tell me and some of the other church people tell me and the welfare people tell me and I even tell myself. But there's no way to earn more than a tiny living when the pay is hardly more than the cost of somebody to watch over your kids."

She collapsed on the sofa, her face angry now.

"You remember, Rev. Isiah, telling me to get educated? And how I got that degree from Detroit Community College? My diploma's hanging in the bedroom. I know how to keep the books for any small business and I can manage an office. But I never make it past the interview. They're all right when I call about a job ad but when they see me…I can see in their face that I'm not what they had in mind. So what good does *education* do me? Huh?"

A cockroach crawled from beneath the couch and started a trek across the old stained carpet toward Jeff who watched, fascinated by its agility and speed and size. The roach grew larger and now was as big as a cat and still it grew, filling his consciousness. Jumping and scooting, the roach lurched to Jeff's chair, miraculously shrinking just in time to disappear in the shadow.

Jeff had no idea what Isiah and Mrs. Horton said while he lived in the cockroach's world. He and Isiah left with her slumped forlornly on the couch, shoes off, legs extended, still wearing her thin raincoat. Her moist eyes were non-seeing, her face sad.

Back on the highway to Ann Arbor in the overcast afternoon's grayness, Isiah was the first to speak, not taking his eyes off the road, voice quiet.

"Hungry?" he asked.

"Yeah, I guess. Sure. Hey, I'll buy," trying to break the brooding mood that infected them both since leaving the Horton apartment.

"Maybe some place with loud, lively music," Isiah suggested. "No, let's skip the loud music. I was only trying to elevate our morale a notch or two above clinical depression."

"Someplace not too noisy and with cheap beer."

Isiah glanced over. "Alcohol's a depressant."

"Well, only a little. And if we can get back to only being a little depressed that'll be progress."

An hour later they each took long drinks from mugs filled from a pitcher with "Rolling Rock" etched in the glass.

"Why'd you take me today?"

Isiah took another swallow.

"Why do you think?"

"I suppose you wanted me to see how struggling poor black people live even in the allegedly less-racist North. To see what some of them are facing every day."

"That all?"

Jeff hefted the pitcher and refilled both mugs. "I don't know. Besides, you're avoiding my original question."

The waitress interrupted with two plates of spaghetti and meatballs.

"Because, frankly, your exposure to that kind of life is exactly zero and I wanted you to see the kind of environment that can create a Stepin' Fetchit or a raging maniac…or Nobel Peace Prize winner Ralph Bunche. I thought it'd be helpful for you to experience, as much as that's possible, the kinds of problems and feelings common to that kind of life."

"I got some idea of what you mean," Jeff said. "I was getting a very strange feeling in Mrs. Horton's apartment just by experiencing the furniture, the crowded living space and the loneliness and despair she was dressed in. Obviously she feels she can't escape."

Isiah stared at Jeff, reached for his mug, and added, "You ain't seen nothing yet, white boy."

CHAPTER TWENTY-SIX

"It was like a trip to Mars," Jeff said the next day, quiet excitement still in his voice. He and Susan strolled hand-in-hand along Main with no specific destination, enjoying the sunny Sunday morning.

"It's embarrassing but I've never been in downtown Detroit before, except on the edges, going to a few Tiger and Lions games. I certainly hadn't been in any inner-city apartments."

"What'd you see? " Susan asked.

"One woman hoping a miracle will produce money for her daughter's college education. Another trying to balance working a crummy job without neglecting her children but her pay barely exceeds cost of a babysitter. She has a community college degree but never gets hired after they realize she's black. She's willing to work hard but can't get hired. Both trying the best they can but are beaten down and discouraged by never-ending, grinding obstacles. They were actual people, real faces, no abstractions or statistics. That's what Isiah wanted me to see; the difference between hearing about something and *experiencing* it. At least a little bit. I wonder about the future of the kids I saw. How will they cope? Can they escape the circular poverty cycle?"

"What struck you the most?" she pressed, as they raised joined hands to split past a parking meter.

"The size of the reality. I was only in two apartments, but we drove through street after street with buildings just like those, with thousands of people trapped in an inescapable mess, like flies on fly-paper. I'm realizing that I grew up surrounded by optimism that things can be better; the idea that if you work hard you can succeed and, I guess, the assumption that opportunities are everywhere. And available to everyone. I got a real sense of how important all that is and embarrassed that I've never even thought about it; just took it for granted. There was no optimism in either apartment. These weren't people looking for opportunities; they don't think that applies to them. And it seems that they're right. These are people scraping by and worried that at any moment they can't even do that. Optimism and hope die when you're locked in like that."

He pulled her to a stop and hugged her before continuing down the sidewalk.

"Overall," he said, "it was extremely depressing."

CHAPTER TWENTY-SEVEN

As usual, Sam burst through the door while still knocking, this time trailed by a stocky, dark-haired stranger. Jeff's head didn't move but his eyes flicked up from the open book on his desk, a pen hovering over a notebook page half covered with scrawlings.

"Hey, ol' Buddy," Sam said, "haven't seen you much lately. Wanna catch a film and ingest a barrel of popcorn? *"La Dolce Vita"* finally made it to Ann Arbor," his eyebrows flicking up and down in a Groucho Marx impression. "Very sexy."

"Sorry. I'm finally making some geologic progress here," Jeff said, eyes returning to the book. "Meaning it's coming extremely slowly."

"Hey, come on, it starts in 38 minutes."

"Nope, sorry. Can't."

"Ok. Oh, I forgot, this is Mel Adkins. Mel, this is my old roommate. Terrible guy to live with. Keeps his clothes neat, seldom makes excessive noises and has fairly good study habits.

"Seldom farts. He set a terrible example for me."

"Hi, Mel," quick wave of the pen hand, trying to discourage the intruders from staying.

"Hi, Jeff," Mel said, rubbing his hands together, leaning close to the window, looking at the falling rain. "Man it's ugly out there. Wind *and* rain. Not fit for man or nigger out there."

Jeff's eyes jerked up to stare at Mel, briefly meeting eyes with Sam.

"It's getting worse," Mel added

"I'd be careful about that," Sam said lightly. "Jeff has several friends of a skin tone that might prompt them to take offense. One of them's big enough to squash you like a bug."

"Oh," Mel said, turning from the window, glancing at Jeff, who was still pretending to read. "I didn't mean to offend anyone," stretching out 'offend.'

"Well," Jeff snapped, staring hard into his eyes, "then you're a complete failure. You're offensive as hell. Haul your sorry ass out of my room right now. You're a fucking idiot."

Sam was already at the door and Mel moved quickly to join him. "Sorry," he said in a low, flat tone. "You've got me all wrong. That's just an expression."

Sam tugged Mel's arm and the door closed quietly. Jeff stood, seething, geology forgotten. He felt his heart pounding and heard his breathing. The intensity of his reaction amazed him.

He snatched his mug from the desk, headed for the coffee pot in the corner. Rinsing the cup he saw himself in the mirror over the sink. The face didn't seem much different from the one reflected in the same mirror during his freshman year when he roomed with Sam for a semester. Maybe a little less boyish? No zits! His smile broke the spell. He poured coffee into his dripping mug and slumped sideways into the large chair, legs hanging over one side, still breathing a little fast.

Two years ago, I'd never have called a perfect stranger a fucking idiot.

CHAPTER TWENTY-EIGHT

The young man in the chair by the door when Jeff came through it was the blackest person he had ever seen; startling him in his own room when he thought it was empty.

"We hope you need a coffee break before diving into a book," Isiah's voice startling Jeff again, coming from the window where he leaned against the sill. His tone implied Jeff would accept. The unexpected presence of Isiah with a stranger in the middle of the afternoon drew Jeff's curiosity even without the hint. He turned back to the now-standing man as Isiah added: "Jeff Martindale, Lamar Jackson," the introductions from 10 feet away, Isiah staying by the window.

Jeff offered his hand a scant second before Jackson and sensed the delay was deliberate, the grasp firm but brief.

"Glad to meet you, Lamar," he said, turning to Isiah. "Since it's your turn to buy, I'll be glad to join you two in a cup."

"We hoped you'd make a pot here," Isiah said. "We brought donuts," hoisting a white bakery bag from the sill.

"Ok, I know a good deal when I hear one," Jeff said, moving to the small bookcase with sliding doors he used as a miniature kitchen, the top hosting an electric coffee pot and several mugs.

He spooned coffee into the basket, realizing Jackson had yet to speak. He plugged in the pot, finally forcing him to turn around, walking to the other chair and sitting, looking at Isiah, who had remained strangely silent. Isiah returned the gaze but said nothing. Jeff looked at Jackson.

This guy isn't really black, more purple-black. Probably my age.

"Are you studying theology, too?" Jeff said, instantly realizing his mistake from Jackson's expression.

"Hell, no," Jackson spat.

Isiah moved to Jeff's desk chair and sat, his silence a heavy presence in the room.

"Actually I'm here to learn as much as I can about the white world before we end it," Jackson's delayed answer breaking the awkward pause.

"What's that mean?" Jeff asked softly.

"Just what I said," his face calm, eyes lancing Jeff.

"The white man is doomed as the dominant factor in this country," Jackson continued, his voice flat-lined. "The rest of us will take what we're entitled to by whatever means required. No more colonies, no more slaves, no more whites killing blacks without consequences. The only good Kluxer is a dead Kluxer. We're gonna do our own killin and we're gonna vote or take over the government however we have to; with ballots or with bullets."

"What in hell are you talking about?" Jeff said, his voice shaky. "Are you willing to destroy the best country on earth?"

"Shit," Jackson said. "This isn't even close to the best country. Who gives a flying fuck if this goddamn country survives?"

"I do." Jeff said, "Any rational person does. We need to fix things, not destroy."

"Sure. *You* have a vested interest. *You're* a beneficiary of this screwed-up system. You'd lose preferences and privileges, but I won't lose a thing, although that's impossible for you to understand. What can I lose? I have nothing. Not even a future. And the present sure as shit isn't worth saving."

"Bullshit," Jeff said, struggling for calm. "This country has lotsa faults and the absolute worst certainly is the shame of slavery and how some people still treat black citizens, but don't give me that crap that you've got nothing to lose. We're all vested; we're all in this together. Together we can fix it. Christ, in many parts of the world you could be shot just for talking the way you do."

He stopped, nearly out of breath, sucking air as he'd been underwater, off balance even while sitting down. He pushed himself from the chair, flushed and embarrassed, moving to the perking coffee.

"I guess we didn't take time for preliminaries," he said. "I'd like to start over," turning to Isiah sitting with his fingers steepled on his lips. "Ok, Sphinx," Jeff said, "this is the quietest you've been since the pancake-eating contest at your church picnic. I imagine Mr. Jackson and I both feel ambushed."

Jackson interrupted even as Isiah began to speak. "Not me," he said emphatically. "I knew exactly where I was going."

"And where was that?" Jeff asked.

"To a white boy's room."

"Look," Jeff said, his anger reheating. "You and I just met. All you know about me is I'm white. All I know about you is you're black. I suppose we could dismiss or even hate each other just on that basis, but I'm not as bigoted as you," surprised that he said it, hearing it for the first time from his own voice. "If skin color's all you need to judge people, then screw you. I'd rather be judged on the color of my socks because that's something I choose for myself," feeling like he was running down a steep hill, out of control, unable to stop or slow down. "Don't file me under 'white boy' because I deserve better than that and so do you. If that's your best thinking, forget it. We've both got better things to do."

Jackson was up, reaching for the doorknob.

"Lamar!" Isiah's voice low but commanding.

Jackson whirled to face Isiah, who was standing now.

Jackson jabbed his finger at Isiah. "Don't you tell me what to do. I shouldn't have come here in the first place and there sure as hell isn't any reason to stay. I'll see you around, Reverend." The last word spoken as if it was an insult.

"You scrawny little licorice stick. I ought to bust your butt."

Jackson looked incredulously at Isiah, who said, "I brought you here to meet a friend of mine and you offer nothing but insults. I expected better from you. I'm disappointed."

Jackson stared silently for long seconds, finally turning to Jeff still standing by the coffee pot.

"Sorry," he half-whispered, seeming unclear what he was apologizing for. He returned to the chair.

"The coffee's probably perked to death," Jeff said, grabbing mugs from the cabinet, beginning to pour. "Cream or sugar?"

"Black for me," Jackson muttered.

Isiah laughed so heartily he startled Jeff and earned a glare from Jackson.

"Honestly, Lamar, you're not even a moderate when it comes to coffee." He laughed again. Jackson focused intently on the desktop.

"Darn, Jeff, I'm sorry to ruin your reputation among the minorities here by revealing that you like your coffee black, too," Isiah's mouth smiling but his eyes serious, going from Lamar to Jeff and back.

Jeff handed both visitors mugs. No one spoke as they sipped coffee, the donuts forgotten.

What's Isiah doing? He tossed me in a barrel with Jackson and neither of us knows what to do.

A knock on the door, which was already opening as Sam-the-dervish blew in.

"Hey, can I borrow your geography notes from Tuesday? Oh, hi, Rev. Booker. I got tied up and didn't….

"Sure, if you can make anything out of them. I need 'em back by tomorrow night," Jeff said.

"Thanks. I'll slide 'em under the door if you're not here."

"Sam, this is Lamar Jackson. Sam Appleton here is a former roommate of mine who, fortunately for me, defected to the Delt house where they put up with him because he pays his dues on time."

Shit, probably not the best introduction.

"Here," he said, handing Sam a red notebook. "Don't forget, by tomorrow dinner."

Sam vanished through the door. Isiah got up and moved to the door, beckoning to Lamar. "Guess we'll shove off too. I'll see you for coffee tomorrow after dinner. 7:30."

A summons. What's with him today?

"Right," Jeff said, offering his hand, noticing again a mini-pause before Lamar's hand moved to take his. "Nice meeting you. Hope to see you again."

Jackson smiled briefly, lips briefly crinkling. "Thanks for the coffee."

The door closed with Jeff realizing Jackson probably believed Jeff's last two sentences were lies.

At least one of them definitely was.

CHAPTER TWENTY-NINE

"Who was that somber hombre here yesterday? Sam said the next day, still only half-way through the doorway. "Here are your notes," dropping the notebook atop the desk clutter before slumping into the chair across from Jeff. "He looked suspiciously like a headhunter. Never said a word or changed expression."

"That's close to true," Jeff said. "He's got a bad case of 'Hate Whitey.' He's a black version of your asshole friend, Mel Adkins; just as big a jerk, just as blind, just as adamant and just as obnoxious."

"Maybe we could get them together, lock the door and let them either convert or kill each other."

"It'd definitely be kill. Neither is going to change his mind and they won't change anyone else's mind either."

"What's this guy all about? What's his big bitch? He just pissed off from waking up one day and discovering he's black or what?"

"I think," Jeff snapped, "it's more that he's fine with being black, but he doesn't like being treated as if he had leprosy and mental retardation because of it."

"Hey, don't get mad at me," Sam said, standing and stretching his arms up and behind his head, trying unsuccessfully to stifle a yawn. "I'm just curious."

"Yeah, me too. I've got a coffee date with the padre after dinner and

I suspect it's to fill me in on this guy. He sprung Jackson on me without warning, sorta bomb-like."

"Anytime you need any more help with geography I'll be glad to borrow your notes," Sam said.

He slipped through the closing door just as the paperback book struck the wall inches away.

CHAPTER THIRTY

Images of Lamar Jackson's dour expression flickered through Jeff's mind the rest of the afternoon as he tried to study. After dinner he plugged in the already prepared coffee pot. The knock came almost immediately.

"Ok, Your Holiness, are you alone or did you bring someone else to ambush me?" Jeff said as Isiah came in.

Isiah laughed from the door to the chair, balancing his feet on a metal wastebasket. "I hope you understand what I did. It was like throwing water and acid into the same bucket; you know they're not going to mix but you want to see what happens."

"Learn anything from using us as lab rats?"

'It wasn't for me, it was for you two. You both met someone way, way outside your experience zone. Very good for the soul, very good indeed," laughing again.

"Where'd you capture him?"

"Yeah, he is a bit undomesticated. Actually he's homegrown—near Atlanta--but right now he's more a bundle of reactions than a person."

"I feel totally misjudged and insulted," Jeff said. "Nothing I said meant anything to him. He came with ideas and he left with the same ones."

"Did he change *your* mind about anything?"

"No," vehemently. "But he certainly made a big impression. I haven't stopped thinking about him. My reactions surprised me and so did some of the stuff I said."

"That's why I gathered you together," Isiah said. "Growing up in Georgia, he's been exposed to truckloads of indignities and hate and discrimination. He lauds black people and black things just as irrationally as white supremacists revere white people and white things. I'm showing him people and ideas that might make him think, even if he doesn't want to."

"Why's he blame me?" Jeff asked. "Am I supposed to feel guilty about something just because I'm white? 'Cause I don't. None of my ancestors owned slaves or were even in America during slavery. I see today's injustices. And I'd like to do something to improve things, but I can't retroactively change anything and neither I nor my family had anything to do with the past. How can he blame me or even dislike me just on sight?"

"Maybe you should ask him," Isiah said, watching Jeff's face.

"He sorta said we're going to have a black and white war. He seemed to look forward to it. Are we going to have another civil war?" Jeff stared back.

"I don't know. Maybe. I hope not. Maybe we're already having one."

World War III?

Jeff covered his surprise by getting up to pour coffee.

"Do you think we'll end up fighting each other? With guns?"

"I hope not," Isiah said, accepting the mug, cradling it in big hands, "but if it comes to anything like that both of us will be considered traitors."

"You're serious."

"Yes, but I'm not as pessimistic as that sounds. It worries me that many people could be caught in the cross-fire of real hostilities and be forced to choose sides based mostly on fear and, in both cases, highly visible, so-called enemies. All the bad guys are black or vice versa."

"Surely things aren't that bad," Jeff said.

"In some places they definitely are that bad. We're either going to have genuine and revolutionary progress, and soon, or we risk a hot revolution the hard way. This isn't 1920 or even 1950. Things can't continue as they are. Too many people won't stand for it any more. They're not willing to suffer crappy separate schools or segregated bathrooms or restaurants. Things are going to change one way or another."

"You're beginning to sound like your friend."

"I've been around him a lot lately but that's not it. The more progressive and modern we become as a nation, the better our communications, the more outraged people are with substandard humanity.

"This fight for civil rights is about *exercising* rights we already have. These aren't rights that can be *granted* by some person or even some state. The U.S. Constitution says every citizen is born with certain "inalienable" rights. It doesn't say some citizens can arbitrarily block other citizens from exercising their rights. Women couldn't vote until a relatively few years ago. Many blacks can't vote now. But that's going to get fixed. It's that simple. And it's inevitable. It just a question of how the changes will come."

"But do you really think the Civil Rights Movement might become a shooting war?"

"It's been a shooting and lynching war for years, but one side has done all the killing. For hundreds of years there have been hangings, shootings, bombing and beatings, all aimed at blacks. I can imagine at some point the victims of these generations of violence will refuse to tolerate it any longer and shoot back or bomb back."

"I've never heard you so pessimistic," Jeff said. "Is it going to be the Mau Mau versus the Rotarians?"

"Possibly." No smile.

"You're cracking up."

"No," Isiah said. "People willing to beat or hang or shoot other people over race may be mentally ill, but you don't have to be crazy to try to stop the insanity."

"I've heard people argue that blacks should train terrorists to intimidate or even assassinate whites committing racial violence."

"I hope that doesn't happen and I don't think it would work. Those are the same things some whites have used against us all these years."

"Then why not?" Jeff said. "Those tactics have *worked.* Particularly in the South, those tactics supported historic and widespread oppression of black people."

"You're right," Isiah said, "that until recently there's been essentially no organized resistance, but that's changing because of the recent marches and sit-ins plus some new groups pushing against racist laws and cultural traditions. Maybe because blacks didn't fight back in any significant way, that confirmed to the perpetrators that they're inherently superior. But striking back with violence is morally wrong and I can't believe it would do anything except provoke a lot more of the same. Don't forget, a white man can kill a Negro almost anywhere in the country without risking conviction or punishment. Terrorism--bombings and murders--would only prompt massive reprisals."

"How about in a limited, selective way? Maybe just execute those who lynch and bomb and kill?"

"That's probably ineffective and indefensibly wrong."

"Damn, Padre, you say non-violence isn't working, or isn't working fast enough, but violence won't work either."

"I didn't say a certain amount of violence might not work in some cases but I said it's wrong. It's divisive and destructive and morally corrupting at its core for everyone involved."

"That's all very nice to say," Jeff said, "but I can understand someone like Lamar Jackson. He's been repressed and humiliated long enough. He's out of patience and believes in aggressive actions."

"Don't mistake patience with weakness," Isiah's voice edged with anger. "It doesn't take brainpower to hate. It takes guts to be patient."

"I'm sorry, but when does patience become acceptance?" Jeff walked to the door and back. "I don't believe justice is inevitable. The belief that there's much justice in the world contradicts reality. I don't mean you or anyone else is weak, but I see parallels between the largely passive responses of American Negroes with that of European Jews during the Holocaust. Could the Germans have killed seven million people if the Jews had been as tough then as they are now? If they'd had more weapons? What if blacks had fought back years ago? I think the Israelis have the right idea by tracking to the ends of the earth every last Nazi they can find. They're still out there hunting. They're relentless."

Jeff paused but Isiah said nothing.

"I think," Jeff plunged on, "the knowledge that justice, even extra-legal justice, has a long memory linked to a fanatic perseverance makes it less likely Jews will be slaughtered in the future. I remember from a class last semester one of the Nazi-hunting Jews saying: "Justice has a way of getting tempered by time. We'll never stop coming for them. It's not just revenge, it's a way to prevent other deaths, other atrocities."

"Yes," Isiah said, looking through the window. "At what point does 'turn the other cheek' become immoral?"

CHAPTER THIRTY-ONE

He found the door to his room slightly ajar and saw Sam tilted backward in a desk chair reading a notebook.

"You suddenly becoming a scholar?" Jeff asked, sitting opposite him. "Reading on a Friday afternoon? Isn't that my geology notebook? You forget where you live or just lost your notebook again?"

"I've turned over a new leaf. Besides I'm party-bound. Don was here when I arrived and I saw your geology notes on your desk. You take better notes than I do."

"You don't take notes."

"Yes I do. They're just not extensive or particularly helpful. There's a party over on Whitmore tonight. I was hoping you'd come along."

"I'm meeting Susan there. Someone in her art history class invited her. She told the padre and he might be there too."

"Great. I'll even let you drive."

"I think I have a six-pack stashed in my suitcase unless you've helped yourself to that too."

"Nope. Plus, I'm treating you tonight" Sam said, pulling a thick book from a canvas bag on the floor and opening it to reveal a fifth of whiskey nestled in pages carved out to frame the bottle. "For us two," he said. "For us three, I mean. I doubt Susan drinks much. She can share your half."

***

The party surprised Jeff by flowing throughout the large house in a neighborhood not known for renting to students. "Guy's parents are in Florida," Sam explained as they tossed coats on a bed heaped with garments. The memory of a similar night when he first met Susan and Isiah reminded Jeff that was more than two years ago.

In the kitchen Sam poured whiskey in a paper cup, handing it to Jeff along with an empty cup. "You've got to be kidding," Jeff said. "I won't drink that much all night; I couldn't drink that in six months."

'That's also for Susan. Fill one with ice and water for chasing." Sam disappeared and Jeff plunked on the living room floor next to a sofa and leaned back. The first sip was followed so quickly by a gulp of ice water that some spilled on his chin.

He saw Susan coming into the room, black ski pants and a white sweater contrasting dramatically with her dark hair, her smile sparking his as she glided to a seat next to him on the floor, arms briefly encircling his shoulders, lips meeting his.

"One of those for me?" nodding at the cups.

"No, well, both of them are. The one's ice and H2O but the other is pretty potent."

She grasped his wrist and passed the glass under her nose. "Wow," she said, "you upgrading from beer?"

Jeff laughed. "Hardly. Sam practically forced this on me. I'll get two straws if you like."

"Sounds pretty old-fashioned," she said in her husky voice Jeff liked so much. "But since I've already shared sauerkraut once, you use one side, I'll use the other."

She sipped and blinked twice at the whiskey's bite. Reaching for the ice water, she said, "There's the padre." They waved as Isiah moved into the kitchen.

An hour later Sam materialized and bent over Jeff and Susan. "Give me your glass," he whispered. "I'm on a refill run."

Jeff, leaning shoulder-to-shoulder with Susan, his eyelids heavy, silently handed him the cup.

"I think I'm already too relaxed," Susan said. "I don't usually drink this stuff."

"Me, either. I may take a nap."

"Yeah. Me, too. Am I awake now?"

"Apparently," he said, looking at her face and feeling warmth separate from the whiskey's glow. "I want to carry you off somewhere but I don't think I can stand up." He kissed her nose. "I love you," he whispered.

"I know. But please keep reminding me." She pushed her face into his shoulder and put her hand on his chest. He covered her hand with his own, eyes closing, body responding to her presence even as his mind blurred under a warm fog.

The voice boomed into Jeff's consciousness. "Hey Susan. What's a girl like you doing in a nice place like this?" the too-loud laugh somehow familiar.

Jeff opened his eyes to see Mel Adkins beaming at Susan, squatting on his haunches, ignoring Jeff.

"Let me take you away from all of this laughter and gaiety," Adkins urged. "Come up to my place and see my National Geographics. It'll be just like high school." He laughed so loudly several people glanced at him.

"You're drunk," Susan said cheerfully. "Jeff, meet someone I went to high school with, Mel Cliché…I mean Adkins."

"We've met," Jeff said quickly, voice flat, barely glancing at Adkins.

"So we have," Adkins said, standing up. "See you around, Susan."

Jeff watched him pick his way slowly and somewhat unsteadily through the living room, disappear into the bedroom and emerge wearing a gray coat. He disappeared through the front door.

Susan turned quizzically to Jeff. "What was that about?"

"Nothing. He's a friend of Sam's and I met him once for about two minutes."

"Long enough to develop hostility? I guess that's not surprising knowing Mel."

"He's a total asshole. I basically threw him out of the room."

"You got him right, and I know him a lot better than you do."

"What was that 'just like high school' remark about? Did you two date?"

"Each other?" she said, eyes widening. "Of course not. I was never *that* young and stupid. He's a jerk on his best day, but we did go to the same high school. I think I'm part of his fantasy world. Let's talk about something else. How about..."

Sam interrupted. "Have you guys seen Adkins?"

"He stopped here briefly, proved again that he's an asshole and left," Jeff said.

"Sorry to mention him, but he's totally blasted and I wanted to be sure he got home ok."

"He was obviously under the weather but he went out the front door a half-hour or so ago," Jeff said.

Sam turned to leave. "You wouldn't believe how much he drank in the last two hours. Amazing."

"Obnoxious seems more like the right word," Jeff said to Susan.

"Let's change the subject again," Susan said. "Who do you think will win the Rose Bowl?"

"Me," Jeff said, passing the cup to Susan, surprised to find the second cup nearly empty.

They sat shoulders together, hands touching between them, grazing each other's thigh, watching people smiling, talking, laughing.

"I think I'm intoxicating," Jeff said finally. "I mean intoxicated," smiling too broadly at his lame joke, then frowned.

"No comment," she said. "I'll confer with you later."

Jeff felt the whiskey pulling a blanket over his body, no thought lingering long enough to grasp, an unaccustomed, uncomfortable feeling. His arm between them was asleep and he couldn't move it. Thoughts came and left, unremembered. He wanted to be somewhere else. Alone. Rest. Sleep. Party noises, droning voices, unidentified music, smoky room, everything crowding in, taking over.

"I need to stand up," he murmured, unsuccessfully trying to rearrange his feet and straighten his legs, finally pushing against the couch to help him up, right arm still asleep and dangling at his side. Nausea seared into his throat and mouth, scarily close to vomiting.

Don't barf!

Susan stirred on the floor beside him and he glanced down at her, the nausea surging. "I'd better wander back to the room and sleep," he said, staring straight ahead, trying to fight the wave.

Seeing the sudden, unhidden disappointment on her face, "I'd like to take you home, but I'm over-indulged. I…just think I'd better…" he finished without finishing, feeling as awkward as he sounded.

Susan nodded uncertainly.

He briefly looked down at her again, momentarily lost in a reeling sequence of unrelated thoughts, finally back to the party. He straightened his shoulders.

'I gotta go, Susan. I don't really want to…but I better..."

"I'll drive you. You're not driving."

"NoNoNo. My car's not far. I'll just lock it up and retrieve it tomorrow. I'll walk home. It's just a couple thousand steps. One at a time. One after another. I gotta go."

"I'll walk with you," she said, standing.

"No. Really. I'll be fine. I just want to get back and sleep. I'm over-sipped."

"Call me tomorrow." She kissed him and hugged him thoroughly before letting him go.

Winter's night air shocked his face. He walked super-carefully down the snowy stairs toward his car nearly a block away, embarrassed at leaving Susan and having her see him this close to barfing.

What a jackass. How dumb…I shoulda just waited…found some coffee.

Nausea swept him again. He desperately wanted to lie down, let the waves pass over him, rest his reeling head.

I'll never make it. Fourteen blocks. Yes I can. One step. One more and one more. Home, sleep, pull blanket over my head, sleep.

Approaching his car the thought beckoned.

Slide in and drive very very very carefully, very very very slowly. I can do that.

He stepped off the curb behind his car, put his left hand on the roof over the driver's side door, pausing with keys in his other hand.

Grab gloves lock car walk walk walk.

The body on the driver's side seat stirred. Jeff stiffened in shock and fear, staring at the figure slumped against the passenger door. The body turned restlessly and Jeff saw the pale, ghostly face of Mel Adkins.

CHAPTER THIRTY-TWO

Jeff wrenched the door open, the overhead light dimly revealing that Adkins was alone except for overpowering whiskey odors flooding the Plymouth.

Jeff grabbed Adkins' shoulder trying to jerk him upright.

He seized Adkins' coat collar with both hands, pulling as hard as he could, shaking him from side to side, finally getting him sitting up, but slouched, his head dangling left.

"Wake up," he yelled. "What the hell are you doing in here? Wake up goddamn it!"

"Good morning," Adkins said, briefly opening his eyes, then closing them and stretching languorously as if accustomed to being awakened on the front seats of strange cars.

"How'd you get in here?"

"Unlocked."

Jeff was angry and woozy, head unsteady on his shoulders, fighting dizziness.

"Get out."

"Need…ride…back to campus."

"I'm not driving back."

"Leaving car here?"

"Youbetcherass."

"I'll drive."

"The hell you will. You're drunk," Jeff said, the bitter taste reinvading his throat and mouth.

"Not drunk. Fine. Ex...tra...ord...in...arily fine. Wonderful nap. Fine. But my ride's gone.'

"Get the hell outta my car!" Jeff yelled and punched Adkins in the shoulder.

Adkins leaned right trying to open the passenger door. Jeff slammed the driver's door and dropped his keys. Reaching into the street to retrieve them the nausea won. He dropped to his hands and knees as great gasping heaves hit him, vomit stinging his throat, retching until his stomach was empty and then still more. Finally, he pushed off his hands, still on his knees. Adkins was standing beside him holding the keys.

"Get in," Adkins said. "We're all right. Rest awhile."

He took Jeff by the shoulder and guided him to the front passenger side, opened the door, assisted him into the seat and closed the door gently. He crossed back to the driver's side and slid in. He adjusted the rear-view mirror. He leaned his head back.

"Try to sit up straight. If you tilt too far you'll barf again. Let's rest here and get our bearings."

Jeff slumped in the seat, his head against the door window, and closed his eyes. The dizziness increased but he couldn't make his eyes open. He sat a little straighter, leaning his head back against the seat at an awkward angle.

Better. Don't think about barfing. Think about...

Minutes later? Hours? He was moving. Brakes screeched, a violent whipsaw thrashing shook him wildly from side to side. He opened his eyes to a blurred windshield as the car stopped suddenly, accompanied by a deafening bang, throwing him forward, driving his forehead into the dashboard, and slamming him back into the seat.

"Adkins! Adkins!"

Who's yelling?

He was screaming. He struggled to sit up. He found the door handle, pulled at it until the door opened. He climbed slowly out, stumbling, almost falling, bracing himself with both hands on its top. He looked slowly around, unsteady, the car's front wheels on the lawn of a corner house, a telephone pole growing from the grille.

"Adkins," he yelled again. He staggered hand over hand on the hood and around the tree to the front of the car but couldn't see inside. The driver's door was open; no one there. He leaned against the car, not knowing where he was.

Looking back toward the intersection he saw a crumpled form in the street. He ran toward it, in slow motion, in a dream. Run, run, he told himself but he could only run slowly.

Approaching headlights grew brighter and brighter sending a long shadow toward him, bouncing along the pavement from the unmoving form on the pavement. Doors slammed and a man and woman materialized as silhouettes in the headlights, only feet from the form.

Adkins was thrown out. OhgodOhgod.

The man in the headlights knelt by the form. Jeff lurched into the lighted scene. The still person on the street was a woman. Jeff slumped to his knees as reality slammed into him.

"I think she's dead," the man said to his companion. "You ran over her," he shouted at Jeff.

"Get a doctor," Jeff shouted, spotting lights coming on in several houses, running awkwardly toward the nearest porch.

"Damned drunk kid ran her down," the man yelled.

CHAPTER THIRTY-THREE

"I can't believe it," Jeff shouted. "That sonuvabitch. That sonuvabitch."

James Martindale slumped in Jeff's room, at late morning after the crash, still wearing his coat after the four-hour drive from Angel Harbor.

"You've got a dandy bruise on your forehead," he said, gently touching his son's brow. Did they take you to the hospital last night to check it out?"

"No, it didn't really show last night and I felt ok. Still do except for some thumping in there. I'll take some more aspirin in an hour."

All right, son. Tell me everything about last night, start to finish." He took off his coat and tossed it on Jeff's bed.

Jeff recounted the previous evening, starting with Sam and the whiskey. He skipped over the details involving Susan and told his dad everything he could remember about waking up in a moving car and the sudden, violent crash into the tree.

"I told the two cops over and over that I wasn't driving and they finally agreed to go to Adkins' apartment and take me along. That sonuvabitch denied the whole thing. He was in pajamas, his hair was a mess. Said he'd been sleeping for a couple of hours, ever since leaving the party. He even looked at me as if *I* should believe him. And I almost could. He really looked like we'd awakened him."

"Someone must have seen him," Jeff's father said.

"Yeah. Several people saw him. They saw him leave the party nearly an hour before I did. I don't know if anyone saw him after that except me."

"You think he'll change his mind and tell the truth?"

"He's not going to change his mind," Jeff said. "He's not that kind of person as far as I can tell."

"God, I hope the woman doesn't die," his father said.

Mention of the victim, the nameless dark form in the street, flooded Jeff's memory with the garish scene as the woman was lifted into the ambulance, vivid crimson blood staining the stark white sheets on the stretcher. He relived the harsh brightness of headlights and the surreal, red, white and blue emergency lights and the stunning realization that Adkins had fled. He remembered the scene at Adkins' apartment and the angry confrontation that left the two patrolmen uncertain and Jeff incredulous and frustrated, before the even more-intense rage that crashed into him later in the night.

The two cops had delivered Jeff to the dormitory, warned him to be available for more questions the next day. Don woke up when the door opened and Jeff told him everything, his anger growing, exploding his brain. Don dressed and disappeared behind a slamming door, returning 20 minutes later, his shoulders slumped. "He completely denies it. He says you're trying to save yourself by blaming him."

Jeff had listened, his fists clenched on his desk. "He says your story is impossible," Don continued. "He says you would never let him drive your car and several people know you dislike him. He says plenty of people saw him leave the party while you were still there. He says Susan and Sam will verify that. He said you were obviously bombed on your butt and that Susan and others would verify that too. He says you'll eventually realize your mistake and take your medicine."

Jeff stared, recognizing the obvious logic. Even his friends would have to support Adkins' story.

"Well," Don said, "we've got ourselves some serious shit, but we'll figure it out," reaching for his Lucky Strikes.

"I'll call my dad in a few hours, closer to morning. And Susan. I left her abruptly last night. What a mess."

Now, hours later, James Martindale sat where Don had been and was taking his turn at trying to sound optimistic. "Let's get something to eat," James said. "It was a long drive."

"Sure," Jeff said, "although I haven't talked to Susan yet. I left a message with her roommate early this morning but she'd already left for a 7 a.m. class."

Isiah arrived as the Martindales were shrugging into coats. Jeff had called him at the parsonage in the pre-dawn hours. He didn't know what he expected Isiah to do but he needed to tell him what happened.

"We were just heading for some grub," Jeff said. "Can you join us?"

Isiah nodded. "I went by the hospital on my way here," he added, pausing at the door. "She, Mrs. Winters, is still in a coma but she hasn't worsened, so at least that's hopeful. She has a broken arm and leg plus some serious scrapes and bruises. The worse thing is she hit her head on the pavement. The doctor refused to tell me anything else except that they're watching her very closely and doing everything they can, but it's mostly waiting for developments."

"Thanks, Isiah. Thank God she's alive," James said.

"What's happening now?" Isiah asked as they reached the street.

"Don talked to Adkins about 3 a.m. and he stuck to his story that he was in bed and that he has no idea what I'm talking about. Same stuff he told the cops last night."

Jeff had told Isiah of his dislike for Adkins during the early morning call, and had been specific about his reasons.

At the café five blocks away, Isiah asked, "What's the legal situation? Are they going to arrest or charge you with something?"

"Definitely with something I guess," Jeff said. "It's just a matter of what, depending on what happens to the woman…to Mrs. Winters. They would have arrested me last night but the cops weren't positive I was driving. It was obvious I had been drinking. And I had a bruise on my forehead plus I imagine my breath could have melted their badges."

"And you were the only one there when the other couple drove up?"

"Yeah. But I wasn't in the car and maybe because I was so insistent that Adkins was driving that the cops decided not to arrest me then. Plus both the driver and passenger doors on my car were open."

"We'll have to convince Adkins to tell the truth," Isiah said. "Shall I go lean on him?" the day's first smile.

"I think just seeing you would scare him into next week."

"We need a lawyer right away to handle this," his father said. "You need a better defense than that you were too drunk to keep this guy you don't like and who you say was also drunk, from driving your car," James said.

Jeff sat, elbows on the table, staring sightlessly into the empty cup, then raising red, teary eyes to Isiah and his father sitting across from him.

James broke the silence. "I'll ask some lawyer friends at home to recommend a lawyer near here. It may be tomorrow before I have a name. You'll need to call whoever it is right away and tell him everything. Don't talk to anyone until you've talked with the lawyer. Have them send the bill home; we'll worry about that later."

"Dad, I'm so sorry about all of…this. I shouldn't have had that much booze. Believe me it was the first time I've been in that condition. Ever. This all happened because I…"

"I believe you, son. That part's done. We've got some serious work to do."

An hour later James started his car for the trip to Angel Harbor. Jeff leaned into the open window, left hand on the car roof, Isiah a few steps away.

"If there are any questions from the lawyer have him call me at the office or home," his father said.

"I will. Dad, I'm sorry…." He stepped back and waved slightly as his father drove away.

Isiah put his hand on Jeff's shoulder. "Tell me everything you know about Mel Adkins."

"I don't know anything beyond what I told you last night," Jeff said as they walked toward the dorm. "I don't like him but I only met him once before last night. Sam brought him by my room and we had words. I actually called him a fucking idiot. Sam's the one who knows him. Oh, and I found out last night that Adkins went to high school with Susan."

"Let's find Sam and start with him," Isiah said. "ASAP. Let me know when. Then let's talk to Susan. We need to know everything possible. Call me," he said, turning off at the church.

Jeff walked without responding, wrapped in a shroud of despair and rage.

CHAPTER THIRTY-FOUR

A pink message slip from Susan was under his door when he returned and they soon converged in the "Java Joint," side-by-side on a faded rose sofa in a back corner of the faux living room; the place mostly deserted on this weekend afternoon.

Jeff, sipping coffee, a storm still thundering inside his head, but not as loud as before, filled her in on everything that happened after he kissed her goodbye the night before. She twisted to watch him, her face in shock but not interrupting.

"And you'll have to tell the police that I was drunk when you last saw me and that Mel had left an hour or so earlier," Jeff said. "It's all true and it looks like shit."

"So does your forehead. You sure you're ok?"

"Yeah. I'm a little banged up and it hurts a bit, but nothing serious."

"The whole thing's unbelievable," she said. "Someone must have seen him get in your car or saw you getting in the passenger side. Something. You remember anyone leaving with Mel or about the time he did?" She got up to pace in front of the sofa.

"No. But I had the attention span of a fruit fly at that point. I saw him close the front door and I didn't see him after that. As far as outside goes, I didn't see anyone so probably no one saw me, although I wasn't very clear-headed. Did you see anyone with him?"

"No. And I'm not even sure when he left."

"He left immediately after he stopped by to annoy us," Jeff said. "I saw him get his coat and go out the front door. Can you make a list of everyone you remember being at the party? Let's do it together, maybe we'll find someone who saw something. Oh, and Sam went to Adkins' room about an hour ago. Sam says Mel's very convincingly claiming that he has nothing to do the accident. Same story he gave Don when he went to Mel's room early this morning."

She put her cup on a side table and took his hand. "Ok, I'm past the 'this-can't-be-happening' stage and now I'm pissed."

Tears moved down his cheeks, draining haunted eyes.

CHAPTER THIRTY-FIVE

It was nine days before Barbara Winters opened her eyes and it was four more before she did it again. Only daily persistence by Jeff eventually provoked the woman's physician into a brief hospital hallway comment that "she may survive but the extent of any possible rehabilitation is impossible to predict."

Jeff returned to his room wishing he could cry, but he didn't. He had visited the hospital daily although it was nearly a week before he stood in the doorway of Mrs. Winters' room and glimpsed her seemingly sleeping peacefully in a sea of white sheets, only the bandages on her exposed arm and most of her head hinting that she wasn't merely taking an afternoon nap.

He tried to avoid her family but eight days after the accident he was sitting in the hallway when they came from her room; two small boys, about eight and ten, and a teen-aged girl, followed by the husband, a stocky, dark man with a prematurely old face.

The man saw Jeff and despite Jeff's quick turnaway, walked over, almost bumping into Jeff, and demanded: "Are you him?"

Jeff stood, not knowing whether to say yes or no. Finally, "I wasn't driving that car Mr. Winters. But you can't know how sorry I am about your wife."

Winters stared for long seconds. "I hope that if you're innocent you can prove it. Doesn't look like it to me. You're going to regret this the rest of your life," turning away. Jeff watched them walk the length of the hallway. All three kids turned to look at Jeff as they turned the corner.

The next day, Jeff saw the doctor and two nurses coming from Barbara Winter's room, talking while walking past his seat in the hallway. The doctor hesitated, then detoured two steps and said: "She opened her eyes a few minutes ago. One time for about 10 seconds," and hurried to catch up with the nurses. After a few minutes, Jeff went to her door for the second time, pushing it partway open. She appeared not to have moved. He stood for several minutes hoping to see even a flicker of life but none came.

Four days later, the doctor said Barbara Winter's unseeing eyes had fluttered open again.

Jeff called Susan from the hospital. "Can you meet me for something to eat?"

Jeff was in a booth when Susan slid in next to him.

"Hi. Howya you doing?" she asked, forcing a light tone. "I'm feeling left out of your life lately. All depression and no play make Jeff a dull boy."

He looked at her and then away, taking one of the menus stacked between the sugar container and a bottle of ketchup.

"What's new?" Jeff said.

"Don't do that," she said. "I'm sorry for trying to sound cheerful. Tell me everything."

Jeff told her about Barbara Winter's eyes opening, the confrontation by her husband and the haunting looks from her children. His voice was flat, coming from a grim face, hands crushing his napkin into a ball.

"Anything new from Mel?" she asked.

"That's hopeless. My lawyer tried to meet with Adkins, but his lawyer said Mel had already told the police what happened and that was that. He said Adkins was astonished that I'd accused him but claimed it's because I don't like him and I'm obviously trying to shift blame from me to him."

"What are you going to do?"

"Same as I've been doing, I guess, wait, hope, worry, cut classes."

"Wait for what?"

"See what happens to her. She's not changing as far as I can tell, still semi-conscious at best, although opening her eyes again even for a few seconds this morning seems like good news. But she's been in a coma for nearly two weeks.

"What'll happen if she doesn't get better?"

"My lawyer says that at worst, if she dies, I can be arrested and charged with some kind of manslaughter; possibly some kind of jail sentence. And possibly a civil suit by the family. I could be liable for a civil judgment that would take the rest of my life to pay. I've got to prove I wasn't driving."

"How? Her voice so low he almost didn't hear her.

"I don't know. I don't *know.* There's just no way to prove what happened. It's my word against his. And I was the only one there when the witnesses drove up."

He pushed his half-eaten tuna melt to the side, lifted his glass and finished a Coke with two deep swallows. He looked around the restaurant, at his empty glass, finally at Susan.

"It'll work out," she said. "It has to. It's too wrong to end this way. Somehow it'll work out."

Jeff nodded slightly, no sign of optimism, looking away.

Barbara Winters died four hours later.

CHAPTER THIRTY-SIX

Bright afternoon sun projected tree shadows on the windows in Jeff's room. He pulled the drapes shut and in the dimness sat, then toppled onto his bed, crying and shaking after Isiah called to tell him Mrs. Winters was dead. His mind denied him mercy; death sat with him and refused to let him look elsewhere.

He had been barely a teenager when his Grandpa Martindale shocked him by suddenly dying. Gone forever.

Forever.

His father came into the bedroom shortly after Jeff had fallen asleep, waking him by sitting on the edge of the bed and putting his hand on his shoulder.

"Jeff. Jeff. Wake up." Then, when Jeff stirred, "I've got some bad news." The 13-year-old searched his father's face, saw his red cheeks, eyes watering; the first time he'd seen his father cry. "Grandpa Martindale passed away a little while ago."

Passed away? Dead. Oh, God!

The boy felt his father's hand slide down his arm to hold his hand. Jeff knew about death. That was when your dog lay still and stiff and cold one morning and you knew it would never wake up again no matter how hard you wished and prayed and denied that there would never be another ball chased across the lawn, another mock wrestling match on the living room floor, another furry head on your knee under the table silently signaling hope for a smuggled piece of chicken.

Death was when you shot a BB at a bright, flitty robin and it fluttered to the ground from his perch in a backyard tree, flapping wings desperately but succeeding only in bouncing awkwardly along the ground until the young hunter, now horrified and remorseful, had to shoot twice more into the bird he had thoughtlessly doomed.

The image river of Grandpa Martindale flooded his mind throughout the long, sweaty night. In the darkness of his bedroom that night and for endless nights thereafter, Jeff imagined his grandfather lying dead in the bedroom of his farm home.

He had never seen an actual dead person although people "died" in the movies and on television, usually after choking out a few last words before a deep sigh and a slump into stillness and peaceful silence. But the vision of his grandfather failed to merge with such dramatic images. He knew dead people were buried in boxes; he had attended a funeral for a friend's cat, closed in a shoebox and buried under a shrub in the backyard.

The vision of his dead grandfather in a large shoebox with the lid closed left Jeff smothering in a hot, heart-stampeding, claustrophobic stickiness. *Not Grandpa Martindale!* His mind rejecting the thought, desperate to not think about it, to block it, to get away from it, to escape. Failing. The image persisted and expanded, leaving him gasping for air, heart pounding out of control, his mind screaming in his ears. His brain was too hot, feverish with despair, overwhelming him, simultaneously freezing and sweating. He sat up in bed, too cold to take off his pajamas, the next second too hot to suffer the blankets, unable to escape his inhospitable body.

He saw himself lying dead. He felt himself being lowered into a confining box and twisted violently when the lid was closed. He wanted to scream, to shriek, but his throat was dry and his mouth didn't open. The heat flamed in his head and his heart tried hammering through his chest. He flopped back on the pillow, fists clenched, eyes streaming tears, legs churning, mouth full of salt. He slipped finally into sleep tormented by a torrent of dreams.

That was death to a thirteen-year-old, but now, in Ann Arbor, death incredibly expanded, swelling itself up until, for a time, it filled his entire body like a gas, squeezing his brain with icy hands. He relived the horror of the momentary glimpse into the open coffin at visitation the night before his grandfather's funeral. The funeral was even worse, keeping his eyes anywhere but toward Grampa Martindale in his coffin, people coming and going, leaning into his face with regrets, milling around the room but unable to erase that unexpected first image lodged in his heart like a bullet for recall whenever he desperately didn't want it.

And now Mrs. Winters was dead. Although he had never seen her fully alive, walking, playing with her children, watching a movie, his mind punished him, allowing him no peace, and keeping him from anything resembling real sleep. He endlessly imagined Barbara Winters as she might have been, in a kitchen, hugging her husband, reading a book, sitting in a church pew, talking on a telephone, driving a car, laughing.

Then pale, semi-conscious, almost dead.

Then dead.

The sequence played endlessly in his mind, trapped in a theater with the same horror movie playing over and over. He got up and walked to the window, parting the drapes with both hands. The sun was blindingly bright but he stared with unfocused eyes.

It's my fault. If I hadn't gotten drunk, my car wouldn't have been in that intersection. Everything was going great and now my life's shit.

He turned, letting the drapes rewrap the room in soft darkness, momentarily blinding him again. He banged his shin on the desk and the pain was hot and sharp.

"God dammit! God has damned me!"

CHAPTER THIRTY-SEVEN

Three days later Jeff's lawyer called. "You've been charged with drunk driving and negligent homicide. I'm sorry, but it's not surprising."

"What's next?" Jeff said hoarsely, his shoulders sagging.

"The arraignment's day after tomorrow."

Waiting on a bench in the courthouse hallway, Jeff and Isiah flanked Winston Bartlett, Jeff's lawyer whom he'd met only once to describe the circumstances of the accident and confirm that Bartlett would represent him if needed. Susan and Don sat together across the crowded hallway.

A bailiff periodically popped from the courtroom to announce the convening of yet another hearing, but Jeff heard nothing.

Then came the summons: "Jeffrey Martindale."

Breath exited his body, leaving him slightly dizzy as they stood and trooped into the courtroom, which intimidated him the moment he came through the huge doors Isiah held open. He'd been in courts before, covering hearings and trials, but this time the rich, dark-wood walls, railings and tables facing the elevated bench were personal, the place where he was charged with killing an innocent woman and where eventually he'd be judged for the crime; where his life might change forever in horrible ways.

Jeff followed Bartlett through the gate in the railing separating the court from observers. They took chairs behind the left of two tables. Susan, Isiah and Don sank onto chairs behind the railing. Bartlett opened his briefcase on the table to extract a file folder and yellow legal pad with hand-written notes. Jeff, in his blue blazer, gray slacks, white shirt and dark-blue tie, felt as if he were dreaming, wanting to run from the courtroom, but paralyzed and panicked.

"All rise," as a tall, black-robed man entered, sat on a mountain top, looked down and gestured to the bailiff.

"The State of Michigan versus Jeffrey A. Martindale."

The words were like a 2-by-4 to Jeff's forehead.

"Is the prosecution ready? And the defense?" getting "yes, your honor" from both tables, two attorneys bobbing up and sitting down almost simultaneously.

The bailiff read the charge against Jeff. "...did carelessly and negligently and without regard for the public safety, drive his car while intoxicated... ending the life of 38-year-old wife and mother of three, Mrs. Barbara Winters...."

"How do you plead?" the judge intoned.

Bartlett rose. "Not guilty your honor."

The judge nodded at the prosecutor who rose immediately. "Your Honor, the state has charged Mr. Martindale with negligent homicide. His automobile struck Mrs. Barbara Winters late on the evening of January 7 of this year. After languishing in a coma for nearly two weeks, she died from her injuries. Mr. Martindale was observed in a drunken state by two witnesses who will testify that they drove up to the scene moments after the impact and saw the injured woman sprawled unconscious in the street. The witnesses and two police officers called to the scene will all testify that Mr. Martindale reeked of alcohol.

Mr. Martindale claimed he was not driving the car when it struck Mrs. Winters even though he is the registered owner of that car. He alleged that another man had been driving when the accident occurred but claimed that person had left the scene.

"That person was interviewed a short time later that night by two police officers and he denied being the driver. He alleged that Mr. Martindale has a grudge of some sort against him. We have other witnesses who will confirm that harsh feelings had been expressed by Mr. Martindale toward this other person.

"We believe there is sufficient evidence to set this matter for trial."

"So ordered," the judge said. "Six weeks from today at 9 a.m." pounding his gavel and vanishing through a side door.

"We have some serious work to do," Bartlett said as they walked to the courtroom door. "Can you be at my office tomorrow at 1 p.m.? Figure on at least a couple of hours."

"Yeah."

Then Jeff saw Mrs. Winter's husband sitting in the last row of benches, expressionless, arms wrapped around his chest, eyes on Jeff's face. Stunned, Jeff stopped, took two more steps then quickened his pace, moving ahead of the others, heading for the last row.

Isiah saw the man and grabbed Jeff's arm, pulling him to his side, a firm hand on Jeff's back propelling him through the door into the hall. Isiah kept his grip on Jeff's arm, motioned with his head to Bartlett and took them all down the hallway to the back door and outside.

"What were you going to do?" Isiah asked quietly, unlocking the car. "You can't be talking to Mr. Winters."

"Jesus," Barlett said, "Is that who that was?"

"I just wanted to talk to him," Jeff said. "I need to tell him again that I wasn't driving the car, that I'm sorry about his wife but that I didn't kill her."

"No. Not a chance," Bartlett said angrily. "You absolutely must not talk to anyone except me, Rev. Booker and your family. That's it. You stay away from Mr. Winters."

"But that's what I would do if I were guilty," Jeff said.

"*And* it's what you must do when you're innocent," Bartlett said. "You've got no choice."

The next day, in a mahogany paneled conference room, Bartlett, in a black suit, described the next steps in the legal process. "Now we need a list of every person you can remember from the party. We need to interview them to see if anyone saw Mr. Adkins get in your car. Or recalls a*nything* helpful."

An hour later, he looked across the polished round table at Jeff and Isiah. "That's it for now. Any questions for me?"

Jeff said aloud what he had been telling himself endlessly since the accident. "I'll be acquitted of this," underlining each word with his voice, leaning forward, fists on the table. "I'm innocent. The only thing I did wrong was falling asleep in my own car. And that bastard drove and he killed Mrs. Winters. I'm not guilty and I have to believe I'll be acquitted," his voice less certain now, whispering. "I understand the circumstances make it look as if I did it, like I was driving the car, but I wasn't. I didn't," bitterness and despair in his voice. Then anger. "We need to get that asshole Adkins on the stand and force him to tell the truth. Let's see if he can lie under oath."

"Why do you think he'd have any trouble lying under oath when he hasn't been bothered by repeatedly denying to the police that he was anywhere near your car that night?" Bartlett asked.

"Because it's the truth," Jeff said, without conviction.

"You know what'll probably happen if we subpoena him," Bartlett said, glancing from Jeff to Isiah and back. "He'll get seven witnesses, perhaps including your friend here and your girlfriend and others at the party, to testify *truthfully* that he left the party an hour before these same people saw you leave. Your friends will tell the truth. And your old roommate will testify that he provided the whiskey to you. "And then," he continued, palms down on the table, cuff-links flashing, "your girlfriend gets on the stand and says you told her you were too drunk to drive."

"I know all that. I *was* too drunk to drive. But I didn't drive. It may not be as plausible as Adkins' story but it's the only story I've got because it's true. If I wanted to lie about it I could have come up with something better than that."

"Really?" Bartlett said, eyebrows arching. "And what could you have dreamed up that's more credible than what you say happened? That you don't remember much of anything? That you got in the car with a guy everyone knows you detest? Even you admit you think he's a jerk. Is it more credible that your car was stolen but you were asleep inside? Let's face it, truth or lie, your story is the only remotely feasible explanation...other than that you were driving the car, which is quite a bit more believable. Do you know the police report says they found vomit on the *driver's* side door."

"Do you believe me?" Jeff asked softly, trying to mask his intent to leave the office immediately if the answer was unsatisfactory. He had no idea what he'd do next if that happened.

The lawyer leaned back in the chair, studying Jeff. .

"If I say no, you'll probably walk out of here and get another lawyer. If I say yes, 'I believe you,' you'll still not know whether I have doubts or not."

"Do you believe me or not? Yes or no?"

"Yes."

Jeff never knew for sure.

CHAPTER THIRTY-EIGHT

Isiah and Jeff walked from Bartlett's office, Jeff's shoulders hunched, hands in his pockets, staring at the sidewalk, silent.

Isiah wanted to grab him by his arm, or by his mind, and yank him from depression but couldn't find the right words or a tone that didn't reek of artificial optimism. Between the arraignment and meeting with Bartlett, neither was in the mood for cliché slogans or pretending that everything would turn out ok. They both knew truth and justice didn't always prevail.

When they neared the dorm, a deeply upset Isiah left Jeff and headed for his church office. A half-block from the church he pivoted, walking briskly back to the dormitory, entering the lobby. He turned right along the hallway, reading names on small, white cards posted on each door. Almost at the end of the first-floor hall, he saw what he was looking for.

129 MEL ADKINS

He moved quickly past the room and down the hall to a door, pushing the release lever, jogging through the side entrance to the sidewalk. He continued for several blocks and climbed concrete steps to the Ann Arbor police station. His heels clicked on the marble floor to a counter with a uniformed cop holding a telephone to his ear with one hand, writing on a clipboard with the other. He nodded at Isiah, giving him a holding look with his eyes before they returned to the clipboard.

The call ended and the cop looked up. "Can I help you?"

"Is Detective Haynes around?"

He wasn't.

***

Damn good chance Haynes won't go for it, Isiah thought, opening the door to his small, sparsely furnished living room. Probably save my neck if he doesn't.

He knelt before a sofa, 230 pounds of bear-like man praying like a small boy. A full five minutes passed before he moved, slowly straightening his body.

The phone woke him before dawn.

"Morning, giant of the cloth. Got your note. What's so important that you wanted me to roust you out of bed this early?"

"What's this? Police brutality?"

"One of your flock in our pokey?"

"No. I want to keep someone out of your hotel."

"Wanna have breakfast?"

Ten minutes into scrambled eggs at Mike's Diner, Haynes parked his fork and looked at Isiah. "You realize you're way out on a skinny limb. You're not built for that. If your rather uncertain plan fails and he blows the whistle on you…."

"And if you help me and I muff it, your neck is way out there."

"Not as far as yours. You're locked into the system and won't be able to lie out of it. In fact, if it goes bad, no one will have seen me. We sneaky types have an advantage."

"Good, because I need help with the sneaky parts. You willing to help?"

Haynes paused before nodding. "Give me a day to think." He reached into a shirt pocket to touch the cigarette pack but didn't take it out.

"It's cut and dried, Billy, one man's word against another's. Problem is all the evidence is circumstantial and on the wrong side."

"You're sure it's the wrong side?"

"Jeff Martindale wouldn't drive drunk and he isn't going to lie. I'm as sure of him as I am of you."

"You mean you don't think I sometimes lie?" Haynes asked.

"I didn't say that."

CHAPTER THIRTY-NINE

Larry Williamson, the Campus Editor, waved at Jeff was he walked into the Daily office. "Broder wants to see you."

"What's he want?"

"Dunno," Williamson said, glancing up briefly then back down.

Jeff paused in front of the closed door with EDITOR painted on the glass. Finally he knocked and got an immediate "Come in."

Jim Broder, a graduate student four years older than Jeff, stood up as Jeff entered.

"Hi, Martindale," Broder said. "Have a seat."

After a short pause, Broder said, "Jeff, we've got a problem. We need you to suspend your work on the Daily until this drunk-driving, negligent homicide thing gets cleared up."

"You're suspending me?" Jeff said, disbelief in his voice. "You think I'm guilty?"

"No," Broder said. "But those are serious charges that can undermine your situation here. And I'm sure you'll need lots of time to prepare to defend yourself."

"But you're suspending me before any problem even comes up," Jeff said, his voice full of anger. "This is bullshit."

"No. No," Broder said. "This is just until your *situation* gets resolved. "Don't forget, you admit you were drunk."

"This is nonsense," Jeff snapped. "Who's pressuring you?"

"I'll ignore that because I understand the strain you're under. Look at this morning's headline," Broder said, holding up the paper. "Student charged in driving death," he read. "Owner of car denies driving drunk."

"That's the god's truth," Jeff said. "It was my car but I wasn't driving it. We'll get this straightened out in court."

"Good. That's what we expect. But in the meantime we need to minimize the damage to the paper's credibility. I'm sure you'll agree with this after you've had time to think about it."

Jeff bolted to his feet, lunging to the door. "And I'm sure when you've had time to think about it you'll realize what crap this is," slamming the door behind him.

His footsteps sounded like gunshots as he sprinted down the hallway, down a flight of stairs to the first floor and out the front door.

Now my job's gone. A great display of faith. Fuck Broder. Goddamn lying Adkins.

***

"Suspended?" Susan said. "Before the trial even starts?"

"It feels like I've fallen down the rabbit hole and I'll never see Kansas again. It's so unfair."

"To hell with Kansas," Susan said. "To hell with Broder. Let's get outta this town for a few days. I'll sign out for the weekend. Let's drive somewhere and it'll be just the two of us for…"

"Not right now," he said. "It wouldn't be just the two of us. There's a dead woman with us. Plus Adkins and Broder. And a trial."

CHAPTER FORTY

The next day and a half passed like a year and a half for Isiah, now pacing his apartment, mentally rehearsing and revising the scene he planned for Adkins while trying to convince himself the project was neither unethical nor a violation of his own values. It deeply concerned him that during all the mental scenarios he'd visualized, even knowing that, at best, it wouldn't happen exactly as planned, Adkins had never reacted correctly.

Late that afternoon, he ended his debate with himself and in a few minutes, was parked in the dormitory lot watching Detective Sgt. Billy Haynes and another man, both in dark coats, striding toward the building entrance. He left his car and joined them. Haynes nodded to him without a smile.

"Rev. Booker," he said with unusual formality, this is my partner, Detective Art Treacher. He's agreed to be nearby if we're needed."

Isiah shook hands with Treacher, a short, sharp-faced man who nodded but didn't speak.

"Change your mind?" Haynes asked Isiah.

"No. You?"

"Let's go."

They paused briefly in the men's room off the dormitory lobby, then they were two doors from **"129 Mel Adkins."** Haynes and Treacher went to the end of the hall, as Isiah paused by Adkin's door. He nodded slightly toward the two men about thirty feet away and knocked twice. No response. As he started to knock again the door opened and Adkins stood there in jeans, an untucked blue and gold Michigan t-shirt and bare feet.

Neither said anything, looking at each other.

"May I come in?" Isiah asked, glancing over Adkins' shoulder, hoping no one else was there.

"Why? I know who you are."

Isiah leaned slightly forward and Adkins moved almost imperceptibly back. Isiah moved a half-step forward and Adkins retreated a full stride. Isiah quickly took two more steps into the room, Adkins retreating in matching steps, enabling Isiah to pull the door almost closed.

"We need to talk," Isiah said. "We have a mutual problem."

"I have no problems," Adkins said, his voice sharpening. "What is this? What'er you doing here?"

"It's about the accident," Isiah said, advancing slowly but directly at Adkins, finally standing less than two steps away, leaning slightly forward, as if to move even closer. Adkins retreated another step.

"Sit," Isiah commanded, gesturing to the couch directly behind Adkins, who briefly looked as if he might argue, but said nothing and remained standing.

"I need to share some thoughts with you," Isiah said.

"I don't need any *thoughts* from you. You need to get the hell out of here," Adkins said, body language shifting from intimidated to angry. "I don't like this one goddamned bit. Get the hell out," his voice rising. "I know you're Martindale's friend."

He started to move toward Isiah but stopped when Isiah didn't move, their eyes challenging each other.

"Let's sit down," Isiah said softly. "You're going to hear me out so we might as well be comfortable."

"I'm doing no such thing. You get out before I call the front desk. I don't think they approve of clergy forcing their way into rooms."

"Go ahead. But you'll be sorry, very sorry. Believe me, this is for your own good."

Adkins didn't move and Isiah took a small step toward him, prompting Mel to sit on the edge of the couch, Isiah immediately dropping into the upholstered chair facing him.

"Please listen carefully," Isiah said quietly, learning forward, into Adkins. "I left that party right after Jeff did and I saw you shove him through the passenger door of his car," pausing for several seconds of intense eye contact.

"And I saw you get in the driver's side and drive off just before the accident." Another long pause. "And I'm telling the police what I saw. Unless you tell them yourself. This is your only chance."

Neither moved nor spoke. The silence lengthened and Adkins stared at Isiah, disbelief and shock on his face like a palm print.

"You're lying," he spat. "I'm not falling for that bullshit. If that story were true, you'd have said so long before now. You're nuts, or worse, you're a lying son-of-a-bitch."

Isiah's giant hands clenched but he made no other move, still in the black overcoat and, even while sitting, looking down at Adkins.

"You'll discover that I'm a very convincing witness. This is, you know, a case of one man's word against another's. Actually it's two men's words against yours. I might be considered an expert in such a dispute. My confirmation of Jeff's story will surely be persuasive, and, as you know full well, an accurate account of what you did.

"But I'm giving you a chance to come clean and hope for better treatment than if you wait for it to be proved in court that you were driving; and that you cold-bloodedly ran away, that you didn't try to help the injured woman, that you cowardly left someone else to take the blame. And that you lied in statements to the police. Then you'll be charged with manslaughter and perjury, plus leaving the scene of a fatal accident, and failing to render aid to a dying woman and who knows what else. Telling the truth now may get you a better deal. If you're honest and remorseful, you may be able to plead to lesser charges and possibly get probation."

"You're lying," Adkins said. "You're flat-out, lying. Nothing changes you people, even having a preaching degree. You're lying to save a buddy. Do you think he'd do that for you?"

"Look, you miserable piece of crap," Isiah hissed, leaning farther forward until their faces were inches apart, "only the fact that I don't want you to have any bruises is saving you from getting tacked up on that wall. I don't care what you think of my motives. You know damned well what

I say is true. You *were* driving that car. The rest of the world will believe me and you need to understand that. There'll be no sympathy for a weasel trying to shift blame to someone else with false testimony."

"Isn't that what you're trying to do?" Adkins snapped, his back pressing hard against the couch cushion. "You never saw me driving Martindale's car."

"You *were* driving."

"I never said that. You didn't see me. You couldn't have seen me because I didn't do it."

"Well," Isiah said, "we'll see who the jury believes. Don't place any bets on yourself."

"You black son of a bitch. You'd perjure yourself just to get your friend off his own hook."

"Screw you," Isiah said, his teeth barely moving. "You play all the games you want. You were driving that car and I'm going to describe it to the jury and they're going to believe me. They're going to hate you when I'm finished. They'll despise you so much they'll hardly be able to send you away fast enough…or far enough…or long enough."

"Putting a Bible in a nigger's hands doesn't make him believable. When the jury finds out you've waited three weeks to say anything, they'll know damn well you're obviously lying for a friend."

"No, actually that helps prove what I'm saying."

"You really are nuts."

"No. I didn't speak up right away because I didn't want to admit that I was at the party. I'm sure you saw me there; I saw you. And I'll confess that I had been drinking a bit, but not too much, and I was reluctant to tell my lead minister. But now I realize what my choices are and I'm coming forward and telling the truth about what you did, even though it's embarrassing and may damage my ministry. I can't keep silent and let an innocent person be blamed, so I'm doing the right thing. And I'm sad and remorseful. As you should be. But I can't protect myself and let you pass blame to someone else. Justice must be served. And it will be. You *will* be indicted. And later I'll probably preach a sermon about truth and justice. And the wonderful part is it'll be the *truth*."

Adkins seemed to shrink into the couch. Isiah could almost smell his fear. Adkins didn't move, looking like a dead man propped up, his eyes sightless. Suddenly his face twitched and he bolted upright, stepping sideways, away from Isiah, his look hot, intense and disturbing. Isiah stood up, feeling the momentum flowing away from him and doubt stabbing him in the chest.

"Fuck you, you nigger preacher. It'll never happen. You two are friends. You'll be disgraced in court."

"Juries don't like for clergymen to be badgered or accused of lying," Isiah said softly, trying to appear calm and confident, standing tall in his black coat. "It'll hold up all right. I'm very believable. And I'll be believed because it's true. You were driving that car and I'll be much more convincing than you because you're lying.'

"You're really over the edge, you know it?" Adkins said. "I don't have to testify against myself."

Isiah pounced. "You're so aware of your own guilt that you're forgetting that you're a witness, not the defendant. You'll be on the witness stand. Under oath; one lie and the perjury trap snaps shut. You'll be the defendant before it's over. I guarantee it." He stepped forward, closing in on Adkins.

"Stay away from me."

"I'm not going to touch you. I wouldn't want to hurt your social acceptability. But you can count on this. I'm going to help convict you and there's nothing you can do about it."

Adkins violently thrust his extended middle finger at Isiah's face, almost touching him. "That's what I think of your threats," jerking the hand toward the ceiling. "You can try to frighten me all you want, but your precious Jeff is fucked. You don't know that I was driving the car and trying to bluff me into blubbering to the cops is stupid."

Isiah tried to recapture some confidence even as Adkins' accusation sounded true; this probably had been a stupid idea.

"Well, we'll see who the jury believes, you, or an ordained minister who puts his career on the line to serve justice."

Adkins, sensing victory, moved even closer to Isiah. "That's right, nigger, we'll see. I predict a big disappointment for you. You'll find out how much you're worth when the jury believes a white man's lie over a nigger preacher's truth. Why don't you just forget the whole goddamn thing and save yourself lots of trouble. I'm not going to the cops and confessing and that leaves you hanging out there. Lynched by your own stupidity. I *was* driving and I *was* completely smashed, but you'll never prove it and no one will ever believe you."

Isiah stepped quickly to the door and pulled it fully open. The two detectives appeared in the doorway, both shoving badges at the startled Adkins. "I think you'd better come with us," Haynes demanded, as Treacher reached out with handcuffs.

Isiah removed his coat and Haynes removed the small recorder taped to the small of Isiah's back, along with the cord running up to his shoulder and down to the microphone taped to his wrist.

Haynes held up the recorder in a triumphant gesture in Adkins' face. "I think this will make it your word against your confession."

Adkins collapsed onto the couch and began to cry.

The relief on Isiah's face wasn't lost on Haynes.

"We're going downtown," Haynes said, roughly pulling the sobbing Adkins to his feet. "This is your last chance to do the right thing and get some credit for it."

"Let's go," Haynes said, leading Adkins into the hallway toward the lobby.

Isiah stood slumped at the other end of the hall, his chin on his chest, his back against the wall.

CHAPTER FORTY-ONE

"Why aren't we somewhere toasting with champagne, or at least a pitcher of beer?" Jeff laughed. "Or more appropriately, iced tea."

"I'm glad that's over," Don said, sprawled on the bed.

"Amen, brother," Jeff said, still flooded with relief mixed with disbelief by the arrest of Mel Adkins. They were both grateful the threat to Jeff apparently had ended but they were drained by the ordeal.

A few minutes before Don arrived, Isiah had called after talking with Detective Haynes, who reported Adkins had hysterically admitted driving Jeff's car and fleeing the accident in a panic. "He seemed relieved when it was over," Isiah quoted Haynes. "And he was devastated that Mrs. Winters died because of him. He's one frightened puppy. He signed a statement to Haynes and Treacher, so that should settle everything. It was darned close for awhile," he said. "Thankfully, his lawyer decided to try to show confusion, immaturity and remorse. They're probably hoping for probation," Isiah said. "The lawyer even said something about Adkins being confused because he bumped his head in the accident. I'm headed for your place."

"Great. Don should be here any minute. I'll tell him you met with Mel and convinced him it was his moral duty to tell the truth. That's all the detail anyone else needs."

When Isiah joined them he looked exhausted. Jeff embraced him and

Don said: "I'm not up to champagne but I'll treat to a celebration pizza. Let's hoof it to the Pretzel Bell."

"I'll call Susan. Hope she can meet us there," Jeff said.

The 15-minute walk, plus nearly two hours of pizza and beer, brightened everyone's mood. As they strolled slowly back to campus, Don said, "I gotta stop by that place where they keep all the books," pausing to hug Jeff before waving and turning toward the main library.

Two blocks later, Isiah began a detour toward the parsonage. Jeff followed for a few steps.

"Just 'thanks' is pretty weak, but you'll never know how much what you did means to me," Jeff said, putting a hand on Isiah's big shoulder.

"There's no need for either of us to say anything more," Isiah said. "Besides, it's small reimbursement for the fishing spots you've shown me," smiling and shaking Jeff's outstretched hand. "That, as the saying goes, is what friends are for."

"This was *way* beyond that," Jeff said, hugging Isiah with a touch of ferocity. "You risked your reputation and possibly your whole career. I'll never forget that. Never. I'll remember this the rest of my life. I can't believe what you did."

He looked at Isiah for a few seconds. "What would you have done if it hadn't worked? What if he'd tried to expose the whole thing?"

"I'm not sure. I may have done what I told him I was going to do."

"Under oath?"

Isiah turned and walked away.

CHAPTER FORTY-TWO

Jeff rejoined Susan waiting on the sidewalk and they strolled hand-in-hand without speaking. At her front door, they held each other tightly for a long time, slightly swaying, not talking. His left hand caressed the back of her head, inhaling the sweet scent of her hair, her face nestled on his shoulder. Several lingering kisses left them both breathless.

He leaned back, looking at her, his arms locked around her waist. "I don't normally get dessert after pizza but that was great."

"Oh, yeah. Terrific, in fact," she said, putting her head back on his shoulder and whispering in his ear,"this is the most terrific I've been in weeks," flicking his ear with her tongue.

"Good grief, woman," he said. "Show some mercy. Tomorrow let's go someplace new for a really nice dinner. Definitely no sauerkraut. Do you think you can chaperone me better than you did last time?"

"I might try to try," she said, tongue flicking again, "or not. No promises." He groaned and pulled her closer.

"Now that this accident mess is over maybe we can get back to normal. Whatever that is," he breathed.

"Hold that thought," she said. "I'll help you search for normal."

A few minutes later, back in his room, the mirror by the door showed him still smiling, looking at someone other than the grim, depressed person who inhabited the mirror only a day ago. He laughed out loud.

He was amazed again by the depth of Isiah's friendship. Thinking of Susan, the face in the mirror grinned back. Moving to the bed, he let himself fall backwards as if onto a trampoline. Crossing his arms behind his head, he stretched his entire body, holding it and relaxing.

I've got a right to feel damned good. It's been a bitch lately.

He dozed and awoke in late-evening when Don returned. Refreshed, Jeff felt an over-powering sense of urgency and after Don fell asleep, he finished a tardy report and reviewed notes for another class before exhaustion captured him at 2:10 a.m. He turned out the desk light and went to the window to watch the quiet, early morning street, a few lights still speckling the neighborhood. The second-floor view reinforced his feeling that he had never before been so confident of an essentially wonderful world.

CHAPTER FORTY-THREE

A few weeks after the Mel Adkins crisis faded in Jeff's mental rear-view mirror, he was caught up with his classes. And his car was repaired, but his impatience with the slow pace of civil rights progress wasn't. His mood had drifted darker.

Although it was early afternoon, a heavy overcast kept the room dim, two desk lamps barely breaking the gloom surrounding Jeff and Isiah in Jeff's room reading for separate classes. Jeff closed his book, rose and walked to the door and back to the desk, pivoted to the door, pacing without realizing it.

"How can we just sit here?" he said, still walking.

"My knee complains when I run," Isiah said, watching the pacing.

"You know what I mean. We're sitting around waiting for hearts to change and the races to start living together in peace and brotherhood. Ain't gonna happen like that."

"I'm not waiting. I'm working," Isiah said. "You're working. You even got your job back at the Daily. And the NAACP and the church you're so critical of lately are working."

"Churches aren't working; they're just doing their rituals du jour. Look at the calendar, perform a ritual," Jeff mocked. "How can you have faith in a church that isn't even united in its own beliefs? Organized religion is sliced and diced into hundreds of denominations and factions, all created by human beings proclaiming with absolute certainty that their rigid dogmas are the only true words. They argue tiny details as if they actually know unknowable things."

"Don't attribute man's confusion to God," Isiah said softly. "With the many shades of Christian philosophies, plus other great world religions, it's unlikely any particular one has all the complete or correct answers to anything. I certainly agree Christians have wasted hundreds of years using the Bible to support individual views, and insufficient time understanding what Jesus is actually saying. He gives us vital principles for life but we're often abysmal at following them."

"Exactly," Jeff said. "Next you'll want the church to practice more and preach less."

"What's making you so bitter these last few months?" Isiah said, getting up to pour coffee. "You seem convinced that churches are bad, not just flawed, but almost evil; that the NAACP and the people who work there are accomplishing nothing and you're the only one who realizes it."

"No one is doing anything of real significance," Jeff said, more anguished than angry. "If there's such a thing as sin, that's it; seeing cruelty and injustice and tolerating them. If Christ was the type of man I've been taught he was, he'd be uncomfortable as hell in any organized church. He'd be where the action is. He *was* where the action was. He *was* the action. And that's certainly not true in today's churches. I think he'd look around, declare everyone hypocrites and toss all of us out on our butts."

Isiah said nothing for nearly a minute, looking through the window. "At the risk of pointing out the obvious, you should be aware that the church…"

"Don't bother," Jeff shot, jerking his hand toward Isiah in the "stop" gesture. "At the risk of being rude, I know all about what churches have done. Basically they haven't done Jack Shit. I'm painfully aware of what organized religion *hasn't* done. It didn't lead the fight for women's rights. And it's never even argued for, let alone fought for legal or moral rights for blacks. It's not telling its members that racial discrimination is wrong, one-hundred-percent, totally wrong, UN-Christian and morally indefensible. The conclusion is obvious; people leading organized churches don't actually believe in equal rights. No words, no actions. No commitment."

"You're being far too negative as usual," Isiah said quietly, rubbing two fingers on each temple. "Churches are groups of people with faults, just like us. And aren't you forgetting that most of the people actively fighting for civil rights are church people, clergy and lay, Christian and Jew? Doesn't that count for anything?"

"Not much," Jeff said. "Most of those people are black or Jewish and the loudest voices in pulpits are northern preachers farthest from the major problem. Southern Christian churches? Hell, they're key parts of the problem; certainly not part of the solution."

Realizing he was talking to a 'northern preacher, Jeff mentally scrambled. "Look," he said,"I know there are lots of exceptions, including you. You've even worked in Mississippi. I certainly don't mean to criticize anyone's faith. I wish I had more of it and maybe someday I will. But I'm angry at those who say they're Christians or otherwise religious, but they don't do, or even say, anything about the huge injustices going on every day. That makes them accomplices."

"You're an uncharitable cuss these days," Isiah said, smiling, trying to wind down the emotions and the discussion. "Have you lost your faith?"

"I was brought up in a Christian church but I'm not sure how much actual faith I ever had," Jeff said, glancing at Isiah and then quickly away. "For sure, I have less now than ever. Maybe none," he added.

"Do you believe God manages details of our lives?" he said, surprised at voicing one of his deepest thoughts. "Do you believe in miracles?" he added. "Do you believe prayer actually works?" his voice lower and lower with each question. "I have trouble believing any of that stuff."

Isiah didn't move, not even an eye blink, staring at Jeff, both frozen where they sat.

"Well," Isiah finally said, getting up, stretching his arms over his head. "Let's get back to this some sunny day soon when we're both fresher. I'm tuckered out, but I understand what you're going through, searching for what you believe. That's a good thing to do."

"I know what I believe," Jeff said. "I'm a realist. The problem is the reality I see is making me sick to my stomach...or maybe sickening my soul....I don't even know if I have a soul."

"You're too young to lose your idealism and turn so sour," Isiah said, gathering his books. "There's lots of undone work and I think you're frustrated by not yet finding an active-enough role for yourself."

"Why wait? When will I be old enough to be a realist?" Jeff asked.

There was no reply as the door closed.

CHAPTER FORTY-FOUR

"Ok, Mr. 'Put-up-or-shut-up,'" Isiah said from Jeff's doorway, "I've got another gig in Mississippi this summer."

Jeff launched to his feet behind the desk. "Mississippi? Why wade back into that racist swamp?"

Isiah stared at Jeff, astounded at his reaction.

"Look," Isiah said sharply, irritated now, throwing up his hands. "You've been bitching that no one's *doing* anything about equal rights. I'm trying to *do* something by joining the national voter registration project this summer. I expected you to be supportive. Are you really criticizing both acting and not acting?"

"I'm sorry, I didn't mean…" Jeff sputtered. "I'm totally freaked by the thought of you stomping around the Mississippi boonies stirring up local racists. That scares the liver outta me. I'm sorry. Will a voter project actually accomplish much?"

"I honestly don't know," Isiah said, leaning against the window sill. "At least we'll register some voters and let people know they're not alone. And we'll show them that our movement is strong. And relentless."

Isiah collapsed in the reading chair under the tall reading lamp, still furious at having to defend himself. He had expected Jeff to be enthusiastic. Jeff's over-flowing frustration had lingered with Isiah, even as he tried to moderate Jeff's growing cynicism. He was tired of Jeff's 'no one's doing anything rant,' but he knew it wasn't completely wrong, and it left him uncomfortable and restless, vaguely dissatisfied with himself. When notice of the summer's voter registration drive in Mississippi, Arkansas, Georgia and Alabama came to the office he instinctively decided to go. His lead pastor had quickly agreed to the nine-week absence that included a week's training plus eight weeks in Mississippi attempting to register black adults who had never voted. He filled out and signed the paperwork, penned a letter home and flung them in a mailbox on his way to tell Jeff.

"Look, I'm really excited about this," he said, softening his tone. "I'm energized and my mind is focused. I'll work with real people who need me. Maybe it'll be a wasted effort, but, even if it is, I'll find that out and can concentrate on something else."

"I know. I apologize," Jeff said, subdued. "I'll be scared shitless the whole time even though I know it's important. But it's a hell of a lot more dangerous now than when you were there two years ago."

CHAPTER FORTY-FIVE

Jeff stooped to scoop The Ann Arbor News from its usual morning place, tossed against his door. He was turning back into the room when he saw the screaming headline and simultaneously recognized the small photo. He didn't remember going to the edge of his bed where he now sat.

* * *

CIVIL RIGHTS ACTIVIST MISSING IN MISSISSIPPI

FOWLERVILLE, Miss. (AP)—A Negro civil rights activist from Philadelphia, Pa., who has been a student and assistant professor at the University of Michigan for two years, was reported missing last night by the head of a voter registration drive in Mississippi.

Rev. Isiah Booker was last seen two days ago. Lee Bowen of Berkley, Cal., organizer of the registration effort, said Rev. Booker did not return to the house where he was staying, but colleagues first thought he had spent the night at another house used by some of the 18 team members attempting to register Negro voters.

The Dixon County Sheriff's office said deputies were investigating but that they had no information about Rev. Booker's whereabouts and didn't know for sure that he was actually missing.

* * *

"Where is he?" Jeff's voice was anguished in Susan's lounge. She hugged her legs drawn up on the couch. Don stood leaning on the back of a chair watching Jeff pace.

"He couldn't just disappear. Someone knows where he is. He wouldn't wander around alone in that cesspool." Jeff paused at the piano and plinked two random low notes.

"Maybe he met someone and they're taking a little R-and-R break," Don said.

"Maybe there's a secret planning session going on to develop strategy," Susan offered.

"Then the leaders would know about it," Jeff snapped. "They're the ones who reported him missing. I didn't want him in that goddamned state. He should have stayed away from those snakes. It's full of evil people who would hate Isiah the minute they saw him."

"Those are the reasons he believed he needed to go," Susan said quietly. "He was willing to take risks to help change things."

CHAPTER FORTY-SIX

***

ANN ARBOR ACTIVIST SHOT TO DEATH IN MISSISSIPPI

Negro Minister *Found Buried; Was UM Doctoral Student*

FOWLERVILLE, Miss. (AP)—The body of Rev. Isiah R. Booker, a Negro minister from Philadelphia, Pa., and a doctoral student at the University of Michigan, was found late Tuesday in a junkyard about three miles south of Fowlerville.

He had been shot three times according to the Dixon County Sheriff's office.

Rev. Booker was part of a voter registration drive being conducted in four southern states this summer sponsored by several civil rights organizations including the National Association of Colored People (NAACP), the Congress for Racial Equality (CORE), and the Student Non-Violent Coordinating Committee (SNCC).

The body was found after an anonymous telephone tip to the Sheriff's office. The body was in a shallow grave in a seldom-used area on the fringe of the Dixon Auto Parts and Junkyard about a half-mile

off State Highway 19, according to the Dixon County Sheriff. No serious trouble had been reported during the first two weeks of the countywide project aimed at registering Negro voters. A spokesman coordinating efforts said 18 civil rights workers were in Dixon County. Lee Bowen of Berkeley, Cal., leader of the voter drive, said Rev. Booker was last seen Monday afternoon. He was reported missing 36 hours before the body was found.

Sheriff's deputies said they were continuing to investigate but had no clues to the killer or killers. They were interviewing the junkyard's owners and residents in the vicinity.

Rev. Booker was ordained in 1958 after an undergraduate career that included two years as a hard-running halfback for Temple University.

After seminary at Harvard University, he served as assistant pastor at a small church near Mt. Pleasant, Michigan, before moving to Ann Arbor to pursue a doctoral degree in theology. He is survived by his mother, Mrs. Robert Booker of Philadelphia, and a sister.

* * *

Jeff slumped onto his desk, face cradled on his arms, sobbing without realizing it, smothered by brutal reality short-circuiting his brain.

The phone rang and he lurched upright, still holding the newspaper, picked up the receiver without speaking.

"Jeff? Jeff?"

"I can't talk, Mom," Jeff choked and hung up.

The radio announcer was asking, "When's the last time you had a really crisp cracker? One with just a slight hint of salt and that rich buttery goodness…"

How the Christ can they have that shit on the radio when Isiah's dead?

The door flew open and Don kicked it shut behind him. He saw Jeff's tears and the newspaper on the floor by his feet.

"I didn't know if you knew yet," Don said, sitting on the unmade bed, then got up and put his hand on Jeff's shaking shoulder. "This can't be happening."

"It's already happened," Jeff croaked, glancing up, his eyes red slits in his flushed face.

The damned phone rang again. "I just heard," Susan whispered. "This is unbelievable. I won't believe it. How are you? Never mind, stupid question," her voice clotted, barely clearing her throat.

"I can't talk about it," his voice flat-lined.

"Meet me at Café Coffee for a cup and a hug," she said. "We don't have to talk."

"No. Please. I can't. I just...I'm cutting the rest of the week and going home," announcing a decision he didn't realize he'd made. "I need...I don't know what I need. Some thinking time. I don't know...I'll call you from there."

"I understand. This is the worst thing I can imagine...I don't ...Oh, Jeff, I love you. Call me when you get home."

"I will. I love you, too. I'm just...The world's all fucked up."

***

His mother seemed unsurprised to see him even though he hadn't called to say he was coming. She said little--none of which he heard--then nodded, understanding when he said he needed to be alone.

He sat on the bed in his old room seeing, as if for the first time, wallpaper with baseball players swinging bats against a light-blue background scattered with team pennants, the matching bedspread; two balsa wood plane models dangling from the ceiling, a battered BB-gun leaning behind the door. He stretched out.

A kid's room! I don't belong here anymore.

He awoke to a tap on the door. For a moment he thought it was...but he was home, in his boyhood bedroom.

"Jeff?"

" Yeah, Dad, I'll be right down."

"Can I come in?"

"Yeah."

His father sat on the bed. "I'm so sorry," he said, a hand on Jeff's arm, "I don't know what to say. This is so incredible. Completely devastating."

Jeff's body shook with silent tears. Finally he rubbed his arm over his eyes and sat up, swinging his legs over the side of the bed.

"How could anyone…? Why would…? He didn't deserve this. He… just…wanted to help people…."

"Yes," his father said softly. After a long pause, he added: "Mom's making dinner."

"I can't face food. I'm going for a drive."

CHAPTER FORTY-SEVEN

Lake Michigan loomed in his windshield, disappearing into the horizon like the inland ocean it is. He didn't remember how he got here but he was glad to see the lake, a place of good memories.

Heavy dark clouds moved overhead as he parked the Plymouth. The air wrapped him in humidity as he walked slowly across the gravel parking lot onto fine white sand leading to the nearest of two piers, 30 yards away. He barely felt the faint mist on his forehead. His shoes made grinding sounds, creating temporary indentations in the sand.

He took a long step onto the massive concrete pier, a gentle wind ruffling the lake on his left, the river on the right flowing like black oil in the expanding gloom. He recalled walking here with Susan and sitting by the lighthouse, enjoying the view and the day. Imagining their future life together.

He remembered other times when the rhythmic foghorn moaned from the lighthouse, sending warnings to freighters and small boats whenever fog spread its gray blanket over the lake. The horn was silent now but the light at the top was already revolving into the dusk. The pier was about 30 feet wide with a raised center section like a trapezoid, the narrow end on top, slides sloping toward the water on each side, stopping at a five-foot flat area where fishermen often sat watching their lines, or stood, casting shiny lures far out into the lake or into the river on the other side.

Reaching the pier's end, blunted to withstand assaults by waves that sometimes matched the storm-tossed Atlantic, he was grateful to find it deserted. Moving to the lake side, he sat on the rough, cold concrete, at the bottom of the slope, hugging his drawn-up knees.

The mist stopped as he watched the lake moving hypnotically along the pier, small waves intersecting and sliding smoothly along the edge, the faintest of rainbows celebrating the rain's demise.

Why are there still rainbows when Isiah's lying dead in a box with bullet holes in him?

The water softly caressed the weathered concrete, spilling shallowly along the flat area, one wave and two, and another, each lazily following another and another, endlessly, forever. Beneath the surface all was quiet and still, peaceful and eternal. The evening was darkening, accelerated by the nearly black clouds shifting slowly overhead, disappearing into the dusk. He was no longer sure where the water ended and the sky began. Everything was dark, a tinge of black seeping into the dark blue of the lake.

The water was content. He knew that even when storm winds whipped the surface into a furious frenzy, sometimes with waves six or eight feet high, not far beneath the turmoil were the quiet depths. Always.

The world above the waves lurched on and changed; often confusing and violent and unfair and battered by man-created winds that came and went. But under the water it was always quiet and peaceful. The soothing waves moving endlessly along the pocked concrete, forever chasing one another toward shore where they turned, returned and came again. And again. They would always be there, gently flowing by or pounding this gigantic concrete chunk for centuries, perhaps forever. The water was forever. Forever, people walked here along the water and continued on, passing into their individual oblivions. And other people always came and went away.

Staring into the hypnotic waves, Jeff rejected the thought even as it developed, as if emerging from a fog. Peace stretched out her arms and beckoned. A massive cynicism washed over him like a tsunami.

We constantly guard our lives. So we can live a long time? For what? To enjoy our fleeting lives? To contribute to society? To leave a temporary mark? To grab some sort of brief immortality? Because we're afraid of death? Death deserves to be feared. It comes at any random moment of its choosing. It's unknown and we fear the unknown.

"It's all for nothing." Jeff's voice startled him, not intending to say it aloud. "There's no point at all," hearing a stranger's voice. "A man like Isiah can't die in vain."

That must be true. What can Isiah accomplish now? Why in hell is he dead? There must be a reason. Was it all a mistake? Is there any point at all? To anything? Does God make mistakes? Does God give a shit? Does God have anything to do with anything? Is there a god? If there is a god, why does he permit this shit?

He sat on the concrete for a long time, feeling the dampness through his jeans, night taking over, town lights flickering on along the coastline, headlights moving on nearby streets. He arose stiffly, brushing the back of his pants, climbing the slight slope to the middle of the pier, walking slowly to his car. Stepping back on the sand bordering the parking lot, he realized his earlier footprints were already gone.

"Whoever it is, I'll kill him," he said aloud.

But he knew he couldn't.

CHAPTER FORTY-EIGHT

The organ moaned its funeral dirge as Susan, Don and Jeff shuffled through heavy, carved-wood sanctuary doors crowded by a slowly moving river of black-clad mourners. The trio sank onto oak pews near the rear, exhausted by the drive from Ann Arbor to the Philadelphia church.

Jeff glimpsed the bronze casket on a maroon-draped, wheeled cart between two raised podiums flanking the front of the sanctuary. A large woman in a black caftan stroked keyboards behind the right podium, two dozen men and women in black choir robes sat opposite her, like solemn ravens on telephone wires.

The funeral blurred past Jeff. A rich, booming baritone reading scripture, another *celebrating* Isiah's life while *regretting* his death and *accepting* God's will, Susan's hand gripping his in her lap, *"Amazing Grace"* by the choir, a soloist singing *"The Lord's Prayer,"* two hymns by the congregation--stand up, sit down--the skirted casket floating down the aisle as if on a cushion of air, flanked by eight black suits and faces as he desperately tried thinking of anything, *anything,* other than its contents. It was like peering through a kaleidoscope while someone else shook it, the view changing abruptly every time he tried to focus.

Hours later, Don was driving toward Michigan, Jeff slumped in the passenger seat, stocking feet on the dash, remembering Isiah's mother after the service, her white hair captured in a bun, her black dress with a white collar framing her round face dominated by huge, profoundly sad brown eyes, the faintest glimpse of smile-induced crinkles from better times.

"Yes, Mr. Martindale," she said when he introduced himself, bowing slightly to take her offered hand; other mourners surrounding them, waiting to hug her, say something to the dead man's mother. "Isiah mentioned you many times. I'm glad to meet you finally," looking away briefly. "Even today," her compelling brown eyes watering.

"Mrs. Booker, I'm so very sorry. Isiah was a terrific person. Wonderful. I believe he was destined to be a great man. I'm proud that he was my friend. I, uh, uh," tears streaming, eyes closing, his throat strangled by invisible hands, his mouth unable to continue. She reached again for his hand, grasping it in both of hers. They looked helplessly at each other, unable to talk, two strangers sharing unspeakable grief. She pulled him to her into a hug.

Jeff shook his head as if denying the reason they stood in a church basement jammed by people with sorrowful expressions, fighting tears, struggling to comfort each other and themselves with rituals and songs, words and hugs.

"God bless you," she said, squeezing his hand. "Thank you so much for coming," turning to another of the circling throng who called her name.

As Jeff merged back into the crowd, ready to escape, looking for Don or Susan in the tightly packed room, a firm hand grasped his shoulder from behind.

"Hi. You're a friend of Isiah's from Michigan."

A very tall, slender black man looked down, offering his hand. His hair was short, the front receding, flashes of white decorating his temples. "I'm Antoine Johnston" he said, still holding Jeff's hand. "I thought I knew all of Isiah's friends from around here," he said, noting the surprise on Jeff's face.

"Yes. We met in Ann Arbor."

"I thought so. Isiah and I went through high school and college together. He was the football player and I, as you might guess, played basketball. We drank beer together, double dated, studied. Pretty much everything."

"Uh, we fished together and talked a lot."

"Bet you mean listened a lot," a brief full-face smile. "Isiah was a major league, hall-of-fame talker. I don't mean that in a bad way," he added quickly. "He was someone worth listening to. And he listened to others. I'm sorry, this isn't coming out right. I know he's gone but I feel like I can still kid him. I *know* he's gone but..." eyes brimming, voice fading to a whisper. "He'll always be my best friend."

"He was a good friend to me," Jeff said. "And a mentor. I've never respected anyone more." Then, abruptly: "He isn't just gone; he was murdered," Jeff said, realizing everyone in the room knew that. "I can't get past it. Is it sacrilegious in church to say I can't forgive his killers? Have you?"

"No. Not yet. Maybe never. Probably never."

Now, as Susan napped in the back seat and Don drove west through the dusk, a light rain added hundreds of tiny mirrors to the windshield between wiper swipes. Jeff glowered through the side window, the world streaming by, as unsorted and incoherent as his thoughts.

"How ya doing?" Don's voice was startling in the closed car.

"Shitty. Thanks for asking." No trace of a smile, not turning his head.

"Yeah. Me, too. Still glad you went?"

"I had to."

"Yeah, it wasn't to feel good, but maybe add some perspective."

"There is no perspective," Jeff snapped, turning to Don. "There is no goddamn perspective. There's murder. Isiah's dead. He shouldn't be. That's it. No horseshit about some *celebration* of his life. That's crap. Perspective my ass!"

"Ok, ok. I'm sorry," Don's voice more hurt than apologetic. "Why'd you want to be there?"

"To honor Isiah. And I wanted to see people who knew him." A silent pause. "I'm sorry. I'm not mad at you. I'm furious at those sonsabitches who executed him and I don't know what to do about it."

"Nothing we can do."

"There *must* be. This can't be all there is. It can't end like this. A thrown away life. They can't get away with this."

"Who's 'they?'"

"Obviously I don't know, but somebody knows. They better get them."

"Another 'they,' Don said. "What if they're never caught?"

"I don't know but this won't be the end. If there's a god....if there's any justice in this world....if... I...."

"You're mad at God, aren't you?" Susan said, straightening in the backseat from an in-and-out doze.

"Aren't you?" Jeff barked, turning to look at her.

She stifled a yawn, stretched her arms as wide as the car allowed, delaying a response. "I don't know. I'm not sure what God is responsible for and what he leaves for us to decide." She leaned forward, massaging his shoulders.

"I know this much." he said, "There is no way God himself can explain this to me. No way in hell."

CHAPTER FORTY-NINE

***

THREE SUSPECTS ARRESTED IN SLAYING OF PHILLY CLERGYMAN

FOWLERVILLE, Miss.—(AP)—Three Fowlerville-area white men were arrested Tuesday with slaying a Negro minister from Philadelphia.

Arrested were Edward P. Bryant, 41, Roy S. Ryser, 40, and Rollin B. Price, 41. They are accused of killing Rev. Isiah R. Booker, whose body was found last week buried in rural Dixon County. He had been shot three times.

Sheriff Lanny Purdy said the suspects were linked to the case by tire tracks near where the body was found. Sheriff Purdy refused to provide any other information.

A grand jury will consider the case immediately, according to Dixon County Prosecutor Walter Stallman.

The Negro Baptist minister was found in a shallow grave in a junkyard three miles south of this Mississippi town of 35,000 people. Rev Booker was part of an 18-member civil rights team operating this summer in Dixon County. The group sought to register Negro voters for approximately two months in preparation for next fall's election.

Prior to Rev. Booker's disappearance and murder no serious incidents had occurred, according to the team's leader, Lee Bowen of California.

An anonymous tip led to discovery of the body.

CHAPTER FIFTY

***

GRAND JURY INDICTS TRIO IN MINISTER'S SLAYING

FOWLERVILLE, Miss.—(UPI)—A Dixon County grand jury indicted three Fowlerville men yesterday in the murder of a Philadelphia Baptist minister five weeks ago.

Charged with first-degree murder are Edward P. Bryant, 41, Roy S. Ryser, 40 and Rollin B. Price, 41.

The murdered man was Rev. Isiah R. Booker, a 32-year-old Negro minister from Philadelphia, Pa. His body, shot three times, was found about three miles south of this Mississippi town of 35,000 people.

Bryant, owner of a hardware store in Fowlerville was linked to the case when sheriff's deputies found tire tracks near the burial site resembling tires on his late-model sedan. He and fellow defendant Ryser are members of the Dixon County White Citizens Council. Bryant is married and the father of one child.

Ryser is an unmarried pharmacist and owns the "Family Drug" store on Main Street in Fowlerville.

Price is a truck driver for Dixon Auto Parts and Junkyard, where

the body was found in a shallow grave in an abandoned part of the junkyard. He is married and the father of four children.

Deputies say Price once owned a 38-caliber pistol. The murder weapon has not been found but reportedly bullets recovered from the body are 38-caliber. Deputies said Price told them his revolver was stolen about two years ago. The theft had not been previously reported.

Deputies said Bryant and Ryser were seen together several times the night Booker disappeared.

Attorneys for the three accused men said "undeniable alibis" would prove the men innocent of the murder. "This is an impossible case," defense attorney Lester Adler said. "This is a terrible, terrible mistake. It's based entirely on circumstantial evidence and on assumptions without a shred of fact to them."

Prosecuting Attorney Walter Stallman refused comment. "We'll try the case when we get to court."

CHAPTER FIFTY-ONE

***

TRIAL OPENS FOR TRIO IN SLAYING OF BLACK PHILADELPHIA MINISTER

FOWLERVILLE, Miss.—(AP)—A jury of 12 men, all white, was selected Monday in the trial of three Fowlerville-area men charged with the slaying three months ago of Rev. Isiah R. Booker, a Negro minister from Philadelphia, Pa.

Testimony is scheduled to begin tomorrow with presentation of the prosecution's case.

***

CAR AND MISSING GUN LINK TRIO TO MURDER

Defense Challenges
Tire Tread Evidence

FOWLERVILLE, Miss.—(AP)—Tire tracks and a missing pistol were used by the prosecution Tuesday in its efforts to convict three white

men for the murder of a Negro civil rights worker form Philadelphia, Pa.

On the second day of trial, Prosecuting Attorney Walter Stallman called a Mississippi State Patrol expert who testified that tracks found near the scene were similar to tires on a car owned by one of the defendants, Edward S. Bryant, owner of a local hardware store.

However, cross-examination of Sgt. Bobby Joe Williams by Defense Attorney Lester Adler forced the State Patrol expert to admit that many other cars with the same Firestone tires could have made the tracks. "Could these tracks have been made by hundreds of other cars?" he asked Sgt. Bobby Joe Williams.

"Yes."

"Thousands of other cars?"

"I suppose so. Yes."

A second defendant, Rollin B. Price, an employee of the old and sprawling junkyard where the minister's body was found, was identified as owner of a 38-caliber revolver. Dixon County Coroner Abbott Simpson testified that his office recovered three 38-caliber slugs from the minister's body. The murder weapon has not been found. Price has said his revolver was stolen almost two years ago. The theft had not been reported to police.

The prosecution included testimony by Peter Barron, owner of the Dixon Auto Parts and Junkyard, where the body was found. He said the remote part of the junkyard where the grave was found hadn't been actively used in "six or seven years or more." The junkyard has been in existence for 32 years and covers approximately 25 acres. The yard office, where used auto parts are sold, is several hundred yards from the shallow grave site.

Defense lawyers commented after the trial recessed that the prosecution's case "was totally circumstantial and amazingly weak."

CHAPTER FIFTY-TWO

Dear Mom & Dad,

I hope you're following the trial in Mississippi. I've memorized the newspaper stories here; and seen the reports on Detroit TV.

I hope those sonsabitches get the death penalty so Isiah's murder won't have been for nothing. If these three are hung maybe it'll help save the lives of others because it'll scare the bigots back under their rocks.

But they'll probably get off. It is Mississippi after all.

Love,

Jeff

***

A few days later he tried to beg off when Susan called inviting him to "dinner on me," but she persisted. Then, at Tony's, he insisted he wasn't hungry. Tired of his gloomy face and attitude, she confronted him as gently as she could.

"It's time to come out of your cave," she said. "Let's get on with your life. With *our* lives," sending him a warm smile and reaching across the table for his hand. "Let's get you out in the sunshine."

"I'm not very good company," he said, not looking at her.

"No, you're not. Terrible company in fact. But we can change that. How about a picnic Saturday afternoon? Just the two of us by the river, maybe stretched out analyzing cloud formations or we could take in a movie with cardboard popcorn at the Empire?"

He looked up at her finally and nodded. "Let's see what Saturday looks like. I'm sorry to be like this…I'm just…." eyes moistening and he quickly looked away and then down again, grabbing his water glass to mask his distress with activity. Finally: "Sorry again."

"We'll go from here," she said. "I understand how you feel."

"I don't think so," he said so quietly she barely registered his words. "I wish the NAACP or CORE would organize vigilante teams to hang race murderers who escape the corrupt Southern justice system. Reverse lynchings." He looked unblinking into her eyes.

"Isn't that exactly the opposite of Isiah's beliefs?" she said.

"Look what it got him."

CHAPTER FIFTY-THREE

***

SEVEN WITNESSES PROVIDE ALIBIS FOR ACCUSED KILLER OF NEGRO ACTIVIST

Testimony Rocks Courtroom; Called 'Devastating' to Prosecution

FOWLERVILLE, Miss.—(UPI)—Seven witnesses gave identical testimony today, providing an alibi for one of the three men on trial in the slaying of a Negro minister from Philadelphia, Pa.

The seven testified in quick succession that defendant Rollin B. Price, was playing poker with them for nearly six hours on the night Rev. Isiah R. Booker was shot three times and buried in a shallow grave south of town.

Price is one of three defendants on trial for the murder. He had been linked to the case because of friendships with the other two defendants, his reported criticism of civil rights workers and his ownership of a missing 38-caliber pistol. The actual murder weapon has not been found.

One courtroom observer called the testimony "devastating"

and predicted acquittal for all three men. Timing of the poker game virtually ruled out Price as a participant in the killing if the jury believes the seven men.

Tire tracks found near the burial site were of the same general type as those on the car of another defendant, Edward S. Bryant, according to previous testimony by a Mississippi State Patrol investigator. Sgt. Bobby Joe Williams also admitted, under aggressive cross-examination by the defense, that the tracks were too indistinct to make an exact match to Bryant's car and that similar tires were on many other vehicles.

Bryant had said before the trial that he was taking inventory in his hardware store until approximately 2:30 a.m. the night of the slaying.

Sheriff's Deputy Cecil Stuart testified yesterday that during his patrols that night he saw Bryant in his store at approximately 9 p.m. About two hours later, the deputy testified, he drove through the alley behind Bryant's hardware store and observed the interior lights on and Bryant's car parked near the rear door.

On a later patrol, at around 3:15 a.m., the deputy said the store was dark except for its normal night lighting and Bryant's car was no longer in the alley. Deputy Stuart testified that he saw the same car parked in Bryant's home driveway around 4 a.m.

CHAPTER FIFTY-FOUR

***

TRIO ACQUITTED IN SLAYING OF PHILADELPHIA ACTIVIST

FOWLERVILLE, Miss.—(AP)—A jury Tuesday acquitted three Fowlerville-area men on trial in the slaying of minister and Negro civil rights activist Isiah R. Booker of Philadelphia, Pa.

The jury of 12 white men deliberated only 22 minutes before returning the not-guilty verdict after closing arguments late this afternoon.

One of the defendants, Edward P. Bryant, 41, turned to his wife in the packed courtroom and said, with a huge smile, "Thank you, God."

The other two defendants were Roy S. Ryser, 40, and Rollin B. Price, 41. All refused to talk to reporters but were laughing and joking with family and friends as the courtroom cleared.

The verdict left the county with no other suspects, according to Sheriff Lanny Purdy.

A courtroom observer commented that the prosecution's case was "completely circumstantial" and so weak that there never was any chance of a conviction. It looks deliberate. This means they can never be tried again," he said. "It's over."

CHAPTER FIFTY-FIVE

A day later, Jeff read Isiah's obituary again and again, folding the battered clipping, keeping it in his shirt pocket, taking it out to torture himself when it called to him while trying, but failing, to study. He read it while eating and when in the bathroom. He thought about it while trying to sleep.

By the second day, he stopped even attempting class work and drifted deeper into a brooding darkness, sometimes staring sightlessly at his desktop for an hour or more. He rebuffed or ignored all attempts from Susan or Don to leave the room. He rejected Susan's daily appeals for coffee or a movie or lunch or a flirtatious invitation to drive to the river. Not even Don's, "let's go jump in a pitcher of beer and soak our way to sanity," brought even a glimmer of a smile.

The next evening, staring at the gathering dusk, he remembered nothing of the day, although he'd watched the earliest hint of dawn from the same window.

Late Saturday afternoon, Don and Susan and bright light invaded the room. As Don opened the drapes, Susan sat next to Jeff on his bed and hugged him from the side, whispering in his ear. Hearing only unintelligible mumbles, she jumped up, grabbed his hand with both of hers and tugged him firmly to his feet, rolling her eyes at Don watching them. She guided Jeff through the door, pulling him by one arm, holding his hand, her other hand pushing his back.

Once outside, Jeff stopped resisting, but walked as if comatose. She held his hand firmly and continued talking, though he didn't respond. Finally they got to the Pizza Barn where he sank into a booth with her. She continued to talk to him but he sat, mostly with his head down, using his forefinger to move his fork from side to side on his plate, the obituary clipping on the table between them until the pizza arrived.

Finally, glancing up, he said: "Isiah's obituary is too brief," he said. "It's barely an outline of dates in his life, it doesn't really tell who and *what* he is…was…the impact he had…or might have had….The kids and others he helped. It doesn't say who he actually was."

"You're right, it doesn't." she said. "It's difficult to do that in an obituary. He deserves more detail, more people talking about him, explaining what he was like. It might take a magazine article. Or possibly a book. Maybe you should write that book."

Jeff looked up into her eyes.

"Me?"

"Sure. You were his friend. You know a lot about him. You have reporting and writing skills. You could interview people who knew him, friends, relatives. You can make people understand how tragic his death is."

"Not me," Jeff said. "And the worst part can't really be told anyway. It's what he *could* have been, could have done. No one will ever know."

"You can make people know him," she said. "You can write what you think he was going to do, what he might have accomplished, what he told you he wanted to do. Did he tell you things like that?"

"I can't do it," he said. "How do you tell people about someone who wasn't finished becoming who he was? I know what he was capable of, but that's not a book. It's an incomplete symphony, an unfinished life," choking, tears flowing. His hands masked his face, gulping for air. Finally he rubbed his face and looked at her. "Am I crying for him or for me?"

***

Later that night, his mind raced as he lay in bed, finally falling into a sleep that brought no peace. In a pre-dawn dream Jeff is an old man.

"Didn't you know that black minister who was killed in Mississippi about 50 years ago?"

"Yes."

"Whatever happened to the killers?"

"Nothing."

CHAPTER FIFTY-SIX

The next day Jeff wrote his own obituary, imagining that he had died and a newspaper published a totally truthful story about him.

* * *

Jeffrey Martindale, 76, died yesterday after a long but not particularly notable life. He was the father of three children, all of whom will miss him quite a bit for a short time and a little bit for a longer time. Martindale was a retired newspaper reporter.

A long-time friend and golfing companion, when informed of Martindale's death, said: "Well, ole Jeff never made any holes-in-one. Of course," he hastened to add, "He never left any really big divots either."

Perhaps the high point of Martindale's life, as best as can be determined, was graduating cum laude from the University of Michigan.

His life's low point appears to have been the death of a black friend at the hands of racial murderers in Mississippi in the early 1960s.

Two friends remembered that Martindale took the death very hard at the time. But, they say, he eventually got over it and the incident was apparently forgotten. The friends didn't recall the murdered person's name but he was one of the dozens who were killed in similar incidents in the 1950s and into the late-1960s, Martindale's widow said.

Survivors include…

* * *

A terrific memorial. What a wonderful life. Barely an actual life. That's the sum total of my existence? Should the world give someone space for 76 years in return for only that? Isiah's name was forgotten! Will I remember it by then? Two lives wasted; one by bullets, the other by a guy just living. I won't let them forget Isiah, what he was and what he died for. Whatever the hell that was. I'll take his place and work for…shit. I'd have better chance of sculpting him in bronze. A premature death. Even he said that was the worst kind. How ironic. He got the death I've been afraid of. Damn Mississippi. DAMN MISSISSIPPI! He said we live on in deeds that affect others, the only real impact we can have. Those effects are unknowable, like trying to track ripples created by a stone tossed in a pond. Hell, I didn't make any ripple in life's pond. Damn fucking Mississippi. Damn you. Damn your ignorant racist murderers. The whole state should be flooded for 40 days and nights so we can start over. Now I'm pretending to be God. As long as I can't do anything I might as well dream about things I can't do as God either. Apparently God can't do anything either.

***

Later that night he put four Pabst Blue Ribbon bottles in the sink filled with ice while Don slept. He drank three, one after another with barely a pause in between. Well into the fourth, he held it toward the dim window to see how much was left. His bedside clock glowed 3:26.

Can't be that late. So what? Who gives a shit? It's too late for everything. ISIAH'S DEAD. He'll never know how the civil rights fight turns out; if there's ever any racial progress. I can't do a goddamn thing about it. Can't do anything about anything. The murdering racist pigs do things. They eliminated forever someone good and kind and wonderful. Someone who would never have considered killing them. Bet they didn't give it a second thought. Firing bullets into him and burying him in a junkyard in the middle of the night.

He raised the nearly empty bottle in mock toast and whispered into the darkness: "Here's to you, you murdering redneck bastard pieces of shit."

Just what the doctor ordered. Take four beers and don't call me tomorrow. Prescription beer.

CHAPTER FIFTY-SEVEN

Jeff was talking before the door was fully open, interrupting Don punching keys on his portable typewriter, books and paper and notebooks littering his desktop, overflowing to the floor.

"I got one of those national summer internships I told you about," Jeff said, waving a letter and envelope.

"Hey," Don said. "Congratulations. This is the best mood you've been in for months. The one in D.C.?"

"No, actually smaller."

"Cincinnati?"

"Much smaller."

"I didn't see the list. Where you going?"

"Fowlerville, Mississippi."

"That's not funny."

"I'm serious."

"Are you're shittin me?"

"No, that's the slot I got. I may be the only applicant who checked it as a preference."

"I can believe that. Why'd you do that? Are you crazy? What were you thinking? What will your parents say? This is stupid. What's Susan say?

"Susan doesn't know yet. I just called her. We're meeting for dinner in a few minutes. I'll tell her then. I'll call home tonight.

"Yeah, but what about my most important question? Are you crazy?"

"Maybe. It was Susan's idea to think about a book possibly telling Isiah's story."

"Did she suggest going to Mississippi? To actual, fucking Fowlerville?"

"Not exactly. Neither of us knew this was a possibility."

"Is that why you're going? To research a book?"

"Why else?"

CHAPTER FIFTY-EIGHT

Susan lost her grip on the cup a quarter-inch above the saucer. It chinked, teetered and she pressed her palm on it, steadying it before it could tip over.

"I don't believe you applied for Fowlerville," her voice rising. "And without telling me? You talked about trying for the Washington or New York internships. You mentioned Chicago or Detroit. You never mentioned Fowlerville. What happened?"

"At the last minute I kept looking at Fowlerville on the list of 92 papers in the internship program," he said, glancing around the room. "It seemed like an opportunity I had to take. You suggested a book," he said, eyes briefly meeting hers. "I don't know if that's possible, but maybe I can at least do a magazine article about Isiah. And I hope to get some insight into how Mississippi thinks."

"You don't need to *go* to Mississippi to write about who Isiah was. You don't have to be *there.* We already know how Mississippi thinks. They're brutal, murdering racist thugs. That's a place I would think you'd avoid like hell itself. You can't do this," she said, pleading, reaching a hand across the table. He covered it with his, staring at their hands, still avoiding her eyes.

"It scares the bejesus out of me just to think about it," she said. "You'd be surrounded by the very monsters who murdered Isiah. If they find out you were his friend they could kill you, too."

"There's no way for anyone to know we were friends," he said. "Isiah's from Philadelphia. That's how he's been identified in news coverage since… since they murdered him. I'll just be a student in town for the summer on a national internship program. They had an intern there last summer."

"They might think you're a threat to them in some way."

Jeff remembered Isiah's reaction only a few months ago when he told Jeff he was returning to Mississippi to help with another voter registration drive. Isiah had said, 'you're the one who's been complaining that no one is *doing* anything about equal rights and the dignity of man. You're the 'put up or shut up' guy around here. Well, I'm trying to do something. I'm going to register black voters. I expected you to be supportive…'

Isiah's image was more real than Susan, who was less than two feet away. She was moving her lips but he couldn't hear her. He felt her anger and frustration and fear. He knew she didn't want him in Mississippi.

But I'm going.

CHAPTER FIFTY-NINE

Jeff's father looked as if his son had announced plans to dance naked down Main Street. He leaned forward in his living room chair.

"This makes no sense," he said, standing up, his voice desperate.

"I have to go, Dad. I need to see where he died. I want to understand what kind of place has people capable of killing Isiah while his hands are tied behind his back."

"What'll you do there? Your mother will crumble. She won't sleep the whole time you're gone and you're talking about three or four months. It's been an unbearably rough time since Isiah was murdered. Horrible beyond belief. All of us, but you most of all, are traumatized. You need some decompression time. Escape for awhile this summer. Just get away. Take a few weeks off when school's out and go camping in the UP. Remember when you wanted to fish the Big Two-Hearted River from Hemingway's book you read in high school? Do it now. Don't go to God-forsaken-Mississippi. Please," his face pinched with fear.

Jeff had anticipated and dreaded the objection but also savored his father's request, another sign of the adult relationship they now had; not long ago his father would have forbidden him to make the trip.

"I waited until mother was gone to tell you because you need to help me reassure her. I've got to go. If I don't get my head straightened out..." he looked away for a long moment. "I gotta know as much as I can about how this happened. At worst it won't be a total loss. I'm hoping to develop a magazine article about Isiah and his murder. And his wasted future. Susan thinks there may be material for a book. We should emphasize to Mom the book or article possibility. That's a positive goal. She'll understand that."

"Susan wants you to go?" doubt narrowing his eyes.

"Not exactly, but she understands what I need to do."

James walked to the living room window, hands jammed in his back pockets. He turned to Jeff.

"I'm not sure your mother can handle this; she'll be absolutely frantic with fear if you're in Mississippi. And so will I," his tone and face begging. "What if those killers find out you're there?"

"I know this seems risky to you, Dad, but it really isn't. And I gotta do this," shifting to meet at his father's gaze. "I won't be reckless. The internship is a real opportunity. I'll see what kind of town Fowlerville is and learn something about how the people think. There's no reason for anyone there to know that I am, was, a friend of Isiah's. He's known as a Baptist minister from Philadelphia. I'll be careful."

"I just can't understand this," his father said. "I'd think you'd never want to go near that place. You need to get your perspective back." "That's exactly it," Jeff said, standing up, rubbing his hands as if to warm them. "I can't do that here. I need to know as much as I can or I'll never be satisfied or at peace. I'll never be able get a perspective on this. I need to see it for myself."

CHAPTER SIXTY

The phone was made of lead and holding it to his ear took conscious effort as Don waited, listening to the rings.

"Susan, we need to talk, somewhere private, without Jeff knowing."

"What? Why?"

"Trust me, it's important."

She was already in a back booth, elbows on the table, hands framing her face, when Don came through the dim room and slid into the cracked, brown vinyl seat across from her; a glass of 7-Up the centerpiece.

"Mississippi?" she asked without preamble.

"Yeah."

"I'm worried, too. That's a disgusting, evil and dangerous place and I don't want him there," she said, reaching for the glass.

"I'm worried about something else," he said. "You're the only person I can talk to."

He saw her eyes narrow.

"Has Jeff said anything to you about revenge?" he asked, his face as neutral as he could make it.

"What are you talking about? He's very bitter about what happened. We all are. Are you asking if he's talked about doing something to those men who killed Isiah?"

"Anything at all," he said.

"I think he'd like to beat the snot out of 'em, but we both know he's not that kind a person. It's just talk. Frustration. Anger. Why are you asking this stuff?"

"I'm worried that he's thinking about burning down their houses…or something. Something big." He paused, looking directly at her. "Maybe hurting them." He was whispering but he felt as if he had shouted. It took three shaky tries with the Zippo before he could light the cigarette.

He felt the power of her stare as she watched him for a long moment. "Hurt them?" she said finally. "Beat them up? Or..."

He waved off a waitress, continuing as there'd been no interruption, but not answering her question. "Sometimes he sounds and looks like someone I don't know. He threatened to kill them the day they were acquitted. He was furious, livid, out of control; not like himself," whispering.

"That's been awhile," he continued, "but he still talks about making them suffer or making them pay. Or sending them to hell. I keep hoping he'll calm down, be able to move on. But he hasn't. And he's still furious once or twice a day, and now this Mississippi trip seriously scares me. He says you suggested he write a book about Isiah, but I doubt you suggested going to Mississippi."

"Of course I didn't," she said. "Never occurred to me. I was stunned when he told me about it. I yelled at him because it's a terrible, senseless idea that frightens me. He'd never mentioned considering going to Mississippi. The very town that killed Isiah! He didn't include me in his plans. I'm still angry about that. The book idea came up earlier when we were mourning Isiah's life being cut short. I suggested that he try capturing on paper what a wonderful person Isiah was; maybe something to inspire others. I hoped something positive could come from this horrific tragedy.

"Going to Mississippi is a terrifying idea," she said, sitting in perfect 90-degree angles. "But I can't believe he's thought *seriously* about killing anyone. I can't imagine anything like that," her voice vehement. "It's not possible. That's his anger talking. He couldn't hurt anyone. Even if he wanted to kill someone, when it came right down to it, he couldn't do it. He's not capable of anything like that," her hands turning to fists on the table, her chocolate eyes pinning Don against his side of the booth.

"I've been telling myself the same thing," he said. "I've known him most of my life and I agree with you," he said, grinding the cigarette in the ashtray. "But every time I convince myself he couldn't take revenge on those murdering bastards, something in his eyes or voice chills me and I wonder."

He avoided looking at her by watching his fingers making endless circles on the table. "I hope it's just frustration talking, but his seeking an internship in that vicious, hate-filled goddamn town scares me. He's changed since Isiah's murder. We all have, but it's been several months and he's angrier than ever. Something keeps bothering me when he talks about Isiah's unfinished life or about how those killer assholes that killed him got away with it and they may do it again to someone else. I…" his voice faded away. "I *know* who he is, but sometimes I *feel* something's drastically different. Like there's a stranger in there part of the time."

She hugged herself. "What specific things has he said?"

He thought a moment, wondering how far he should go, feeling he'd been working without a parachute since he'd called her. "The worst, most specific thing was when the acquittals happened. He came in shouting about corrupt southern justice and several versions of 'it can't have been for nothing…I'll make them sorry…' and then something I'll never forget as long as I live, 'I'll make them fucking dead!'"

She froze for a long second. "And since then?"

"A couple of times recently he's declared black death squads should hang Isiah's killers in public; that Negroes shouldn't be so accepting of oppression. Several times he said that since there's obviously no justice in the southern system it'll have to come from somewhere else, maybe from vigilantes or someone willing to deter others from killing more innocent people. It's usually when he's worked up, ranting and particularly bitter about Isiah being in his grave but the shitheads who killed him are still alive, still with their families and friends, heroes to the people there."

"He mentioned vigilante teams or something when he was so depressed over Isiah," Susan said. "I didn't think for a second that he was serious. I don't know what to think now. I can't believe Jeff could kill someone. Even those murderers. So why am I so nervous now?"

Neither spoke for several minutes.

"We need to talk to him," Don said. "I'm afraid Isiah's murder is so traumatic that he's at least thinking about doing something major, something otherwise unimaginable to him and inconceivable to us. The two of us together talking to him is the most powerful approach. He'll be stunned that we even think he would do anything drastic. He'll probably convince us that we're just nervous Nellies. I hope he can. He might lie to us but I think we'd know."

"God, this is completely bizarre," she said, dabbing tears with a napkin. "We're seriously talking about Jeff possibly thinking about murder; and about lying to us."

"Isiah's murder devastated all of us," Don said. "It still seems impossible, but it happened. If another tragedy is even remotely possible, we need to confront it; we must try."

He caught her eyes as she glanced at him, her face red and scrunched.

"I can't cram all this into my head," she said. "But you're right. We gotta talk to him. But how?"

"I'm not sure," he said, both relieved and disappointed. He had desperately hoped she could show him he was mistaken. Now they needed an action plan.

"We need a reason to talk to him," he said, "and, I guess, a place that's private, uh..." simultaneously talking and thinking. He looked at her the way a drowning man looks at a life preserver just out of reach.

"Maybe," she said, "we tell him up front that we want to chat about the Mississippi trip because we're worried. That's true, although he'll think we're only worried about the physical danger."

"Perfect," he said, voice bordering on admiration. "We want to do that anyway and we'll get to the other worry at the right moment."

He resumed drawing finger circles on the table. "Why don't you invite him to a picnic at Forest Hills Park Saturday," he said. "Emphasize the picnic and the setting so that'll seem most important, but that we want to talk about the Mississippi trip. That'll be true and explain why it'll be just the three of us." He searched her face for approval.

"Okay. I'll call you," she said, already sliding out of the booth, shrugging into her coat.

They walked through the restaurant and to their cars without speaking. He watched her get in and back out.

He got in his car and sat staring into the darkness, foreboding flooding his thoughts. He turned the key, listened to the motor humming and shook his head, wondering if their darkest concerns about his life-long friend were true.

CHAPTER SIXTY-ONE

The weathered wood picnic table was almost in the water, perched on a slight rise less than a foot above the Huron River.

Don was sitting on the tabletop facing the river. Gray clouds hung low overhead threatening rain, the humidity already heavy. He heard doors slamming and turned to see Jeff carrying a cardboard box, Susan waving, in olive shorts and a white, short-sleeved blouse that seemed inadequate in the cool, early spring air. A white sweater's arms hugged her waist, her hair tucked under a black Detroit Tigers cap.

Need help?" Don asked, finger-killing his cigarette and walking toward them in jeans and dark-blue sweatshirt with gold "Michigan" across the chest.

"Nope, this is it," Jeff said, nodding at the box. "We got cheeseburgers, we got fries, we got apples, we got cokes, we got crème sodas, we got beer and we got Twinkies."

Can he really be this cheerful? He knows we want to talk him out of Mississippi. This just an act?

Holding a Stroh's bottle aloft in one hand, opener in the other, Jeff's face asked the question.

"Sure," Susan said, the cap already hitting the tabletop.

Don sat on the table's attached bench, his back to the river, watching Jeff intently as he sat down, Susan next to him, maybe an inch apart. She emptied the box onto the table.

Chewing his first bite, Jeff put the cheeseburger on a napkin and broke the uncomfortable silence.

"Okay, look, I know you guys want to convince me not to go to Mississippi. I understand your worries, but you're both way too nervous. I'll be fine," looking briefly at Susan, then at Don.

"These men have murdered before," Susan said. "What happens when they find out you were Isiah's friend?"

"Well, I'd be proud if that happened, but it's the last thing I want. And it's unlikely. There's been no mention of Ann Arbor in the national news reports of Isiah's murder or of the trial. He's always described as being from Philadelphia. I'll just be another rookie reporter in town for the summer."

"But that alone makes you stand out in a town like that," Don said.

"Naw, they had an intern there last summer, the first year of the national program."

"Where was last year's intern from?" Don asked, tented fingers supporting his chin.

Jeff stared at his cheeseburger, then put it back on the napkin. "Alabama. So, yeah, I know my Midwest accent won't blend in as well as his, but when I saw Fowlerville on the list I knew I should apply," his voice low.

"A voice in your head," Don said, taking a small twig from the ground and snapping it into small pieces, his unwrapped sandwich still on the table.

"Not exactly," Jeff said, glancing at Don, then re-inspecting his burger. "I want to experience the place and the people. I want to understand their thinking. I've tried to imagine a town so full of vicious hatred that they can murder someone—someone they knew nothing about except his skin color—and then acquit the killers. And everyone involved, the murderers and the jurors and the judge, are heroes? They'll probably erect a statue to them. I want to understand that. If I can."

For a long moment they all heard the river on its journey downstream.

"I keep trying to imagine how this could happen," Jeff said, anger reddening his face. "What goes on in their minds, how they could have slaughtered Isiah. Erased him from the planet. Had no respect for him as a human. They shot him in cold blood and disposed of him like a dead hamster. I need to understand how people can do that."

"What are the chances," Susan said, "you'll find any answers?"

"I don't know. I want to try."

"Then what?" Susan asked.

He shifted toward her, meeting her relentless eyes.

"Whata ya mean?"

"After you find out as much as you can about the people and the place and the attitudes that produced those murdering bigots, what happens then?"

"I don't know. Maybe nothing. Probably nothing," voice drifting softer, eyes shifting to the river. "Maybe I come home and try to live the rest of my life without every day imagining what it was like for Isiah to feel the bullets hitting his body. Maybe I'll be able to write that book you suggested," glancing at Susan then back at the river, "about Isiah's stolen life and also the scum who murdered him. Maybe. I don't know," his voice intense and defiant.

"Have you thought about revenge?" Don was nearly inaudible.

"Revenge?" Jeff's voice rose and he glanced briefly at each of them. "Revenge? You mean poisoning their dogs? Bombing their cars? What?"

"Are you thinking about that?" Susan said.

"You mean an eye-for-an-eye? I don't believe in revenge."

He slid off the bench and walked a few steps to the river's edge, his back to them. He bent and scooped a handful of small gray-black pebbles in his left hand, selected one with his right and hurled it as far as he could into the river. Then another. He abruptly underhanded the rest of the stones into the river, wiped his hands on his jeans, and turned back to the silent pair standing, watching him, Susan hugging herself with both arms, Don's hands in his jean pockets.

"At first, all I thought about was revenge," Jeff said. "Now I want meaning. Are you asking if I might kill those murderers?"

Susan walked to him, shrugging into her sweater, and moved to hold him from behind, her hands clasped over his chest, her chin on his shoulder. "This has been an unbelievably traumatic time. We're worried about you being in that Mississippi cesspool. And we're worried about you."

"Worried that something'll happen to me or worried that I might do something to take revenge on those assholes? Which?"

After a silence, Don said quietly, "Both," looking at his sneakers, avoiding Jeff's face. "You're not yourself since this happened; and no wonder. We're wondering if you're thinking of doing something you couldn't have imagined a few months ago. Maybe seriously thinking of something …? Are you thinking of hurting these people?"

"These *people.* They aren't *people;* they're not human. Human beings can't do shit like that. Have I thought about hurting 'em? Hell, I've thought about killing 'em."

Susan's arms tightened around Jeff

"What are you thinking now?" Don asked.

"What are you, some kind of goddamn shrink? Two frigging psych classes and you're guessing what's in my head? Hell, I don't *know* what's in my head," he said, shrugging off Susan's encircling arms, moving to the end of the table farthest from them, turning away, leaning back against the table.

Susan and Don walked to him, one from each side, Susan hugging him from the front now, the side of her face on his shoulder, her eyes closed. Jeff rebalanced his weight on both feet, slowly reaching around her with both arms, his face disappearing into her hair, his eyes closing. Don stopped two steps away.

Jeff pulled Susan closer, his quiet sobs shaking both of their bodies, his arms tightening like steel bands around her, hoping hugging could change the world.

"I don't know what to do," Jeff whispered. "I don't know what I'm going to do. I…I don't know what's right or wrong."

He loosened his arms and she did too, both stepping back. He couldn't see clearly, tears streaking his face, eyes squinting. His shoulders slumped so suddenly Don thought he might fall but he climbed on the tabletop, sitting with feet on the bench, elbows on knees, head down, staring at the gravel between him and the river.

Susan stepped up on the bench and sat touching his left side, her arm around his shoulders. Don book-ended on Jeff's right and the three of them sat there like silent mourners in a pew.

"Let us help you," she said finally, pulling his shoulder toward her. "We both love you. Help us understand what you're thinking."

He straightened his back and noticed the river. "Everyone wants to saw the top off my skull and see what's in there." He rubbed his eyes with shaking hands, blinked rapidly, hands smearing tear traces on his cheeks. His body trembled as he scooted backwards on the table, away from them, crossing his legs to sit yoga-style, arms crossed on his chest.

"I don't know what I think. Can't you understand that? My thoughts are like marbles that I'm trying to organize on a table with one short leg. Everything's rolling around and I can't get anywhere."

"You're trying to make sense of Isiah's murder," Don said, "but...."

Jeff cut him off. "I'm trying to make sense of Isiah's *life,"* he snapped. "His life!"

"I understand," Don said softly. "But his murder drastically changed *your* life. It's changed all of our lives. And it's ripped out a chunk of your soul. Ours too."

"His life can't be wasted," anguish twisting Jeff's face into a stranger's. "It's cosmically wrong. How can any kind of god let those pieces of shit murder Isiah?"

"We don't know what purpose God may have," Don said. "We never can know."

"Well, screw that," Jeff said, waving a dismissive hand. "Don't patronize me. I don't think there is a god or a *purpose.* If there's a purpose from this, someone else is going to have to provide it."

"Who do you mean? *You*?" Susan asked, sliding back on the table next to him, gently rubbing his shoulders and back of his neck.

"What if Isiah's killers all died?" Jeff said, his voice low and flat. "Wouldn't that discourage shit bags like them from murdering more civil rights workers?"

"Died? What do you mean 'died'?" Susan said. "You mean if someone killed them?"

"Whatever. Killed by God. Struck by lightning. Killed by unknown person or persons, run over by a truck or shot down in a junkyard like Isiah was. Regardless of how, if they died *because* they killed Isiah, wouldn't that make other redneck bastard crackers afraid to slaughter people?"

He was talking so fast he stopped to catch his breath. "What if Isiah's murderers were assassinated? And what if the assassin was never identified or caught? And what if those southern savages who think they have the right to murder people like Isiah, became afraid to do it? Wouldn't that save innocent lives? And give meaning to Isiah's death? Isn't that justice? We can't bring Isiah back, but maybe someone can prevent future murders. Maybe Isiah's death can still accomplish something. Maybe his martyrdom can help win the fight."

"Are you thinking of doing something like that?" Susan said, leaning forward to peer back at him. "Are you?"

"Do you think I could?"

"No. Of course not. No rational person could. It wouldn't work. It's the opposite of everything you are."

"It's actually very rational if you think about it," he said, looking away from her. "Those sonsabitches cold-bloodedly put bullets into a special man, a person whose only goal was ministering to others. The killers deserve death for that crime…which everyone, including the corrupt morons on the jury, knows damned well they committed," his voice harsh, teeth so tightly clenched they could hardly hear him. "And in exchange, truly innocent lives are saved because potential killers are afraid they'll actually be held accountable; something they don't fear now.

"Nothing in Mississippi's so-called justice system has anything to do with justice. Everything from the police to the courts is totally corrupt. That trial was not only a foregone conclusion, it was deliberately weak so those three killers can never be tried again, thanks to double-jeopardy laws. They could confess today and still be safe. The guys who tortured and killed Emmitt Till, that black teenager accused of whistling at a white woman in Money, Mississippi, about seven years ago, told Look magazine how they did it. And they got paid for it.

"If somebody fixes that problem and then lynchings and murders decrease, isn't that rational? Bad guys die, good guys live. Justice over evil. What's the crazy part?"

"It's all crazy," she said softly. "You can't make sense out of nonsense. This isn't you talking. It's not *you*."

A long pause so silent he realized all them were holding their breaths.

"You're serious about this, aren't you?" Susan whispered. "You're actually thinking about killing them?"

"God," Don said, "I wondered…but I didn't…Jesus H. Christ. You can't…."

"*Could* you kill someone?" Susan said, moving closer. "Actually kill them? Could you look them in the eyes and shoot them? Bomb their houses? Could you possibly live with that? With yourself?"

"Maybe," he said. "I don't know."

Don practically shouted. "Are you willing to throw away *your* life as well as Isiah's? What if you accidentally kill innocent members of their family? If you burn down a house you can't know who'll get hurt. You'd spend your life in prison. In Mississippi you'd probably hang." "That's the whole thing," Jeff said, sounding enthusiastic. "It only works if the person doesn't get caught. And besides, we're all condemned; it's just a question of timing." He looked at Don, then back at Susan, waiting for them to see the point.

"You're obsessed right now," she said. "You're not thinking straight. Wanting revenge is natural. We all have some feelings like that; but that'll pass."

"It already hasn't passed, but it's *not* about revenge," he snapped. "It's about justice. I'm not saying I'm going to do something like that, but I admit I've thought about it. Saving other lives makes sense, brings some meaning to this…tragedy. I've thought about lots of things, but I don't know…."

"If Isiah were here he'd grab you and not let go until he convinced you not to do anything like that," Don said. "He'd absolutely not want you to do anything involving killing people."

"One of the first things I ever heard Isiah say was something like 'I'm pretty sure I'd respond violently to an attack on me or my family or some other human being.' He said non-violently pursuing civil rights doesn't mean you have to offer yourself as a human sacrifice to some 'hate-filled, bigoted son-of-a-bitch.' That language surprised me so much I've never forgotten it. It was the same night I saw Susan anywhere other than at the Daily office," turning to her, taking her hand in his.

"Even if you could actually kill someone," Susan said, "is taking a life ever morally justified? That's contrary to everything Isiah believed."

"Don't be so sure of that. He and I discussed war and how it's considered morally right to defend your country by killing the enemy. We train people to kill whoever's our enemy at the time. Everyone approves. We honor soldiers as patriots. And we should. Churches sanction wartime killing. They provide chaplains to bless soldiers and what they're doing. Is it hypocritical to be against murder but also admire people who kill in war? War justifies killing. War *requires* killing. Isn't this war? Truman dropped atom bombs on Japanese civilians to shorten the war and save the lives of American and Japanese alike. That was preventive killing on a massive scale. How is this different? Aren't we in a war for basic human rights in our own country? Our own citizens are oppressing other citizens."

Don jabbed a finger in Jeff's face. "An individual overturning a court decision—no matter how awful the verdict—and taking the law into his own hands? You're describing vigilantism."

"Israelis are still hunting Nazis from World War II," Jeff said. "They captured Eichmann last year and are planning to hang him. How is this different? How can you talk about over-turning a court verdict?" waving a hand dismissively, his voice mocking. "Shit. That wasn't a real trial. That wasn't justice," he said, his voice staccato with anger. "It was a corrupt play. Everyone played roles. It was a goddamn fucking fraud from start to finish and you both know it. Everyone knows it but no one does a goddamn thing about it. It's a heinous sin against humanity. We're all to blame, from the president and congress to us. It's a national hypocrisy and someone's gotta fix it.

"If I had been there when they were killing Isiah, and if I'd saved his life by killing them instead, that would have been a good thing, right? I'm wondering if getting rid of them wouldn't be a good thing for the same reason, saving some other victim's life. It's too late for Isiah." He stopped, out of words, his energy drained.

"I can't believe you're saying these things," Susan said. "You don't know what would happen. What would your family think? You could lose everything, your life, your family and friends...me. It's a life sentence even if you're not caught…or killed. You'd live with it every day. It would corrode your soul. You'd never escape it."

"I can never escape what's *already* happened," Jeff said. "But maybe my life'd be worth something if I could make Isiah's death count for something. Now, he's dead, they're alive and who knows how many other people will be murdered by these sonsabitches and people like them?

"We have two cultures in this country so fundamentally opposite that they can't co-exist. How can you reconcile two views, one of which is I'm willing to tolerate and respect and live with you, but you believe you must kill me because I'm a different color, a sub-human? There is no middle ground there; no way to compromise. There's no way to live and let live. While I'm respecting you, you believe it's ok to kill me."

"Is what you're thinking about actually justice?" Don asked.

"In Mississippi there is *no* justice," Jeff said, staring at Don.

"Then what's accomplished? Isn't it just plain revenge?"

"Deterrence."

"But they would be dead."

"Being dead makes it one-hundred-percent certain they won't murder anyone else. But we know there are other killers out there. What's going to stop them? Nothing's ever stopped them; not for two-hundred years. The system keeps rewarding them, makes them into heroes," Jeff said, sliding off the tabletop looking over their heads, then watching as they stood on the other side. "But maybe they can be deterred."

He began putting trash and the uneaten food in the cardboard box and, when the table was clean, he looked at them for a moment.

"I once heard Isiah ask himself a question: 'Exactly how much evil has to happen before we act to stop it? Exactly when is it immoral to turn the other cheek?'

"You guys know the answer?"

CHAPTER SIXTY-TWO

Jeff ground the Plymouth into first gear, following Don from the parking lot. It was raining gently, the low clouds finally delivering on their promises. Susan shivered and tugged her sweater closed, unsure whether it was the cooling air or her inner fears. Neither spoke for several miles, staring straight ahead, dusk flowing into darkness, Bobby Darin delivering *Mack the Knife* through the radio.

"Please promise me we'll talk about this some more," Susan said softly. "I need some hope."

"Hope about what?" he said, not looking at her. "That I'll come to my senses, change my mind, not go to Mississippi? Or that I'm still worth being hopeful about?"

She stared out the side window, seeing her own reflection with the landscape whizzing by in another dimension.

"Back there," he said, "you were worried about my safety in Mississippi and about what I might do there. Which worry is the biggest one?"

"I can't rank my worries," she said, clipping off the words. "Mississippi is a dangerous place and I'm scared to death. And I'm stunned that…that you're thinking about hurting, maybe killing those men. This isn't the real you. Not the *you* I know. I love *you*.

"I told you guys I don't know what I'm thinking," he said, "let alone what I'm going to do. My mind's like the messy glove compartment in front of you, disorganized and overflowing."

Wiper blades swishing the windshield made the only sounds.

Then Jeff was whispering. "I was on the pier the evening after they found Isiah's body," causing her to turn to look at him. "I thought about slipping under the waves and just letting myself go." He focused rigidly over the steering wheel, sensing her breathing stop for an instant.

"Do you still feel like that?"

"No. I still feel like shit, but I want to do something rather than give up."

"So you're going to Mississippi possibly to kill those men."

"I don't know. Maybe. I honestly don't know. Do you think I'm a bad person?"

"If you do what you've been thinking about I might not know you at all."

"You do know me. But things have changed. I'm changing. I know lots of things I had no idea about before. Now I understand how things really are."

"I guess," she said, "that leaves me trying to see what *I* can understand and what it all means," she said, her voice flat, distant.

"I'm not saying it's logical or…and I'm not…. I don't know what I might do, but you can't deny that drastic action might save others from being murdered. You remember that night we first met and Isiah said: 'We don't know what we're capable of until our moment confronts us.'

"I think this is *my* moment."

CHAPTER SIXTY-THREE

That night he is in his grandfather's tiny boat tied to the end of an ancient, weather-battered wood dock. Lightning flashes inside swirling black clouds as vicious winds slam the little rowboat against the pilings. Waves of wind-driven rain cascade over him again and again. He sees Grandpa Martindale on shore, feet planted wide apart, frantically waving his arms over his head, mouth moving but no sound penetrating the storm. Fishing rods, lunch boxes, a thermos, the cement block anchor and the old wooden oars remain on the dock. The small boat yanks violently at its bow and stern lines and suddenly both ropes snap, sounding like gunshots. The lake, already massively white-capped, becomes a river, pulling the weathered little green boat spinning into the current toward what sounds, over the wind and overhead thunder, like a waterfall.

CHAPTER SIXTY-FOUR

Lake Michigan's blue-green surface was smooth, only small waves of polished mercury moving rhythmically, intersecting the pier at an angle, white puffy clouds dabbed on the bluebird sky by an artist's brush; the air a potpourri of fish smells, humidity and seagull droppings.

Don and Jeff sat beside each other on the pier's concrete incline, their feet on the flat surface that ended where the lake began; both resting forearms on thighs. Several fishermen were spaced along the pier casting far out into the lake, no one close to the pair of hunched over friends. The great lake was calm. Don was not. Jeff watched him pull his cigarette pack from a shirt pocket, extract one, then put it back.

"Ok, I know you're off to Mississippi day after tomorrow no matter what I say," Don said, turning to Jeff's profile, his tone intense, face more sad than angry. Jeff looked at him and Don locked their eyes, as if daring Jeff to look away. "But I want to know your plans," Don continued. "Your real plans. You need to level with me. And maybe with yourself. What are you going to do there?"

Jeff turned his eyes back to the lake. "I told you before," he said. "I don't know. I'm not sure...."

"Cut the shit." Don said, getting up and stepping into Jeff's line of sight, "You've been dancing around that question for two weeks. What are you thinking right this minute? Are you planning to kill those guys?

That's a simple, yes-no question. We've been best friends forever. You owe me the short answer."

"There is no short answer, goddammit," Jeff said, looking at the concrete between his shoes. "I'm not *planning* anything," seeing rough patterns in the concrete surface, a decomposing minnow inches from his left foot, tiny fish scales glinting in the sunlight like spilled sequins. "I'm going to Mississippi, to that goddamn town, and I'll see what I see. That's all I know for sure."

"Is killing them in your mind? Is that a possibility?" Don asked, sitting down again, studying his own piece of the pier, the two of them bent over, looking like old men.

"I can *imagine* it," Jeff finally said. "I can't help thinking about it. Part of me wants to hang the sonsabitches. Or shoot them. Sometimes I think I can. Sometimes I dream so vividly that I'm shooting them that when I wake up it feels like I've actually done it. I wake up sweating and panicked."

"Jesus H. Christ," Don said, sitting bolt upright. "Are Isiah's murderers taking my best friend?"

"Maybe," still studying the concrete

"Remember all the great times we've had out here," Don said, sweeping his hand over the pier and the lake. We've got to get you back," putting his left hand on Jeff's shoulder, squeezing it twice.

"I can't go back," Jeff said. "There is no back. *That* Jeff is gone. Changed. Grownup. Finally. I'm trying to figure out who I am now. I don't know for sure, but I'm working on it. Shit, man, I was the most innocent, most naïve bastard in the Western Hemisphere. Isiah changed me just by being around him, talking with him, watching him work, understanding how things really are. Imagining those crackers murdering him has ripped open the rest of my mind. My life before is gone. I can't ever be the same. I don't want to be the same," finally looking at Don, his eyes moist in his distraught face, beseeching Don for understanding.

Don walked a few feet up the pier, facing the water but not seeing it. Jeff looked down again, resuming his visual autopsy of the dead minnow. Don folded his arms over his chest, walked a few more steps, thrusting his hands in the back pockets of his jeans, finally turning back to Jeff.

"You look terrible," Don said. "And you're depressed," walking back and sitting beside Jeff. "And no wonder. You need to see someone; talk to a professional. Try to get your head straight."

"Go to hell," Jeff said, straightening his back but not looking at Don, focusing on the horizon. "My head's finally straight for the first time in my life. I don't need a sugar pill and I don't need any more advice."

"I'm just trying to help," Don said. "Let me in. That's a big shit pile you've got on your plate."

"Am I depressed because I can see that pile of shit? Because I see how wrong everything is? Do you know that when Isiah was missing the sheriff's department there started dragging the river. They found six bodies. Six! All of them wired or roped to something heavy. All black. Six human beings murdered and discarded in the river.

"Am I wrong? Or crazy? Or am I finally clear-eyed and realistic?

"Did I tell you what Isiah prayed when he visited our house? He gave thanks for the meal and friendship, blah, blah, blah. And he asked God for help in knowing his will and in making our lives count for good through positive deeds and not for evil through action or inaction. He prayed for that. For positive deeds to defeat evil."

"You can't walk around outraged every minute of every day," Don said. "You need some faith that…" Don said.

Jeff cut him off. "My cup of faith hath runneth out," he snapped. "Completely dumped on the ground."

Don looked stunned at Jeff's outburst.

"Isiah showed me the possibilities of what one person can do. What we can be when we fiercely desire something and work for it. I wish I had your faith, I told him once. I wish I had it now. But I don't. And by the way," Jeff added, "I don't need cheering up. I need to *do* something. That's why it's called *spending* your life."

They headed back along the pier toward shore, not looking at each other, walking in silence a few feet apart.

CHAPTER SIXTY-FIVE

That night it seemed like dreaming, but he was conscious, prostrate on his bed, eyes closed, visioning fragments from the past, each snippet as sharp-edged as a cut diamond.

"So much blood has been poured on the ground." Isiah answering Susan a lifetime ago at a long-past party. "If you're asking if I believe in violence as a means to an end, no, I don't. I didn't say some violence might not work, but it's wrong, it's divisive and destructive and morally wrong at its core... Peacefully seeking a worthwhile goal through peaceful means doesn't mean one has to offer himself as a human sacrifice to some hate-filled, bigoted son-of-a-bitch."...It's already a killing war, but one side has done all the killing. For over two hundred years...lynchings, shootings, beatings and bombings of blacks...At some point victims...will shoot or bomb back."

"A white man can kill a Negro with no fear of being convicted or punished."

"I understand turn-the-other-cheek"...but I know in my bones Jeremy was wrong."

"Should we have to wait still more years, hoping for hearts to change so we can vote without harassment, beatings, losing our jobs...even death?"

Susan: "Isn't that exactly the opposite of Isiah's beliefs?"

"Look what it got him."

"We don't know what we're capable of until our moment confronts us," Isiah's voice fading from the edge of the vanishing vision.

"It's time to find out what I'm capable of," Jeff's eyes wide open now.

CHAPTER SIXTY-SIX

His mother's stare pushed Jeff deeper into the sofa. She sat in the matching chair by the fireplace, her spine straight.

"Why choose the very town that murdered Isiah?" her eyes boring into his. "You could have gone somewhere else in the South. You're leaving tomorrow and I still don't understand why. And I'm absolutely terrified," her face anguished, eyes shining with tears.

The deafening ticking of the mantel clock filled the silence. He focused his eyes and ears on the clock just above her, "Regulator" in bold gold letters, the swinging pendulum sounding louder and louder, apprehension hammering inside his head.

"I've already explained it, Mom," he said, his voice low, tinged with frustration. "Sorry, I didn't mean it that way, but I've already told you. And Dad. And Susan. And Don. I want to see what it's like there. I'll…" his voice trailing off, eyes returning to the clock as if hours had passed since he last checked.

She crossed the living room on bare feet, throwing herself next to him, pulling his head to her shoulder, momentarily cradling him awkwardly in both arms.

"It's ok," she said. "I'm just so worried about you. It's ok. It's going to be ok," as if he were a child again and she was comforting him over a skinned knee.

"No! It's not ok," he said, more frustration in his voice. "And it's not going to be ok. The whole world is screwed up; Isiah should not be dead. Americans shouldn't be dying just because they want to vote or eat in a public restaurant. We can't make it ok just by talking about it."

She was quiet for nearly a minute. "I guess I understand that," she said, getting up. "But I don't want my son dying for this," she murmured as she left the room, smearing teary cheeks with her fists.

CHAPTER SIXTY-SEVEN

The next morning, he awoke before 6, the aroma of frying bacon already in the air and Susan's voice from last night still in his brain. "I'm trying to understand what it all means to you. And to us. Where're you're headed. Where are we headed? You're obsessed and you're frightening me."

When she said it she'd thrown him into icy water.

What did she mean? Where are we headed? Am I choosing between Susan and justice? For some convoluted idea of deterrence? Can I risk that much?

He threw on jeans and t-shirt, needing only to toss in his toothbrush and close both suitcases. Susan was already on a kitchen stool, elbows on the counter watching his mother mixing enough pancake batter for a hungry Army platoon.

During breakfast, conversation was largely limited to his father twice reconfirming the travel route he already had asked about three times before, and his mother reminding him to write regularly and call at least once a week. "Collect," she said again. "I'm going to worry every minute that you're in that place. Every single minute."

Susan said little. Jeff caught her staring at him every time he glanced her way. They had driven back from the park the night before in silence, each smothering in conflicting and depressing thoughts, trying to re-cross bridges already damaged, if not burned.

"More coffee?" his mother said standing at his side with the glass pot.

"No thanks, I'm wired," he said, seizing the opportunity to stand, ready to leave, but seeing Susan staring at him again. "I gotta get on the road if I'm going to get even half-way there by tonight."

Susan and his father pushed chairs back and stood up. Susan went to the sink, put her hands on the counter, leaning toward the window, staring at the backyard. Jeff watched her back for several seconds.

What the hell am I doing? Maybe I am nuts.

His dad followed him to the bedroom on the pretext of carrying one of the suitcases. "Please, son, be very careful down there. And call at least twice a week; let us know what's happening."

"I will, Dad. This isn't that big a deal. It sounds scarier than it really is. I'll be careful," he said, aware that everything had already been said and repeated, snapping the last latch and they each lifted a suitcase.

His mother intercepted him in the kitchen and motioned him into the living room. She sat on the sofa and he joined her. She took his hand.

"I'm going to try not to worry but I will anyway. Stay in touch, call every day if you want. It'll help me sleep. I desperately hope you won't go. If you change your mind while driving there just turn around and come home," she said. "I'll make spaghetti," smiling slightly.

"I'll call, Mom, I promise. And I'll be just as careful as I would if you were there with me," getting up and pulling her with him. She grabbed him in a fierce hug and he hugged her back for a long time, not wanting to let go until she did.

They walked into the kitchen. Susan stood by the refrigerator, seeming smaller than she really was. "I'll walk with you to the car," she said, going through the door without waiting for a response.

Jeff hugged his mom again. She was crying again when he finally stepped back. "We love you," she muttered and left the room.

Jeff and his dad embraced for a long minute. "Be safe," his dad said. Jeff picked up the suitcases, went to the garage door and stopped, looking back. "I'll be fine and I'll call. I promise."

Susan was leaning against the Plymouth's driver-side front fender, arms crossed over her chest. He went quickly to her, dropped the suitcases and they hugged for a long time without speaking. Then he felt her shaking and loosened his arms, leaning back, realizing she was crying uncontrollably.

"I'll be fine," he said. "This is something I need to do. We'll have lots to talk about when I get back."

"Who will you be then?" she asked, her throaty voice low as she turned her wet, red face to him. He barely recognized her. His own eyes spilled over and he pulled her to him. Finally they stepped back and stood face to face by the car, holding each other's hands, glistening eyes searching. He realized he was gripping her hands too tightly and loosened his fingers, hands dripping wet.

"Are we ok?" his voice barely audible.

She said nothing for several eternal seconds.

"I don't know," she said softly. "I wish I knew. I wish I knew who we are."

They clung to each other again before he released her and put the battered brown suitcases in the trunk and slammed the lid. He opened the door, pausing before getting in, leaving the door open. She stepped forward, pushing the door closed but not hard enough to latch it. She pulled the handle, re-opening the door a bit and closed it firmly.

His eyes never left hers as he cranked the window open. She put her hands on the sill and leaned forward. They kissed with only their lips touching and she stepped back, Jeff still staring at her. "I love you," he whispered, fishing keys from his pocket, starting the car. She nodded and stepped back.

He backed slowly down the driveway, pausing a few seconds before continuing into the street, moving achingly slowly until he could no longer see her in the rear-view mirror, standing in the driveway like a sculpture.

CHAPTER SIXTY-EIGHT

Suddenly the town crashed through the windshield into his brain like a movie projected directly onto his eyes. Jeff's lips locked in a tight, horizontal line. Momentarily braking as if to avoid a collision, his arms braced straight and taut, jamming his back into the seat, keeping his death grip on the wheel. He aimed the Plymouth across a narrow, barely two-lane bridge, Neil Diamond singing "*What will I do?*" on the radio.

Maybe it was the ever-present, searing memory of the horrors this town had inflicted on him, or perhaps it was the icy, piercing reality that he was finally at the actual scene. And on duty. He didn't resist the crushing darkness trying to again gain control of his mind. He welcomed the retreat into the blackness that had inhabited his head for months. He blew out his cheeks, realizing he'd been holding his breath.

Mid-afternoon light painted lengthening shadows on the worn and uneven road, intensifying the multi-shaded gray shacks lining each side. The tiny houses of unpainted, weathered wood created an antique black-and-white photograph; even the black river, running along the left, reflected only a few flashes of light.

He steered the dark-blue car several more blocks, slowing briefly to study the one-story brown brick building: "Post Office, Fowlerville, Mississippi."

A few more blocks of snapping glances right and left at each intersection and the downtown business section appeared. He crept along, passing office buildings and stores. Three blocks more and a massive stone building of classic Greek design sat astride the street directly ahead of him, seemingly blocking the street. Then he saw that traffic in front of the building was diverted into a one-way, counter-clockwise pattern wrapping around the "Dixon County Courthouse."

That's where the trial was. Where that corrupt jury spit in Isiah's face.

Slowly cruising the square, he saw large windows with gold letters, *Fowlerville Herald,* across from a side entrance to the courthouse.

He turned right, driving several blocks from the square. Everyone he saw was black. Two men in gray shirts and overalls trudged the dirt street; no sidewalks. Neither looked up as he passed.

Several blocks later, three white children played tag in the fading sunshine and he spotted a "ROOM for RENT" sign leaning against a window in a small, one-story house virtually indistinguishable from its neighbors, all fronted by narrow porches. He pulled off the street and stopped, staring at the house a moment. Vines and bushes nearly hid a waist-high, wood fence embracing the one-story home.

He stepped out, arching his back, arms stretching skyward before jamming his hands in the back pockets of his jeans, rotating his head from side to side, trying to shake off two long days behind the wheel. From the car to the gate the powdery dirt was free of vegetation, no grass, no bushes, not even weeds. Pushing open a latchless gate, he wondered if there were people in any of the houses; no movement anywhere. The house had once been light blue with white trim, the blue faded into gray-blue, the trim more gray than white. Two wood steps took him to the porch running the width of the house, sheltered by an overhanging roof. Twin terracotta pots overflowed with red and white geraniums flanking the doorway obscured by a wood screen door. The porch floor looked freshly scrubbed.

He rapped softly on the screen door, hearing his own breathing, imagining that anyone within a hundred feet could hear the air pumping in and out of his lungs as if he had been running. He knocked again, a bit louder and glanced back at the dirt street. The dusty red soil looked like a carpet from the street to the fence; still no visible people. The fence, bushes and vines had married into a single entity, each dependent on the other.

The vegetation was carefully trimmed on the side facing the house and was so thick it wasn't clear if was holding up the fence, or vice versa.

"Can Ah hep y'all?" asked a quiet voice directly at Jeff's side, startling him. Then he saw the small human form behind the screen, less than a foot away. The form might have been there since he came onto the porch for all the noise it made arriving. The voice was so soft he wouldn't have heard it had there been any other sounds in the neighborhood.

"Yes, I'm looking for a room to rent."

"Ah thought so," the voice said as the screen door squeaked slowly open.

The voice came from the smallest adult human he had ever seen, not a dwarf but a scale-model of a woman somewhere between 80 and 180 years old. Her extremely white and deeply wrinkled face seemed carved from an albino walnut. Despite the warm spring evening a white knit scarf over her shoulders partly covered a dark blue dress splashed with small white dots.

"Y'all come in please."

"Thank you," he said stepping in as carefully as he could, feeling 12 feet tall. "I'm Jeff Martindale," he said, unsure whether to extend his hand; she didn't and he didn't.

"Ah'm Mrs. Emma Harris," she said. "Ah'll show you the room," she said, gliding silently down a dark hallway. On the left the living room looked like a museum display. Everything was old and over-stuffed including an old man in a white, sleeveless undershirt and suspendered dark trousers slumped in a chair staring at a television flickering across the room. The man didn't move or look up as the tiny woman and the intruder passed along the dark hall.

Dead and stuffed?

She fumbled with the left wall, and a door opened. A gentle smell greeted him, a potpourri of dust, old paint, old carpets and darkness.

Mrs. Harris pushed a round button on the wall bringing to life a naked bulb hanging from the ceiling by two twisted-together wires.

Jeff stepped inside, inventorying a partly open closet door on the right, a bed with black wood foot and head boards, two chairs, one straight-backed, the other wearing upholstery from his grandparents' era, a table and dresser, a brass reading lamp and a small table by the window. A worn brown rug covered most of the wood floor; ancient, flowered wallpaper. A tall, narrow window glowed in the wall opposite the door, a mottled, dark-tan shade pulled to the sill, hiding whatever was on the other side of the glass. A hotplate rested on a scuffed dark-brown wood cabinet under the window.

"Bathroom's in there," she said softly, tiny arm waving to a door next to the closet. "We're asking eight dollars a week or thirty dollars a month," she said looking at him apologetically.

"I'll take it," moving in another step. "I'll be here at least through the summer, probably about three months."

"In advance," the woman added softly, as if embarrassed at the talk of money.

"The whole three months?" Jeff asked quickly, surprised.

"Oh no, just the first month," she said hastily, voice even softer.

"Fine," Jeff said, retrieving his wallet and handing the miniature woman a twenty and a ten.

She said, "I'll get you a receipt," she said, scurrying to the door.

He didn't move, absorbing the flowered bedspread, the dark wood of the sparse furniture.

At least it's clean. Except for the dust. Must have been closed up awhile.

"Ah'll dust the place while y'all are at work," the woman said from the doorway, having magically materialized for the second time. Then, as if to dispel the idea that she had been reading his mind, "Y'all be starting work tomorrow or Monday?"

"Uh, Monday," Jeff said. "I'm working at the Herald this summer. But don't worry about the dust, Mrs. Harris. I'll take care of all the cleaning. It'll give me something to do."

She nodded slowly, as if puzzled, then smiled. She gave him a scrap of paper and a key. "This is for the room, the front door is always unlocked." Then she vanished again. He tucked the receipt in the pocket of his plaid, short-sleeved shirt.

He waited a few minutes then returned down the dark hall, out the front door to his car. He unlocked the trunk and extracted his suitcases.

He slammed the trunk lid, and walked to the house, his shoes sending up angry puffs of red dust with every firm, fierce step.

The overstuffed man hadn't moved.

He put the suitcases in the closet and stretched out on the bed, fingers laced behind his head. The ceiling had once been white but now was the yellow-white of old paint.

For a long time he remained on his back, hands clenched tightly behind his head on the old bed that slanted slightly in from both sides, his jaw and neck muscles flexing as he visualized photos of the three men he had traveled to Mississippi to see. And possibly kill.

CHAPTER SIXTY-NINE

About a half-hour later, a leg muscle twitched him awake. He combed his hair in the dingy mirror, locked the door behind him, and walked quietly down the dark hall. The television still flickered in the living room but no one was visible.

That old guy must not have been dead.

He drove a half-block to an intersection. Free of the towering trees lining the street, he saw the courthouse cupola, which helped him find the most direct route to the Square, only five blocks away, where he circled again, taking in the stores, offices, a café and the Fowlerville Herald office. He made a second lap around the courthouse and found an open parking spot in front of the Herald.

Not even a parking meter.

He parked the Plymouth, opened the door to the familiar screechy metallic complaint from its hinges, and stepped out, scouting the street in both directions. He looked older than his 21 years, khaki pants topped by a blue short-sleeved shirt. Only a few people were visible, three or four walking nearly a block to the left; a clot of two standing and three seated, denim overall-clad men topped with gimme caps several doors to the right, looking like uniformed members of a club.

He took several deep breaths, as if rehearsing lines before stepping onstage, then walked purposefully to the Herald's front door.

The interior's huge open space was daunting, the entire first floor a single room. A chest-high counter 10 feet from the door ran the width of the room, like a dike restraining flood waters. At each end of the counter an opening led to an informal path created by the ends of desks running in rows the length of the gymnasium-sized room. Except for two glass-fronted offices along the left, the huge room was unwalled and housed thirty or forty assorted desks, some metal, others battered wood of various shades. Overhead signs dangled from ceiling wires over the front counter.

CLASSIFIED ADVERTISING
DISPLAY ADVERTISING
CIRCULATION

Two middle-aged women held phones to their ears at desks under the advertising signs and a younger woman leaned on the counter under "CIRCULATION" talking to a bearded man in jeans, work boots and blue t-shirt.

Halfway to the back of the room more hanging signs signaled:

NEWS
SPORTS

Moving left and around the end of the counter, his eyes methodically scanned the room the way he had been taught to hunt deer, taking in everything he could see, registering the scene, cataloging the parts. Stopping at the only occupied desk in the NEWS cluster, he spoke to the red-haired young man who had watched him approach from the corner of his vision.

"Excuse me, is Mr. Kennedy in?"

"Sure, that's his office over there. The one on the left."

"Thanks."

Walking to the office, he felt curious eyes following him. He saw "Managing Editor" stenciled on the window, stopped at the open doorway and waited to be noticed by the stocky man with close-cropped black hair behind a desk making quick pencil marks on typed sheets of paper. Finally he knocked gently on the doorframe.

The man looked up and smiled broadly.

"Are you by chance Jeff Martindale?"

"Yessir."

"Come on in," his arm beckoning, then outstretched as he stood up, his grasp firm and enthusiastic, gesturing to the chair at the end of the desk. "When did you get in?"

"Thanks. A couple of hours ago."

"Great. We're looking forward to you being with us this summer."

"Me, too. I really appreciate the opportunity."

"Hey, we'll have plenty of fun. And plenty of work. I guess you can call that an opportunity. You got a place to stay?"

"Yeah, over on Fifth Street, uh, pretty much north of the courthouse. It's in a home, seems clean and quiet. I don't need much."

"Quick work," Kennedy said. "You'll be ready to start work first thing Monday morning?"

"Yessir, Mr. Kennedy, I…"

"Hey, none of that 'yessir, nosir stuff. I'm Bobby Ray to everyone here and pretty much to everyone in town."

His voice dropped a bit. Jeff noted the wrinkled, short-sleeved white shirt; tie loose at the neck, perspiration stains in the armpits, several unmatched pens jutting from the pocket, leather suspenders. His florid face tilted forward, turtle-like, sitting neckless on his shoulders.

"I kinda avoid the 'Kennedy' part anyway. If my folks had known that the Attorney General of these United States would have almost the same name someday they'd have called me "Billy Joe' or "Claude' or some other damn thing. It's not much fun bein' "Bobby Ray Kennedy these days, I'll tell ya. Not around here." He laughed heartily, watching Jeff's face.

"I can imagine," Jeff smiled briefly, then quickly serious again. "What time is 'first thing" Monday morning'?"

"First thing is 6 a.m. Being an afternoon paper our final deadline is noon-fifteen. We'll have some things for you to do when you get here Monday. Plan on jogging across the street to the courthouse by 6:35 a.m."

Kennedy stood up, gestured toward the door. "Let's get you introduced to the only member of the news staff still here this late on a Friday and I'll give you a short tour of the building."

"Yessir, sounds…"

Bobby Ray's arm shot up, palm facing Jeff.

"I mean, you bet," Jeff grinned. "Sure."

Bobby Ray was already through the door headed for the redhead's desk, where he put his hand on the young man's shoulder.

"This here's Jeff Martindale, the intern from up north I told y'all was coming for the summer. Jimmy Waller here's been writing for the Herald since he was in ninth grade starting with little stories about junior high football and basketball games. He's gotten a lot better since then, particularly his spellin," patting Jimmy's shoulder.

"Please introduce Jeff to the staff Monday morning when he arrives. Be sure he meets everyone, and doesn't get lost. And take him to the courthouse for early mornin cop rounds."

"You bet, Bobby Ray. Glad to help. You have any questions, you let me know. I'll get you started Monday. See you then, pointing his right hand at him as if it were a pistol. "I gotta run," he said, turning to Bobby Ray. "I'm taking Linda to Catfish Castle and '*Judgment at Nuremburg.'* That's gotta be a bad movie for a date," he said, grinning.

"Thanks. Have a good time. See ya Monday."

"Let's go out back and I'll show ya where to park," Bobby Ray said.

He led Jeff to the back of the room, through double, swinging doors like the entrance to a restaurant kitchen, and down a hallway lined on both sides with doors garnished with JANITOR, MAINTENANCE, CONFERENCE, MEN, WOMEN, Bobby Ray pointing at "MEN."

"You'll need to be able to find that one." Another big smile.

They went through another set of large doors to a bedraggled asphalt parking lot that appeared to be a weed farm.

"Park near the alley so you can get in and out easily. You'll be coming and going several times a day."

"Ok, Mr...Bobby Ray. I'm really looking forward to getting to work."

Bobby Ray's face flushed with laughter. "'Mr. Bobby Ray.' Now that's a new one. You can practice over the weekend."

As they re-entered the news area Bobby Ray strode to the front door. At the counter he took a business card and one of three pens from his shirt pocket and wrote on the card. He pulled several copies of the Fowlerville

Herald from shelves under the counter. He handed the papers and card to Jeff.

"My home number's on the back. Call if you have any questions or need anything before Monday mornin. The papers will give you an idea of recent news and what on-going stories we're dealing with. There may be a pop quiz Monday afternoon after deadline."

He moved to the front door and held it open for Jeff.

"Ok, Bobby Ray. Thanks. I'm really looking forward to working here."

They shook hands. Jeff pulled keys from his khakis and went to the car. Bobby Ray turned to the door, then pivoted back to watch Jeff drive away in the dusty car, noticing the license plate was so covered with dried mud he couldn't tell what color it was.

CHAPTER SEVENTY

Saturday morning Jeff sat up in the creaky bed in the small room. After washing his face and brushing his teeth, he put on jeans and a short-sleeved shirt, snapped off the light and walked quietly down the dim interior hallway seeing no signs of anyone. He drove slowly around the retail and business district surrounding Courthouse Square, trying to memorize the neighborhood, the trees and flowers and houses.

He parked near the intersection where houses ended and commercial buildings began, then ambled slowly along the sidewalk, peering in windows, stopping frequently, pretending to examine displays.

Ron's Grocery. Lantern Bar. Satellite Bar. Salvation Army Thrift Shop. Bea's Café. Ben Franklin. Piggly Wiggly.

At Family Drug Store on the corner he went in, walking past birthday cards and cosmetics to a long lunch counter flanking the left side; a dozen empty, round, padded pedestals. He sat on the stool closest to the large windows with a view of the street to the left.

A bony blonde with a wrinkled and leathery face only years of cigarettes and sun could have created, brought water with two listlessly floating ice cubes.

"Yessuh?"

"Coffee, please."

He pretended to study the menu as she retreated into the kitchen. From his perch most of the store repeated itself in mirrors in front of him.

His eyes flicked to the menu but held longer on the view of the store, a few customers roaming aisles hunting aspirin, hairspray, vitamins.

Bony Blonde returned with coffee, pad and pencil. "What would y'all like?"

"Grilled cheese, please, and a chocolate malt," barely looking at her, rehearsed lines but sounding hesitant; a harsh voice following the syrupy southern smoothness of her words.

No sense trying to pass as a native.

"Early lunch, Hon?" she said, looking at him, sliding the pad into her white apron.

'Uh, yeah," as if he didn't know the answer to the unexpected question.

Nothing happening on the sidewalk. He swiveled from the stool and went to the magazine and newspaper rack near the door. He picked up a Dixon County Dispatch, *"Your Weekly Look at All of Dixon County."*

Returning to the stool, he glimpsed a white-jacketed man on the telephone behind the prescription counter.

Roy Ryser! Looks just like his damn photo.

Jeff spread the weekly Dispatch on the counter glancing at it, then up and around the store, then back to the paper. The school board was meeting to set an annual budget; someone shot a hole-in-one at the Dixon County Country Club; all stories the daily Herald had already published.

Boney Blonde brought his sandwich and malt. "Enjoy, Hon."

He ate and read, keeping a mirrored surveillance on the store. A few people came and went, mostly picking up prescriptions from Ryser.

He was nearly finished with the grilled cheese and most of the Dispatch when the white coat appeared in the mirror, coming directly at him. Ryser slouched onto a stool at the far end of the counter before murmuring to Bony Blonde who was already bringing a white mug of coffee. Ryser was smaller than Jeff expected, five-seven or five-eight, maybe 145 pounds; an open-neck blue shirt showing beneath the white jacket. Jeff thought the man was studying him in the mirror.

An elderly woman came in, walking slowly toward the back.

"Hi, Miss Lottie," Ryser said, getting off the stool. "Here for your heart pills?"

"Yes, Roy. They ready?"

"Sure. Wait here and I'll get 'em and meet you at the register."

"Thanks, Roy," she said after paying for the pills, returning a small black change purse to her handbag.

"Bye, Miss Lottie. Y'all take care."

Jeff walked to the cash register as Roy held the door for Miss Lottie. Ryser looked at Jeff for a moment.

"Food ok?" he asked, as Jeff handed him the check and a $5 bill.

"Yes, thanks," Jeff said, reading the nametag on the man's chest. "Roy." The tag didn't include what Jeff knew. Roy Ryser, 37, unmarried pharmacist; member of the Dixon County White Citizens Council. An acquitted murderer.

Jeff's mind was screaming inside his head. He took his change and tried to walk casually to the door, not calling attention to himself. He escaped to the sidewalk and walked up the street, careful to look anywhere but through the pharmacy window.

I was so close to him! I could have touched him. So damn ordinary. Scrawny murdering coward. Mousy. Doesn't look like a killer. But he is!

Coinette Laundry: 10 Cents Dry! Cook's Stationery. Pete's TV Repair. Hill's Department Store: For the Entire Family. Bryant's Hardware-Sporting Goods. Johnny Reb Pawn Shop.

Jeff paused at the pawn shop then returned to the hardware store window inspecting electric drills, a keg of nails, three gleaming brass light fixtures and a pair of football shoes with a football teed-up in one.

He pushed through the glass front door, a bell announcing his arrival. He walked slowly, scanning the store, looking at aisle signs hoping for one where he could pretend to be shopping. Three customers were in the store, one looking at paint samples, one bent over a lawnmower.

Jeff slipped into the "Housewares" aisle, finding himself amid coffee pots and frying pans. A large man went by the end of the aisle in a blur, then reappeared and approached Jeff.

"Can Ah help you find sompin?"

Ed Bryant. He looked even bigger than in the Associated Press photo with the acquittal story in the Detroit Free Press; stocky, a full, round face, brownish buzz cut going gray.

"Can Ah help?" the man repeated, his paunch hanging over suspendered jeans.

"I, uh, was looking for light bulbs. Need a hundred-watter."

"Bulbs? Sure, right down here. Package of two?"

"No, just one, thanks."

"Ok. Anythin else?"

"No. That's it. Thanks."

"Twenty-one cents," Bryant said, turning back down the aisle, heading for the cash register at the front.

Jeff took his change, grabbed the small brown sack Bryant handed him and fled for the second time in five minutes, his car three blocks away. He willed himself not to run, walking slowly, glancing at windows, seeing only his own reflection, looking at his watch but not seeing the time, glancing across the street then at the sky.

A redneck grizzly! Bigger than Isiah. A monster. A bully. I felt his evil just standing near him. Bet he's got an extra-extra-large sheet with eyeholes.

* * *

Back in the car, he drove south on Highway 19 for a few miles until he saw the sign pointing to Dixon County Auto Parts & Junkyard. He turned left and jarringly quickly came to the junkyard's entrance, framed by two huge posts covered in old hubcaps. He drove by slowly, then reversed and went by again. Before returning to the main road, he stopped without pulling over, put his forehead atop the steering wheel, framed by his hands, and sobbed until a pickup came from behind him and honked.

CHAPTER SEVENTY-ONE

Dawn was a pale glow as Jeff drove to the Herald office at 5:40 a.m., hoping for a few minutes in the newsroom before the rest of the staff came in and he'd have to meet them all at once on his first day. Jimmy Waller was already jabbing at his battered black typewriter with the bold gold Underwood label, using two fingers on each hand. The rest of the huge room was uninhabited.

"Hey, Jeff, good mawnin," Jimmy said, glancing up, apparently noting Jeff's blue blazer, white shirt, maroon tie and tan chinos. "First thing you need do is lose that coat and tie. Our Mississippi (pronouncing it 'Mississippih') weather discourages coats and ties unless you just enjoy swimming in humidity. I made coffee in the conference room," pointing his hand pistol. "And that's your desk right across from me," nodding at the chipped black desk top.

"Thanks," Jeff said, putting his bagged sandwich in a desk drawer. "I'll grab some coffee and you can tell me what to do next."

The morning blurred by as soon as Jimmy shoveled Jeff a stack of press releases to rewrite into short news stories. Jimmy introduced staffers as they arrived and Jeff tried to memorize names and faces of the nine reporters, two photographers, a news editor who designed the newspaper's pages and three others introduced as copy editors. They all seemed glad to see him but had no time for conversation.

A few minutes later, Jimmy motioned him back to the lunch-conference room where he outlined the rest of the morning.

"I'll walk you through the courthouse and introduce you to everyone we can find, from clerks to judges, and specially to desk people in the cop shop. We talk to them several times every day. We try to make them into friends but they live in their own world. I'm gathering string for several longer stories and you can help me with that for a couple of days.

"We'll do the same at the city and police building. You'll mostly be on your own after that. We'll be each other's backup while you're here but you'll concentrate on city government stuff—city hall, town cops and school district--and I'll mostly do county government and the sheriff's office. We both need to be alert for feature stories wherever we are. They can be the most fun anyway.

"Oh, and tonight there's a city council meeting so your first day's gonna be a long one. We'll go together and I'll get you introduced. I'll do the main story and you can do the sidebars on assorted agenda things or anything that comes from the audience. By the time they meet again in two weeks you'll be flying solo."

CHAPTER SEVENTY-TWO

After the evening City Council meeting, Jeff and Jimmy headed for the parking lot, the cloudless sky blue-black, the Mississippi air hot and still, smelling faintly of hot asphalt and fried food. City Hall was a red-brick, two-story box of offices with the Police Department occupying most of the first floor. A two-stall fire station was tacked on the right.

"Did we eat supper?" Jimmy said. "Wanna a burger?" pointing down the street where a neon "Darryl's Café" was visible. "Darryl makes some dandy ones if you like 'em greasy, or juicy as he describes 'em. He says the same thing about his fries."

"I just realized I'm starved," Jeff said. "And tired," looking at his watch. "Can it really be almost 10 already?"

"Sure. Time flies when the pay's this good," Jimmy laughed, already striding toward the café, the frying fat aroma approaching industrial strength. Jimmy pushed through the door and headed for the first of six green vinyl booths on the right. A counter with stools ran the length of the left side ending at a large grill backed by coffee pots, tea jugs, napkins, stacks of plates, cups and saucers. A pie case on the counter sheltered a lonely slice with a whipped cream pompadour loitering on the second shelf.

"Yo, Darryl," Jimmy shouted, waving at the short, balding man scraping the flat grill with a spatula. "I've got a new victim for you if you're still open. I think he's brave enough, or suicidal enough, to try one of your juicy burgers."

"Perfect," the man said around a toothpick jutting upward from the side of his mouth. "I'll have to clean this damn grill again, but anything for you, Jimmy. Almost anything," tossing them a brief half smile, the toothpick barely moving.

"There ya go," Jimmy said, pointing his hand pistol at the cook.

The man turned and bellowed: "Agnes, get your skinny butt out here. We got customers."

An obviously weary woman in her late '40s came from the back, starting to shrug into a flowered apron then, her face brightening at spotting Jimmy, dropping the apron on the counter. She wore white nurse shoes, jeans and a pink flowered blouse. Her hands briefly smoothed both sides of her dark-brown, shoulder-length hair, growing younger as she came closer.

"Cousin Jimmy, it's a pleasure to see you even though I was only five minutes from being in my pickup headed home to my beloved."

"Lock the front door and change the sign to closed," Darryl grumped, limping to the booth, wiping his hands on a stained apron.

"How y'all doin," he drawled, holding his hand out to Jeff and simultaneously thumping his left hand on Jimmy's shoulder.

"I'm Jeff Martindale," half rising, shaking hands.

"Y'all just get out of the Council meetin'?" looking at Jimmy.

"Yeah. Jeff's a college guy from up north, here for a few months learning how we experts do things in real life. I'm going to teach him everything I know and someday he'll be as famous as me."

"Yeah, you're the most famous cousin I got," Agnes deadpanned, "except for the one in that Arkansas prison for the criminally insane," turning the key in the front door lock and flipping the sign. "Good luck to you, Jeff, hanging out with this semi-literate retard who claims he's a writer."

"Reporter, reporter. I keep telling ya," Jimmy said, flashing his ever-ready smile. "If you're finished whupping up on me, we need some grub. Any chance you got some burgers left or are ya sold out?"

"Two burger baskets?" Darryl asked, already turning back to the grill,

Agnes close behind. Jimmy glanced at Jeff, who nodded. "Two of your specialties and two RCees," Jimmy said. He leaned both elbows on the table, looking at Jeff. "How was your first day?"

"Only been a day? Feels like a week. I hope I can use you as a crutch when I forget something or need a reminder of who does what at City Hall."

"No problem, I'll usually be right across the desk from ya."

Agnes plunked two plastic glasses of RC Cola on the table, tousled Jimmy's hair and retreated.

"You have other cousins in Fowlerville?"

"About half the population," Jimmy said, finger-combing his hair. "My family's been around here since great-grand-daddy Earl Waller packed up his wife and their five kids in Virginia and headed west. This is as far as they got. He opened a laundry and planted the Waller family roots before there was much of anything in Fowlerville."

"What's the town like now?" Jeff said after Agnes brought two red plastic baskets lined with paper, cradling massive burgers nearly covered by mounds of fries. "What's it like to live here? Changed much since you were growing up?"

"It's a bit bigger but still feeds mostly off regional farmers," Jimmy said, covering his fries with a thick layer of ketchup. "There's some light manufacturing, mostly a mobile home factory and a school bus builder west of town. And the Fort. Not so big anymore, but it still employs bunch of locals. And lots of churches. Lordy, lordy, you won't believe how many churches we got. They provide a lot of the social life, along with various lodges and clubs."

"You like it here?" Jeff said, lifting the burger with both hands, creating a sanctuary behind it while wondering if Jimmy was insulted by the question's implication.

Jimmy's eyes flicked up and then back to the burger he was lowering from his mouth, chewing for several seconds before answering.

"Yeah, I do. I love the area. Hell, I love Mississipih," he said. "There are beautiful little towns along the Gulf that smell of salt water and boiling shrimp and gardenias all glomped together. And I love driving through the farmland that makes me wish I had grown up on a farm although I hate farm work, but I love the look of the rich dark dirt and it smells wonderful when it's wet and the flowers are blooming and the willows are dancin in the wind.

"Fowlerville's my home. I know most of the people here and not just relatives," he smiled. "The girl I plan to marry was born here and I doubt Linda would leave. Plus, being a reporter means you meet practically everybody from the mayor to the governor passing through; folks in jail and folks at church picnics," fingers extracting three ketchup-soaked fries from the pile and biting them in half. "And sometimes those are the same folks."

"Yeah, I'm from a small town, too," Jeff said, spanking the ketchup bottle to create a red pool on his plate. "I wonder what similarities there are between Fowlerville in Mississippi and Angel Harbor in Michigan. What differences will I notice?"

'I've never been to Michigan but I'm sure y'all will find a bunch of stuff the same as your town plus a pot-load of differences. Our language must sound like another country. You'll be sorta bi-lingual by the time y'all leave," stretching out his drawl.

"What about the people?" Jeff said.

Jimmy put both hands on the table's edge, looking straight into Jeff's eyes before glancing around the café.

"You might find more differences than you expect," his voice lower. "A lot of southerners have separate and distinct personalities and attitudes that are in conflict with each other. More so than just the normal public and private behavior you may be used to. But you could be here all summer and never see both sides of some of these folks."

"Whata ya mean?"

"I think you know some of what I mean but maybe not as clearly as you will soon enough."

"I'm still in the dark," Jeff said, dabbing two fries into the ketchup pond, looking quizzically at Jimmy.

"Race," Jimmy said, again glancing toward the rear of the restaurant. "Race makes a lot of things different here, even 100 years after the North invaded us, as people in the South say. People in my part of the country are either still fighting the Civil War or believing that they won every which way except militarily."

"What do you believe?"

"I believe that's a question needing a longer answer than we have time for right now," glancing at Darryl scraping the grill. "Let's pay Darryl and head for the barn. Another busy day tomorrow. We can discuss our cultures sometime over Dixie longnecks. Some of it ain't purty."

CHAPTER SEVENTY-THREE

Just hearing Susan's "hello" warmed him and he wanted her to talk to him forever, about anything at all. He wondered if she was as glad to hear from him. He had called her three days earlier on his first evening in Fowlerville, crammed in a phone booth at the Sunoco station.

"I'm here," he had said.

"I'm glad you made it safely," she had said, tonelessly. "Are you ok?"

"Yeah. Tired of driving but I've rented a room and I start work Monday morning."

"Good. Let me know how it goes."

The mutual silence stretched out until he ached.

"I better go. I'll call again in a few days."

"Ok."

"I love you," he said and waited again.

"You, too."

"Bye."

Did I cut her off?

Now, three days later, back in the same booth between the street and the gas pumps, he jumped in quickly when he heard her voice.

"Hi. It's me," he said, hoping for the same enthusiasm he'd always heard when he called her in Ann Arbor to see if she were hungry or needed a study break or just to ask her to share her day. "I covered my first city council meeting last night with another reporter who's showing me the ropes. He seems smart and interesting. We had burgers after the meeting and I got to the room late and had to be at the office writing early this morning…" sounding breathless.

"Are you ok?" she interrupted, "You seem frantic."

The concern in her voice heartened him.

"I'm fine. I needed to hear your voice and I just started babbling and…"

"You're doing it again," her laugh throaty.

That's wonderful.

"You talk," he said. "How's it back in Glen Falls?"

"I miss you. I wish we could talk in person. I wish…"

"This is almost in person," he said. "And I have a pocket half-full of quarters. Talk as long as you want. Please talk."

"Let's not talk right now," she said. "Don't say anything. We've said we want to share our lives. Let's try to share the experiences you're having there. Let me know what happens. Let's try to understand each other."

He searched his brain for a response, not sure what she meant.

"And Jeff?"

"Yes."

"I know you, possibly better than you know yourself these days. I trust you to figure out what's right. I love that guy I know. Let's talk after you've had more time there. Let's talk often. As often as you can."

"Ok. I'll fill bags with quarters. I love you, too."

* * *

Later, back in his room, sitting on a chair, stocking feet braced against the mattress edge, he pondered without resolution:

"I love that guy I know. I trust you to figure out what's right."

Am I still that guy? What's right? How the hell do I figure that out?

* * *

Dear Mom & Dad,

I'm enjoying the job and have met a few people so far.

Weather's great except for the humidity.

I'm working from early morning until late evening most days. Lots of things to cover. I hope you're both fine. I'll call Sunday afternoon.

Love, Jeff

CHAPTER SEVENTY-FOUR

A gentle wind mixed hints of flowery perfume with heavier, earthy smells of unmoving water and lily pads and skunk cabbage as Jeff and Jimmy retrieved fishing rods, an armful of newspapers and a white cooler from the Plymouth's trunk, walking carefully on the damp soil through waist-high cattails and swamp grass to the lake's edge.

They rigged lines with hooks, tiny sinkers and small garden worms, attached floats and cast as far as they could. Jimmy parked his jeans on a half-inch stack of old newspapers spread on the moist ground.

"Cold beer?" Jeff asked.

"If you insist," Jimmy said, adjusting a blue ball cap on his red hair, tugging the brim lower, almost covering his sunglasses. "But only because it's so miserable hot the humidity's raining down my arms."

Jeff pulled long-neck Dixie Beer bottles and a rust-spotted opener from the cooler, opened them and handed one Jimmy, before sitting on the cooler top.

"Not as strenuous as fly casting," Jeff said.

"Nope, more time for thinking," Jimmy said, tipping his bottle back for a long drink, wiping his mouth with the back of his hand.

"I can't believe I've been here five weeks already," Jeff said, flicking a mosquito away from his ear. "I'm just working, eating, mostly off the hot plate in my room, and sleeping. I see my landlord about once a week. Feels like I'm just grinding away."

"Yeah, I get like that sometimes," Jimmy said. "It's been particularly busy so far this summer. Linda, my intended, gets cranky when I work three or four nights in a row."

"The first day on the job," Jeff said, not looking at Jimmy, "you said race hangs over pretty much everything around here. What did you mean?"

Jimmy didn't immediately respond, staring into the distance over the lake. Finally: "In the South the Civil War hasn't really ended here. It's in the water, in our blood. It permeates our culture. We don't even always call it the 'Civil War.' Sometimes it's the 'War Between the States.' Or, my personal favorite, the 'Yankee Invasion.'"

"That was almost a hundred years ago," Jeff said.

"You don't understand the bizarre point of view," Jimmy said. "For example, when the so-called Civil War was just starting, a Virginia militia was using slaves to build an artillery base across from the Union's Fort Monroe. The slaves were forced to work right under the Militia's flag, which said: 'Give me liberty or give me death.' I doubt that any of the Virginians saw any irony whatsoever."

"Are you telling me," Jeff said, "that some Southerners wouldn't see the irony today? Is Bobby Ray one of those?"

"Bobby Ray's caught in the middle. He doesn't talk about his feelings in the newsroom, even with me and we're close, almost father and son, since I started at the Herald 10 years ago. But I know him well enough that I think I understand him. He's a good man, but he can't publicly advocate school desegregation because most of the community is fiercely against it. I think he believes it's gonna happen, it must happen, but he's terribly worried about the community splintering and the likelihood of more violence before there's anything resembling acceptance. You know there was a murder here last year?"

"Yeah, I read about it," Jeff said, putting the long-neck to his lips.

"I agree with Bobby Ray," Jimmy said. "It'll probably take at least a generation for much change. More probably two. He thinks every citizen should be able to vote, even though it's obvious that ain't gonna happen just because everyone joins hands and sings gospel songs. He works hard to keep our coverage of racial issues pretty straight forward, but the paper's owner is an original member of the White Citizens Council. That means Bobby Ray is dancing along a high-wire without a net."

"It's incredible to me," Jeff said, "that after all this time there's no reconciliation, that the culture is so toxic and openly violent."

"Don't you see?" Jimmy said, with a hint of impatience, "The South *won*. Lincoln may have saved the Union. And technically he freed the slaves, but most of their descendants are still in chains made of dollars and are fenced in by legal discrimination. By state law. Life hasn't changed that much. Whites and blacks live even more separately now than when the blacks were all in shanties on plantations. There aren't any slaves in physical bondage now, but the coloreds are still prisoners of economic and cultural slavery. They're still a major part of enabling the so-called genteel southern lifestyle and attitude that people are so proud of. And if it takes an occasional cross burning on the lawn of some uppity black wanting to vote, or an occasional bullet or two through someone's windows, well, that's just not talked about in polite company. That's the flip side of the Mississippih that I dearly love in so many ways. It's also the place that's been called the most-violent and dangerous place on earth."

"That's brutally blunt," Jeff said. "And crystal clear."

"There ya go," Jimmy said, firing his hand pistol right between Jeff's blue eyes.

CHAPTER SEVENTY-FIVE

Three weeks later, after work, Jeff retrieved a suitcase from the closet and stepped into the bathroom to pull off a foot of toilet paper. He inserted a jackknife blade into a corner of the suitcase lining, prying outward until the lining separated slightly from the case. Grasping the loosened portion with his fingers, he gently pulled several inches loose. Using the toilet paper to cover his hand, he pulled out three envelopes, all sealed and stamped. He took the top one and replaced the others in the lining.

The next morning, a humid August Sunday, he drove 40 miles to Jackson and found a mailbox on a street corner. He adjusted his cap and sunglasses before covering his left hand with a Kleenex. He kept the hand in his pocket until he was standing at the box, noting that mail wouldn't be picked up until Monday. Looking casually in all directions, he pulled the envelope from his shirt pocket and put it in the fold-out door. The envelope plunged edge-first into an apparently empty box.

When it hit bottom it made a surprisingly loud noise for such a small envelope.

CHAPTER SEVENTY-SIX

Ed Bryant stood at full rigid military attention behind the rear counter of his hardware store, glaring at the one-page letter; the envelope on the counter where he had dropped it. He re-read the two stark sentences for the fifth time when the cigarette in his left hand burned down to his fingers. He dropped the butt, jammed two fingers in his mouth to cool the burning and muffle his curses as he stomped the fallen cigarette to death on the grimy floor.

MURDER WILL BE PUNISHED.
YOU WILL PAY FOR YOUR CRIME.

The store's bell signaled an entering customer. Ed folded the letter along its original two creases, slipped it back in the envelope and slid it under the phone book beneath the counter.

"Hi, Paul, what's up?" he bellowed, walking toward the front, his deep voice even louder than usual, irritated that Billy, his clerk, was busy helping a customer on the far side of the store.

"Not a whole hell of a lot, Ed. Need new hinges for my old shed."

As Paul left with his hinges, Bryant strode quickly from the cash register to his small office in the rear of the store, sticking his burned fingers back in his mouth briefly, then grabbed the black phone and dialed from memory.

"Roy? Ed. I've got sompin to show ya. Let's have lunch here. Bring me a tuna melt and some chips. I got sompin you need to see. Never mind what. Just get here. Twelve-thirty." He hung up without waiting for a reply.

At exactly 12:30 Roy Ryser came through the front door in his white pharmacy jacket carrying two brown bags. Even with the white coat it was unlikely anyone would mistake Roy for a doctor or a dentist although that's why he wore the coat all day, no matter where he went. He didn't realize that, except when he was behind the prescription counter, people who didn't know him would more likely think the small thin man with the weak chin and slightly oversized nose was the town barber.

Roy was worried when Ed yelled at Billy to watch things and herded Roy to Ed's office directly behind the rear counter and slammed the door. Roy sat in one of two chairs in the small room, under the Confederate flag displayed on the wall, wondering why Ed was so agitated. But before he could open his bag, Ed thrust the envelope at him.

"Read this," he instructed, putting his own sandwich on the desk but not sitting. Roy pulled his reading glasses from the jacket pocket, annoyed when Ed barked: "Read it. Hurry up."

Roy re-read the two sentences three times, panic nailing him to the chair. He looked up at Ed, fear pinching his face. "What the hell is this? That's it? Nothin else? No signature?" rubbing the end of his nose with two fingers, as he often did when worried. "No nothin?"

"Of course that's all," Ed barked, glaring. "You can see that's all there is. You don't think somebody'd sign that shit, do ya? Just two sentences. Plain envelope. All typed. Mailed in Jackson on Monday. Came this mornin, addressed to me at the store. Not even a street address. That's it! Whataya think?" Ed sucked on a tooth.

"Oh, hell, it's just a crank. Just somebody gettin kicks," Roy wanting to sound hopeful.

"I don't think it's a joke," Bryant said, voice quiet, suddenly understated, the bark and glare gone.

"Oh, Christ, Ed, I hope you're wrong," Roy said, feeling and sounding desperate. "Who would do something like this? What does he mean? What's he going to do?"

"How the fuck do I know?" Ed snapped. "It's prolly some liberal fag communist who thinks the jury was wrong. Somebody who cares whether or not the jury was wrong."

They were silent for several minutes, individual fears yanking them back into the same courtroom.

"How do you find?"

"Your honor, we find the defendants not guilty."

"If it's a joke," Bryant said, "there's a good chance some fucker is out there right now laughin his ass off because you're here. Maybe even a bunch of guys having a good laugh at our expense."

He pulled the Camel pack from his shirt pocket, shook it, lipped one out and flicked his lighter.

"You think someone's watching us?" Roy whispered, face narrowing in panic as he stood up.

"I'll bet that's it," Ed said, ignoring the question, exhaling the first puff almost into Roy's face, baritone booming again. "That must be it. Hell, it could be Ronnie at the bar or…."

"Jesus Christ, Ed," Roy said. "What if it ain't someone at the bar? What if it ain't a joke?" his voice rising, eyes darting around the room, arms thrashing, as if drowning. "What if it's dead serious?" lurching toward Ed in a half stumble.

He was stunned by Ed's backhanded slap to his shoulder knocking him back into the chair, tipping it over, dumping him on the concrete floor. He sprawled there, his heaving breaths the only sound.

"Get up, you little asshole," Ed ordered, standing over him. "Goddamn you, you can't panic like that. Be a man for once! It could be lots of people."

Roy sat up, rocked several times before getting slowly to his feet. He righted the chair and sat, brushing his thin hair back over his pink scalp, staring at the floor, angry now but afraid to show it.

Ed continued talking as if nothing had happened. "And if that's what's goin on, the best thing we can do is ignore it, act like nothin's happened. But I can't imagine anyone we know would do this. This ain't funny. Not one goddamn bit."

"I hope you're…we're wrong," Roy said, voice low but trying again to sound hopeful, even though Ed was talking in circles. "Some people'll do anything for a joke. You said it might be Ronnie; he's big prankster. What should we do?"

Bryan decided. "Roy, we gonna just pretty much ignore each other for awhile. No lunches together. No comin over to the house until we see what's going on. You shouldna come here today," he said, making it sound like it was Roy's idea. "You scat now and forget it. We'll just act like nothin's happened. Don't mention this to anybody."

Roy's shoulder ached and he was insulted, as he often was when Ed blamed him, even when he'd done nothing wrong. Ed had hit him before but that was when they were still kids. Except for that time on the worst night of his life. He was stunned and angry. Ed was ordering him around, as usual—'You scat now'--as if they were still sixth graders.

"I'll call you if anythin comes up, or in a few weeks when it's blowed over," Ed said, handing him the uneaten sandwich and ushering him to the back door. Roy was halfway out when Ed said, "Be real careful. Let me know if anythin' comes up."

What the hell does that mean, Roy thought, walking without seeing. Being "careful" sounded like Ed was taking this more seriously than he was letting on. He suddenly felt as conspicuous as an elephant in the white jacket. Back at the drugstore he spent almost as much time putting sugar in his coffee as drugs into prescription bottles. I'm glad he got the letter and not me, he thought. Glad it wasn't me.

His letter came precisely one week later.

CHAPTER SEVENTY-SEVEN

Jimmy flung himself into the back booth across from Jeff, shooting sharp looks around Darryl's Diner before hissing: "What the hell are you doing?"

"What's got you all riled?" Jeff's eyes searching to see if anyone was close enough to hear, desperately hoping this wasn't what it sounded like.

"I know that minister who was murdered here last year was studying at Michigan when he was killed," Jimmy said, anger contorting his face. "I know you *knew* him. You *wrote* about him."

A waitress interrupted for their orders, neither of them looking at her. Jeff forced a smile, trying to appear calm, but he was stunned by Jimmy's ferocious accusation.

"Don't mess with me, goddammit, Jeff," Jimmy spat, his eyes piercing, leaning as far across the table as he could, arms extended as if reaching for Jeff. "I reread our clipping file on the case, including some wire stories that didn't run in our paper. One at the very beginning said Rev. Booker was in a doctoral program in Ann Arbor. All the other stories called him a Philadelphia native and a Temple graduate. I called the Michigan Daily and got a student to read me headlines from Booker's file. There was only one story before the murder and you goddamn well know whose byline was on it." He sat back, fists balled on the table edge, furious eyes still accusing

Jeff. "You never mentioned that before. Why not? What are you up to? Why're you here? You better level with me and right goddamn now."

Jeff's eyes skipped over the room again. "I'm sorry, Jimmy, I really am. I didn't know you at first and then, uh, now that I do, I haven't known quite what to say." He scooted forward on the seat, in a face-lock with Jimmy. "Yeah, I knew Isiah…Rev. Booker," trying to sound casual even though his body was rigid with tension, hoping Jimmy couldn't hear his heart ka-thumping in his chest.

"Hold it," Jimmy interrupted, raising a hand to Jeff's face as the waitress approached with their sandwiches. "Marge, put those in a go-bag. We gotta get movin."

* * *

Jimmy pulled onto the highway, away from town. In about a mile, he parked under trees shading the far corner of a sawmill parking lot. Rolling down the windows to lessen the blistering mid-day heat, Jimmy turned to Jeff and demanded: "All right, what's the truth? I want it all and no bullshit."

"I met Isiah at a party," Jeff began, briefly glancing away before speaking directly to Jimmy. "He was the most interesting person I ever met and I profiled him for The Daily. We fished together several times. We drank coffee and talked about everything you can imagine. I took a class from him. He painted details of blacks living in the segregated South that's so perfectly designed to suck every ounce of humanity and self-respect from their souls. He showed me the hopelessness of Detroit's ghettos. He ripped my mind open to cruel realities I hadn't even imagined. I was so unbelievably naïve, criminally naïve, that I'm embarrassed to think about it. I matured ten years in the first year I knew him. He was my friend and he was like a second dad to me. I admired him, bordering on worship, for dedicating his life to serving others. He was an amazing teacher and a terrific person. When he was murdered I was devastated, I…," Jeff's blue eyes moistening, throat muscles trying to swallow to liberate his voice.

"I, uh, I wanted to know what kind of place, what kind of people could, uh, do such a thing. Murder Isiah. What the hell kind of place is this?" Jeff's voice was barely a whisper. He didn't wait for an answer.

"I'm thinking about writing a book about Isiah and about the town that murdered him, shot him in cold blood and acquitted the killers. And then celebrated the murderers as heroes."

"That's the truth? You wanna write a book about that?" Jimmy said, pausing but hearing no answer except for cicadas clicking from nearby brush. He pulled a sandwich from one of the bags on the seat. "You're either insane or terminally stupid," gnawing a corner from a grilled cheese sandwich without taking his eyes from Jeff.

"It's possible I'm both," Jeff said, breaking Jimmy's stare by glancing into his bag, pretending interest in his lunch.

"You have no clue what you're doin," Jimmy said, glaring him. "None. You think you're on some high-minded mission to honor your friend, but you're driving a hundred miles an hour straight into a complete fuckin disaster.

"You don't know what this place is really like under the skin; what these people are like when they're not being so sickeningly polite that sometimes even I want to slap them upside their heads. This is the South, man. The *Deep Fucking South.* People here don't want anyone asking the questions you have. You dig in their magnolia gardens and you'll find more than just worms. You mess around in racial issues and you'll be stunned by the ugliness under those sweet, mint-julep exteriors. Mississipih's like a woman so stunningly beautiful she takes your breath away and then suddenly she's swearing like a sailor while stomping kittens to death in her high heels." He focused through the windshield for nearly a minute.

"Around here you can see god-fearing people singing in pews on Sunday and maybe see them again on Thursday organizing a cross-burning."

"I want to *know* about stuff like that," Jeff said. "I need to know why he died, what the killers were thinking. How did they feel justified? I want to know how he died...."

"Whoa, whoa," Jimmy interrupted. "I get it. But you poke around in that shit pile and you'll be just as dead as he is. Sorry. But you can't be asking those questions. A lot of people will be incredibly pissed off and seriously threatened by anyone resurrecting that case."

"I don't want to retry the case," Jeff said, anger in his voice. "I know that's over. You and I both know there never was a chance in hell of actual justice here in your precious *Deep Fried South.* That fake trial ended last year without ever beginning. It was a farce. I'm way past that. I just want to know the truth."

"Same thing," Jimmy said. "People who can kill civil rights workers won't hesitate even a second before killing some Yankee invader looking for the *truth.* That's as threatening to those people as that army of outsiders trying to get black folks to vote," his face grim. "You think they want a book exposing details and motives?"

"I understand that…" Jeff began.

"No you don't," Jimmy shouted. "No! You! Don't! You dumb shit. You can intellectualize all you want but you don't…you can't even *begin* to understand any of this. This is drop-dead serious. You're obsessed. You need to get UN-obsessed. Wouldn't your black friend want you to move on? Would he tell you to flush your life down the toilet hoping to better understand what happened to him?" he said, waving grilled cheese like a flag.

He stopped for a moment, frozen, glaring at Jeff. "It's not that shining a spotlight on these people would be the worst thing that ever happened. And maybe a book from afar would kick this town's ass down the road a little toward the future that's coming no matter what people here believe or want. Maybe. But it ain't gonna happen," his voice barely audible.

"Look," Jeff said, "can't we just forget this whole conversation? I'm doing a good job at the paper. Anything I learn from being here this summer, meeting people, seeing how things work, is a bonus. It may lead nowhere. I may not get enough material for a book or even an article, and I'll head back home, finish school and get on with my life. My internship only has a few weeks left. I had no way of knowing anyone here would discover that Isiah and I knew each other. Can't we just go back to that?" Jeff said, staring through the windshield, unable to meet Jimmy's eyes.

Jimmy didn't respond, chewing another corner of sandwich, eyes unfocused toward the steering wheel, the silence growing.

Finally Jimmy turned to Jeff and they measured each other for a long time.

CHAPTER SEVENTY-EIGHT

"He found out you knew Isiah? That he was your friend?" the horror in Susan's voice was intense over the long-distance line. "What did you tell him? Does anyone else know? You've got to get out of Mississippi. Start driving home right now. Are you..."

"Wait," he interrupted, sounding too loud in the cramped booth. "It's not that bad. Jimmy was really pissed about my not telling him I knew Isiah, but I explained your original idea of a book or magazine article. I said I wanted to know how Isiah could be slaughtered and this town approves of it. I told him I applied for the internship here because I wanted to understand the local thinking."

"But this won't stop now," she said. "Fowlerville's his hometown. He grew up there. He's one of *them.* He's going to protect it and..."

"Maybe," he said, "but he got over some of the shock and even wondered out loud if it might actually be good for the town if a book or magazine article confronted the dark side of the culture that they keep hidden."

"You think he's serious? Or is he trying to learn more and then betray you?"

"I don't believe he's like that. He knows the South's sometimes unbelievably vicious and cruel. He believes it's gotta change. He started out really angry at me. We've spent a lot of time together at work, fishing, eating, having a beer and just talking. I think he's a good guy, but I just don't know…There are so many layers here, so many things that aren't real…I didn't figure on anything like…"

"That's the whole point," she cut in. "You can't guess everything that could happen. Don told you that before you left. He mentioned it again yesterday. He still calls me every few days for an update on what's happening there. "Come home," she said, her voice staccato. "We *know* that's a dangerous, murderous place. They killed Isiah. You don't understand those people and probably never will, but that's ok. You can still write about Isiah. Please pack up and come home. Today. Please. Or, I can take the bus down there and we'll drive back together. Please. Jeff. Come home. Before it's too late."

"I love you, Jeff," Susan said, whispering. "Please Jeff, don't leave me behind. I don't want to lose you."

Silence.

The connection went dead in Jeff's ear.

CHAPTER SEVENTY-NINE

Opal McCormack limped into the Herald's library, as she did two afternoons every week, to file stories clipped from each day's paper.

Opal was 44, but had the steel-gray, hair-in-a-bun of an older woman. She had always seemed older than she was and it wasn't only because of her limp, the result of her left leg being a half-inch shorter than the right. A plain girl with a serious expression had matured into a plain woman with a serious face. A graduate of Fowlerville High School, she earned her teaching credentials in a two-year program at Ol' Miss, the only time she lived anywhere but Fowlerville, where she taught English at her old high school. For nearly 20 years she had gone to the Herald on Tuesday and Thursday afternoons, filing into the evening for minimum wage, usually alone in a room jammed with file cabinets holding musty, yellowing clippings.

Today she was glad to see Jimmy Waller. He was a nice kid and she liked him. He was always polite: "Thanks, Miss Opal." "Have a nice day, Miss Opal."

He'd been in the library several times recently.

"Can I help you find something, Jimmy?"

"No, thanks, Miss Opal."

"Ok. Let me know if I can help."

"Sure thing, Miss Opal."

He disappeared into the maze of cabinets and she heard a drawer opening and closing. A few minutes later he reappeared and headed for the door with a folder.

"I'll be right back. I'm just going to Xerox a couple of clips. I'll bring 'em right back." This was something he and other reporters did frequently, although usually they mentioned what they were working on, even if they didn't need help finding it. He returned with the folder and vanished back into the maze, returning a moment later, pointing his finger-gun at her as he left.

"Thanks, Miss Opal."

She picked up several envelopes she had been updating, limping into the rows of cabinets to replace them. She saw a drawer not quite closed near the bottom of a cabinet and went to give it a nudge. Must have been where Jimmy was working, she thought. As she pushed the drawer closed, she noticed it was the one containing only clippings and materials from coverage of the murder last year of that Negro minister and the trial of three men, including her favorite cousin, Ed Bryant, member of the Fowlerville White Citizens Council and son of the founder of the Dixon County Ku Klux Klan.

CHAPTER EIGHTY

"I *know* you said we shouldn't be seen together but now I've got a letter. We gotta talk," Roy was nearly hysterical.

"Yeah, just like your'n. Identical. Came to my store. I…acourse I'm not going to say anything I shouldn't. I need to talk to you about it. We gotta do somethin," pleading in his reedy voice, massaging his nose with two fingers, rubbing round and round.

"Nine? Ok. I'll drive by the back door and pick you up."

At 8:55 p.m. Ryser's white Chevy sedan waited behind Bryant's hardware store. Four minutes later Ed came out, got in and leaned into Roy's face.

"Nine o'clock, I said. Nine, goddamn it," his face flushed, eyes boring into Ryser who leaned as far back as he could. "Sitting out here you might as well be wearing a neon sign. Damn it, Roy, when I say nine, I mean nine," pulling Camels from his shirt with one hand, searching his pants for his lighter with the other.

"Don't worry," Roy's voice plaintive, "I've picked you up hundreds of times. No one's gonna think twice about it. Besides, there was no one else while I was here." The car was moving as if on its own to the end of the alley.

"Just because you didn't see nobody don't mean nobody saw you. Nine. When I say nine I mean…"

"Ok! Ok!," Roy interrupting for a change. "Let's not fight ourselves.

I got the same letter today. It said the same thing. Exactly. Except it was mailed in Meridian. We gotta figure out what's goin' on."

"How the Christ would I know what's goin on?" Ed snapped, rubbing his crew cut as if he'd never noticed it before.

He's shook up, Roy thought, with a trace of smugness since Ed was always crudely disdainful of Ryser's emotional reactions. During the trial Roy had despised Ed's condescending attitude, interrupting him, ignoring his questions or occasional suggestions, dealing with the lawyers as if Roy didn't exist.

"Just shut up, Roy," Ed said once, right there at the defense table where everyone could hear. "Let me handle this. Just do what I tell ya."

"Look," Bryant said now, exhaling smoke, staring straight ahead, "We gotta figger whoever sent these letters ain't kiddin. We can't take no chance that they're not. Otherwise the only way we'll find out is if one or both of us is dead."

An icy thought, the very idea Roy was struggling not to think about, squeezed his chest, sucking the air from his lungs.

"So we're gonna have to be ready for anythin," Ed said, glaring at Roy. "Maybe some nigger-lovers decided we shoulda been convicted. Maybe they're trying to scare us or...worse." We havta beat 'em at their own game."

"Game? What game?" Roy's panic moving to anger. "We don't know shit about any *game.* We don't know anything about what in hell's happening. We don't know if it's one person or a mob. We don't *know* a goddamn thing." Roy felt his moist hands slipping on the wheel and rubbed his palms on his pants, driving aimlessly. "What if there's a whole bunch of 'em? What are we going..."

"Shut up!" Bryant snapped. "If it's a group it'll have to be niggers. That's the way they operate. If it ain't them it's got to be some nigger lover. Or maybe it's someone funnin us. If there was a gang of niggers we'd know about it. And they wouldna waited this long. It's got to be one or maybe a couple of niggers or maybe some of those activist fuck-heads stirring up trouble again.

"Our letters came from different towns," Ed added. "And both came to our stores. Maybe they didn't know our home addresses. Maybe it's nobody around here. Just somebody trying to harass us about the trial. Maybe...."

Roy recognized the familiar rambling recitation of uncertain possibilities and it scared him. For once he hungered for Ed to be decisive. The laundry list of possibilities squeezed his heart, sending his thoughts bouncing off in all directions, never landing anywhere. Ed didn't seem certain, confident, the way he usually did, Roy thought.

Is he trying to convince us both?

"Suppose Roll got a letter?" Roy asked. "If somebody's after us he'll go after Roll too."

"I'll call him," Ed said. "If he has one we'll all figger out what to do. Meantime I'm carryin my gun and you better, too." He pulled the small stainless-steel automatic from its holster behind his back, showing it to Roy who barely glanced at it.

"No use playing bulls-eye for some nigger," Ed said. "And you better not walk up behind me quiet like," exhaling another smoke cloud into the car.

Talking down to me again, Roy thought, slowing to swing the car around in the middle of the dark highway, no headlights coming either way. He made a K-turn on the narrow road, feeling Ed's unspoken criticism, his judgment that the turn should have been completed without backing up in the middle of the road. They drove in silence for several minutes, each contemplating the prospect of being the prey of an unknown hunter.

"What if Roll doesn't get one?" Roy asked.

"Shut up! We'll handle it."

They rode silently the rest of the way to town, Roy seething at Ed's misdirected anger. The sedan stopped in the alley behind the store and Bryant started to open the door, then turned, looking Roy straight in the eyes, "I'll call you. Don't call me unless you get another letter. Keep alert. And protect yourself."

Then the door closed quietly and he was gone. Roy drove off without waiting to watch Ed unlock the store's rear door and disappear.

***

Ed locked the deadbolt behind him. Only the display lights from the front windows invaded the dim recess of nails, screws, pipes, baseball bats, camping gear, toilet bowl floats and bulk rope. He walked through the semi-darkness as assuredly as if it were daylight. He lit another cigarette before grabbing the receiver.

"Hi, Roll. Ed. Fine. Yourself? Good. Say, has anything unusual happened lately? Anything related to, uh, the uh, thing from last year? Oh, good...no, nothing special, just a funny thing and I wanted to be sure it was just, uh, funny, you know? Yeah, well...sorry to bother you. See yuh Friday night at the Legion? Good, see yuh then. Right. Bye."

Ed hung up, stood with one hand on the receiver. In the dark store his mind accelerated.

If Roll doesn't have one, then maybe somebody knows something. But Roy got his a week after the first one. Mine. What if Roll sent them? That's stupid. Roll is just as glad as anyone all that's over, forgotten. Maybe it was that tipster who called the sheriff. Still don't know who...Maybe this is just a crank or a joker or... But why so long after? Keep cool. Keep that chicken-shit Roy calm. Can't have him falling apart now after the worst is over. He's such a pussy. Just keep my head. Keep the gun handy.

He stopped his unconscious pacing behind the counter and walked through the dark store, his footsteps keeping him company to the back door. He left, pausing only to relock it before quickly crossing the alley to his car.

Keep calm. Keep your head.

The gun heavy on his belt.

CHAPTER EIGHTY-ONE

Rollin Price wondered who sent it. He couldn't look away, holding the letter and envelope in his hand. A quick mental survey of his friends discounted all of them as likely suspects.

Is this what Ed called about last week? 'Anything unusual happen lately?' That's what he said. 'Anything related to the stuff from last year?' Did Ed send this? Why would he? Ed's the last person to think it's funny. But he must know something about it, why else'd he call? Ed must have gotten a letter like this. What about Roy? What'n hell?

Roll read the letter yet again, still standing in the kitchen where he had pulled the plain white envelope with his name and "Personal" on it from the slim stack of mail. No return address but postmarked Vicksburg. Thank God he'd gotten home before Arlene returned from picking up the kids from school, and glee club and baseball practice. What would she have thought? She's still a mess from back then.

MURDER WILL BE PUNISHED.

YOU WILL PAY FOR YOUR CRIME.

He stuffed the letter into the envelope, folded it and put it in his shirt pocket. He took a sheet of paper and a pencil from the neatly organized little desk by the refrigerator, where Arlene paid the bills, and wrote, as legibly as his big, thick fingers could manage:

Hon, I forgot about a committee meeting at the lodge.

Be gone awhile, will catch a bite to eat there. Sorry, R

He didn't like lying to her but he knew she'd fall apart if she saw the threatening note.

She can't handle this kind of crap. I thought it was over. It was over. And forgot. We all want to forget.

He drove faster than usual, the battered brown and yellow pickup bouncing in and out of potholes in the long, gravel driveway, then spurting onto the road, spraying gravel, barely a glance either way to look for traffic.

The booth door clumped shut and the dime tinkled irritatingly slowly into the machine's guts. He wasn't used to phone booths and he didn't like this one. With his stocky build and broad shoulders he was claustrophobic. He dialed carefully, then looked around, seeing the Sunoco pumps and small cement-block store across the pocked pavement next to the air pump. It was dark and he felt spotlighted inside the booth but was afraid to leave the door open in order to shut off the light because he was afraid someone might hear; although there were no vehicles within 50 feet. Not enough air. Sweating like a hog. Finally the ringing stopped.

"Ed. Roll. I got somethin today I need to talk to you about. Yeah. One page. At the store? Right, fifteen minutes."

Damn, oh damn, Ed knew about it. He knew it was a letter. That means he got one, too. He'll know what to do. Christ.

He parked in the alley behind Ed's store and got out as Roy's sedan pulled behind him.

***

The two men got out, nodding, not speaking, hearing the door unlocking.

Ed re-locked the door, leading them to his office where they couldn't be seen from the street even if someone peered in the front windows. Darker outside now. He closed the door and switched on a small gooseneck lamp on a shelf about head high. Not much light, but better than total darkness. The confined space smelled of stale smoke and dead cigarettes..

Like we're in a cave, Roy thought, pulling a metal folding chair from against the wall, flipping it open as Roll slumped into an old oak chair that looked like it belonged around a dining room table.

Ed turned and leaned backwards, butt braced against the edge of a work bench.

"What ya got, Roll?" he asked. They all knew.

Roll pulled the folded envelope from his green work shirt and handed it to Ed. "From Vicksburg," he said.

Ed opened the single sheet, glanced at it and passed it to Roy, who held it away from him, toward the dim light and handed it back to Ed without comment or changing his grim expression.

"I guess you got one a these too," Roll said, looking at Ed, then Roy, hoping to hear 'no' but knowing it was 'yes.'

"Yeah,' Ed said, "both a us," pulling his letter from his shirt pocket and putting it on the work bench alongside Roll's. "Ours came a week apart. That was a couple of weeks ago. You're right on schedule. On someone's schedule."

Roy took his letter from his windbreaker pocket--no white jacket tonight--and laid it next to the other two. "They're identical," he said, realizing he was pointing out the obvious. "But Ed's was mailed in Jackson, mine in Meridian and your'n in Vicksburg.

"Who in hell's sending 'em?" Roll asked. "What's goin on?"

"I dunno," Ed said, looking over the heads of the seated men, into the dim storeroom, as if the answer was hidden in the darkness.

Roy thought*: Not his usually superior, arrogant self.*

"Well," Roll said, "we swore we was never gonna talk about...you know...but is some sombitch having their jollies with us or is that nigger's family after us or what?"

"I told ya, I don't know," Bryant snapped, straightening up, taking a step right, then about facing, looking uncertain about where to go; the small room confining them in the semi-darkness with only their uncontrollable thoughts.

Assuming the question was aimed only at him. As usual. Even when he doesn't have the answer.

"But we gotta protect ourselves," Ed continued, his voice unusually low. "If it's someone who's serious about this we can't be sittin ducks."

"I'm thinking of moving away," Roy interrupted, irritated at being ignored. "I can always get a job and this town gives me the creeps not knowing who's out there sending letters. I never did much like this town anyway," he said, "even when we was growin up," knowing the others knew it was a lie.

"Oh, that'd be just great," Ed said sarcastically, voice rising. "Just pack up and run like a scared bunny and what good'll that do? Unless you change your name and completely disappear for the rest of your life they'll find you eventually. You might just as well say you're guilty. We already proved in court we're not."

"They?" Roy shot. "*They'll* find me? Who? You talk about not being sitting ducks. How we gonna do that? We got no idea who the hunters are. We *are* sitting ducks. I don't want to be a *dead* duck. Somebody doesn't believe the jury and has decided to play judge and jury by himself," surprising himself with the anger he seldom showed.

"Himself?" Ed mocked. "We don't even know if it's a 'they' or a 'him.' We don't know nothin about who or why?"

"Yeah?" Roy shouted, jumping up, not feeling like himself, excited, talking in machine gun bursts. "That's my whole point. This don't feel like a joke to me. I think somebody means business. I think someone's after us and I'm scared shitless and not afraid to admit it. So are you guys; you're just pretending like you're cool."

Roll pulled a silver penknife from his pocket and began to clean under his blunt fingernails. "Goin to pieces may be just what they want, Roy," Roll said gently,

"I don't give a rat's ass what they want. And who? That's the point. Could be any fool."

"Naah," Roll said. "Most likely someone who thinks we killed that nigger and got away with it. Did the nigger have a brother or somebody who might want revenge? Or one of them Yankee pricks who keep comin down here tellin us how to live? Could be one a them fuckers."

The silence was as dark as the room, each of them traveling without a map.

Ed finally spoke. "Let's be calm 'n logical about this," he said, slipping his hands into his pockets, walking to the other side of the room, into the darkness and back. "Let's forget the crack-pot idea or the joke idea. If it's one of those, this'll go away cause there's really no problem. Somebody will have a few laughs or will think they put a scare into us and then move on. That'll be that."

"Yeah," Roll said, pulling his Marlboros from his shirt pocket. "Whoever it is oughta get his head split."

"Forget the joke idea or that it's only a bluff," Ed said. "Let's figger the letters mean just what they say. That it's some kind of real threat, although it could be just a judgment, you know, like God himself sent 'em, someone basically tellin us we're gonna rot in hell. But if the letters mean they plan to punish us here, then it's either an individual or a group."

"Christ you're smart," Roy snapped, sitting on the folding chair again. "Next you'll figger out that it's either a black group or a white group. None of us knows shit."

"That's exactly right," Ed said, glancing at Roy, then at Roll, not outwardly angered by Roy's unusual insult. "We havta look at every angle. If it's a buncha niggers they probably plan to kill us or frighten us inta admitting we killed that nigger minister. Or maybe scare the shit out of us for the rest of our lives. Anyways, we can't be tried again and since we ain't goin to be scared into nuthin, then it's gotta be for revenge. If it's a black bunch then they'll be easier to spot. If it's a single nigger we're going to have one hell of a time finding out who it is. Unless it's a stranger, not one of our niggers."

"What if it's a bunch of whites from up north or somethin?" Roll asked.

"That'd be a bad problem too, because they's lots of strangers in town. There's that construction crew working on the bridge and there's always new soldiers at the fort. And a few of them self-righteous, northern know-it-alls are back. God, you'd think they'd stay away from here after what happened last year. But it's more likely some nigger or nigger group who wants a scare us."

"Or kill us," Roy said.

"We gotta be goddamn careful, that's all. That's all we can do," Ed said.

Ed pulled up his shirttail to reveal the small silver automatic stuck in a tan leather holster hooked inside the waist-band of his pants. "I'm bein as careful as I can and I'm not afraid to use this."

"What about Claire?" Roll asked. "What's she think bout you toting a gun?"

"She don't know nuthin. Since the trial I've always had a gun in the car and one in the store. I just keep the one from the car with me now."

Roy stood up, right hand going to his side, under the windbreaker, pushing it to the side, showing a blue-steel revolver in a black holster on his belt. "Hell, I'd have a hard time hitting you from here," he said.

"Then go practice," Ed snapped.

Roll's face stayed calm. "I guess I better pack one, too. But it'll be hard to use against somebody we don't know is a problem until they make a move."

No one answered. The other two had already reached the same conclusion.

"Who the hell is it?" Roy asked angrily for what felt like the nine-hundredth time. He swung his left hand backward, against the wall behind him.

That was stupid. Show you're pissed and scared. Damn hand hurts. Nothin's going right. That really hurt. You stupid asshole.

He hoped the others didn't see the pain in his eyes. He hoped it didn't show on his face but knew that it did; his face always gave him away.

"I can't think a nothin else to do," Ed said. "Maybe now that we all got one of them letters this'll all go away. Maybe they'll think we're all shittin our pants and that's what they want."

"They'd be right," Roll said with a brief grin. "I'm going to need all new underwear if this keeps up."

Ed took two steps to the door and said, "We'll wait and see. But keep your eyes open. Anyone sees or hears anythin, he tells the others."

Ed turned off the gooseneck lamp and opened the door but they stood momentarily in the darkness until their eyes began to see the dim light from the main part of the store. They walked quietly to the rear door.

They paused in a clump for a few moments. Then Ed nodded and the others nodded back; Roy wondering what they were nodding about. Roll turned to his pickup, Roy to the white sedan. All of them feeling someone watching.

***

Ed went back to his office and closed the door. He dialed the Sheriff's department and asked for Cecil Stuart.

"Cecil," he said when the deputy came on the line. "I need ta show you sompin. In private. Can ya drop by the store? As soon as you can. Back door," he said and hung up.

Less than ten minutes later, Cecil started to knock at the alley door but heard the deadbolt unclicking. He looked Ed who motioned to follow him.

As soon as the office door closed, Cecil said: "I didn't like how you sounded on the phone, and now you look like you're standing in cow flop up to your nostrils. Somethin wrong?"

Ed pointed at the letters on the counter.

The deputy looked at the letters and then at Ed. "What the hell's this?"

"We each got one; me, Roll and Roy. Mailed a week apart, mine from Jackson, Roy's from Meridian and the last one, Roll's, from Vicksburg. We don't know nuthin else."

"Shit, Ed, it's gotta be about last year but..."

"We figgered out that much," Ed snapped. "But who sent 'em. What do they mean?"

Cecil looked at the letters again, as if they'd changed somehow. "I got no idea," Cecil said. "Could be anybody; prolly not anyone from around here. Maybe somethin cooked up by one a them nigger organizations trying ta spook ya."

"Well, it's workin. Roy's spooked outta his pea brain," Ed said. "And Roll and me are damned nervous." He lifted his untucked shirt to show his pistol.

"Good idea. Roll and Roy got guns?"

"Yeah, but Roy's dangerous when he's armed. I hope he don't shoot one a us by mistake. He's pracly hysterical. Don't walk up behind him. Maybe we should give him some blanks."

"I'll drive by your houses real regular just to be safe. I'll have other deputies do the same."

"No," Ed said. "This is just us talkin. I don't want nobody else involved; keep it quiet."

"Ok. If you say so. I'll keep an eye out for cars or trucks with outa-state plates. You seen any strangers around lately? Anybody hanging around your store or cruisin your house?"

"No, but I'll watch out. What else can we do? Any way you can find out who's out there?"

"We all better keep our eyes peeled for anyone suspicious," Cecil said, "although I'm not sure what that is. Let's stay alert and see if this blows over. That's prolly what'll happen," his voice less certain than his words.

"Yeah, ok, thanks. Remember, nobody else needs to know bout this. Just atween us two. I'm not gonna say anythin to Roll or Roy."

"Gotcha," Cecil said, opening the office door, anxious to leave. "I'll be watching. I'll check on any foreign plates I see. If I see anybody at all suspicious I'll pull their ass over."

Ed accompanied him to the back door. Then he returned to his office, locking the door behind him. The three letters and envelopes were lined up on the workbench. He angrily crumpled them in one huge hand, staring at the paper ball for a few seconds, then put it in the coffee-can ashtray and set it ablaze.

CHAPTER EIGHTY-TWO

Jeff hoped he was driving fast enough to appear normal to anyone seeing the dirty blue car with mud-caked plates, but slow enough to get a good look at the woods and fields surrounding Ed Bryant's home and at the long driveway between the road and house. This was his third run along the country road not far from town and he knew he was increasing the risk someone would notice his car.

The driveway was barely two tracks, flanked with tall trees planted years ago, 25 feet apart, their tops grown together into a tunnel. On the first drive by he focused on a wooded area ending less than 50 feet from the left side of the antebellum house, part of a quarter-mile band of tall trees and bushes running beside the road.

On his second pass, about a mile from the house, he watched the right side of the road for a battered sign he had spotted earlier: DIXON COUNTY Department of Parks. He swung onto the narrow road, flanked by grass and brush, and followed it several hundred yards to a weed-infested, dead-end cul-de-sac flanked by two weather-battered picnic tables, a disheveled outhouse and a rusty trash barrel.

This'll do.

He parked and pulled a screwdriver from the floor under his seat, got out and walked to the passenger side, scanning in all directions for moving vehicles, farmers in nearby fields or anyone walking.

He dropped to the ground, rolling his upper body under the car, back pressed into the ground, reaching up with the screwdriver. He removed four screws from a metal box welded to the frame just ahead of the right-rear wheel. Hand-applied grease and accumulated mud and dust from the road made the box almost invisible even to someone lying under the car looking for it. He removed a small, tightly folded canvas bag protecting a tattered, blue hand-towel. He unfolded the towel revealing a pair of thin, black-leather gloves wrapped around his grandfather's pistol. He rubbed the ancient revolver with his forefinger, finding no dirt or dust before rewrapping and taking it into the car with him.

CHAPTER EIGHTY-THREE

Jimmy tried aiming his red-white-and-rust pickup between potholes in his gravel driveway, but they still jolted his hands through the steering wheel. His butt rode the truck seat bucking like a rodeo bull. Heavy rain in the evening darkness overwhelmed the wipers and blurred his vision as he snaked into the little house's carport, offering only partial shelter from the downpour. Warm clothes and a cold beer beckoned as he slid from the truck, trying to dodge water pouring through the flimsy carport roof. Wind pushed raindrops over the edges of the carport, creating splash puddles in the gravel, a musty rain smell mixing with oil and exhaust fumes from the truck's last, gasping exhale.

The savage blow to his shoulder knocked him sideways so violently that his head smashed into the edge of a plywood work bench, crashing him full-length onto the wet ground.

Darkness.

Then the voice.

Talking to me?

So close to his head it seemed to come from inside him. Consciousness came and went.

"Wake up. Wake up, you red-headed turd."

Me?

"Come on, God Damn You! Listen to me! You hear me? Wake up! Sit up! Open your eyes, you shithead!"

Me? Am I not sitting? Where am I?

Pulled upward by his shoulders.

"That's better. Keep those eyes open. Listen! You mind your own business. Got that? You unnerstand me? Huh?"

Why the hood?

Then, aloud: "Why…hood? Who?"

"Never mind, you stupid fuckhead. No questions. Just listen. Here's all you need to know. Butt the hell out. Mind your own goddamn business. Stay the hell out of old stuff. That's over and done. We was all innocent. Get me?"

Darkness.

"Wake up. You hear me? Wake up!" the burly hooded figure kneeling, shaking Jimmy by the shoulders, limp as if boneless. "Wake up. Shit. Oh, shit! Oh, shit! Oh My God," shoving Jimmy away as if he were covered with spiders.

"Oh Jesus," the big figure said, jumping up, vanishing into the black downpour, lightning and thunder exploding overhead.

CHAPTER EIGHTY-FOUR

It's my fault. Oh, god, Jimmy wouldn't be dead if he hadn't met me. I brought death right to him. I killed him. Dead. Isiah's dead. Now Jimmy's dead. This place is hell itself. I've made it worse. I should have been straight with him. He warned me. I should have warned him. But how could I know? What have I done? Without me this wouldn't have happened. I killed him.

***

The newsroom staff grieved in the newsroom while scrambling for details of Jimmy's death, seeking to know if this was a tragic accident or murder. Mourners without a cause.

"Go through his desk, look at all his notebooks," Bobby Ray croaked to Jeff while leaning on the edge of Jeff's desk, so close that Jeff saw the red veins in his tortured eyes. "I want to know every, and I mean *every,* story he was working on or even *thinking* about working on," anger and grief distorting his voice, a hint of alcohol drifting toward Jeff.

"We're going to find out if Jimmy slipped in his wet carport and banged his head or if some sonuvabitch did this to him," Bobby Ray said, his face haggard, a hundred years old. "God, I hope he just fell. That's tragic enough, but if he's been murdered..." his voice fading as he straightened up. "He was like a son to me...He...Why would anyone kill Jimmy? Jimmy for god's sake. This must be an accident." A long minute passed before Bobby Ray regained his voice and straightened up. "Ok, everybody. Get to work."

* * *

An hour later, Sheriff Lanny Purdy filled the conference room door looking at a clipboard, his tan uniform freshly starched. "Jeff Martindale?" he said, looking up from the list of Herald staff members Bobby Ray had given him, then removing his Stetson and his glasses, putting them on the table between them as he sat heavily into the chair opposite Jeff, the only person in the room.

"You understand I'm talkin' to everyone at the Herald to see if there's any reason to think Jimmy Waller didn't just get out of his truck, lose his footing in the rain and crack his head on that work bench."

"Yessir."

"Good," the sheriff said, studying Jeff's face as if memorizing it. "What can y'all tell me? I understand from Bobby Ray that your desk is right across from Jimmy's and y'all backed each other up on some stories. What was he working on?"

"That's what I'm looking for," Jeff gesturing to the long table half covered with notebooks and papers. "Bobby Ray told me to go through Jimmy's stuff and list everything he was doing."

"What have you found so far," the sheriff asked, glancing around the table, beefy arms jutting from his short-sleeved shirt.

"I'm sorting things to get organized," Jeff said. "It'll take a while to sift through the debris," instantly regretting the reference to a dead man's things.

The sheriff stood, retrieving his hat and glasses. "Let Bobby Ray know immediately when you have a list, or anything that looks interesting, and he'll contact me. Now I gotta go talk with his parents and girlfriend. Good lord," he said, pausing at the door. "You have *any* idea of stuff he was working on?"

"Only the usual things," Jeff said. "County commission meetings and budgets and other business. Nothing special that I know of."

"Ok," the sheriff said. "Work as fast as you can."

***

"Ed? This is Cousin Opal. Did, uh, did…did something happen last night?"

"Shut the hell up. Are you crazy, woman, callin me with sompin like that? Nothin happened. I'll call you if there's sompin to talk about," slamming the receiver in the phone cradle so hard it bounced back onto the table in his office. He grabbed it and jammed it in place.

CHAPTER EIGHTY-FIVE

"The sheriff asked you if Jimmy was working on something that might have gotten him killed?" Susan sounded panicked.

"Not exactly. They're looking for any indication this wasn't just an accident. He asked if I knew what Jimmy was working on. He wants me to go through his desk and files. Bobby Ray had already told me to do that; seems logical to do in an investigation. I sit, sat, right across from him. We covered some stories together. They don't have autopsy results yet and it sounds like there may not be any definitive evidence. They may never know if he slipped and fell or if someone killed him."

There was no sound on the line.

"Oh, God," he said, "I hope this has nothing to do with Isiah's murder…or with me."

CHAPTER EIGHTY-SIX

Jeff arranged Jimmy's notebooks in a chronological pile on the long table, guessing about some of them since Jimmy wasn't meticulous about dating his notes.

He riffled through the other stacks of paper he'd retrieved from Jimmy's desk top and drawers. It all appeared routine and of little interest; press releases from various companies and government bodies, miscellaneous clippings of stories Jimmy had written that might need future follow-ups.

Taking the most-recent notebook, Jeff began reading, nursing a bottle of RC Cola and occasionally reaching for a potato chip from the small bag half-spilled on the table. An hour later he'd identified nothing that seemed relevant.

At first, the second notebook seemed just as routine, but eleven pages into it were notations that popped off the page because they made no sense. There were no dates or indications of what subject or story they might refer to.

MD-fe-J (JB)

RIB

MIJ

MJ

UPAA

What's this stuff? Abbreviations for something? For what? Coded references?

If so, why coded? Where's the key? Was he hiding something so that only he understood? If so, why? Is this related to Jimmy's confrontation about my knowing Isiah? What could it mean?

***

At that moment Wayne Jenkins, a general assignment reporter, came in and slid two sheets of paper toward Jeff. "Here are carbons of my story from the Coroner's office. Thought you might want to know about this. Gotta run," he said, disappearing back into the hallway.

***

Reporter's Death Ruled Accidental

Coroner Abbot Simpson issued a preliminary ruling today that Herald reporter Jimmy Waller died accidentally during Tuesday night's heavy rainstorm.

"There's no indication whatever of foul play," Simpson said. "The carport where the accident happened was very wet from the storm. He may have been hurrying to get into the house and out of the rain.

"He apparently slipped and fell against the wood work bench in the carport, hitting his head and fatally injuring him," Hawthorne said. "There was blood on the edge of the bench. Full autopsy results will be available in about a week."

Waller was found dead Wednesday morning on the carport's concrete floor with a severe gash on his right temple. He had been a reporter at the Fowlerville Herald beginning as a sports writer while in ninth grade. He graduated from Fowlerville High School...

***

Jeff returned to his list, trying to make sense of it, looking for relationships or patterns, trying to decipher even one item, hoping that would provide a key to the rest.

MD-fe-J (JB)
RIB

MIJ
MJ
UPAA

What could MD-fe-J(JB) possibly mean? And "RIB?" Whose rib? None of this makes sense? MJ? Four "J's"? A reference to me? But "JB?" as if that explains the "J" preceding. What's the "B" for? "MIJ?" '

He read and re-read through the list hoping to recognize anything. More RC Cola. More staring at the far wall, mind flickering but not able to translate the cryptic notes. He scanned the list again and finally focused on the last entry.

UPAA.

UP could mean Upper Peninsula. AA could be auto club or Alcoholics Anonymous or, oh shit, Ann Arbor. That's it. Two references to Michigan. These must be notations from Jimmy's tracking down that I knew Isiah. Maybe MIJ means "Michigan Isiah Jeff." But "RIB?" Wait, "IB" must mean Isiah Booker. That's it. The "R" could make it "Rev. Isiah Booker." Of course. Hot damn.

MD-FE-J(JB)

He stared at the entry for a long time, guessing at the "J" and "JB" parts but couldn't figure it out. He started again at "MD" and finally guessed "Michigan Daily" which then quickly made a possible connection with "FE" as "feature" and the "J" as referring to himself. But "JB" remained opaque and then there it was. "JB" was probably John Bolton, the young Michigan Daily student who may have read the feature to Jimmy over the phone.

He was referring to checks he was making of Isiah's Michigan connections, which is how he found out I knew and had written about Isiah. Were these cryptic references a way to avoid any explicit information in case someone saw the list? Are there actual notes expanding on the list? Is this just all a short-hand system that he used? Nothing like that in the other notebook.

He riffled quickly through seven more notebooks without seeing another list or indication of short-hand or coding.

Seems to be just this one topic. Maybe more details somewhere with specific references that could lead to me. Maybe he kept sensitive stuff at home. What if the sheriff or someone finds details? How can I explain? Should I destroy this notebook? Will the coroner's ruling end the investigation?

He stood and retrieved his coat from a chair where he'd tossed it. He picked up the notebook with the cryptic notes and put it in his jacket. Then he slung it over his shoulder, walked to the parking lot and put the jacket and notebook in his trunk.

Hiding evidence? Did I just jump into quicksand?

* * *

Someone killed Jimmy. That was no accident. I don't care what the autopsy shows. He was killed because he was looking into Isiah's murder...because of me. How can I live with that? I'm going to stop those racist bastards from murdering more innocent people. I'm risking everything for that...but Jimmy's dead because of me...Am I making things worse? Am I really only thinking of deterrence? I hate these people. I want to kill them. I will kill them. Isn't that vengeance? Is it ok to want revenge if it also scares murderous racists away from violence? Will that actually happen? Jimmy was innocent and he's dead. Oh, God, I wanted it to be an accident. What god was I praying to? Right this second I want revenge. Goddammit. That's not my mission. Sometimes my lust for revenge overwhelms my head, but I know bringing justice to cold-blooded racist murderers is a good thing. We have to kill the enemy in a war. This is war. Everyone knows that. Am I fooling myself? Which self?

CHAPTER EIGHTY-SEVEN

Ed Bryant dried dinner dishes as Claire washed and put them in a rubber rack in the right-hand sink.

"Eddie and I should be home before nine," she said, "particularly since the kids will be there and it's a school night. No regular PTA business this time."

"I'll probly still be shufflin inventory cards," he said. "I hate this crap but gotta do it," putting a dried glass on the counter, then moving it to the kitchen table next to the Jim Beam bottle he'd already put there.

Claire scrubbed harder at the last pan in the soapy dishwater, her lips tight, eyes almost shut. She disliked it when he drank alone. She wondered if she'd return to find him sleeping, face on the table and she'd have to wake him, hoping he'd sluggishly wander down the hallway to bed. Or if, when she came home, he'd be awake and in a rage over something she could never understand.

Eddie burst into the room, hair still damp and freshly combed, his six-year-old body exploding with excited energy.

"Can we go now, Ma? Can we? You ready?"

"Almost. Did you brush your teeth? Your hair looks nice."

"Yep," he said, either answering her question or agreeing with her observation.

"Hey," Ed said, flipping the towel over his shoulder and squatting down, arms out to his son. "Come 'er."

The boy ran to his father, colliding with him, almost pushing him over backwards with his exuberance.

"Hey, Eddie, ya know what you need? A little aftershave so you'll smell real nice and grownup. Whata ya think?"

"Yay," the boy yelled, running down the hall to the bathroom, his father close behind. It was a ritual usually reserved for Sunday mornings before the three of them headed for church.

In the bathroom Ed knelt on one knee, pulling the top off a white bottle of Old Spice as his son closed his eyes, pointing his face up toward his father who gently patted a few drops on the boy's soft checks.

A few minutes later Claire and Eddie left and Ed, at the kitchen table, poured Jim Beam as the sound of the Buick disappeared down the driveway. He reached for the stack of blue inventory cards.

CHAPTER EIGHTY-EIGHT

The knock on the front door surprised him. He glanced through the window at the shadows of dusk fading into night. The clock said seven-twenty, way too early for Claire and Eddie to be back. They'd only been gone 30 minutes. Probably that stupid paperboy, he thought. Another late delivery and it's not even collection week. He scraped the chair back and headed for the front door. He paused when he arrived at the solid, windowless door.

"Who's it?"

"Roy," the muffled voice answered.

"What the hell you want now?" he snarled, yanking the door open.

The man in the doorway pointed the gun right at Bryant's face, stopping his instinctive movement toward the holstered pistol on his belt under his shirt, over his right hip.

"Inside," the gunman said. "Back," he said, his arm extended, gesturing with the gun. Ed retreated two steps and the gunman moved forward, closing the door behind him. The man glanced at the door long enough to spot and click the button that would prevent a key from opening the lock from the outside.

"Over there and sit," the flat command emphasized with a jerky wave of the gun.

Bryant backed up and sat in one of the kitchen chairs. He's just a kid, he thought. And white. A holdup? No, that would be at the store. He noticed then, for the first time, the black hat and gloves. And the dark clothing. Terror wrapped his body.

He's the letter writer. Shit. Why in Christ did I open the door without being sure?

***

His grandfather's gun was heavy in Jeff's hand and he felt as if he were dreaming. It was finally happening. He had seen Mrs. Bryant and the boy leave and guessed from their clothes that they were going somewhere for at least a few hours. Long enough.

"You know who I am?" Jeff asked, his voice and face masked by a lack of expression.

"Whata you want?" Bryant barked. "I got no money here so it's senseless to hold me up."

"This isn't a holdup and you know it. You remember my letter?"

"Letter?"

"Don't act stupid, Mr. Bryant," Jeff snapped. "I'm here because you murdered a friend of mine and because a jury of your redneck friends set you free while he rots in his grave."

"We was acquitted," Ed shouted. "We're innocent. They couldn't convict us of that shooting because we didn't do it. Seven men testified for us and every one a them told the same story."

Jeff's began speaking so rapidly that it sounded like a single sentence.

"You erased a life that wasn't finished being lived. The man you killed was worth a thousand of you. I'm going to kill you to make others afraid to do what you did; that's the only way to stop this insanity; no one will know *who* killed you and your friends but they'll know *why;* people will realize someone is bringing justice when the courts are corrupt; I want you to know that. You understand? Do you understand?" jabbing the pistol almost into Bryant's nose.

Jeff was breathless, as if he'd been running.

Bryant sounded calm even though his eyes were locked on the gun barrel and he seemed to be talking to it.

"All I unnerstand is that you bust your way in here with lies about stuff that's been decided in court. You can't come in my house and kill me in cold blood and claim it's for justice. You're trying to take revenge," Bryant voice was rising, face flushed. "I didn't do nothin! We had witnesses! You've no right," looking up at Jeff.

"Oh, you're guilty all right," Jeff said, over-pronouncing the words. "You and your friends slaughtered an innocent man. Three bullets into an unarmed man. What did he say to you? Which one of you shot him?"

Bryant sat numbly, desperation holding as effectively as ropes.

"Which one of you shot him?" Jeff repeated, shouting now. "Answer me you miserable cracker asshole. Who?"

"You got this all wrong. We was in court. We was cleared there."

"Did he fight you? Why'd you kill him? He wasn't here to hurt anyone."

"They was all down here to stir up trouble and that's what they got. But we didn't do it."

"I'm not going to debate you," Jeff said, straightening up and extending the gun arm again, keeping the old revolver aimed at Bryant's right eye. "I want you to understand this and I think you do although you're trying to pretend that you don't. You cheated the world of a good man and I'm sure you won't hesitate to do it again. There are others like you and I'm going to use your life to discourage them. Did you kill Jimmy?"

Bryant moved slightly in the chair. He dropped his hands to his sides.

"You murdered Jimmy, too, didn't you?"

"Coroner said that was an accident. Waller slipped in the rain. That old carport leaks like a sieve."

"How do you know what that carport is like in the rain?" Jeff said. "You were there. You killed him."

They stared at each other.

"Tell me how it was with Isiah," Jeff said. "Tell me about killing him."

Bryant continued staring silently at him.

"Tell me," Jeff said again, more demandingly. He stepped closer to the seated Bryant.

"I can't tell you anything when I don't..."

"Shut your goddamn mouth," Jeff screamed. "Shut up!"

His face was in flames, as if sunburned. He felt himself losing control and his scream came from someone else; the voice harsh and ugly. He took two steps closer to Bryant. He wanted to smash the gun into his face. He visualized the man pointing a gun at Isiah and pulling the trigger. How did Isiah look? Scared, like Bryant looked now?

Each man's eyes focused only on the other, as if trying to see into each other's soul; each seeing the other as unrecognizable, foreign, as incomprehensible as creatures from different planets.

Jeff felt his anger subsiding even as he realized the danger was growing. He had come with a mission, a crusade. How long had he been inside the house? When were the others returning? The time was now.

Do it. Now. Pull the trigger. Now. Get it over with. Finish it. This is war. Do it now now now.

He took another step forward, their feet almost touching, dimly realizing that moving closer was forcing the issue, making the decision, determining exactly when was now now now now.

The knock on the door was loud as a thunder clap.

As Jeff's head involuntarily jerked briefly to the side, toward the door, Bryant reached behind him for his own gun, pulling the pistol from the holster under his shirt as Jeff's head snapped back toward him.

Jeff saw the arm moving and the pistol coming from behind Bryant and lunged to grab it with his left hand, forgetting his own gun. Bryant's gun came forward and up as the force of Jeff's lunge jammed it straight up under Bryant's chin.

CRACK!

The small pistol in both their hands barely recoiled, the shot scarcely louder than breaking a small tree branch. Jeff yanked the gun from Bryant's hand, surprised when there was no resistance. Bryant's face was inches from Jeff, who saw amazement melting from the man's face, as if made of wax. Jeff staggered back, still holding Bryant's gun and leveling his own now-remembered pistol to cover the man who was sliding sideways, his eyes open but expressionless. He tilted and hit the floor on his shoulder, sprawling backward, feet pointing at Jeff, blood leaking from his chin and spreading along his neck onto the floor. The acrid smell of gunpowder assaulted Jeff's nose. He stepped left, watching the unmoving form. He had never seen anyone die before. Bryant's chest was unmoving.

After a few seconds, Jeff moved closer, trying to avoid the blood river, bent and dropped Bryant's pistol by his right hand. He shuddered and stood up, still staring at the body. He felt detached, as if only an observer.

He almost shot me. He nearly killed me.

He looked again at the blood, light-headed but unable to look away.

Who knocked on the door?

The question aroused him from his stupor. He glanced at the kitchen window but the black night revealed nothing. His legs wobbled as he went to the door and listened. No sound except his own pounding heart.

They must have heard the shot. I've got to get out of here. I've got to get away from this.

He clicked off the lock and looked back at the dead man and the blood. Sticking the gun into the top of his pants, he opened the door, peering cautiously in all directions. No one. He stepped out and pulled the door closed behind him. The lock snapped shut. He took a step across the porch toward the darkness when his right foot brushed something. A folded newspaper lying where it had bounced off the door.

He darted across the porch, skipping the stairs and jumping to the ground, landing in full stride. He sprinted up the long driveway toward the blacktop road. No car lights in either direction. Running hard.

Just as he reached the road, the gun fell from his pants and clattered to the ground. He stopped, eyes searching frantically. Nothing. Then he saw a slight shine in the grass at the edge of the driveway. The pistol. He snatched it up realizing at the same moment that a car's headlights from the right had caused the reflection; still at a distance but in his flight path.

He threw himself behind the short row of bushes lining the driveway, flat on his belly, head in the dirt, the gun-less gloved hand covering his face. The headlights were practically there. He peeked through his fingers enough to see the car pass the driveway and continue down the road.

He pushed to his feet before the taillights vanished, squeezed between the bushes, scrambled down and then up the shallow ditch paralleling the road and dashed down the blacktop toward his car, a mile away. Soon he was gasping from the insane pace, one hand bizarrely waving the gun, dashing through blackness, feet pounding asphalt.

Finally: DIXON COUNTY Department of Parks.

He ran more slowly on the gravel path to the picnic tables, his car at the back by the portable toilet. He leaned on the car roof trying to catch his breath. Looking momentarily at the sky, stars flickered, a slice of moon riding through the clouds. His trembling hand couldn't find the lock on the first two tries but finally the door opened and he slammed it behind him in a panic to extinguish the interior light, which flashed briefly. He pushed the door lock down and slumped forward, forehead on the steering wheel.

Crack and you're dead.

His mind ricocheted hysterically in his brain, like the ball in a pinball machine that never stops. He wanted to cry. Then laugh.

Stop it! Get hold of yourself. Where? Great advice but where do you grab? How do you get a grip on yourself?

His laugh grew and filled the car until he was shaking with great gasping sobs of laughter.

Bang. You're dead.

His ribs ached with unstoppable, hysterical laughter.

Stop it. Stop it. Stop it. Goddamn it, stop it.

He put the key in the ignition and the engine sound focused his mind. Partway to the boarding house he steered onto a small side road he had selected earlier and, with the aid of a flashlight, wrapped the gun in his gloves and replaced it in the metal box under the car.

Back in his room, he closed the door. The persisting, hysterical laughter tried to bubble up again. In the tiny, dark bathroom he flooded his face with water, holding it against his eyes with his hands. He gulped two glasses of the luke-warm water, choking, then leaned forward, hands gripping the sides of the sink, arms stiff, face inches from the old mirror and barely visible in the dim light leaking in from the bedroom.

Who are you? he asked the unfamiliar visage looking back at him. *Who the hell are you?*

He flopped backward on the bed, still wearing his clothes and shoes. It was the loneliest he'd ever felt.

I did it! The sonuvabitch is dead. Just like Isiah. God, that was horrible. All that blood. And his eyes...My life's ending, too, spiraling down. I've jumped off the cliff and there's no unjumping now.

He stayed awake until early morning when sleep finally closed his eyes but sent him only nightmares.

As he ran he stepped on a stick and a sharp breaking noise released a torrent of blood which splashed on him and he kept running but the blood kept coming and it was catching him.

CHAPTER EIGHTY-NINE

Wayne Jenkins dashed through the back door shouting. "Ed Bryant committed suicide last night," causing everyone in the newsroom, including Bobby Ray, to surround his desk as he arranged his notes and began to type.

***

Ed Bryant Found Fatally Shot,
Coroner Simpson Suspects Suicide

Edward P. Bryant, 41, well-known local businessman and a central figure in last year's sensational murder trial, was found dead in his home Friday night with a bullet wound to the head.

County Coroner Abbott Simpson issued a preliminary ruling this morning that Bryant's death was suicide. Simpson said Bryant apparently shot himself under the chin with a small-caliber automatic pistol that he owned. He added that autopsy results will take several days.

There were no signs of a struggle or of forced entry, Sheriff Lanny Purdy said. The sheriff said the house was locked when the victim's wife and the couple's young son returned from a PTA meeting. Bryant's body was found on the kitchen floor, the death weapon by his hand.

Mrs. Bryant could give no reason for her husband to kill himself,

Sheriff Purdy said. He added that Mrs. Bryant said her husband had "seemed fine," and had not been despondent. "I would have known," the sheriff quoted Mrs. Bryant, who was unavailable for further comment.

The sheriff said his department will continue its investigation into the apparent suicide.

Bryant was owner and operator of Bryant's Hardware and Sporting Goods of Fowlerville, a family business for 45 years. He had apparently been working on the store's inventory reports just before his death. It's unknown if the store was having financial problems.

Bryant was one of three Fowlerville men who were tried and acquitted last summer after the shooting death of a Philadelphia-area Negro Baptist minister who was part of an 18-member team from out of state trying to register Negro voters in Dixon County. Rev. Isiah R. Booker's body was found in a shallow grave on…

***

Jeff grabbed a copy as soon as the presses thundered in the huge pressroom only a brick wall from the main offices. He took the paper to the men's room, secured himself in a stall and read the story. He read it again and stood up, reaching behind him to flush the toilet even though he hadn't used it.

Then he noticed the dime-size spot of dried blood on the toe of his right shoe. He dipped toilet paper in the bowl and scrubbed the shoe again and again, until it appeared cleansed. He dried the spot with more toilet paper and flushed again.

That evening, on the way home he stopped at a small store for a few groceries plus another copy of the Herald. He drove to the Sinclair station on the north edge of town to buy four out-of-town newspapers for more reports on Ed Bryant's death. Back in his room he carefully folded two copies of the Herald, as if they were valuable documents, putting them in one of the suitcases in the dark, back corner of his closet, zipping them into a small area designed to keep shirts separate from the main compartment. Now he was locked in his room re-reading the story for the fourth time.

Suicide. Not what I planned. Do the other two think it's suicide? Probably not. Maybe Ryser and Price will be scared enough to tell the police about the letters. Maybe Bryant already did. No rumors of that. Maybe the story in the paper is a lie; cops saying suicide to throw me off. Maybe a trap. Suicide. He shot himself. I didn't even really pull the trigger. He had a gun. He took the letter seriously. That wimpy pharmacist looks like he'd call the cops. They can't guard him forever. I can't leave it now. It doesn't mean anything yet. Gotta finish my mission. It can't end up looking like he killed himself. Maybe this is good. A suicide will divert attention. As long as when it's over everyone knows someone delivered justice. Eventually, everyone's got to realize Bryant was killed for his crime. And the others too. What are those two thinking? Probably shitting their pants. They'll really be on guard.

He dampened a wash cloth from the bathroom then knelt on his left knee to rub furiously at the toe of his right shoe.

CHAPTER NINETY

Roy was trying to convince himself not to leave town but he desperately wanted to be somewhere else, anywhere else, as long as it was far away; almost hysterically afraid to be here, in his own kitchen. He had two, almost-full suitcases spread open on his bed, the clothes thrown in.

Ed's dead and they're coming after all of us, Roy thought, the afternoon Herald sprawled on the floor while he listened to unanswered rings on Rollin Price's home phone. Roy's panic was expanding in his head. Through the window, night's cloak was already closing in.

Maybe something's already happened to him. Maybe they're coming after me right now. Maybe they're already here. They're going to kill us all. Ed wouldn't have shot himself. Whoever sent those letters killed Ed and made it look like suicide. Where in God's name is Roll?

The soft knock on his back door three feet away was deafening. He stood up, holding the still-ringing phone.

"Roy, it's me, Roll. Open up."

Sounds like Roll. But what if...oh, Christ!

He put the receiver in the cradle, pulled the revolver from his holster and went to the door, standing well to one side, fearful of shots coming through the door.

"It's Roll. Open up. Hurry."

Leaning toward the door as little as possible, leaving the night chain in place, Ryser unsnapped the lock and opened the door a crack, prepared to shoot if it wasn't Roll.

"Let me in," Roll said, trying to push the door open, stopped by the chain.

Thank you, God!

Roy unfastened the chain and Roll was inside, brushing Roy aside. Roy slammed the door shut, locked and re-chained it before either man said a word. Roll turned to the kitchen table and sat, looking at Roy with despair, eyebrows and jowls sagging, eyes darting around the room.

"I called the drugstore and they said you'd gone home sick." He stared at Roy. "You look like you don't believe Ed shot himself," he said.

"Do you? Do you?" Roy's demanding voice a mixture of hope and fear.

"I can't imagine Ed killing himself. I…."

"Me, neither," Roy cut in. "He wouldn't never quit like that. He'd shoot you or me, but not himself."

"I don't know anyone I'd be more surprised at than Ed."

"That's what I think, too," Ryser said, walking in little circles in the tight space of the old kitchen. "I just don't believe it. Somebody got in there and killed him with his own gun."

"Well, that's pretty far-fetched too," Roll said softly, fisted hands on the table. "Ed's unlikely…was pretty unlikely to be shot with his own gun without a fight. The paper said there was no sign of a fight. Ed was just lying there dead with his gun practically in his hand. He was shot right under the chin. Who coulda done that to Ed? It sure looked like suicide from what the paper said."

"Yeah, well, I don't believe it," Roy said, dropping into a chair opposite Price.

"Me neither."

"Oh shit, I hope to hell he killed himself."

"Yeah."

"He wouldna killed himself in his own kitchen for Claire and Little Eddie to find him. He wouldna done that."

Roll stared at Ryser for long seconds. "We got no choice now. We gotta figger Ed was killed by whatever sent them letters. We gotta be really careful."

"Damn you, Roll. I know that. I want to know how. We can't protect ourselves and you know it. If they got Ed in his own house they can get us. We don't even know if it's a 'they' or a 'him' what done it. We gotta get out of here. I ain't gonna just sit and wait for somethin to happen. I'm goin nuts. This is so stupid; all because of that goddam nigger. I'm getting out and I'm not even going to tell *you* where. I can sell the store without ever coming back here. I want to keep living and if getting outta here is what it takes, then I'm gonna be gone just as soon as I can get that way."

"That's great for you, but I got a family and besides, ain't no letter-writing, nigger-lover gonna run me outta my own town," Roll said. "They don't know what really happened. Even if somebody killed Ed they're gonna have one hell of a time killin me."

"Yeah," Roy said sarcastically, "that's probably what Ed thought and right now he's stretched out in Blackburn's funeral parlor. Not me! I'm packed. Goodbye. I'm never going to see you again."

"Maybe we should talk to the sheriff," Roll said. "Or Cecil."

Doesn't pay me no attention. Just like Ed.

"We can tell Lanny about them letters," Roll continued, "get us some protection. Tell him we need his deputies to guard us. Tell him to find out who sent them letters. Maybe we ought to make the whole thing public, scare away whoever's doin this." Roll looked hopefully at Ryser. "Where are the letters? Didn't Ed keep all a them? Maybe Purdy has found 'em."

"Don't matter," Roy said. "Lanny can't protect us all the time or forever. Whoever sent the letters had no way of knowing we wouldn't go to the sheriff right from the start. Maybe they thought we did. Maybe they thought we would, maybe even hoped we would, get some publicity. Nobody can protect us forever. You do what you want. I'm getting out."

"Look," Roll said quietly, "why don't you hole up for a few days while we think of something. Maybe Lanny'll find something at Ed's place. Maybe they'll catch somebody. Maybe it *was* suicide. At least wait till Simpson's finished with the autopsy. See if anything turns up. Be real careful."

"They shot Ed in his own kitchen, with his own gun," Roy repeated.

Ryser picked an empty beer bottle off the floor next to the table. Raising it questioningly at Roll and getting a nod, he put the bottle in the trash under the sink and got two more from the refrigerator, prying off the caps and putting one on the table in front of Roll. Roy drank in hurried gulps, walking around the kitchen again.

"Ok," Roy said, "Maybe I'll think on it for a day or two, but I'm not going anywhere at night and I don't think I'm changing my mind. And I might already be gone the next time you call. As long as I'm here, no sombitch better come around after dark unless they're looking to get shot."

Roll left his unfinished beer on the table and went to the door, removing the chain. As Ryser let him out, gun in his right hand, anxious to close the door, Roll looked down the alley in both directions. "I wonder who he is and where he is," he said softly.

"Or they."

"Yeah," slipping into the alley and his car, which started immediately and moved quickly down the alley before the headlights came on. Roy didn't see Roll enter the car because the door was locked and chained the instant his friend cleared it.

CHAPTER NINETY-ONE

"I need you to interview Ed Bryant's wife," Bobby Ray said the next afternoon, suddenly appearing next to Jeff hunched over his typewriter.

Jeff looked at him, his face frozen, trying not to look shocked.

"Me?"

"Yeah," Bobby Ray said. "And right away. I know them from church and I've talked to Claire. She's pretty shook up but she agreed to talk about her husband if we can get there in the next twenty minutes and promise to be gone before five."

Jeff glanced at the wall clock. "It's ten after four already," he said, standing up.

"Right, so get going. Here's the address. It's about 15 minutes from here, not far out of town. She wouldn't agree to photos so just get what you can. Maybe she has a family picture she'll let us run with the story. Ask her about Ed's life, growing up in a well-known family, son of the famous Bull. If there's time and she seems ok, ask what she thinks happened, if he was down lately, under stress of any kind, although she already told the sheriff he seemed ok. Everything you can think of between here and there," he said, turning away. "Go," over his shoulder.

OhMyGodOhMyGod

Jeff grabbed a notebook and walked briskly, but in a daze, to his car. He already knew how to get to the Bryant house.

Back in that kitchen? Ask the widow questions? Without me she wouldn't be a widow. How'd you feel when you found him, Mrs. Bryant? You know, after I killed him, Mrs. Bryant. Did your son see his dad's blood on the floor, Mrs. Bryant? Did he see his father's blank eyes staring at the ceiling? Do you think he'll ever forget that, Mrs. Bryant? Will you? Will you be able to stand living in house? What are your plans for the rest of your life, Mrs. Bryant? And for your son's life?

She opened the door at his first knock, her face ravaged by grief and tears. She looked questioningly at him, but was already moving aside so he could step into the kitchen where he'd been less than two days ago.

"Mrs. Bryant, I'm Jeff Martindale from the Herald and I'm so sorry to intrude on you at this terrible time. I'm sorry for your grief. I'll be as brief as I can," not looking at the room, desperately wanting to flee.

She nodded, turned her back to the kitchen, where cooking smells filled the air and three women were chopping and stirring. He followed Mrs. Bryant to the living room through an archway on the right.

Don't look! The blood must be gone. Did she mop it up?

She sat in one of two chairs flanking a small table, her hands stretched along her thighs. She waved Jeff to the other. She still hadn't spoken, her eyes focused a thousand miles behind Jeff.

"Mrs. Bryant," Jeff said, her face shifting to him, eyes blotchy red, squinting as if into a bright sun. "Tell me about your husband. What did he like to do? What were his favorite things?"

"Ed's a family man," she said, glancing at him. "He loves his family. He's…was," her eyes moistening and spilling over, voice trapped in a throat that couldn't swallow. She stared again into the silent far distance over Jeff's shoulder.

"He doted on little Eddie," she said finally, voice almost inaudible. "Just before we left for the PTA meeting he put some of his after-shave on Eddie. He does that before church, makes a ritual of it. Just pats a few drops on Eddie's little cheeks. Eddie loves that, it makes him feel grownup. Ed took him fishing and went to his Kid's League games. He…Ed's…a good husband and father. He grew up with a tough but loving father and I think he's a softer version of Bull," her voice hoarse, tears free-flowing again.

"When we came home and found..." She sat without speaking for several minutes; Jeff unable to say anything. Finally, "I'm sorry," she said. "I can't do this. I just can't. I…." standing now, her face beseeching him. "Maybe some other time. Please tell Bobby Ray…"

He lurched to his feet, tears in his eyes. "It's ok, Mrs. Bryant, I understand," he gasped, desperately trying to hold back his own sobs, refusing to even glance at the table or floor as he moved through the kitchen close behind her to the door. She opened it and nodded helplessly, both hands trying to wipe away the free-running tears staining her cheeks.

Then he was outside, stumbling down the porch stairs half-blinded by his own tears, sprinting to the car.

CHAPTER NINETY-TWO

He began talking immediately.

"Have they reported there what happened here last night? Have you heard?" He was trying not to sound as frantic as he felt.

"Of course," Susan said, her voice soft but agitated. "Don called an hour ago. He's scared that…I hoped you'd call. What happened?"

"Well," he said, his voice so flat and low that she had to listen carefully, "the police and coroner say Bryant shot himself under the chin with his own pistol in his own kitchen while his wife and son were at a PTA meeting. That's pretty much all that's public."

"Are the police speculating that this might be related to Isiah's murder?"

"I don't think so. The Herald story mentioned the trial as part of his past, but didn't quote anyone saying his death might be related to that. His wife said he hadn't seemed depressed and that she would have known if he had been. And she told police the door was locked when she got home. And the guy who delivers the Herald threw the paper on the porch within an hour of when the shooting apparently occurred and he said there were no vehicles in the yard except Bryant's pickup."

"So it definitely looks like a suicide?" she asked, speaking slowly, as if reading the question from a piece of paper.

Was that relief in her voice?

"Yeah. Yeah, it does."

They heard each other breathing on the line, neither saying anything.

Finally, whispering, she asked: "Are you ok?"

"No. I don't know what I am, but it's not ok."

"What happened?"

He heard his heart thumping in his chest, sure she could hear it. He saw the blood pooling on the floor behind Ed Bryant's head, empty eyes staring accusations at him.

"Jeff?"

"Oh, god, Susan, I was there…I was yelling at him to tell me what happened that night with Isiah and he was denying everything and…"

She interrupted. "Did you believe him?"

He continued as if he didn't hear her question, his voice quickening. "We were arguing and then he pulled a pistol from behind him and I grabbed it by the barrel and the gun fired but it was pointing at him and he fell on the floor and blood was coming from his chin and was running all over, almost to my shoes, and he…and then he was dead and his eyes were wide open looking at me and I got out of there and ran to the car and now they believe he killed himself," gasping hysterically.

"And this afternoon Bobby Ray sent me to interview Mrs. Bryant. She fell apart while I was there and…."

Their breathing merged over the line, each hearing the other as clearly as if in the same room, the tempo for each increasing as if synchronized, each afraid of their thoughts, worried about the other.

***

Dear Mom & Dad,

Everything's very busy here.

Still working about 12 hours per day but I'm learning lots. But I'm still not enjoying the humidity, ha ha.

Love, Jeff

CHAPTER NINETY-THREE

The next night he returned to his room after a Planning Commission meeting carrying the black plastic zippered pouch he used for notebooks, pens, folders with information for on-going stories. Without turning on the overhead light, he pulled a pint of Southern Comfort from the pouch and put it on the table by the upholstered chair. Retrieving a white coffee cup, he sat and twisted the bottle cap, pouring the cup half full.

He sipped, feeling the fruity warmth start in his mouth and seep down his throat.

Only a dim glow made it through the shade over the single window and the room was nearly dark. He tilted his head back against the chair and closed his eyes. He saw Ed Bryant's face, eyes open but blank, blood spreading under his head onto the kitchen floor. And his grandfather and Isiah and.... He sat up, back straight and rigid. He reached for the whiskey and swigged a mouthful from the bottle.

I did it! One-third finished! And they're not even looking for a killer! Why do I feel like shit? I didn't think I'd feel this bad. I killed a man. But he deserved it. He stole Isiah's life. He was a stone-cold murderer. And I paid him back. Made him pay. I executed him for a righteous reason. Now he can't kill anyone else. There'll be fear and panic all over the South. When it's understood what happened. I've got it started. But I killed him. More or less. No, I killed him. Without me, he'd still be alive. And without him, Isiah would still be alive and we'd be fishing together somewhere. Or talking. Or he'd be helping people register to vote. Without him, Jimmy would be alive. The big sonuvabitch deserved it; he killed Jimmy. I know he did. And, he pulled the trigger on himself. I just helped him. Maybe that's suicide. Technically suicide? You could say it was an accident. It's my fault, but it's his fault, too. I'm not sorry! Not one bit. One down, two to go. Can I do this again? Twice?

CHAPTER NINETY-FOUR

In his dream, his hands are cuffed behind him in a courtroom filled with people, mostly strangers, and a judge in a black robe, plus his father and mother, grandparents, Susan and Don. Ed Bryant is crumpled on the floor inside a chalk outline. Everyone is frozen in place, no motion except where a woman and a small boy are kneeling in the flowing blood pool growing on the courtroom's polished wood floor. Every face is contorted, every mouth open as if shouting or screaming at him but he hears no sound. He looks at his feet and sees the expanding blood engulfing his shoes but no one else's. Susan walks toward the door, Don by her side, followed by his grandfather and grandmother holding hands. His mother and father walk together, the procession looking like an exiting choir. Leaving him behind. He wakes up sweating and panting and leaps from the chair, looking wildly around the room, momentarily wondering where he is.

CHAPTER NINETY-FIVE

This far from town the cloudless night sky is black. The sliver of silvery moon can't slice open the darkness. Countless stars are tiny diamonds spilled on infinite black velvet; sparkling reminders of insignificant human mortality. The rich earthy smell of Mississippi soil is seasoned with whiffs of a distant wood fire. Despite the warm, late-summer night, he wears black pants and a long-sleeved, black t-shirt. And black gloves. His pockets are empty except for a single car key and his grandfather's pistol. A wind picks up and clouds begin invading the clear sky, moving slowly and silently, like the thoughts in his mind.

He sits on the ground, arms clutching his knees, behind low bushes clustered around trees near a garage. The luminous watch says 10:10. He's been here surrounded by shrubs since 9:30, time so slow it seems not to pass at all. He's thinking about time so intently the waiting seems eternal. He tries not to look at his watch for the hundredth time, trying to think about anything else, but he knows the dangers of losing the steely focus he needs to keep his mind from asking questions he doesn't want to answer.

He imagines that his mother and father, and Grandpa Martindale, plus Susan, can see him crouching in the dark, the revolver in his front pocket. Their voices overlap and over-flow in his head. His heart pulses out of control.

Are you going to stain my pistol with this man's blood?

Son, can you see yourself? Hiding there in the dark so you can kill someone? Please God, don't let Jeff murder this man and kill his own soul!

Jeff, I love you, but I don't understand what you're doing. Save yourself. Save us. Please!

He takes the ancient revolver from his pocket and looks at it in the dim moonlight, rubbing his thumb over it, feeling and smelling the fresh gun oil on the scarred blue-steel barrel. He hefts the heavy gun in his hand for a moment and replaces it in his pocket.

Almost an hour later, lights flicker from the right, out on the road passing the driveway a hundred feet from his hiding place. The house, about 50 feet away, has been dark since a half-hour after he crept so carefully, hunched over, sometimes on hands and knees, hoping not to hear a dog barking, into the underbrush near the detached garage.

The engine propelling the approaching headlights sounds powerful, possibly the pickup he awaits. The lights are near, winking wildly through trees along the road. He sees glimpses of the actual headlights but mostly the light is a flickering, jumping, here-then-there creature adding a fleeting, three-dimensional texture to the darkness. His heart accelerates as he hopes to see the lights turn down the long driveway to the garage, a few feet from his hiding place. This is the seventh vehicle, or maybe the eighth, to flash from tree to tree along the road. Lights sweep the driveway without pausing and then it's even darker with only the fading sound of the engine reminding him why his hands are damp with sweat and his pulse echoes in his ears.

Twenty minutes past midnight and lights flirt with the trees again. The vehicle approaches slowly, the lights reach the driveway, slow and turn onto the gravel. Through the thick band of bushes Jeff watches the lights coming closer, finally pausing about thirty feet from the garage doors, and equidistant from him, before turning slowly sideways and pausing again.

Then he sees the unilluminated lights on the car roof and SHERIFF painted on the door. His breathing stops in mid-inhalation as he points his face down, between his knees, trying to become part of the shoulder-high bushes he sits behind, hoping not to hear a car door open. No sound comes for a long minute, his lungs clamor for air, his brain desperate to see what's happening but his mind is shooting silent instructions: Don't move, don't breathe, don't move....

Tires finally crunch on the gravel as the patrol car slowly completes its u-turn, its headlights briefly flashing over his shrubbery and heading back toward the road. Jeff tilts his head upward a few inches, watching retreating taillights. Then he gulps night air into panicked lungs, his mouth dry and gasping.

A half-hour more and he crouches lower as bouncing lights briefly illuminate one side of the driveway, then the other, the driver struggling to keep the truck on a straight path. The lights sweep past him, the silhouetted truck stopping in front of the garage. As the engine dies, Jeff is already sprinting across the grass, moving quickly toward the pickup. A figure seen only in outline climbs from the truck, pausing by the front fender, head bowed and putting a steadying hand on the front fender.

Jeff slows behind the man, walking cautiously now. He pauses at the open truck door.

"Mr. Price."

The figure whirls unsteadily toward the quiet voice, half stumbling.

Jeff is startled by the silhouette's rapid movement and realizes he is too close, only a lunge away from the man, and steps back.

"Get in the truck, Mr. Price. Please don't yell, I don't want to involve your family."

The silhouette doesn't move or speak. Jeff realizes the man can see him plainly in the light reflecting from the garage door. He motions with the gun in his right hand.

"Get in."

The figure remains motionless. *Drunk?* Then it moves toward Jeff who quickly takes two more steps back and motions again with the gun. He is relieved to see the figure turn toward the truck.

"Stop," Jeff's voice firm.

The figure freezes. Jeff takes a tentative step forward.

"Put your hands on top of the truck."

The man leans forward, hands on the roof, his face looking at the gravel.

Jeff eases closer, putting his left hand on the man's shoulder, a finger tense against the pistol's trigger. His left hand pats the man's chest and sides, immediately finding the revolver tucked into the belt at the small of his back. Jeff puts the gun in his pants pocket.

"Get in. Close the door and keep your hands at the top of the steering wheel. "

As the door closes Jeff backs quickly around the front of the truck, keeping the gun pointed at Price through the windshield, seeing him clearly for the first time, seemingly staring at the steering wheel. Reaching the passenger side, Jeff opens the door, slides quickly onto the seat and closes the door, gun riveted on Price.

"Back out slowly and quietly."

Price is still staring at the steering wheel. A yeasty beer aroma perfumes the truck.

"Now!"

Price glances briefly at Jeff and the gun, starts the engine, puts the truck in gear and backs up, twisting around to see out the rear window to turn around. Jeff's finger tenses against the trigger. Then they're at the road and the truck slows.

"Left," Jeff says, motioning with the gun away from town. "Slowly."

Price speaks for the first time. "You the one what sent them letters?" His voice low and gravelly, as if he needs to clear his throat.

"Yes."

"You kilt Ed?"

"He was trying to kill me at the time. He pulled the trigger himself. He didn't mean to shoot himself. But I went there to shoot him and he got shot."

"You gonna kill me?"

Jeff is unprepared for the stark question.

"Yes."

The truck cab shrinks; they are less than two feet apart. Neither speaks. Headlights pierce the blackness. In about a mile Jeff spots the small dirt road he's looking for.

"Turn right."

Five minutes later the rough dirt road ends at an old dump, thousands of cans winking in the headlights. Small, bright beads shine, then disappear and reappear as dark forms scurry out of the invading lights.

"Turn it off," Jeff commands.

Price switches off the engine.

"And the lights," Jeff says.

The dark silence covers them both.

The angry speech Jeff has mentally rehearsed for months stalls in his throat.

He's one of the killers, possibly the one who pulled the trigger. It was his gun. Make him suffer and grovel and beg so he'll know he's not the man Isiah was.

"Well?" Price says suddenly.

Jeff is so startled he flinches.

"Shut your goddam mouth," he snaps.

"You think I helped kill that nigra minister," Price's voice flat. He stares at Jeff's face, barely visible in the darkness.

"Did you?"

"No."

"Who did?"

"I wasn't there. We proved that in court," his voice calm.

"Who did kill him?"

"I told you. I wasn't there. I swear to God."

Anger and frustration collide in Jeff's mind. "The same crap Bryant gave me," he spits. "Swear to God?" he mocks. "What god could *you* know and still kill a man like Isiah? You piece of shit. It makes no difference whether you tell me the truth or not...except that I want to know because the man you killed was a good friend and a great man."

"You're kiddin me and yourself," Price says, a defiant tone edging his voice. "You goddamn well *do* care. If you're right and I was at the killin then shootin me will keep you from ever knowin what you want."

"You admit being there?"

"No, goddamn it! I wasn't there. You're talking about doing to me just what you claim I did to your nigra."

"You warped sonuvabitch. *My nigra.* Your bigoted brain can't even imagine the truth. We were *friends.* He was the best man I ever knew. I didn't *own* him. And stop saying nigra. It's bullshit. The word you mean is nigger, so say nigger. It's time to tell the truth. Cut the crap and the denials. We both know you were there.

"I wasn't. I ain't never kilt nobody. Never!"

"Watching or helping is just as bad as shooting."

"I ain't never seen no one kilt neither."

"Was it your gun that killed Isiah?"

"I don't know."

"You lying sack of shit. How could you not know? You know why I brought you here? Because a dump is a good place for you to end up."

"What if you're wrong?" Price's voice low and calm, still gravelly.

Jeff stares at the cluttered dashboard; an open Marlboro pack, sunglasses, a short pencil, two ballpoint pens and scraps of paper, a coffee mug wedged in the corner left of the steering wheel. Raindrops begin sliding down the glass.

"What if you got this all wrong?" Price repeats.

"I don't. It's obvious what you racist hillbillies did. It took seven liars to get you acquitted. Actually, under southern justice you were never in danger of being convicted, no matter the facts. I'm bringing justice to you. You know what good you're going to accomplish?"

"I ain't good at riddles."

"You know what people like you will think when you three are all dead?"

"They'll think somebody took revenge on us for somethin I didn't do."

"No. They're going to be too damned scared to murder people. They're going to realize they can't get away with murdering black people and civil rights workers. Those cowards are going to figure out that some unknown someone delivered *real* justice. And this is the best part. By dying, you're going to help protect the very kind of people you murdered. Pretty ironic huh? Does it makes you shit your pants to think about it?

"You're nuts."

"No, I'm not. It would be easier if I were. But I'm not and it's going to cost me a lot. It already has. It may cost my life. But I'm going to do it, and I'm going get away with it, so other cowards like you know someone is around with a gun when Lady Justice gets fucked southern style."

Price stares at Jeff, then his eyes drop to the old pistol, dimly visible in the shadows and aimed directly at his chest. "It won't work. They'll catch you and it'll all be for nuthin. You're throwin your life away. And you'll be more guilty of murder than me because I ain't never kilt nobody. And I ain't never helped nobody kill nobody neither."

"Don't deny it again," Jeff said. "That's bullshit. I'm not throwing my life away. A valuable life has already been thrown away by you and your worthless racist friends. I'm going to guarantee that Isiah's life wasn't wasted. You're going to give the only thing you've got that's worth spit."

"You got no right to decide who lives and who dies."

"Neither did you!" Jeff shouting, fury heating his face.

"I didn't kill nobody! Never!"

"You bastards are all alike. You won't even admit guilt on your deathbed."

"For God's sake. I didn't kill nobody," Price was pleading now. "Didn't you ever think you could be wrong? I *was* playing poker that night. I shouldn't have been arrested at all. The jury was right. We proved it."

"I think the jurors didn't need any so-called evidence. Everything was right except the verdict. The jurors damned well knew you sonsabitches were guilty, they just didn't care. But I care. And I'm doing something about it." He felt the bile stinging his throat as if he might throw up.

"You're wrong." Price turns slightly to look out windshield, into the blackness. "You're going to regret this the rest of your life."

"I'm already regretting it, but not for the reasons you think. I have other regrets. Lots of 'em. You murdered a good and decent man. You've kept him from spending his life doing good things for people. And all because you couldn't, and still can't, see him as a human being; just like you. Only better than you." Jeff's voice rises again, tears streaming down his cheeks.

Price reaches for his cigarettes on the dashboard.

The blast overflows the truck. Jeff is momentarily blinded by the flash and deafened by the sound; the harsh smell of gunpowder stings his nose.

Then he sees Price slammed up against the driver's door, his face turned to Jeff, eyes piercing. They stare at each other. Neither moves. Jeff sees Price's right hand pressed just under his armpit, blood seeping through his shirt and between his fingers.

"You're wrong," Price says quietly, his eyes never leaving Jeff's. "You've judged me but you're wrong."

Jeff can't speak. His ears are ringing and he leans slightly forward, left hand on the car seat, and looks down. The bloodstain on Price's shirt grows larger. Jeff raises his eyes to the unwavering stare of the other man. Price's face is softer now, sad and less defiant.

"Isn't it time for the truth?" Jeff's voice is barely audible to either of them.

"You don't believe the truth. Now you're a killer. You don't seem like a killer."

Price turns his head and coughs several times, the sound surprisingly quiet. He looks back at Jeff.

"Please tell me what happened." Jeff is begging, no longer furious, no longer hating the man slumped against the door, looking at him.

Price slowly raises his right hand from the bloody shirt and moves it, covering Jeff's gloved left hand on the seat between them.

Jeff can't move or look away. He sees the bloody hand on top of his. Then he feels a slight squeeze. He looks up at Price, who is watching him. Without a change of expression, Price's eyes become opaque and unseeing before closing as his head tilts slightly sideways against the window.

Jeff flings the truck door open and leaps out, stumbling briefly when his feet slam on the ground. He runs down the dirt road, pausing twice to look back before the truck dissolves in the darkness and the quickening rain.

After several minutes of full-out running, he slows and begins the lope that will take him to his car, parked on a side road a mile away.

Hut, two, three, four, hut, two, three, four, hut, yeo, three, four.

He counts the bizarre cadence. No hysterics this time. No laughing, no out of-control stream of consciousness. Hut, two, three, four. Turn here? Wrong road, hut, two, three, four, there it is, three, four, there's the car, three, four.

He kneels, attempting to clean the blood from his glove by rubbing it hard against tall grass by the road. Key from pocket and finally he's driving toward town, wipers echoing the cadence. Flap, two, three, four, flap, two, three, four.

Get to room and rinse these muddy clothes. And scrub my hands.

CHAPTER NINETY-SIX

The Plymouth rolls quietly to a stop and Jeff is out, pushing the door lock down, easing the door closed, moving quickly to the porch, carefully opening and closing the screen door, hoping the old couple is asleep, tiptoeing down the hallway, unlocking his door and slipping inside, turning on only the small reading light, blowing out his cheeks and pacing in the small space.

After a few minutes he sits on the bed and looks at the ceiling before slumping forward, eyes closed, his head and shoulders bowed, hands clasped between his knees, breathing deeply again and again. Opening his eyes, he stares without focusing at the old brown carpet between his feet. Rollin Price's face materializes from the scuffed rug, the way objects sometimes appear in clouds. Jeff blinks, lurches upright and the dead face vanishes. He strips off the black clothes and his underwear and moves back into the tiny bathroom, almost totally dark, the small white sink and stool barely visible.

Let there be light, pulling the short chain dangling in front of the mirror, momentarily blinded by the 60-watt bulb visible twice, then sees his flat, dead eyes, his lips tight and pale, hair mussed from pulling off the t-shirt--*You look like shit*--pulling the chain, pitch black again, turning sideways to shoe-horn himself into the coffin-like shower stall, trying to shut off his mind while letting the hot water run until it turns cool.

You don't believe the truth. That's what he said. Did he mean I wouldn't believe it if I heard it? Or I've heard it, but refuse to believe it? I'm a killer. And a jury. And a judge. And God? Grandpa's gun has blood on it now. And it's on me. Inside and out. I pulled this trigger by myself. How can something this right feel so horrific? I've crossed a one-way bridge I can never re-cross. I'm on the dead side. No more things to decide. The Army of One is marching. Finish the job. And then?

***

Now I lay me down to sleep,
I pray the Lord my soul to keep.

CHAPTER NINETY-SEVEN

Susan, in Glen Falls, felt the full horror in his voice despite trucks thundering nearby.

"What I wanted for them is happening," he said, speaking rapidly, almost hysterically. "Two of 'em are dead."

He paused, but she said nothing; both apparently hoping for something from the other that they couldn't identify.

"I gotta go," he finally choked out. "I'll call again later."

But he didn't hang up.

She slumped in her bedroom chair, receiver to her ear.

Oh God. Did he really do it? Kill that man? Shoot him? Actually pull the trigger? Will his next call be from a Mississippi jail? This is the end of everything.

"Susan? Are you there?"

Silence.

"I don't think so," she said.

Another long minute of telephone silence.

"No," she said, emphatically now. "I'm not *there* and I can't get *there.* Not ever," her voice more sad than angry. "Wherever *there* is. Wherever you are in your mind. I don't understand how you can be doing this. Your parents and your own friends wouldn't know you now. I've loved you. We've loved each other, but I don't know *you* anymore. Not now. You've become someone else. Something else."

"Susan. Don't say that. My internship's over in two days. I'm trying to stop the cruel violence...and maybe get some justice. And I'm coming home...and we can talk about..."

"No, Jeff," she interrupted softly. "You've gone somewhere I can't imagine. You're rationalizing revenge by calling it justice. Or a deterrent. It's neither of those. Why can't you see that? You're playing God. No one has that right. You used to know that. You're living in a sick, twisted perversion of moral reality."

He heard her sobbing and then she said: "I kept telling you not to go. I pleaded with you to get out of there. Now it's too late. You've murdered two men. And possibly killed a third. Your friend Jimmy is dead probably because of your vigilante crusade, or whatever it is you think you're doing. I'm sorry," she said. "I'm so sorry. I'm devastated. Exhausted. I treasured all of our plans together. They're all dead. You killed them, too. You've left me. Left *us*. You changed and went somewhere I can't follow. I begged you not to go."

He didn't speak and after long silence she said: "I miss you so much... but you're not the person I loved. I desperately miss that person. He couldn't imagine what you're doing or how you're thinking. And neither can I. I can't support you. I can't...Remember when you thought about suicide right after Isiah died? When you were on the pier? I think maybe you're committing suicide now. I just know that the Jeff I loved is gone. Forever. He died with Isiah."

"But Susan, I know...I'm just beginning to think my life is finally making sense...."

"Goodbye," she gasped. "Please don't call me. Jeff ...I...Goodbye."

CHAPTER NINETY-EIGHT

The dial-tone had pierced his head. Now his eyes didn't see the dead phone slowly twirling inches from his face. Sitting on the floor, knees jammed against his chest, claustrophobic in the small, closed booth, he rubbed tear-streaked cheeks, noticing both bloody hands for the first time.

The endless dial tone still droned after Susan's last words telling him he was someone she didn't know. Telling him he was a murderer. Telling him he had killed his friend, Jimmy. Telling him not to call her. Telling him she didn't love him. Not the person he'd become.

He had let the receiver drop and smashed his fists into the phone box before slumping to the floor. Suddenly the booth had no air and he tried to stand up to open the in-folding door. It took two tries and he was hyperventilating when the door finally opened. He lunged out, stumbled to the Plymouth and leaned outstretched bloody hands on the hood, still gasping.

***

I've got to talk to her. I can explain everything. The unknown lives I'm risking so much to save. She's got to listen. She must. Goddammit, why can't she understand? She doesn't believe me, but I thought she believed in me. *How can all of that be gone? Face-to-face I can make her realize what I'm doing. Protecting lives. She's got to understand. I can't lose her. Without her I…don't know…Oh, God, please don't let me lose her! Now I'm asking God for help?*

This cause is stealing Susan from me. I should have...Isiah's killers ruined my life. I'm ruining my life. I've already done it. She's right. It's too late. The rest of my life? What's next? Is there…can there be anything else? Maybe I should go to the cops and get a trial where I can publicly explain everything so everyone understands. Announce that others like me are out there. Would saying it make it true? Spur others to fight back? Bring justice and fear to racists planning lynchings and shootings? Would that scare off those ignorant sonsabitches? Or would a trial look like they won? Is everything I've done for nothing? I'm not finished. I have one more to go. Am I insane? Maybe Susan's right; I'm crazy. Is that my legacy now? A killer driven insane by bigoted murderers? Would Isiah agree with Susan? That I'm insane? He said you don't have to be insane to try to stop insanity. Would he see the sense and logic in what I'm doing? She doesn't love me. She loves someone else. Someone who used to be me. But not me. BUT I LOVE HER!

CHAPTER NINETY-NINE

Arlene's voice was worried.

"He didn't come home last night."

She paused. Roy said nothing, pressing the receiver to his ear with both hands..

"He hasn't done this in a long time, Roy," she said. "You know he's not like he used to be. Back then. I hoped he might have gone to your place after the meeting."

"Well, no, Arlene, he didn't. Fact is I left before Roll did. He, uh, may have...probably got in one a them card games and they all stayed there all night. Safest thing to do, you know, Friday night and all. You know how he likes his poker. We had some drinks, so maybe he thought it would be better than driving home. I bet that's it," trying to sound casual and optimistic.

"I hope so, Roy. But it's late afternoon. Where is he? Who was there? I'll call some people," her sad voice pleading.

She always sounds like a little girl, he thought.

"Heck, Arlene. Let me call. I'll bet I track him down in fifteen minutes. I'll give you a call back."

"Thanks, Roy," unsure but hopeful.

He dialed, hoping he'd find someone from last night who knew where Roll was, but desperately afraid he wouldn't. Six calls later, he was positive. Roll had vanished between the meeting and home.

CHAPTER ONE-HUNDRED

Roy quietly closes his back door, hefting his last suitcase.

I'm the only one left. Whoever they are, they won't find me. I'll find a place. Any someplace is better than a coffin in the graveyard. There must be somewhere.

He carefully goes down the three steps, then his shoes crunch the alley's gravel where his car waits. He unlocks the trunk, struggling to lift the suitcase over the bumper. He pushes the trunk lid down with both hands, then again with all of his weight before it closes.

The night is dark and only dim street lights and neon signs reflecting from the nearby business district make it possible to see at all. The white sedan glows in the dimness against the dark jumble of trash barrels and cardboard boxes waiting for pickup. He reaches for the door handle and pulls at the door.

"Don't move, Mr. Ryser."

Icy fear replaces the blood in Roy's body as the voice and the cold spot on his neck come simultaneously.

He vomits. Great convulsive gasps, the sharp bile surging in his throat and nose, the smell magnifying his nausea. He doesn't try to escape the cascading vomit, which runs down the partly opened door, splashing onto his pants and shoes.

Jeff moves back involuntarily, the pistol at his side, pointing at the ground. He watches the bent-over pharmacist gasping for breath, shivering and gagging, attempting to expel every last molecule from his stomach. Meatloaf revisited.

Momentary relief following regurgitation sweeps over Roy, his face cold and damp. He partially straightens, turning to face the voice.

Jeff whips the gun to point like an angry finger at Roy's nose.

Roy leans weakly back against the car. The partly open door slams shut. He staggers and nearly falls.

Jeff's finger tightens at the sudden movement. "Turn around. Hands on top of the car."

Jeff steps around the vomit, leans forward and runs his left hand over the man's clothing, removing the small, blue-steel revolver holstered on his hip. He puts it in his jacket.

"Get in the car," his voice is quiet but authoritative.

No thought of disobeying, Roy turns, opens the door, sits tentatively on the seat, staring at Jeff. Vomit oozes down the door as he closes it.

Jeff points the pistol through the windshield at the man in the driver's seat, staring right at him, hands gripping the wheel. Jeff circles the front of the car, alert for any movement inside. He pulls the passenger door open and gets in.

Roy is racked with rapid-firing hiccups; the absurd sound unbelievably loud.

"Shut up," Jeff orders.

Roy shakes his head helplessly, apologetically, and continued to twitch uncontrollably.

"You know why I'm here?" Jeff says.

Roy nods miserably, eyes locked on the dashboard. "You're the one… who sent…the letters…you're…blaming us for that nig…"

"Nigger?" Jeff says.

"…minister's death," Roy finishes.

"Yes.

"Did you kill Ed?"

"Which one of you shot Rev. Isiah Booker?" the question sounding like a courtroom indictment. Jeff tries to enforce the question, leaning toward Roy, shoving the pistol closer to the hiccupping man. "Which one."

"You…don't unnerstand…we didn't…"

"Don't give me any lies. Not one. You have only a few minutes left, you may as well tell the truth." Then, his voice harder, hisses, "Which of you miserable cowards shot him? What did he say?"

Ryser's mouth tastes of vomit and bile and he is close to gagging again. He grips the wheel with both hands to keep them from shaking.

"Who…are…you?" Hiccupping again.

"I'm just a friend of the man whose life you stole. I'm nobody. As far as you're concerned, I'm the jury you can't bribe."

"But you don't know how it was," hiccups lessening, his voice pleading. His eyes shift to the gigantic gun a few inches from his face.

"How did it happen?" Jeff demands. "Tell me how it was. What did you say? What did Isiah say before you killed him?"

"Look, you didn't know Ed. You don't know what kind of man he was."

Headlights stab through the windshield, startling them both. The beams bounce off one side of the alley at the far end then straighten, its lights freezing Jeff and Roy in an unrelenting stare.

I should have made him drive away from here. Maybe they'll go on by. What if they stop?

"If that car stops, you say nothing," he spits at Ryser who is staring into the approaching lights. "Whoever it is, you just give 'em a wave and drive away. Start the car. Do it now!"

Ryser turns the key.

"If you do anything stupid I'll put a bullet right in your ear. Think about it. And another bullet in whoever that is. Don't kill another innocent person."

Ryser sits numbly as the car draws alongside. Both men's hearts jump to see the **FOWLERVILL POLICE** seal on the door and the light bar on the roof.

The cruiser stops window-to-window with Ryser's car. A uniformed man rolls down his window, gesturing to Ryser.

"Roll your window down," Jeff whispers, "and imagine a bullet in your ear!"

Ryser cranks his window down just as the vomit smell assaults the officer's nose.

"What'n hell? What happened here, Roy? You sick?

"No. We had a few drinks and I guess Bob here couldn't handle 'em tonight. I'm all right."

"What about your friend?"

"I'm fine officer," Jeff slurs, his chin down, face shrouded in the semi-darkness.

"Sounds like you guys better behave yourselves," the cop says, peering at Roy for several seconds before rolling up his window, his nose filled with the stench, and then his car is rolling slowly down the alley.

Jeff and Roy sat silently for several moments.

"Drive till I tell you to stop."

Jeff quietly gives directions as they drive; "turn right at the next corner…straight ahead…keep going."

DIXON AUTO PARTS & JUNKYARD

The car winds through aisles between dead and abandoned cars and trucks, dark carcasses of manmade ghosts in above-ground graves. Finally, at a corner of the property about two hundred yards from the main roadway, "Stop here. Turn off the lights and engine."

In the darkness the deceased junk looms dark and heavy, like mountains faintly silhouetted against the night sky.

"Why here?" Roy whispers.

"It's important that people understand that what happens to you started here," Jeff says. "Why didn't you yell for help from that cop?"

"I didn't want to get him killed. Or me neither. I don't want to die," glancing at Jeff, then looking to his left, hands still on the wheel. "I thought about throwin the door open. For all you know, I may have signaled him."

"What difference does it make to you if he got shot?"

Roy turns to Jeff. "You think I go around shooting people? Or not caring if people get shot?"

"Do you?" Jeff says sharply. "Do you shoot people?"

"No. Course not."

"The murder," Jeff says, jabbing the pistol into Roy's side. "Were you there?"

The long silence fills the car. Neither man moves.

"Sorta…yeah…not for the actual…I was…I heard….I kinda knew."

"Tell me about Isiah Booker. Tell me how you shot him."

"I didn't shoot him. I never shot nobody."

"Then who did? Price? Bryant?

"Ed."

Jeff puts the gun against Ryser's earlobe. "This one goes first unless you tell me the truth. Right now." His teeth hurt from the tension.

"Ed said, 'We gotta stop these niggers from taking over.'" Jeff can barely hear him.

"'We got to show 'em they can't run this county,'" Roy continues.

"When was this?" Jeff demands, pushing the gun barrel against Ryser's cheek.

"When the voter drive started, when those agitators came here from up north. Ed and me was drinking coffee at the drugstore, at the end of the counter. This nigger girl came in, all bold and everything, sat right at the counter and had a soda, just as big as life. Just like she belonged there. And we had to serve her. I didn't want no trouble.

"'Looka that,' Ed said. 'A year ago they wouldna dared try that. They think they own the place now, can go anyplace they want. We can't have that. We gotta do somethin to stop this shit.'

"'Yeah, but what can we do?'" I said. "We was just talkin, you know?" shooting another glance at Jeff. "Then Ed said: 'They got the whole federal goviment with 'em since the sit-ins and the fucking Supreme Court says we let them into our schools, our kids and them. You know what'll happen around here? If they register all those niggers and some son-of-a-bitch from up north gets 'em organized, they can elect a nigger sheriff or a nigger judge or any goddamn thing. They could do it. We're outnumbered right here at home. You know they out-breed us. If things keep up, our kids *will* be schoolin with 'em. Our wives and daughters will get pulled over on dark roads by nigger deputies. We're losin all our rights. They're thinking they're better'n us. We gotta do somethin.'"

"'It's a losing fight,'" I told him. "'Things are changing."

"'They sure as shit are, but that don't mean we gotta sit still for it. We can beat all this. Not just stall it, beat it. We can keep this county the same as it's always been, the way it's supposed to be, the same as when we was boys. We'll get the knights together and…'

"Then three more people came in. Two white college boys and this nigra minister. We'd seen his picture in the paper. Big guy, older than the others. I guess you know how he looked," glancing at Jeff who jammed the gun hard against Ryser's temple, pushing his head sideways against the window.

"They was all northerners from their talk. Like you. 'Look at that big buck of a nigger' Ed said.

"They waved at the nigger girl at the counter and went over and sat by her. They was all talking and excited but it was hard to figure out what they was talking about. I remember the minister didn't say much. Seemed mostly to listen and once in awhile say something. He was looking around the store. He saw we was looking at him. The girl was sitting between two white boys. That pissed off both of us.

"'Looka that,' Ed said. 'Bet she's a nigger whore from one of those fancy colleges.'"

Jeff leans backward against the door. Both men are turned, facing each other, but trying to get as far away from the other as the car allows.

"After awhile they left," Ryser continues without prompting. "Ed was furious. And I was too. Always someone coming from outside, someplace else, people thinking they's better'n us…can't stay home and take care of their own problems. Come to our town to make trouble. We had no trouble till these agitators started coming. Our niggers was happy. White boys and nigger girls; and vice versa? We can't have that. And a nigger minister right there watching the whole thing. Can't even trust the church. Used to be the nigger churches kept their people happy. They got no right to be here in our county, at the counter in my drugstore and they shoulda known it would cause trouble. They shoulda known," his voice a whisper.

"That evening I went to Ed's store for a drink. We was just talkin, shootin the shit, ya know, but Ed had a few snorts and was getting' madder and madder. 'Them goddamn nigger-lovers are fuckin up the whole state,' he said. 'They gotta learn to stay home. If they want to live with niggers that's fine with me, but they got no right to cause trouble here. They're gonna find out we won't put up with it. We gotta teach 'em a lesson; scare the holy crap out of 'em.'

"He was really loud. 'Take it easy, Ed,' I said. 'What's a handful of 'em going to do? They'll get tired of beating the bushes and tramping around in the heat and the dust and they'll go away.'

"'Goddamn it, Roy, we ain't gonna let 'em shove this shit down our throats. We gotta make 'em too damn scared to come down here. Let 'em fuck their nigger whores up north. Leave us the hell alone.'

"He was really worked up and I was getting scared myself. Two things usually made Ed mean, drinking and niggers. He was scaring me bad. I wanted outta there.

"'Come on Ed, let's go home,' I said. 'No sense us getting all riled up.'

"'Horseshit. If we don't get worked up and don't get crackin we're gonna get run over by these animals. Nuthin'll be the same. Won't be how it's supposed to be. You can't never get the cream out of the coffee once it's mixed.'

"He took a swallow right outta the bottle. Never saw him do that before. He was getting more and more pissed, acting crazy.

"Come on, I'll drive you home,' I said.

"'I can drive myself,' Ed said.

"It'd be better if I drove you and I'll pick you up in the morning and bring you here after I freeload breakfast offa Claire. Come on.'

"I helped him lock up and we left in his car. It was already pretty dark. I think everything would have been ok 'cept suddenly, he said, real soft-like, 'Pull over. Pull over. Stop the car."

"I did. I thought he was sick. But then I saw that big Negro minister coming right at us, down the sidewalk on the same side of the street we was on. He was just walking along. He didn't look like he was in a hurry or nuthin.

"Ed said, 'We'll fix that black bastard. We'll make 'em all afraid to come here. Lemme get Roll's gun.'

"We all carried guns in our cars. Roll had given Ed one of his pistols.

The black preacher walked by us as Ed was trying to get the gun from under the back of the seat. He finally got it.

"'What are you gonna do?'" I was afraid he was gonna shoot at him."

"'We're gonna scare the black sumbitch. Go round the block and stop when we're close to him. I'll tell you when.'

"I was really afraid he was gonna shoot at him but I went around the block. I remember hoping not to see him, but he was crossing the street when we came around. He noticed the car and I think he recognized it as the one parked at the curb before because he stared at it as he was walking across. The minute I got close, Ed said 'stop' and jumped out and pointed the gun at him.

"'Nigger, get over here,'" he said.

"He could tell there wasn't no use in runnin. He didn't even try. But he didn't move. He just stood there looking at Ed. Ed kept the gun pointed at him and moved quickly until he was real close and stuck the gun right in his face, like he was gonna shoot him. I didn't know what to do. I couldn't think of nothing to do. I didn't know how to stop him. I couldn't believe he was gonna shoot him, but it looked like he was gonna do it and I just didn't know what to do," Ryser's voice rising, reliving the panic of his indecision, talking more to himself than Jeff.

"I'm sure the nigra…the minister…saw it too. I couldn't see his face very well but he just stood there and didn't say nothin.

"Ed was shoutin. 'You're time's come, nigger.'

"I blew the horn. I had to do somethin, so I hit the horn. I don't know how, but the preacher jumped at Ed and wrestled him down. He was a big man; almost as big as Ed. The minister was trying to twist the gun outta Ed's hand. He was sitting on Ed's chest and he had Ed's wrists in his two hands. Ed was cursing and jerking around, but he weren't getting anywhere. He screamed, 'Hit him, Roy. For Christ's sake, hit him.'

"I grabbed the big flashlight off the back floor of Ed's car and got out. They were still thrashing around in the street and when I got to the other side of the car I hit him with the flashlight. I just hit him once, but the sound was terrible and he fell right off to the side. I only hit him once. Just that one time. I didn't know what else to do. Oh, God, I wish it hadn't happened. I wish I hadn't….Ed jumped up then and he was breathing hard and he was real excited. 'Help me throw him in the back,' he said. 'Come on! Help me tie his hands.'"

"He was so big it was a real job getting him in the trunk. Then we got back in the car and Ed was driving.

"Where we goin? What are we gonna do?"

"Ed just kept driving. Finally he said: 'We gotta get rid of him. We'll scare these nigger-lovers right back up north and they'll never come back.'

"We were driving out of town and I couldn't figure out what was happening. I wanted it to be a bad dream, but I knew that nigra was back there in the trunk. I wondered if he was dead. I kept hearing the sound when I hit him with the flashlight. He just fell over. I can still see it. What's Ed talking about? Where we going? How did I get into this? I didn't want to be there. Then we was driving into the junkyard, just like we did tonight. It was real quiet. The tires on the gravel sounded like an army was coming. Ed drove like he knew where he wanted to go. We ended up way in the back, right around here somewheres, and then he stopped. We hadn't had the lights on since turning off the road.

"'Let's go,' he said to me.

"'Where? What you gonna do?'

"'We gotta get rid of that nigger. Come on!'

"He got out but I stayed in the front seat. I was mixed up. I was real scared. I didn't want to do nuthin. I didn't know what I could do. I knew Ed was gonna shoot that nigger, but I didn't know anything to do. I turned around and looked out the back window but the trunk lid came up and I couldn't see. I heard some noises and then two quick shots. Then there was another one. Then it was real quiet. I pretended I was just sitting at home. I just sat there for a long time looking out the windshield. I guess it was a long time. Then Ed's voice was right there at the window beside me. I almost wet my pants it scared me so much.

"'Come on, damn it," he said. We gotta bury him. Get your ass outta the car.'

"I got out but I walked to the front of the car. Ed was hollerin something at me and I went back there but I couldn't look. But then I did look and the nigra was on his back in the trunk and his face was bloody and I looked away and I never looked at him again.

"'Grab his feet,' Ed said. 'Hurry up. We gotta get this done. Come on.'

"But I didn't want to. I swear I didn't want nuthin to do with any of it. We carried him quite a ways and I never once looked at him. Then Ed said 'here' and we put him down and Ed started to walk away. I started to go with him.

"'You stay here. I'm gonna get the shovel outa the trunk."

"'I ain't staying here.'"

"'Oh, for Christ's sake,' Ed says. Then he slugged me in the face and I was on the ground before I knew it. I touched my face and my hand was covered with blood. My nose was bleeding and I couldn't hear nothin. I staggered up while Ed got a shovel from his trunk. I got in the car. I wasn't getting outta that car again. And I didn't.

"After a long time he came back and he drove to the highway, put on the lights and came back to town. We went to Ed's store and he called Roll, but he wasn't home. Then I went to my house and Ed said later he talked to Roll in the morning and told him to say his pistol was stole a long time ago if anyone asked about it. He said he didn't tell Roll anything but that he understood. I don't know what he did with the gun. Not to this day. I don't know. We never talked about it."

Ryser stops talking, exhausted and weak, collapsing against the door. The words had poured from him like the vomit had spewed earlier. He stares through the windshield, looking beaten, worn out, face resigned, his chin tilted down.

Jeff feels like he's been crying for hours and he straightens his back. Now he knows how Isiah died. Three shots heard, but not seen. Blocked by a trunk lid. That was the way the world changed. A chance encounter on a Mississippi street and a grave dug in the night. After a long time, Jeff hears his own voice coming from far away.

"What about Roll Price?"

"He knew afterwards. He could tell from Ed's tellin him about the gun but that's all. He just sorta knew, but not the details. I think he understood that Ed did the shooting but no one ever said so. We never talked about it. We didn't want to even think about it. We agreed we'd *never* talk about it. And we didn't, not even during the trial, not until your letters came. Roll's playing cards that night saved us all, I guess. Roll knew nuthin about…about the…the thing. He wouldn't have gone along with that. He wouldna. If he'd been there he might have been able to stop Ed. He wasn't like that. He didn't like niggers, but he wouldn't kill anyone. I'm sure of that. I wouldn't neither but…" and, after a silence, "I'm not that kind. I always kinda wondered if Roll mighta phoned in that tip about the body, not realizing they might link Ed's tire tracks to the killin. Roll wouldna wanted that to happen. Maybe Ed wanted the body found. You know, to send a message. Maybe it wasn't neither of them…but who else knew?"

"One of the wives?" Jeff asks.

"Oh, Christ, no," Roy is vehement, sitting up straight. "Not Claire or Arlene. I don't think either of 'em ever knew...and they definitely…they might have suspected…they wouldna done anything even if they knew. No chance."

"It wasn't you?" Jeff asked quietly.

Roy doesn't answer, sagging back against the seat.

"If you hadn't hit him with the flashlight he'd probably still be alive," Jeff whispers, before slumping into the corner, his eyes unseeing through the windshield, his face slack, feeling beaten, defeated and drained, his right hand loosely holding his grandfather's heavy revolver.

I executed an innocent man. Not totally innocent, but he had nothing to do with Isiah's actual murder. He deserved prison but not the death penalty. I decided his fate; I told him he was sentenced to death. I executed him. I was wrong. I self-righteously murdered an innocent man. I decided he was guilty and I killed him. He told me the truth and I killed him.

He feels something on his left hand and looks down. Roll's bloody hand is again dripping blood on Jeff's wrist and hand. Jeff jerks back violently against the car door.

"Get away from me, get away, don't touch me," he shouts, willing his eyes back to the windshield. "I'm sorry…so sorry, I never could have…I didn't know…believe you…" his entire body sobbing.

Did I say that out loud? Am I thinking or screaming?

"What?" Roy says, jerking his head to look at Jeff, huddled in the corner, his chin tucked into his chest.

Jeff straightens up, the pistol forgotten in his lap, tears glaciating down his cheeks.

"Start the car and go back to the road," Jeff's voice is barely a whisper. Ryser looks at him before turning the key. He turns on the headlights and drives slowly through the gravel paths to the road, the only sound is the car easing over the gravel. At the highway he turns right, the car seeming to drive itself toward the distant glow of town lights.

At the edge of town, when the first store signs become readable, Jeff says, "Stop here."

Ryser stops without pulling to the side of the road. They sit for a long time, on opposite sides of the car, unseeing eyes fixed, each entombed in his own fleeting thoughts, unaware of each other. Two unconvicted murderers not talking to each other. Each knowing how to destroy what remains of the other.

Finally, Jeff leans toward Ryser. "We'll never see each other again." Then he slips out, closing the door quietly. The car lurches as Ryser drives away.

Jeff walks rapidly through the darkness toward his car several blocks away.

He knows he needs less than ten minutes to throw his already packed things in his car. And go. Somewhere.

###

Other Books By This Author

BIBLE-BASED HISTORICAL NOVELS
Series of 8: *They Met Jesus*
Ongoing Series of 8: *Intrepid Men of God*
Series of 10: A Child's Life of Christ
Series of 10: A Child's Bible Heroes
Series of 8: A Child's Bible Kids

TOPICAL
Applied Christianity: Handbook 500 Good Works
Christianity or Islam? The Contrast
The Holy Spirit: 592 Verses Examined
Inside the Hearts of Bible Women-Reader, Audio, Leader
Revelation: A Love Letter From God
Worship Changes Since the First Century
Worship the First-Century Way
365 Life-Changing Scriptures Day by Date

DEVOTIONAL – TOUCHING GOD SERIES
365 Golden Bible Thoughts: God's Heart to Yours
365 Pearls of Wisdom: God's Soul to Yours
365 Silver-Winged Prayers: Your Spirit to God's

EASY BIBLE WORKBOOKS – O.T. & N.T.

Genealogy: How to Climb Your Family Tree Without Falling Out
Volume I: Beginner-Intermediate
Volume II: Colonial-Medieval

COVER AN ORIGINAL WATERCOLOR BY
BETSY KEMP THOMPSON
https://watercolorsbybetsy@wordpress.com

Copyright © 2018
Katheryn Maddox Haddad

NORTHERN LIGHTS PUBLISHING HOUSE

ISBN- 9781792696565
All rights reserved, including the right to reproduce this book or portions thereof in any form. No part may be reproduced, stored, transmitted, or distributed in any form or by any means without prior written permission from the author. The only exception is for a brief quotation in a printed review.

Printed in the United States

365 Golden Bible Thoughts: God's Heart to Yours

Touching God Series 1

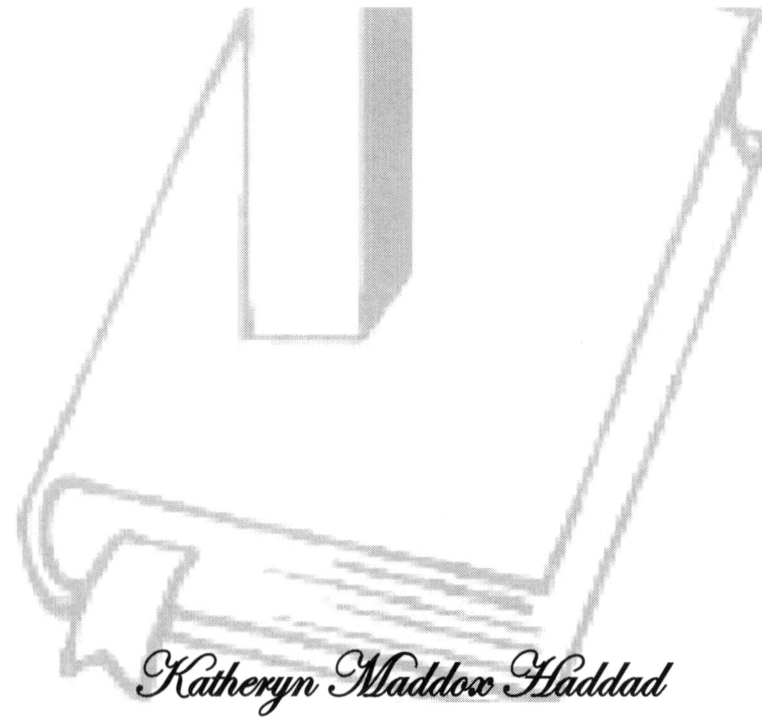

Katheryn Maddox Haddad

ABOUT THE COVER ARTIST

Betsy Kemp Thompson

The Detroit Institute of Art, with a collection valued at over 8 billion dollars and 100 galleries of art from around the world was the home away from home for Betsy Kemp Thompson from the time she could ride the bus alone and on into adulthood. The DIA is among the most visited art museums in the world, especially by Betsy.

Every Saturday for years ~ some 500 trips ~ Betsy went to the DIA and spent all day meticulously studying the 8'-and-10' tall oil portraits, scrutinizing the paintings by world-renowned artists, and studying landscapes covering entire walls in both galleries and massive hallways.

As an adult, she hosted a television show in Nashville, Tennessee ~ *A Brush with Art* ~ teaching watercolor methods.

Some of her many watercolors are for sale on her website at **https://watercolorsbybetsy.wordpress.com**

She has resided in Nashville for nearly forty years where she and her husband, Sam (the love of her life) have spoiled three children and numerous grandchildren. They have done inner-city work together in Nashville for thirty-eight years.

Table of Contents

Read this First

This is Book 1 in the trilogy *Touching God*. Each book provides a different way to touch God day by day throughout the year.

Book 1 ~ 365 Golden Bible Thoughts: God's Heart to Yours
Book 2~ 365 Pearls of Wisdom: God's Soul to Yours
Book 3 ~ 365 Silver-Winged Prayers: Your Spirit to God's

Just a brief explanation of how these inspirational thoughts were organized. Each daily scripture was based on the date. For example, March is the third month. Then on March 16th (3/16), the scripture for that day is John 3:16. You get the idea.

Other than the above, the daily thoughts are not in order, such as with a story or building a theme. Therefore, you can begin using this book at any time of the year.

May you feel as inspired in the reading as I was in the writing.

January

1st - The scripture for today, January 1 (1/1), is **John 1:1f, 14a** as found in the New Testament of the Bible:

"In the beginning was the Word, and the Word was with God, and the Word was God. He was with God in the beginning.... The Word became flesh and made his dwelling among us."

Genesis 3:8 says God walked on earth in the Garden of Eden. When Jesus came, God once again walked with us. But when Jesus left, did he leave us with no one to walk with?

Jesus said in John 14:17 that he was going to send another Comforter ~ the Spirit of Truth. And in John 17:17 he said God's Word is Truth. So, just as Jesus was the Word that people could watch, the Spirit is the Word that people can read.

We do not have to guess what God is wanting us to do. We have it written down to read, and consider, and contemplate, and re-read as many times as we want.

If you have a Bible in your home, why not read it through in a year beginning today? There are suggested schedules on the internet. Or you could even divide up the number of pages in your Bible by 365 to know how many pages to read each day.

Just remember, every time you get out your Bible and read it, once again God is walking with you.

2nd - The scripture for today, January 2 (1/2, is **3rd John 1:2** as found in the New Testament of the Bible:

"Dear friend, I pray that you may enjoy good health and that all may go well with you, even as your soul is getting along well."

Your health may be bad, your finances in an upheaval, your home damaged by wind or water, your job about to be lost. But, amidst your frustrations and tears, you can still smile. You can still rejoice that your "soul is getting along well."

When problems come into your life ~ and they do ~ remember the most important thing is your soul. No one and no thing can touch your soul as long as you are safe in the arms of Jesus.

So, when problems do come, you can still with confidence rejoice that your "soul is getting along well."

3rd - The scripture for today, January 3 (1/3), is **Jonah 1:3a** as found in the Old Testament of the Bible:

"But Jonah ran away from the Lord and headed for Tarshish."

Do you spend your life running away from the Lord? Do you do it with busy-ness, with resentments toward people, with anger that God does not make people stop being bad to you, with boredom at the thought of worshipping him, with refusal to believe he even exists?

Is it even possible to run away from the Lord? Eventually it is. But for a long time, the Lord runs after you just as he did by causing a storm at sea where Jonah was on board his escape ship. He does things to get your attention too.

Perhaps there are storms in your life. Have you ever thought of them as God trying to get your attention? Perhaps you run here and there day after day, too busy to even think about God. But when disaster hits, do you suddenly remember God so you can blame him for your hardships?

Yes, perhaps you sometimes do blame God, but at least you're thinking of him. Perhaps it's been years since you have thought seriously about God.

He has big shoulders. Go ahead and blame him for a while, then remember how he loves you and just wants you back.

But don't wait too long. God only runs after you for so long. Eventually, he gives up. Don't wait so long that God gives up on you and treats you the way you have been treating him.

"God, I'm coming back. Help me."

4th- The scripture for today, January 4 (1/4), is **Philippians 1:4** as found in the New Testament of the Bible:

"In all my prayers for all of you, I always pray with joy."

Are you sad about something? Do your prayers consist mostly of give me this, help me with that? Begin today to keep an on-going list of your prayer requests for the year, and another one of thanksgiving for when those prayers are answered. Begin today to tell God, "Thank you."

Also begin today to look around at your circumstances ~ whatever they may be ~ with joy. There can be some kind of joy in every situation if you look at it through eyes of joy.

The above quotation is from a letter to Philippi in northern Greece bordering today's Bulgaria. Here, a majority of the citizens were barbarian-looking warrior Thracians. But these rough semi-professional warriors also brought the world joy with their beautiful sculptures.

Philippians is a book about peace and joy. This is the book that says, "And the peace of God which transcends all understanding will guard your hearts and your minds in Christ Jesus" (4:7)

This is also the book that says, "I can do everything through him who gives me strength" (4:13).

From now on, tell God, "Thank you," and in the process rediscover your joy.

5th- The scripture for today, January 5 (1/5), is **Colossians 1:5** as found in the New Testament of the Bible:

"...the faith and love that spring from the hope that is stored up for you in heaven and that you have already heard about in the Word of Truth, the gospel."

Does your faith have its ups and downs? Is it strong sometimes and weak sometimes? When things sometimes go so wrong you have trouble having faith in God, you can still hope. Do you grow angry at God sometimes? You can still hope. During such low times when faith does not come easy, you can still hope. Hope is the springboard of faith.

And stay close to the Word of Truth, for John 14:17 says the Comforter is the Spirit of Truth, and John 17:17 says Truth is the Word of God. Read when you don't feel like it. Ephesians is what I go to. David tells of his own faith problems in Psalm 42.

When your emotions are pulling you down and you feel only the darkness of confusion inside, rely for a little while on your logic, your intellect, until your emotions heal. Read things proving God exists. Read things about other people's love for God Do not drop out of the church; you need your Christian friends. It may be hard for you to believe right now but someday you will heal.

So, keep on hoping ~ the springboard. Eventually, along the way, your hope will return to faith.

6th - The scripture for today, January 6 (1/6), is **Titus 1:6f** as found in the New Testament of the Bible:

"An elder must be blameless, the husband of but one wife, a man

whose children believe and are not open to the charge of being wild and disobedient. Since an overseer is entrusted with God's work, he must be blameless ~ not overbearing, not quick-tempered, not given to drunkenness, not violent, nor pursuing dishonest gain."

This is quite interesting. God does not leave us to guess the qualifications of a church leader. We don't have to hold conferences or synods to decide on qualifications for this office, because God has already given them.

Something surprising here is that the word **elder** is used interchangeably with the word **overseer** (sometimes also translated **bishop**). The word elder comes from the Greek word ***presbyter***. The word overseer/bishop is from the Greek word ***episcopos***. Elder and overseer and bishop all are the same in this passage referring to the same office!

Here's something else interesting about the elder/overseer/bishop: The word **pastor** comes from the Greek word for shepherd, ***poiman***. In Acts 20:17, Paul sent for the **elders** of the church in Ephesus to talk to them. When they arrived, he said, "Keep watch over yourselves and all the flock of which the Holy Spirit has made you **overseers**. Be shepherds [**pastors**] of the church of God which he bought with his own blood." He called them by three titles.

Do you see the overlapping of the same office being called by different names? It's kind of like father and papa being the same.

Titus 1:6f uses elder and overseer for the same office. Overseer is the same in Greek as bishop. **Acts 20:17** uses elder, overseer, shepherd (pastor) for the same office.

In our daily lives we have different words meaning the same person; such as father, parent, dad, papa ~ all names for the same position in the family.

So, too, for the family of God ~ the church ~ all these words overlap as names for the same office! And the qualifications for this office are found in our scripture for today, Titus 1:6f. Indeed, how interesting!

7th- The scripture for today, January 7 (1/7), is 2nd **Timothy** 1:7 as found in the New Testament of the Bible:

"For God did not give us a spirit of timidity, but a spirit of power, of love, and of self-discipline."

Have you discovered some "new truth" in the Bible? Perhaps you have read it a hundred times but never noticed it before.

People fear the unknown. Do not fear it. Embrace it. Then share with others this new-found truth. The word "timidity" is sometimes translated "fear." Remind your friends of that "new truth" you discovered enough times that it is no longer an unknown and no longer something to be feared.

Do you fear reprisal among your church friends or leaders if you stand up for some "new truth" no one noticed before? God can help you. God can give you the courage to speak out with power, with love, and with self-discipline as you explain that new-found truth.

Then be patient. God said, "My word will not return to me

void" (Isaiah 55:11).

8th - The scripture for today, January 8 (1/8), is 1st **Peter 1:8** as found in the New Testament of the Bible:

"Though you have not seen him, you love him! And even though you do not see him now, you believe in him! And are filled with an inexpressible and glorious joy!"

Ah, the memories Peter had of being with Jesus when they all were young. Now he was old and people were dying out who had seen and heard Jesus in person.

After Jesus returned to heaven, it was the job of his Apostles to tell people about him and repeat his words. They spent the rest of their lives doing just that. What joy they found when people believed, even though they had not seen him. They not only believed, but they also loved him

Thank God, the Apostles wrote the New Testament so we would never have to guess what Jesus was like and never have to guess what his words were, even after the Apostles died. In fact, we have the advantage because we do not have to wait for an Apostle to come visit us and tell us. We can read about Jesus for ourselves over and over as many times as we like right in our home.

Yes, we have not seen Jesus. Yet, with his life and words before us, we believe! And we love him. What inexpressible and glorious joy!

9th - The scripture for today, January 9 (1/9), is **Joshua 1:9** as found in the Old Testament of the Bible:

"Have I not commanded you? Be strong and courageous. Do not be terrified; do not be discouraged, for the Lord your God will be with you wherever you go."

Fear can paralyze. Just ask Joshua. He had just been given the job of conquering horrible people who practiced prostitution as a religion, self-mutilation and sacrificing their children to the fire god. Plus, his spies said those bad people were like giants and his army was made up of the children of former slaves with no experience.

Guess what God said. "Go anyway. Conquer anyway."

What do you fear? A few people fear spiders and night time and heights and such. A lot more of us fear changing a bad habit that has us in its claws and won't let us go. Even more serious, do you fear telling a neighbor, someone in a club, a relative about Jesus' willingness to save them from hell and get them entrance into heaven? To all this, God says, "Go anyway."

Some of you reading this live in countries where it is dangerous to be a Christian. Do you fear being arrested, tortured, killed for your faith? God tells you, "Be strong! Be courageous! Do not be terrified!" Why. Because "the Lord your God will be with you wherever you go."

What keeps the fear under control? "Perfect love casts out fear" (I John 4:18). Love yourself, love your neighbor, love God.

Today, whatever it is holding you back, "Go anyway,

Conquer anyway."

10th - The scripture for today, January 10 (1/10), is **Colossians 1:10** as found in the New Testament of the Bible:

"And we pray this in order that you may live a life worthy of the Lord and may please him in every way: Bearing fruit in every good work; Growing in the knowledge of God."

Are you always doing some good work for other people? Does it fill your thoughts and life? Or are you always delving into the Bible to gain more knowledge of God? Does it fill your thoughts and life? Good for you.

But we see here, we must have a balance. James 2:17 says faith without works is dead. On the other hand, Romans 10:2 says certain people were zealous for God, but their zeal was not based on knowledge.

We have to add to our Bible-based faith, good works. We have to add to our zealous good works, the knowledge of God from the Bible.

It's hard to get out of a rut, no matter how good it is. Maybe it's time to examine yourself. Maybe it's time to add the other requirement to your life. Don't you want to be spiritually balanced?

11th - The scripture for today, January 11 (1/11), is **2nd**

Peter 1:11 as found in the New Testament of the Bible:

"And you will receive a rich welcome into the eternal kingdom of our Lord and Savior Jesus Christ."

How often do you forget that earth is not your home? As an old gospel song says, "We're just traveling through." Do you really believe that?

If someone told you tomorrow you were going to die, would you go into a panic? Would you beg God to let you live another ten or twenty years? Would you feel this was the beginning of the end?

To a true Christian, your dying is the end of the beginning. You have a whole "life" ahead of you in heaven. A never-ending life. Do you live like you believe it? Will you die looking forward to it?

Are you even a Christian yet? What is your life like? Do you even know what is in the Bible, God's messages to you? Does the thought of heaven sound boring to you? Do you even like God?

Stop and listen to the empty place in your heart (Ec. 3:11). Do you hear it? Shhh. Listen... God is calling you.

12th- The scripture for today, January 12 (1/12), is **James 1:12** as found in the New Testament of the Bible:

"Blessed is the man who perseveres under trial, because when he has stood the test, he will receive the crown of life that God

has promised to those who love him."

How loyal are you to God? Is your relationship up and down, depending on how your life is going at the moment? If you pray for something and don't get it, do you feel like God is punishing you? If everything seems to be going wrong, do you blame God instead of Satan? Do you pray over and over for God to relieve you of a particular burden, but relief hasn't come so you've decided to quit the church?

Quit grumbling! God has assignments for you. What kind of soldier of the Lord are you? Do you tell the general you don't like what he has assigned for you to do? Where you are today is where God wants you. Your job is to stay loyal no matter how difficult things get. Be brave. Hold fast. Stand your ground.

Why? To prove that love is stronger than hatred. To prove that good is stronger than bad. To prove that right is more mighty than wrong. To prove that God is stronger than Satan. Ephesians 6:12 says Our struggle is not against flesh and blood, but against the rulers, against the powers, against the world forces of this darkness, against the spiritual forces of wickedness in the heavenly places.

Determine today to thank God for whatever state you are in, even if you do it in tears because it goes against all your emotions. And, even though you may feel helpless to do anything about it right now, in your helplessness, persevere!

13th - The scripture for today, January 13 (1/13),

is **Habakkuk 1:13** as found in the Old Testament of the Bible:

"Your eyes are too pure to look on evil; you cannot tolerate wrong."

This pretty much explains why no one deserves heaven. Going to heaven has little to do with doing so many good works God will feel obligated to admit you.

It's all about sin. Only sinless people can be in heaven, for God cannot coexist with sin and still be God. Of course, you cannot be sinless. If nothing else, you have sins of attitude and neglect.

For thousands of years, God let mankind try any way they could to be perfect. Some people he gave the Law of Moses to, and some people he continued to let try on their own. Neither worked. No matter how hard we tried, no one could get it right.

The wages you earn for sinning is death (Romans 6:23). Remember in the Garden of Eden God warned, "The moment you sin, you die." He was talking about souls dying and eventually bodies dying. Satan was now holding mankind hostage. Satan causes death, so sinners collect the wages Satan pays for following him.

But mankind was still being held hostage. He demanded the highest ransom imaginable: The death of God. Satan wanted to e God and this was the only way he could carry out his plan.

God held Satan off temporarily: He told them to kill an animal to die in their place. Even collecting the wages of sin, Satan still held mankind hostage. Mankind had to have all the chances possible to be perfect. But after millenniums, mankind still could not.

Galatians 4:4 says, "When the time was come, God sent his son." Finally, when mankind understood everyone needed outside help, God sent Jesus. Hebrews 4:15 says Jesus lived the perfect life that was impossible for anyone to live; he was completely free of sin.

Then God seemingly gave in to Satan's ransom demand to free mankind. God offered his son ~ God in the form of mankind. Finally, Satan got his wish ~ the ransom he had demanded: The death of God.

So, Satan freed mankind from his prison of soul death. But Satan was in for a surprise. His gloating came to an abrupt stop. God tricked Satan. You cannot kill Life. God returned to that human body and came back to life.

It was too late. Satan had already freed mankind.

That done, God ~ who can only dwell with sinlessness ~ is now able to allow obedient, faithful believers in Jesus into his home, heaven. For, through Jesus, we become sinless. Glory of glories!

But something terrible happened after that. People began selling themselves back into slavery to Satan (Romans 6:15-23). No! No! This cannot be! So God, through people who have resisted Satan's lures of fun and riches, power and beauty, continually call out, "Come back! Come back to God! Come back. I miss you. God misses you...."

14th - The scripture for today, January 14 (1/14), is **Hebrews 1:14** as found in the New Testament of the Bible:

"Are not all angels ministering spirits, sent to serve those who will inherit salvation?"

Have you ever wondered if the Bible really mentions guardian angels? Well, here it is. How wonderful! How reassuring! But the angels do not minister to everyone ~ just to the saved who will inherit salvation.

As much as they minister to us, however, we are not to worship them and we are not to pray to them. For a while ~ and still some today ~ it was popular to collect pictures and statues of angels. Some people were saying there is no God, but there are guardian angels. Some people who do believe in God bypass Him and ask angels to help them, kind of like going to the peasant instead of the king.

Where do they think angels come from? God created them to be the servant class. We are not to adore, worship or pray to angels (Revelation 19:10; 22:9).

So, yes, we do have guardian angels. Let us be grateful God loves us enough to send the angels to minister to us until we reach his home, heaven. Then, we and the angels will bow down together to the God of the universe and Him will we worship.

15th - The scripture for today, January 15 (1/15), is **Galatians 1:15f** as found in the New Testament of the Bible:

"But when God, who set me apart from birth and called me by his

grace, was pleased to reveal his Son in me so that I might preach him among the Gentiles...."

Isn't this amazing? God knew before you are born what you can be doing for him later in life. He sets aside work for you to do, but he does not force you to do it. You may set aside a certain amount of money to spend on food but you end up spending it on clothing. Being set aside does not mean something will end up doing what it was set aside for.

God has given you certain talents and set you aside to use them for Him. Do you? Is your thinking even oriented on things that can endure through eternity? Or do you think only of the next day, or the next year?

You do not have to guess what God has set you aside to do. Read the scriptures. He has messages for you all through them. Find someone in the Bible with your personality and use that person as an example. Find advice in the proverbs. Find advice in Jesus' teachings, and in his apostles' teachings. It's all there. Pick one and do it.

If you are willing to follow God's advice and not man's, then decide today to accept the work God has set aside for you to do. Or maybe you're already doing it and don't realize it.

You may not think your life has been very exciting. You may be waiting for God to give you a big important job to do for him. But the truth is, you ~ in your seemingly mundane life ~ may already be doing what God set aside for you to do.

Never under-estimate yourself and what God can accomplish through you.

16th- The scripture for today, January 16 (1/16), is **Ruth 1:16ff** as found in the Old Testament of the Bible:

"Don't urge me to leave you or to turn back from you. Where you go I will go, and where you stay I will stay. Your people will be my people and your God my God. Where you die, I will die, and there I will be buried. May the Lord deal with me, be it ever so severely, if anything but death separates you and me."

Although Ruth was talking to her mother-in-law after the death of her husband (Naomi's son), this can be and sometimes is quoted by the bride and groom at their wedding. If only it were quoted more often. Not only at weddings, but at anniversaries. At birthdays of children and parents. During arguments, and low times and hard times and discouraging times.

Even deeper, it could be said when Satan attacks us. Just change you to him. *Don't urge me to leave him or to turn back from him. Where he goes, I will go, and where he stays, I will stay. His people will be my people and God will always be my God.*

These are the words of love ~ deep genuine, unselfish love. Let us so love one another that deeply. Let us love our God that deeply.

17th- The scripture for today, January 17 (1/17), is **James 1:17** as found in the New Testament of the Bible:

"Every good and perfect gift is from above, coming down from the Father of the heavenly lights, who does not change like shifting shadows."

Do you sometimes feel slighted because other people get more gifts on special occasions (or even between special occasions) than you do? No need to feel that way. Christians get the goods ones. Christians get the perfect ones. We get them all! And our heavenly Father will never stop showering us with those "good gifts," those "perfect gifts."

Ah, Lord God, my creator, my life, lover of my soul. With you, I am never hungry, I am never cold, I am never in pain, I am never in want. With you I have all that I need for my soul is filled with your love, I am warm in your embrace, everything is good within my being. You, who died in my place are even now waiting for me at your door. I will be there soon. And we will be together for eternity."

God's gifts are good and perfect because they are forever gifts. And what can be better than that?

18th- The scripture for today, January 18 (1/18), is **Isaiah 1:18** as found in the Old Testament of the Bible:

" 'Come now, let us reason together,' says the Lord. 'Though your sins are like scarlet, they shall be as white as snow; though they are red as crimson, they shall be like wool.' "

When did this become possible? Revelation in the New Testament explains in 7:14 we make our robes white by washing them in the blood of the Lamb.

What lamb? John the Baptist introduced the world to the Lamb. When he saw Jesus walking toward him in front of a crowd, he announced, "Look! The Lamb of God who takes away the sin of the world!" (John 1:29).

How did Jesus become the Lamb of God? Romans 6:23 says the wages of sin is death. In the Old Testament era, God allowed us to kill an animal in our place whenever we sinned. So, for centuries, we would sin and sacrifice an animal, sin and sacrifice an animal and on and on, for we never could stop sinning.

Finally, God offered one last sacrifice for all times. This is what Satan wanted. In order to redeem us from our soul death, Satan wanted God to die. When Jesus instituted the Lord's Supper (Communion), he did so during the Jewish Passover feast where they ate their meal of lamb. There is no mention that Jesus and his apostles ate the usual lamb. Instead, he passed around the usual wine and said from now on it represented his blood as the sacrificial Lamb. And he passed around the usual bread and said from now on it represented his body as the sacrificial Lamb. (Mark 14:12 22-25).

Then Jesus ~ God on earth ~ went out and paid our ransom by dying. Then he tricked Satan and came back to life on Sunday, overcoming death forever.

Sunday is the most special day of the week for Christians. Why? The early Christians under guidance of Jesus' apostles "broke bread" for the communion every first day of the week (Acts

20:7). May we always make this the central part of our worship on this special day.

It is snowing where some of you live. Look out your window or find a picture of snow. So white and pure and sparkling. So soft and quiet and peaceful. Oh, my Savior. You can make my soul this white? Whiter? I fall at Your feet and worship You.

19th- The scripture for today, January 19, is **James 1:19a** as found in the New Testament of the Bible:

"Everyone should be quick to listen, slow to speak and slow to become angry, for man's anger does not bring about the righteous life that God desires."

There was a book published a few years ago entitled, *Hurt People Hurt People.*

Has anyone ever tried to console you by saying, "I know how you feel"? Did you lash back at them saying something like, "How dare you think you know how bad I feel!" or "How dare you think you understand the ordeal I went through!" or "How dare you treat me like that!" ?

Those are accusing words. And what do they accomplish? It's almost like bragging. "My hurt is so far above your hurt, you could never come up to my superior level."

You may feel justified in explaining how badly you were treated by someone. But, in reality, it makes the hurt keep going and going and going.... Perhaps this is an accusing cycle you've been in for a long time with someone.

Which one of you is going to stop the cycle?

Satan is the accuser (Revelation 12:10). God is the forgiver. Even Jesus forgave his killers When you have been hurt, be ready to listen to the other person's hurt instead of accuse. And in the process, "bring about the righteous life that God desires."

20th - The scripture for today, January 20 (1/20), is **2nd Peter 1:20f** as found in the New Testament of the Bible:

"Above all, you must understand that no prophecy of Scripture came about by the prophet's own interpretation. For prophecy never had its origin in the will of man, but men spoke from God as they were carried along by the Holy Spirit."

Isn't this interesting? It's a definition of prophecy. Prophecy is Scripture. It isn't just telling the future. It's telling the mind of God. Sometimes in the Old Testament God warned his people that if they did so-and-so, this would happen, but if they did such-and-such, that would happen.

Still, ultimately all prophecy was telling people how much God loved them and wanted them in the long run to be happy. The Old Testament has much of that in it, and all the New Testament does. It is your Creator's Words.

1st Corinthians 13:8 says prophecies were going to cease and they did when we got the entire Word of God, the entire Bible.

If someone prophesied today, it would be unfair to the rest of the world, for prophecy is scripture. The rest of the world would be cheated out of knowing the complete Word of God.

You are so blessed that you do not have to guess what is on God's mind. Many other religions have to guess ~ Hinduism, Buddhism, and so on. But you have God's very own words in black and white to read over and over whenever you like ~ prophecy which is Scripture.

Read it. Absorb it. Love it. It was written by the Lover of your Soul.

21st- The scripture for today, January 21 (1/21), is **Job 1:21** as found in the Old Testament of the Bible:

" 'Naked I came from my mother's womb, and naked I will depart. The Lord gave and the Lord has taken away; may the name of the Lord be praised.' "

Wow! Is he for real? Job had every reason to turn against God. In one day his entire wealth was stolen from him, nearly all his servants were killed by an invading army, and all his children died in a storm. Why hadn't God protected him if he loved him so much?

Amidst tragedy, do you sometimes forget that Satan exists also? Job understood that whatever Satan does, God can undo.

Satan is the accuser (Revelation 12:10), but God is the forgiver. Satan can cause you to get sick, but God can heal. Satan can cause you to die, but God can bring you back to life.

Satan can make you miserable in this world, but God can take you to a better world.

Shall you leave God to fight Satan alone? You were made in his image. And how do you fight Satan? The same way Job did. Romans 12:21 says, "Do not be overcome by evil, but overcome evil with good."

Romans 8:28 says, "And we know that in all things God works for the good of those who love him." There's more....

In all these things we are more than conquerors
through him who loved us.
For I am convinced that neither death nor life,
Neither angels nor demons,
Neither the present nor the future,
Nor any powers,
Neither height nor depth,
Nor anything else in all creation
Will be able to separate us from the
Love of God
That is in Christ Jesus our Lord.
(Romans 8:37-39)

How can you be "more than a conqueror" unless you have something to conquer? How can you have "victory in Jesus" unless you have something to be victorious over?

You have periodic assignments from God. What bad thing has happened in your life lately? That is your assignment.

22nd - The scripture for today, January 22 (1/22), is **Ephesians 1:22** as found in the New Testament of the Bible:

"And God placed all things under his feet and appointed him to be head over everything for the church, which is his body, the fullness of him who fills everything in every way."

What makes this so interesting is that the church is the body of Christ. What else is the church?

Colossians 1:18 says...

the church has only one head on earth and in heaven ~ Jesus. (Some people claim to love his head but not his body. Hmmm.)

Matthew 16:17-18 says...

the church is the kingdom of heaven.

Ephesians 5:25 & 32 says...

the church is his bride.

Revelation 21:2, 9-10 says...

the church bride is the new Holy City Jerusalem.

And what does Jesus think of the church? You already know this one. Ephesians 5:25-27 says he loved the church so much that he gave himself up for her, to make her radiant ~ no stains, no wrinkles, no blemishes.

Oh, that last part: I must have missed it before. Me radiant? Human, sinful me radiant? And no stains, Lord? No stains either?

23rd - The scripture for today, January 23 (1/23), is **Romans 1:23** as found in the New Testament of the Bible:

"....and exchanged the glory of the immortal God for images made to look like mortal man and birds and animals and reptiles."

Well, the opposite has happened in our millennium. Instead of worshipping many gods, people are worshiping nothing. They declare God does not exist. They declare the existence of the universe just happened for no reason and that their minds have reason for no reason. One of their arguments is that they cannot see God.

Do you ever wish you could see God, touch God, look God in the eye? Everyone has. And we may wonder why we can't.

If this were the case, then God wouldn't be God. He wouldn't be omnipresent (present everywhere). He would only be able to listen to one prayer at a time, and the rest of the world's prayers would go unheard.

Besides, God is too big to see. It is like facing a building half an inch away. We have no way to know what the building looks like because it is so big. There are over two trillion galaxies out there, and God is larger than them all because he made them all. It is impossible to see God he fills the universe and beyond.

Let us be grateful our God is so great He cannot be limited. He is so great, he cannot be pictured or imagined. He is so great He fills our hearts and our souls.

24th- The scripture for today, January 24 (1/24), is **Jude 1:24** as found in the New Testament of the Bible:

"To him who is able to keep you from falling and to present you before his glorious presence without fault and with great joy ~ "

Yes, it is possible for Christians to fall because we have free will. But fall from what? God is perfect, and so cannot dwell with faults and imperfection. We have faults. Romans 3:23 says everyone sins. And Romans 6:23 says the wages we earn for sinning is death. Satan was holding our souls hostage in his realm of death. But God always has wanted us to live with him. What a dilemma!

God solved our problem at great expense. His Words descended to earth in a human body so he could live the faultless life for us. Then God offered Himself to die in our place, to pay the ransom to get souls out of Satan's death existence. Amazing.

But God wasn't through yet. He tricked Satan and came back to life. After that, God told the world He would consider us "without fault" vicariously through Jesus. We even today have a choice. We can enslave our souls back to Satan("fall") or we can grab hold of our spiritual freedom, spiritual life and hang on to it.

Deep down, who have you chosen?

25th- The scripture for today, January 25 (1/25), is **James 1:25** as found in the New Testament of the Bible:

"But the man who looks intently into the perfect law that gives freedom and continues to do this, not forgetting what he has heard, but doing it ~ he will be blessed in what he does."

A lot of people do not understand that there was the Law of Moses with over 600 commands in the Old Testament, and the Law of Jesus with very few commands in the New Testament. Religious leaders use the Law of Moses to justify adding fancy or fun things to worship or a separate priesthood or tithing, or whatever they like.

But they leave out stoning for adultery or disobeying your parents, killing someone who killed your relative, knocking the eye out of someone who knocked your eye out, giving a third of your income (not just a tenth), killing animals to sacrifice, etc. It's all part of the same Law!

Romans 7:4-7 says Christians have been released from the Law. Hebrews 8:13 & all of chapter 9 say the first covenant (testament/law) of Moses had regulations for worship but is obsolete in favor of the new covenant (testament/law). James 2:10 says if you try to live by the old Law but fail in just one point, you are guilty of all of it.

But how are you to know what was in the Old Law of Moses besides the fancy or fun things today's religious leaders like? There is only one possible answer: Read it. Plow through Leviticus and all those minute codes. Then you will understand.

Let us truly let loose of the old Law of Moses and cling to the "perfect Law that gives freedom" in Christ.

26th- The scripture for today, January 26 (1/26), is **1st Samuel 1:26f** as found in the Old Testament of the Bible:

"And she said to him, 'As surely as you live, my lord, I am the woman who stood here beside you praying to the Lord. I prayed for this child and the Lord has granted me what I asked of him.' "

Wow! Hannah prayed for a baby and God gave her a son! Then she told everyone. How often do you tell someone God has answered your prayer, big or little?

Or do you wander aimlessly from prayer request to prayer request, and let the answers drift away from you unnoticed? Or worse, do you ask others to pray for something, but after once or twice you stop praying for that thing yourself? A year later, someone tells you they are still praying for your something and you have completely forgotten it.

Begin today to keep a list of your prayer requests. Write down the date you first began to pray for each. If your requests are all about yourself, expand. Begin including your neighbors, your co-workers, people you attend church with, your relatives, schools, people in the newspaper.

Then begin a second list of your answers and the dates. You will be amazed how fast your Prayers Answered list grows. Do not let the answers drift away from you unnoticed.

Notice them.

Claim them.

Tell others.

And spend the rest of your life telling others and thanking God over and over and...

27th - The scripture for today, January 27 (1/27_, is **James 1:27** as found in the New Testament of the Bible:

"Religion that God our Father accepts as pure and faultless is this: To look after orphans and widows in their distress and to keep oneself from being polluted by the world."

A lot of people never lie, never cheat, never steal, never murder. Wow! That person deserves to go to heaven! Not! The greatest sin of most people who are "good" is the sin of omission. We are basically "good for nothing". We don't do the good things we should be doing.

Do you hear of someone whose relative just died? Do you call them? What about the person who is home sick: Do you send them a card? What about the person who needs a ride to the doctor: Do you give them a ride? What about the mother who sits in church with wiggly children and finally just leaves during the service out of embarrassment: Do you move over and sit with her? What about that children's home where the "orphans" would love a card, a gift certificate, a gift?

Oh, Lord God. I never thought. I have been heedless to their silent cries. I have traveled on the other side of the road from them so my perfect life is not interrupted. Lord, open my blind eyes, open my deaf ears, open my hard heart.

28th- The scripture for today, January 28 (1/28), is **1st Chronicles 1:28** s found in the Old Testament of the Bible:

"The sons of Abraham: Isaac and Ishmael."

Are you a parent with a grown or nearly-grown child who is going in the wrong direction? Have you tried everything you can think of, and nothing is working? Do you know in your heart that you have been a good example and things shouldn't have turned out like they have?

Abraham has been called the Father of the Faithful. Yet he had one son who followed Jehovah ~ Isaac ~ and one son who followed idols ~ Ishmael. Certainly, Abraham tried everything he could to "talk some sense" into Ishmael. Certainly, he prayed earnestly for Ishmael. So, what went wrong?

Just as God has given each of us free will, our children also have free will. Just as God will never force us to follow him, we cannot force our children to follow God. You did not refrain from having your children because they may have difficulties in their life, and neither did God. And when our children rebel and break our hearts, imagine what God goes through when we rebel and break his heart.

Who knows? Perhaps your child will return to God some day in your old age, or even after you have died. If your child deep down has a good heart, that is enough for God to work with.

Keep hope alive.

29th - The scripture for today, January 29 (1/29), is **Colossians 1:29** as found in the New Testament of the Bible:

"To this end I labor, struggling with all His energy which so powerfully works in me."

Wow! Hyperactive Paul, Paul who preached even while in jail, Paul who went back to preaching after he'd been beaten and told not to, Paul with the "A-type personality" said he got all that energy from Jesus Christ (see verse 28).

Who provides your energy? It depends on what you are being driven to do. It depends on what consumes you. It depends on what you're spending your time doing and what is on your mind all the time.

Think about it today.

On what things do you use the energy of Jesus?

30th- The scripture for today, January 30 (1/30), is **1st Corinthians 1:30** as found in the New Testament of the Bible:

"It is because of him that you are in Christ Jesus, who has become for us "wisdom" from God ~ that is, our...

...righteousness,

...holiness and,

...redemption."

Me? Sinful me? Considered right and holy? But I'm not right and holy. How can that be?

Let's look at these words of reassurance backward. When we are redeemed (bought back from Satan, our accuser and punisher), we gain God's holiness and God's rightness. But I am not holy and right. God, don't you understand this?

"Yes, my child," God answers. "But My Son knew how, and so became sinless for you."

I cannot let what He did for me drift by. Jesus traded. He took my sinfulness and gave me his sinlessness. He took my punishment and gave me redemption. Now, at least in the eyes of God, I am holy.

I think on this and the more I do, the more amazed I become. Me, Lord? Unworthy, sinful me? I am awed into silence and worship.

31st - The scripture for today, January 31 (1/31), is **Genesis 1:31** as found in the Old Testament of the Bible:

"God saw all that he had made, and it was very good. And there was evening, and there was morning ~ the sixth day."

Oh, how God loves to spoil us! He didn't create a barren earth and then order us to get to work and plant something. He got everything just right. And then.... And then.... Then his crowning glory ~ he created us! Special us!

However, as perfect as he made earth, he left some joyful things for us to create ourselves, for he made us like him ~ creative. He left the jewels unmined, the buildings unbuilt, the songs unwritten, the paintings unpainted, the ships unmade, the sculptures uncarved....

Here we are surrounded by everything we need to imitate one special part of God ~ his creative side. Today, create something!

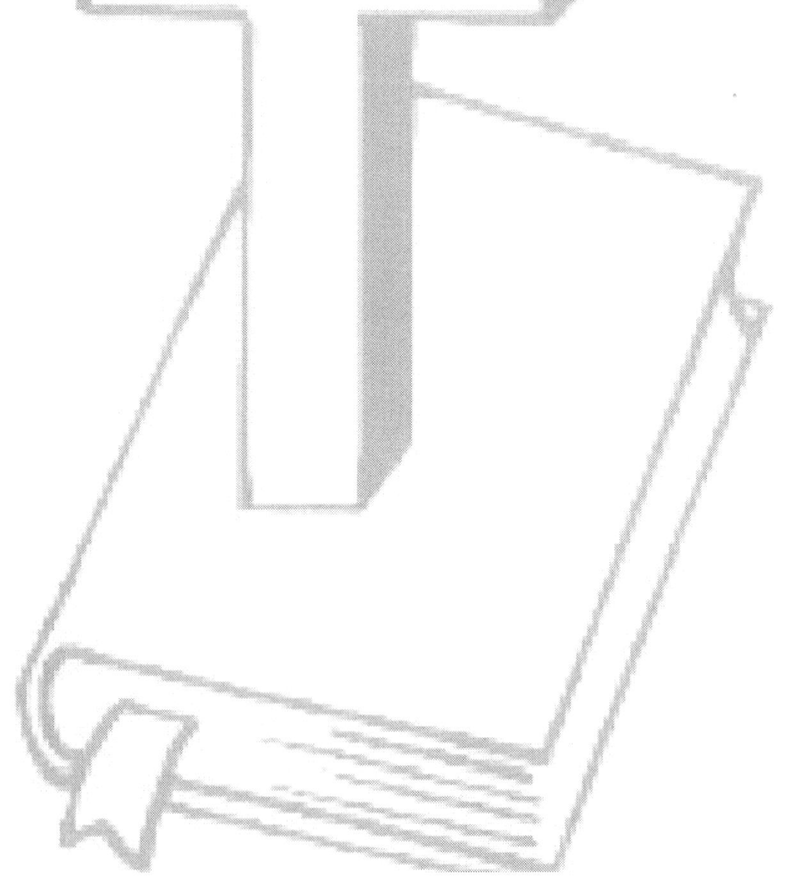

February

1st- The scripture for today, February 1 (2/1), is **Mark 2:1** as found in the New Testament of the Bible:

"A few days later, when Jesus again entered Capernaum, the people heard that he had come home."

Just think of it. Jesus coming home. The place where his family lives. The familiar places he'd seen walking around town in earlier years. The familiar faces. Hearing a voice in a crowd and recognizing it and automatically knowing s/he is a neighbor. Being able to walk through a market almost blind folded because the same shops are in their same places selling their same goods.

Has Jesus come home to your heart? Is it familiar to him? Does he recognize you? When he hears your prayers, does he automatically know who you are? Can he walk beside you as you walk through life, knowing the places you will be visiting? Does he live with you?

When he is in your heart, is he home?

2nd- The scripture for today, February 2 (2/2), is **Matthew 2:2** as found in the New Testament of the Bible:

"[the Magi/Wisemen] asked, 'Where is the one who has been born king of the Jews? We saw his star in the east and have come to worship him."

There are people who believe the "star of Bethlehem" was in the east. But the star wasn't in the east; the wise men (Magi) were.

The Christmas carol says the star led the wise men the whole way. But Matthew 2:9 & 10 says, "After they had heard the king [Herod], they went on their way, and the star they HAD seen in the east went ahead of them until it stopped over the place where the child was. When they saw the star, they were overjoyed."

They rejoiced when they saw the star again, not because it had been with them the whole time, but because it had reappeared.

The Christmas carol also speaks of them as "We Three Kings." First, there were three gifts but could have been an entourage of ten or twenty or more. Second, they were not kings. It wasn't until 600 AD that someone named them as the king of Arabia, king of India and King of Persia. The original language calls them Magi which is a tribe of astrologers and priests in Babylon and Parthia.

By the way, the manger scenes show the wise men there with the shepherds on the night Jesus was born. Jesus was around two years old by the time the wise men figured out the meaning of the star and traveled over 1000 miles to get there, following by boy babies killed ages two and under. Then there are the carols that say the angels sang are wrong. Angels do not sing. Christians do, but angels do not. Check it out. There are so many things about the Bible that we have heard all our lives and just assume are true.

Here's an idea: Investigate things for yourself! Why take a teaching about the Bible for granted? You're smart. You can do it. Will you?

3rd- The scripture for today, February 3 (2/3), is **Philippians 2:3** as found in the New Testament of the Bible:

"Do nothing out of selfish ambition or vain conceit, but in humility consider others better than yourselves."

This is probably among the top ten hardest-to-keep commands in the Bible. It's right up there near loving our enemies.

Do we consider people who stand and speak in front of an audience superior to the listeners? Even though the one up front may be all talk and no show? Even though someone in the audience prays for others more than the "leader"? Even though someone in the audience is often awake all night caring for someone who needs him? Even though someone in the audience goes down to the seedy part of town wearing rags and tells about the love of Christ to people in the cellar of life?

But we give in to it. We praise the one standing before an audience and envy all their attention and their title. Oh, my friend, who is the true leader ~ the audience or someone standing up front? Can we judge ourselves and each other as God does? Can we act as God does?

Jesus was always a server, helping others to be better. The last time he ate with his apostles before his death, he put on an apron and went around washing their feet. Apparently, none of them felt they should stoop so low as to do it. So, the Son of God did it.

4th- The scripture for today, February 4 (2/4), is **1st Timothy 2:4** as found in the New Testament of the Bible:

"[God]...wants all men to be saved and to come to a knowledge of the truth."

Some people say, "You don't choose God; God chooses only certain ones to be saved and keeps out all the other people of the world." But God wants to choose us all. He wants everyone to be saved. So, in what sense does he choose us?

He is like an employer who is looking for people to fill certain positions. He chooses those who qualify. He doesn't have to choose anyone. By the employer's grace, he chooses to hire help and give them part of his money. But we must qualify to be chosen.

I Timothy 6:11 says we were called to eternal life but have to take hold of it. II Peter 1:10 says we are to make sure his calling and choosing us. Hebrews 6:4-6 says those who fall away crucify Jesus anew.

So how do we qualify for God's grace? Certainly, atheists do not qualify, for they would not love God. People who worship another so-called god or nature do not qualify, for they would not love God. People who do not want to be looked upon as a goody-

goody would not qualify, for they would not love God.

So, again, the question: How do we qualify? First, we never deserve it. We can never do enough good works to qualify because we still sin. We can qualify to be selected for heaven only if we are sinless. Impossible! Yes, for us it is. But, because God loves us, he has given us a few things to do to qualify and be sinless in his eyes.

Believing is just the first step to qualifying. Admitting we sin and repenting is another step to qualifying. Read Romans 6 and Acts 2. Explaining what baptism is for. Not many things, but they are necessary. Look them up. Check them out.

And remember 2nd Peter 3:9 ~ "He [God] is patient with you, not wanting anyone to perish, but EVERYONE to come to repentance."

When we make ourselves God and say the Bible doesn't mean what it says so we can sneak into heaven our own way, how our Lord's heart must ache.

5th- The scripture for today, February 5 (2/5), is **Ephesians 2:5** as found in the New Testament of the Bible:

"[God] made us alive with Christ even when we were dead in transgressions ~ it is by grace you have been saved."

Every time you sin, your spirit ~ your soul ~ dies a little more. Every time you steal, cheat, torture, murder. You say you don't do such things. Well, how about every time you stretch the truth (lie), go over the speed limit (disobey the laws of the land), close your eyes to someone you know is in need (selfishness), lose your temper, indulge in coarse talk, call someone names, refuse to forgive (sins of attitude)?

It is true that all have sinned and come short of the glory of God (Romans 3:23) and your wage you collect from Satan every time you sin is death (Romans 6:23). That is what you earn. That is what you deserve. You certainly do not deserve to live with a sinless God. Nor can you. But by his grace, he made a way possible to consider you sinless.

In Old Testament times, people killed a perfect animal to die in their place, but it was only a temporary fix. Then God sent his perfect Son who never sinned ~ the Lamb of God ~ to lie down on the altar of the world at the cross. There he died spiritually and physically in your place for the things you in the world did wrong, all while the world raged at him.

Yes, while we were still enemies of God by sinning, Jesus died for you and me. That was his amazing part. His amazing grace part. He can also make you spiritually alive. If you will actively seek him. That is your part.

6th - The scripture for today, February 6 (2/6) is **Jonah 2:6f** as found in the Old Testament of the Bible:

"To the roots of the mountains I sank down; the earth beneath barred me in forever. But you brought my life up from the pit, O Lord my God. When my life was ebbing away, I remembered you, Lord, and my prayer rose to you, to your holy temple."

This is what was going through Jonah's mind as he was swallowed by the great fish and on his way to certain death.

It is never too late.

As long as the breath of life is in you, it is never too late to cry out to God. You may be in the pits of your life. You may feel you cannot sink any lower than where you are now.

But look up! God is watching you with tears. You are not only breaking your own heart, but you are breaking the heart of your Maker who loves you so. God wants to lift you up out of your pit.

Still, he cannot do it without your help. What is your part? You must lift up your hands so God can grab hold of them.

Look up! God is right there within your grasp.

7th- The scripture for today, February 7 (2/7), is **Proverbs 2:7** as found in the Old Testament of the Bible:

"He holds victory in store for the upright, he is a shield to those whose walk is blameless."

Do you feel like a loser sometimes? Once someone gets into that mindset, it is hard to break out. One dream after another has been shattered. One goal after another has been blockaded. One effort after another has been a failure.

The world can be a cruel place in which to live. It is ruled by Satan.

But look up! Victory is still possible! There is an old song called "Victory in Jesus." We may be losers to our friends, but victors to Jesus. Just remember, we cannot have victory in Jesus unless we have something to be victorious over.

Life is hard. But each day problems face us and we refuse to give in, that's victory. Each day we search God's Word for answers in the right places, that's victory. Each day we refuse to give up on Jesus despite opposition to him by those around us, that's victory.

Satan hates it when you don't give up. Satan wants you to, not only give up on yourself, but also give up on God.

Do not give up. Never give up. Turn to God who can help you with all your sins be blameless and victorious. Keep on fighting and walking, fighting and walking until at last you walk right through the gates into heaven and are given the crown of a victor.

8th - The scripture for today, February 8 (2/8), is **Genesis 2:8** as found in the Old Testament of the Bible:

"Now the Lord God had planted a garden in the east, in Eden; and there he put the man he had formed."

Just think: Mankind's nursery was a garden. How God wanted to spoil us, his children. And dote on us.

He even visited us sometimes. He walked with us in the cool of the evening through the beautiful home he had given us. It was the first of many times in the future he would walk with man. It was a beautiful time.

Then jealous Satan appeared out of the shadows of time and lied to us. He claimed God was our enemy. How could he say that with God providing tasty food to eat and sparkling water to drink beautiful flowers and trees and... Well, we had everything.

Satan knew he couldn't deny that, so he planted in their minds what they did not have. "See that tree over there? God doesn't like you or he would let you touch that tree. See that fruit over there? God doesn't like you or he would let you eat anything you want." Oh, and the biggie. "God doesn't want you to be as smart as him. Evil is fun, but he is keeping you from knowing what evil is. It's the most wonderful thing in the world. If God hates you that much, then hate him back."

So, they did. And Satan laughed. They were so gullible. Too late they discovered God had been trying to protect them.

Do you believe God doesn't want you to have any fun? That is not true. God does not hate you. God is not trying to keep you from having a good time. The real good time is in heaven and he is trying to get you there.

Do not listen to Satan. He is the one who hates you. Do not wait until it is too late. Turn around and try once more listening to God. See, he is running after you. He wants to protect you. He loves you beyond comprehension. And wants to spoil you. In heaven.

9th - The scripture for today, February 9 (2/9), is I **Corinthians 2:9** as found in the New Testament of the Bible:

"No eye has seen, no ear has heard, no mind has conceived what God has prepared for those who love him."

This amazing promise applies to us today. It also applies to eternity. Indeed, it is difficult to conceive of heaven. That is why so much of Revelation is symbolic. The symbols are beautiful. Why not try going one step beyond reading how Revelation describes heaven, and make a drawing of what you think it looks like. Here is a link to a drawing of an imagined heaven:
https://casagrandechurchofchrist.com/what-color-is-heaven
Then colorize with all those beautiful hues. Revelation 21:12,13,21:

Each of the 12 GATES is named after one of the Tribes of Israel, and has an angel guarding it. Make the gates pearl. Make the angel over the gate white or yellow.

Revelation 21:17, 18a: Make the WALL jasper, which is a light see-through green.

Revelation 21:16, 18b: Heaven is full of many MANSIONS (John 14:2). Make them a translucent (see-through) gold.

Revelation 21:21: The STREETS of the city are like crystal and gold. Make them a translucent (see-through) gold also.

Revelation 22:1: The RIVER OF LIFE runs through heaven coming out from the throne of God. Make it blue.

Revelation 4:6a: The CHRYSTAL SEA is in front of God's throne. Make it blue.

Revelation 22:2: The TREE OF LIFE grows on both

sides of the River of Life. Make it green and brown.

Revelation 22:2: The ALTER OF INCENSE from Christians' prayers is in front of the throne. Make it gold

Revelation 21:23: God's THRONE is jasper and the glory of God is so brilliant, there is no need of a sun. Make the area of the throne silver/white.

Revelation 4:5: Around the throne of God are the seven SPIRITS of God, symbolized by seven lights. Make them yellow.

Revelation 4:3a: Near the Spirits there is a ruby red GLOW around the throne of God. Make this inner arch red.

Revelation 4:3b: There is a RAINBOW over God's throne. Make the arch at the very top over the throne emerald green.

Although this is all symbolic, doesn't drawing and coloring in the symbols help understand a little bit more of how beautiful heaven will be!

10th - The scripture for today, February 10 (2/10), is **James 2:10** as found in the New Testament of the Bible:

"Out of the same mouth comes praise and cursing. My brothers, this should not be."

Do we pray on Sunday and curse on Monday? Do we sing on Sunday and lie on Monday? Do we recite a scripture on Sunday and mock someone on Monday?

On the other hand, do we use this as an excuse not to go to

church? Do we refuse to attend because there are hypocrites in the church?

Do we refuse to go to work because there are hypocrites there who talk behind the boss's back? Do we refuse to go to school because there are hypocrites there who would skip school if they could? Do we refuse to sit for two hours in a boring airport because there are hypocrites there smuggling things in their suitcases? Do we refuse to go to sporting events because there are hypocrites there that would literally "kill the umpire" if they could?

Even Jesus had a hypocrite among his 12 Apostles ~ Judas. That didn't stop him from doing what was needed to save us from hell.

In a sense we are all hypocrites because we go to church and sing songs about giving everything for Jesus, then we go home and don't. Or we sing songs about going into all the world and teaching the gospel, then we go home and don't. Or we talk about the importance of praying for everyone around us and their loved ones, then we go home and don't.

Perhaps Jesus was the biggest hypocrite of them all because he, who never, ever sinned, took the blame for your sins and went through excruciating body and soul death in your place. Oh, my Lord Jesus, how can I worship you enough? How can I thank you enough? How can my spirit touch your holiness? Get Satan away from me, for I am weak and need you.

11th - The scripture for today, February 11 (2/11),

is **Ecclesiastes 2:11** as found in the Old Testament of the Bible:

"Yet when I surveyed all that my hands had done and what I had toiled to achieve, everything was meaningless, a chasing after the wind, nothing was gained under the sun."

King Solomon wrote this. He tried everything to bring deep happiness and satisfaction into his life. He had both the money and power to do it. He tried writing books and songs. He tried having a thousand women. He tried working hard with his hands. He tried building big fancy buildings with grand gardens to surround them. He tried investing his money and becoming the richest man in the world. Nothing worked. He wandered through all his luxury feeling empty. He still couldn't achieve the deep happiness he longed for.

There was a book published a few years ago entitled, *How to Want What You Have*. Is the deep contented happiness you crave always just around the corner? If you could just get that promotion, if you could just get married, if you could just get a pay raise, if you could just be on the winning team, if you could just have children, if you could just get that next house or car or....

Always IF. Is the problem that, once you attain what you believe will bring you happiness, you just want the next promotion, the next pay raise, a different marriage partner, the next house, no children, the next car?

What was Solomon's conclusion? He suspected what it is in 3:11: "God set eternity in the hearts of man." In other words, there is a God-shaped emptiness in man's heart. Then, after he had tried everything his own way, he had only one choice left. He spelled it out in the final few verses of his writing: True happiness comes from a heartfelt relationship with God. How's your heart today?

12th - The scripture for today, February 12 (2/12), is **2nd Timothy 2:12** as found in the New Testament of the Bible:

"If we endure, we will also reign with him. If we disown him, he will also disown us."

God loves us, but never forces us to love him. He has given us a beautiful world to live in full of excitement and challenges and comforts. He has given us family and friends. He has given us his Son to take our punishment for our sins so we can live with him in his home ~ heaven. He is constantly calling to us, "I love you! Come to me for safety!"

But being the Gentleman that he is, he never forces himself on us. Instead, he lets us lead the way so to speak. If we don't want to listen to God's words, God doesn't want to listen to our words. If we don't want to spend extra time on God, God doesn't want to spend extra time on us. If we don't want anything to do with God in this life, he will not want anything to do with us in the next life.

He never forces us. But oh, how he weeps when we walk away from him.

13th- The scripture for February 13 (2/13), is **Philippians 2:13** as found in the New Testament of the Bible:

"For it is God who works in you to will and to act according to his good purpose."

Here is another related verse: "The Lord opened her heart to respond" (Acts 16:14). God the Father moved people's hearts throughout the Bible ~ Old Testament and New Testament. But he never moved hearts to do what they were not already inclined to do. He does not go against someone's will, for he gave everyone free will.

If you are struggling to know the will of your religious leaders and friends, you struggle alone. If you are sincerely struggling to know God's will and do it, the Father will help you.

If you are struggling to act according to the purpose of your religious leaders and friends, you struggle alone. If you are sincerely struggling to act according to God's good purpose, the Father will help you.

If you have a sincerely open heart, God can move you closer to himself so that he can work in you and through you on earth.

He will always tell you what to do through his Word ~ the Bible. You do not have to guess. It covers every possible situation you could ever face and shows you his good purposes.

Choose one of those purposes and do it. God the Father will work in you if you are willing. Are you?

14th - The scripture for today, February 14 (2/14), is **Colossians 2:14** as found in the New Testament of the Bible:

"[God] having canceled the written code with its regulations, that was against us and that stood opposed to us; he took it away, nailing it to the cross."

It is beyond my comprehension why anyone would want the Law of Moses unless they don't want to obey ALL 600 commands but want an excuse to justify the one or two HERE AND THERE they do want.

They want the part that says to tithe so they can get people's money. (Actually, the good Jew gave one-third, not one-tenth.) Or they want a separate priesthood so they can feel important. Or they want showy things in worship like candles, incense, musical instruments (though they were only allowed the harp, lyre and cymbal) so they can enjoy themselves more.

Hold on! If we obey one command, we are required to keep the entire Law of Moses ~ all 600 commands. Galatians 5:3 and James 2:10 say so. Are you up to it?

Our verse for today says the Law was against us; that is, it was impossible for us to keep perfectly. Try wading through Leviticus in the Old Testament. That's where most of the old Law ("the written code with its regulations") is.

It's tedious. It regulated nearly every part of everyone's daily life. It involved what we could and couldn't eat, having to kill animals to die in our place whenever we sinned, stoning adulterers and rebellious children to death, having a separate Levite priesthood, giving a third of your income, reporting to priests as long as we had an open sore, use of candles, having to go to the Temple in Jerusalem three times a year, spreading blood on our door posts, and on and on.

The book of Hebrews in the New Testament was written to help us understand that God's new Law of Grace is much more spiritual. Read especially chapters 8 & 9. We have to make a choice: Old or New.

Hebrews was written about the time the Temple in Jerusalem was permanently destroyed, thus making it impossible to obey several things in the old Law. And a little time later the Jewish genealogies were destroyed, thus making it impossible to prove who was a Levite and eligible to be a priest.

But wait! Does that mean Christians should never read the Old Testament? The Old Testament of the Bible is not the same as the Law of Moses. The Law is a small part of the Old Testament. The rest of it is wonderful praise, amazing wisdom, accounts of people who did or did not try to follow God, and those astounding prophecies of Jesus all through them. Plus, it doesn't hurt to wade through those old laws just as a reminder of what we have been set free from.

So, let us not neglect the Old Testament as so many people do. Thank God for the Old Testament.

15th- The scripture for today, February 15 (2/15), is **2nd Timothy 2:15** as found in the New Testament of the Bible:

"Do your best to present yourself to God as one approved, a workman who does not need to be ashamed and who correctly handles the word of truth."

"Do your best," Paul told a younger co-worker. "Do your best."

This was an apostle speaking. This was Paul who had endured multiple beatings with rods and lashings with whips. This was Paul who no one could stop.

He had endured floods and snowstorms, hunger and robbers on the road. Still, no one could stop him. He endured ship wrecks and even treading water a day and night in the sea. Nothing could stop him.

It seems with Paul, it was never enough. He was driven. When he was stoned and presumed dead, he got up and went back into the city! When he was imprisoned, he defied the magistrates who put him there and sang his sermons to the other prisoners. Nothing could stop him. Nothing could shut him up.

When he wrote this, he was now in prison. He had done his best. Now it was time for the next generation. He was handing the torch over to Timothy and the others.

"Do your best, Timothy. Don't let them stop you. Never let them stop you. They are lost and don't know it. Tell them, Timothy. Keep telling them, no matter how terribly they treat you. Keep telling them and keep telling them. Don't stop, Timothy. Do your best.

"Some will stop what they are doing and listen to you. They will turn their life around. They will be there with you when it is time to be presented to God. They will be there with you, and with you they will say, "I did my best."

16th- The scripture for today, February 16 (2/16), is **2nd Thessalonians 2:16** as found in the New Testament of the Bible:

"May our Lord Jesus Christ himself and God our Father, who loved us and by his grace gave us eternal encouragement and good hope, encourage your hearts and strengthen you in every good deed and word."

Who were these people the apostle Paul was writing? They were suffering. Physically they were suffering. Some in their group had even been killed for their faith. Mentally they were suffering. Would they be next? Would it be worth everything they were going through?

Spiritually they were struggling. The apostle Paul, who wrote this, had been through such struggles many times himself. He wanted to make sure their faith did not waver.

How? By praying that their persecution would stop? At no time in the Bible do we have an account of Christians pray that the persecution stop. What did they pray for? Boldness.

They could be bold if they knew Jesus Christ loved them personally. They could be bold if they knew God the Father loved them personally. They could be bold with eternal encouragement, strength.

"Just keep doing what you've been doing," he told them.

With the strength God gives you, keep doing good deeds, good spreading the Word." Persecuted? Yes. Frightened? Yes. Frightened? Yes. Cowering? Never.

How about your life?

God's encouragement never ceases. It is always there. There when you feel alone, when you feel forsaken, when you are frightened, when you feel helpless, when you feel hopeless.

God gives good hope. Sometimes things in your life may be going so badly you have trouble having faith in God. But you can still hope. The candle of your faith may be flickering, but your hope can still be a flaming hope, a large hope, a good hope.

17th- The scripture for today, February 17 (2/17), is **1st John 2:17** as found in the New Testament of the Bible:

"The world and its desires pass away, but the man who does the will of God lives forever."

Have you lost anything very important to you lately? Has it left you feeling empty?

Were you injured and cannot participate in a certain sport or your bones are getting old and you have to get around in a wheelchair? Did you lose a savings or part of your income and no longer can buy fancy clothes, a shiny car, a big house? Did you miss out on being an official for a committee or community and all the importance that comes with it?

The previous verse in the KJV says there are three basic

types of sins: Lust of the flesh and eye, and pride. Is your loss devastating to you? Do you now feel worthless? Do you sometimes even have fleeting thoughts that life is no longer worth living?

Or, perhaps you recently obtained your heart's desire. Were you satisfied? Or did you begin to look higher wanting a little more? Take a deep look at yourself? Do you think you will ever be truly satisfied?

What are your cravings? Are they all that important? Are they all that valuable?

Only one thing can ever give us what we truly crave ~ doing the gentle will of God. He is our Creator and he knows what will make us happy. Then we can have all we ever craved ~ forever.

18th - The scripture for today, February 18 (2/18), is **Hebrews 2:18** as found in the New Testament of the Bible:

"Because he himself suffered when he was tempted, he is able to help those who are being tempted."

Do you find yourself caught up in some kind of sin over and over? Is the temptation always there? Do you commit the sin and then curse yourself for your weakness in giving in to the temptation? Do you see no way out?

A lot of people never think of Jesus ever being tempted. He was too good. But he had a human body and was tempted in every way that we are (Hebrews 4:15).

Try to imagine Jesus with your particular haunting temptation and imagine how you think he would have resisted it. Jesus used to get angry at temptation, which of course is caused by Satan. In other words, he got angry at Satan. One time when tempted, he declared, "Get behind me, Satan!"

Temptation is not the same thing as sin. Temptation is when we want to commit a sin, but haven't decided yet to do it. Jesus faced Satan (temptation) head on. Once when he went through over a month of harsh temptation alone in the wilderness, Satan gave him all the reasons he should do certain things and made them look so good and reasonable; then Jesus gave all the reasons he should not do those things.

Hebrews 4:15 says, "We do not have a high priest [Jesus] who is unable to sympathize with our weaknesses, but we have one who has been tempted in every way, just as we are ~ yet was without sin."

Jesus stood up to Satan. Jesus was a spiritual warrior. Today, be a warrior.

19th - The scripture for today, February 19 (2/19), is **Ephesians 2:19** as found in the New Testament of the Bible:

"Consequently, you are no longer foreigners and aliens, but fellow citizens with God's people and members of God's household."

Let us pretend there is a nation called Occland and we want to become a citizen of that nation. Of course, citizenship would not be automatic. And in the same way, citizenship in the Kingdom of God (being a Christian) is not automatic.

Just living in Occland would not automatically make us a citizen of Occland any more than just living in a Christian nation automatically makes us a Christian.

Owning a copy of Occland's constitution would not automatically make us a citizen of Occland any more than owning a copy of the Bible automatically makes us a Christian.

Going to meetings of parliament or the senate every of Occland every time they met would not automatically make us a citizen of Occland any more than going to meetings with other Christians every Sunday automatically make us a Christian.

It just is not automatic. We would need to be invited into Occland, and then do things to accept Occland's invitation. God invites us into his kingdom, but we must do things to accept his invitation. Romans 6, Acts 2 and 1st Peter 3 in the New Testament are good places to check it out. Do so.

Oh, to be citizens in the kingdom founded by the Creator of the universe. Is it possible? Really possible? For me too? For me too? It's not automatic, but it is possible.

20th - The scripture for today, February 20 (2/20), is **Galatians 2:20** as found in the New Testament of the Bible:

"I have been crucified with Christ and I no longer live, but Christ lives in me. The life I live in the body I live by faith in the Son of God who loved me and gave himself for me."

The apostle Paul wrote this. He had been an angry, spiteful, and hateful man in his younger days. He had been a terrorist and had even declared holy jihad against Christians He had gone around the country rounding up Christians and sending them either to prison or to their death. He hated Christians.

But once Jesus got his attention and Paul realized he was persecuting those who could tell him the true way to heaven, he switched sides. Jesus had to do it himself because all the Christians were afraid of him. Then Paul, so to speak, crucified his old self, and let Jesus and his words live in him instead. All his tremendous energy that he had used for hate was now used for love, and he turned his part of the world upside down for Christ.

Is there someone in your life or that you know of who is angry, spiteful, and hateful? Dare to talk to that person and tell them how much God loves him/her. S/he will argue with you and maybe even be meaner to you than ever. But when things calm down, try saying something else, perhaps about what Jesus did or said once in his life.

It may take you months or years. S/he will be curious why you keep coming back when s/he is being so mean to you. And eventually, this same person who uses all his enormous energy in a negative way, just might turn that same enormous energy around and use it for Jesus in a great way.

Give it a try. If you are crucified with Christ, then nothing anyone says can hurt you because your ego is dead. Keep trying to reach this enemy of Jesus. Keep trying to help this person become Jesus' friend and defender.

You may be the only one in his or her world with the courage to do it. Keep trying. Cry in private after the insult, then take a deep breath and try once again. And once again. And again. Never stop. Who knows?

21st - The scripture for today, February 21 (2/21), is **Daniel 2:21** as found in the Old Testament of the Bible:

"He [God] changes times and seasons; he sets up kings and deposes them. He gives wisdom to the wise and knowledge to the discerning."

It seems there is always some amount of restlessness within each nation regarding who is ruling. Some people like the ruler, some do not. Or people may start out liking the ruler, but later dislike him. Some rulers are okay, a few are considered outstanding, and a few others are outright evil.

But God sets up the rulers of nations and deposes them. Many places among the prophets of the Old Testament, God explains that he may raise up a cruel leader just because he is strong enough to get rid of other cruel people. After that, God deposes the cruel leader.

In the midst of all this, innocent people are always hurt. That is why it is important for us not to complain, but to bear up under a hard government with patience and courage. It is in hardship that the true heart of a Christian is revealed. And it is in hardship that many people turn to God who might never have done so.

God knows what he is doing, even if we do not understand ~ at least, on this side of eternity. Remember Romans 8:28 ~ "All things work together for good to those who love the Lord." Life is a mosaic of many colors ~ sometimes bright and sometimes dark ~ but in the end, it can be beautiful.

22nd - The scripture for today, February 22 2/22), is **Ephesians 2:22** as found in the New Testament of the Bible:

"And in him you too are being built together to become a dwelling in which God lives by his Spirit."

Another place in the New Testament, 2nd Corinthians 6:16, says we are the temple of God. A lot of things in worship under the Law of Moses were a literal version of what Christians someday would enjoy in a spiritual and deeper sense.

We have no need for the temple in Jerusalem, for now God dwells in Christians. We have no need for the altar of sacrifice at that temple because Jesus was our final sacrifice (Hebrews 10:4-12). We have no need for the cymbals, harps and lyres played in worship, because Christians play on the strings of their hearts (Ephesians 5:19).

We have no need for the priestly system in the Law of Moses with the special vestments and titles because all Christians are priests (1st Peter 2:5). And how do we serve as priests? Romans 12:1 explains it: "Offer your bodies as living sacrifices."

What a concept! God does not dwell in temples or church

buildings!

He dwells in Christians.

He lives and moves through Christians.

What a privilege.

What a responsibility.

23rd- The scripture for today, February 23 (2/23), is **1st John 2:23** as found in the New Testament of the Bible:

"No one who denies the Son has the Father; whoever acknowledges the Son has the Father also."

When you speak into a tape recorder and your voice then comes out of that machine for other people to hear, that doesn't make you two. You are still one; you have just chosen to put your voice in something where you can be heard by people away from you. That tape recording is just another form of you. You can also put your voice and body in a movie. That doesn't make two of you ~ one on the screen and one in your physical body. You are still one.

God is One, and yet he revealed a part of himself in a burning bush to Moses just like you revealed a part of yourself in the tape recorder or movie. Does that mean there were two Gods ~ one in heaven and one in the bush? No. God can and has sometimes revealed himself in different ways. Remember how he walked with Adam and Eve in the Garden of Eden?

Some say, "If Jesus was God on earth, when he died, God was dead." No. That temporary body was dead, but God's Spirit,

God's Soul, God's being continued to live. Jesus, the Word of God, did not depend on a body to be alive.

Why would Jesus be called the Son of God, since he was not a son created in the literal way we have sons? You have thoughts and those thoughts have existed as long as you have. But you still created those thoughts. When your thoughts become hearable or seeable, people call that your "brain child". In that same sense, Jesus was God's "brain child" ~ God's thoughts in hearable and seeable form.

How was he the only begotten Son? God has only one Word ~ the Bible. "In the beginning was the Word, the Word was with God, and the Word was God...All things were made through Him, and without Him nothing was made that was made" (John 1:1-3). When God spoke the world into existence, that was Jesus. Every time God spoke, that was Jesus.

"For unto us a Child is born, unto us a Son is given...Wonderful, Counselor, Mighty God, Everlasting Father, Prince of Peace" (Isaiah 9:6). God has always been one.

24th- The scripture for today, February 24 (2/24), is **1st Peter 2:24** as found in the New Testament of the Bible:

"He himself bore our sins in his body on the tree, so that we might die to sins and live for righteousness; by his wounds you have been healed."

Many people do not understand what Jesus dying on the cross has to do with us going to heaven. After all, if we don't murder, steal, abuse others and only lie a little, God has no choice but to take us into heaven. But God is perfect, so cannot co-exist with imperfection ~ even one tiny sin.

Romans 3:23 says all have sinned and come short of the glory of God. And Romans 6:23 says the wages of sin is death. So, all through the Old Testament era, whenever we sinned, God allowed us to kill/sacrifice a perfect animal and spill its blood to collect the death wages in our place. Notice, the animal had to be perfect and this was a temporary fix.

Eventually God sent his own Son to come to earth and live in a human body and be tempted in every way that we are (see Hebrews 4:15). Jesus resisted all temptations, and lived his entire life sinless. He was perfect morally, just as the sacrificial animals were perfect physically.

Then as the perfect Lamb of God (John 1:29), Jesus became the final sacrifice. He died in our place. He took the terrible wages of death for our sins. On the cross, he died spiritually (forsaken by God) and physically with blood dripping from the wounds in his hands and feet. Then God basically told the world, "I will consider you perfect too; all you have to do is believe in and follow my Son."

It is explained further in Romans 6:3-4. Just as Jesus died bearing our sins, we die to our sinful nature ~ the part of us that sins and doesn't care. Then just as Jesus was buried in his tomb, we are buried in the watery tomb of baptism. And finally, just as Jesus rose up out of his tomb the Savior, we rise up out of our watery tomb the saved ~ born again to a new life.

Indeed, by Jesus' wounds we can be healed. We fall at his feet and say, "I am a sinner and so unworthy. Thank you."

25th - The scripture for today, February 25 (2/25), is **Revelation 2:25** as found in the New Testament of the Bible:

"Only hold on to what you have until I come."

Several years ago my 91-year-old mother left this life. Some say that at the moment of death, one's life flashes before their eyes. In the case of my mother, at the moment of her death, her life flashed before my eyes.

I suddenly imagined her as a baby in her mother's (my grandmother's) lap. Then she was a toddler playing in their yard. Then I saw her in school, then as a young bride to my father, then at home with her husband and children gathered around her. Then I saw her as launching a career after we were grown, then retiring, then eventually going into the nursing home.

And when that brief moment of envisioning her whole life was gone, I whispered, "You made it, Mother! You made it! You never faltered. Through all those years of ups and downs, you never wavered in your faith in Jesus Christ. You stuck it out. And now you're home!"

May we all live our life in such a way that, despite our ups and downs, we never wander from Jesus. We stick with him through every storm, every flood, every blast of tragedy, every tumbling of dreams. Let us hold on to what we have until the day we leave this temporary life and enter our true eternal life.

26th - The scripture for today, February 26 (2/26), is **Ecclesiastes 2:26** as found in the Old Testament of the Bible:

"To the man who pleases him, God gives wisdom, knowledge and happiness, but to the sinner he gives the task of gathering and storing up wealth to hand it over to the one who pleases God. This too is meaningless, a chasing after the wind."

Are you happy regardless of how much wealth you do or do not have? Do you require things in order to be happy? Solomon, who wrote the above scripture, was the wealthiest man in the world, but he found it to be meaningless, a chasing after the wind. In another place in Ecclesiastes (5:10) he said that a man loving money never has enough.

Indeed, centuries later, the highly educated and intelligent apostle Paul, who did not own a home or much of anything else, explained his happiness: "I have learned to be content whatever the circumstances. I know what it is to be in need and I know what it is to have plenty. I have learned the secret of being content in any and every situation, whether well fed or hungry, whether living in plenty or in want" (Philippians 4:11b-12).

If you lost everything tomorrow, would you panic? Or would you use God's wisdom and knowledge to create a new happiness? Might you look around and begin doing something you have always wanted to do but were too tied down with things to do? If you lost everything tomorrow, might it bring a new freedom to you or paralyze you?

27th - The scripture for today, February 27 (2/27), is **Jeremiah 2:27** as found in the Old Testament of the Bible:

" 'Why do you bring charges against me? You have all rebelled against me,' declares the Lord."

More and more people are blaming God for bad things happening in their life. That is their excuse for rebelling against God and declaring he does not even exist. Their view of God is a Santa Claus or Genie in a Bottle who grants their every wish and keeps them from all harm. No one ever dies, no one ever sins, and it is heaven on earth.

Other people sometimes blame God for bad things happening in their life because blaming is one of the ways they handle their grief. They don't really want to blame God because they want to think God loves them. But there is no one else to blame.

No one else to blame? Oh, yes, there is. There is Satan. We tend to forget Satan is out there too. It is Satan who causes bad to happen, not God.

Is that what you've done lately ~ blame God for bad happening, then rebel against him? Or do you know someone who is going through many problems not of their doing or choosing? Are they blaming God and rebelling against him? Help them. Remind them of Satan.

People want to blame someone. They will be relieved to be reminded that Satan exists. Now they can put the blame where it belongs.

Let us not blame God for the bad. Instead, let us thank Him for the good. Ah, yes. God does love us after all and is the source of everything good.

28th - The scripture for today, February 28 (2/28), is **Jeremiah 2:28** as found in the Old Testament of the Bible:

"Where then are the gods you made for yourselves? Let them come if they can save you when you are in trouble! For you have as many gods as you have towns, O Judah."

Today we think the whole thing is ridiculous. How could people believe in a multitude of gods? Further, how could people make statues of them as though anyone knew what the gods looked like? On top of that, many of them looked like dumb animals.

Apparently it was the popular thing to do. In fact, a person discovering yet another god would be highly esteemed. And it seemed logical that the more gods one believed in, the more holy a person was. Or the bigger the statue of a god in one's home, the more dedicated a person was.

We today call them myths ~ things that were made up out of people's imaginations. Yet they thrived in their time. Why? Because of "mass hypnosis" in a sense. Humans are social beings and we don't like being ostracized. We want to be accepted.

Do we do the same thing today? There are evangelists on television who draw crowds of hundreds and thousands. They seem so right and so holy. Yet they contradict each other. So it cannot be a measure of rightness and holiness that a lot of people believe something.

The measure must be the Bible. Many religious leaders in antiquity and up to today have duped peopled because they look and act so holy. Remember, no matter how many thousands upon thousands follow a religious leader, that leader will be judged by God just like everyone else.

There are a lot of religious contradictions out there. We cannot say "all religions are right in their own way". Is it ever possible to sort through all the contradictions and come up with what is the truth? Is it possible to know for sure?

Let us read the Bible for ourselves. Let us study the Bible for ourselves. Let us not search the scriptures for something to prove our opinion right, or a certain leader right, or our family right, or a particular religious idea right. Let us try to erase all our pre-conceived religious notions, and read with an open mind what God himself has to say to us. It is possible to know for sure.

29th - The scripture for today, February 29 (2/29), is **1st Samuel 2:29** as found in the Old Testament of the Bible:

" 'Why do you scorn my sacrifice and offering that I prescribed for my dwelling? Why do you honor your sons more than me

by fattening yourselves on the choice parts of every offering made by my people Israel?' "

This is God talking to the high priest Eli. The high priest who held his office until he was a very old man. The high priest who raised one of the greatest prophets in history, Samuel, to manhood.

As successful as Eli seemed, when it came to choosing between his family and God, he chose his family. His sons were priests and taking more than they were allowed of the people's offerings at the tabernacle. God finally punished them himself because Eli never did, and God's punishment was much more severe.

But Eli did not want to hurt the feelings of his sons. Eli didn't want to alienate his sons. Eli wanted his sons to like him.

Did he not think about the fact that he was hurting the feelings of God? Did he not care that he was alienating God? Did it occur to him how serious it was to let his sons have their own way instead of letting God have his own way?

Is that what is happening in your family? On Sunday mornings, if your family would rather watch a favorite TV program than worship God, who do you give in to? On Sunday nights, if your children think it's more important to get school clothes or supplies than worship God, who do you give in to? On Wednesday nights, if some family members want to participate in a team activity instead of learning what to do to save their eternal souls from hell, who do you give in to?

"What good is it...to gain the whole world, yet forfeit [your] soul?" (Mark 8:36)

March

1st - The scripture for today, March 1 (3/1), is **1st Thessalonians 3:1,5** as found in the New Testament of the Bible:

"So when we could stand it no longer, we thought it best to be left by ourselves in Athens....For this reason, when I could stand it no longer, I sent to find out about your faith. I was afraid that in some way the tempter might have tempted you and our efforts might have been useless."

In Thessalonica there had been a riot, and the man who had given Paul and his helpers a place to live was hauled into court. Paul just couldn't put his host through that so "when we could stand it no longer" he left the city and went off by himself so he wouldn't jeopardize anyone else.

Still the great Apostle Paul ~ who went everywhere preaching non-stop for decades; who stood up under beatings, stonings, hunger, and ship wrecks; who explained to church leaders how to lead their congregation; whose letters were prophecy and became scripture ~ the powerful Apostle Paul still felt very tenderly toward his fellow Christians.

He worried about how they were getting along spiritually.

And when he "could stand it no longer" he wrote back to Thessalonica to find out how they were doing.

Tender love is a powerful love. A strong love. A love that will never, ever let go. Do you feel this way about the spiritual well-being of other people? Is there someone you need to call or write to today because you want to find out how they are? Do you have any words of encouragement for them? Any at all?

2nd - The scripture for today, March 2 (3/2), is **2nd Corinthians 3:2** as found in the New Testament of the Bible:

"You yourselves are our letter written on our hearts, known and read by everybody."

As important as it is to read the Bible for yourself and determine for yourself what you will follow, it is equally important to put those things into your heart at the ready for practical life application on a moment's notice. But isn't knowledge of truth enough? Just giving our heart to Jesus as Lord isn't enough?

James 2:19 says that even demons believe, but they are still demons and still bound for hell. It takes more than faith. There are things to do.

Are you a letter from God to people around you? Or do you have a double standard, acting one way around worshipers and another way around non-worshipers? People read our hearts by our words and actions. What do people read in your heart?

Do you absolutely and completely believe people will go to

hell without Jesus? Do you absolutely and completely believe people have to rise above demons who believe but who are still going to hell? Do you absolutely and completely believe you could be the only one in your family's and friends' lives who cares enough for their soul that you will actually say something ~ put your heart letter into words?

Do you love them more than yourself? Do you love anyone more than yourself? Do you love them enough?

3rd - The scripture for today, March 3 (3/3), is **Genesis 3:3** as found in the Old Testament of the Bible:

" 'But God did say, 'You must not eat fruit from the tree that is in the middle of the garden, and you must not touch it or you will die.' "

This is a conversation Eve is having with Satan in the Garden of Eden. She was a little put out by God that he would withhold even one item from her. So she misrepresented God. What God actually said was....

"You are free to eat from any tree in the garden; but you must not eat from the tree of the knowledge of good and evil." Eve had added to what God had said: "You must not touch it."

Do we do that? When we get put out by someone, do we embellish a little and add a few little things to an event in order to make the other person look worse than s/he really is? Are we in the habit of making ourselves a victim so we can get other people's sympathy and maybe get other people to act on our behalf? Or perhaps we do it to "brag" how great our adversity it over and above all others' adversity, thus gaining admirers?

1st Corinthians 13:5 says love does not keep a record of wrongs. If you have a feud going with someone, try breaking the cycle. 1st Corinthians 13:7 says love protects, always trusts, always hopes. Had Satan convinced Eve to stop loving God?

It's easy to do when God is made "the bad guy". It's easy to stop loving others if they are always the "bad guy". What are we missing by not extending love even to those who are not nice to us? Who knows? Are we giving up paradise?

4th- The scripture for today, March 4 (3/4), is **James 3:4** as found in the New Testament of the Bible:

"Take ships as an example. Although they are so large and are driven by strong winds, they are steered by a very small rudder wherever the pilot wants to go."

James, in this scripture, is talking about the tongue being a small thing, but it can get our entire lives into a lot of trouble. Once we say things, we cannot take them back.

What do you spend your day saying to people? You do have a choice. People do more good things than bad things. Do you respond to them with more good or more bad words? It is your choice.

When you compliment someone, they will take heart and try

to do that good thing even more. When you berate someone, they will lose heart and probably do the bad thing again. Years ago there was a saying, "You can catch more flies with honey than vinegar." Are your words honey or vinegar?

Jesus said out of our heart comes our words. If you normally say nice things to others, it shows you have a nice heart. If you normally say hard things to others, it shows you have a hard heart. Jesus also said, "Do to others as you would have them do to you."

Starting now, when you launch out into a new day, go of your way to say small nice things to people. The rudder of your tongue may be small, but oh how powerful it is. You may even provide a rudder to help someone out of a private storm. How powerful your words are.

5th - The scripture for today, March 5 (3/5), is **Titus 3:5** in the New Testament of the Bible:

"He saved us, not because of righteous things we had done, but because of his mercy. He saved us through the washing of rebirth and renewal by the Holy Spirit."

God is perfectly good and cannot dwell with imperfection. How, then, could we ever live with him in his heaven? After all, as hard as we tried, we could not be perfect. Mankind was held hostage by Satan.

God loved us so much that he solved our dilemma. He sent

his Son to live that perfect life that is impossible for us to live. Then, his perfect "Lamb of God" took our punishment for our sins by paying the ransom to get us out of the clutches of Satan.

Romans 3:23 says the earnings of sin is death ~ physical death (separation from this world) and spiritual death (separation from God). Jesus took it all for us. And that included being completely separated from God. At the worst of it, Jesus cried out to God, "Why have your FORSAKEN me?" That's when Jesus died spiritually for a while. It was we who deserved to be forsaken by God.

Sin and its power now destroyed, God said if we go "through the washing of rebirth" we will be renewed by the Holy Spirit.

But how? God did not leave us guessing, for in Acts 22:16 he said through Peter, "Arise and be baptized and wash away your sins" and in Romans 6:4 he said through Paul, "We were therefore buried with him through baptism in order that...we too may live a new life [rebirth]." Then we could start over pure and washed.

God took care of the hard part. He gave us the easy part. And so we worship him.

6th - The scripture for today, March 6 (3/6), is **Proverbs 3:6** as found in the Old Testament of the Bible:

"In all your ways acknowledge him, and he will make your paths straight."

Is your life full of twists and turns, short cuts that never work out, detours, mountains to climb and valleys to make your way through? Welcome to the human race. Life on earth can be hard. Did you know the Bible calls Satan the god of this world (2nd Corinthians 4:4) and ruler of this world (John 12:31)?

Your path to heaven is another matter. Your path to heaven is straight. God has done everything in his power to straighten your path and make it easier for you to reach him. How? By providing his Son to die in your place for our sins, and by providing you with His Word to read any time you see trouble ahead (Psalm 119:105).

Do you see a mountain ahead of you that is impossible to climb or valley so full of darkness you cannot bear the thought of entering it? Do you see a curve in the road ahead of you and dread knowing where it will lead you to?

Colossians 1:13 says God can rescue you from Satan's domain of darkness and transfer you to the kingdom of Jesus Christ. There God takes control. There God says, "Hold on a minute, Christian, while I lower than mountain, brighten that valley, straighten that curve."

The path to heaven ~ thanks to our merciful God ~ is straight. What path are you on?

7th- The Scripture for today, March 7 (3/7), is **Titus 3:7** as found in the New Testament of the Bible:

"So that, having been justified by his grace, we might become heirs having the hope of eternal life."

Being "just" means being correct, being law abiding, being perfect. No one is. Romans 3:23 says "All have sinned and come short of the glory of God."

But God wants you to live in his home so much, he was willing to overlook your sins and pretend you are correct, law abiding, perfect ~ just. When you follow God and obey the few commands he has for you in the New Testament to become a Christian and stay a Christian, in his eyes you become just.

Not only just, but God has put you in his last will and testament, what we call the New Testament. It contains his guidelines and what you will inherit. Your inheritance is explained in large part in Revelation ~ God's heaven. And what an inheritance!

But, back to the overlooking part. God does so to the same extent you overlook the sins others commit against you. Yes, even if they do it over and over, just like you commit the same sins over and over and expect God to forgive you. Now, where is your inheritance?

8th - The scripture for today, March 8 (3/8), is **Philippians 3:8** as found in the New Testament of the Bible:

"What is more, I consider everything a loss compared to the surpassing greatness of knowing Christ Jesus my Lord, for whose sake I have lost all things. I consider them rubbish that I may gain Christ."

Wow! Paul, who wrote this, considered everything he had previously owned and every position he had ever held as rubbish ~ garbage ~ compared with belonging to his Lord.

Paul apparently came from a well-to-do family since he was born in today's Turkey but went to school in Jerusalem. He also apparently held a position in the Jewish ruling body, the Sanhedrin, since he could vote on whether to execute someone. So he probably owned a lot of things and had an honored position. The King James Version of the Bible says he considered it all as dung ~ manure.

Where are your priorities? What do you spend most of your time on? The stuff you just have to own, exciting things you just have to do, the power you just have to claim? All to enhance the little inch of your life on earth?

What if a storm destroyed your house, your car and all your stuff tomorrow? What if you were banned from a sport you love tomorrow? What if a rumor destroyed your career with all its power tomorrow? Then what?

Do you think you would consider suicide as so many of the wealthy did during the Great Depression? Or could you consider the deep and unconquerable love of Christ Jesus your Lord the most valuable thing in your life? Could you accept your loss, take advantage of it, and unleash a different kind of life for Jesus with no regrets?

9th - The scripture for today, March 9 (3/9), is **Ephesians 3:9f** as found in the New Testament of the Bible:

"To make plain to everyone the administration of this mystery, which for ages past was kept hidden in God, who created all things. His intent was that now, through the church, the manifold wisdom of God should be made known to the rulers and authorities in the heavenly realms, according to his eternal purpose which he accomplished in Christ Jesus our Lord."

Ever wonder why God created the world? Here it is: The "mystery". The" mystery" can be discovered by making a chart each time "mystery" appears in the Bible along with who understands it and who does not.

The "mystery" as expanded upon in this letter to the church in Ephesus, is Jesus paying the ransom for us sinners and setting us free from Satan. It is complete and full forgiveness.

Who does God desire to explain this "mystery" to? Rulers and authorities in heavenly realms ~ angels, demons and Satan. You see, angels don't seem to get it, and Satan does not want anyone to be forgiven.

Satan spends a lot of time and energy convincing people good is bad and bad is good. He doesn't want to be the only one going to hell. And he wants to prove he is stronger than God. But even when Satan is successful and we sin, God just negates it and forgives us. There is nothing that Satan can do that God cannot undo. That enrages Satan.

Oh, the grand "mystery". It is God's love demonstrated by the death and resurrection of his Son so we can be set free. This "mystery" is revealed through the church who has believed it. Open the door to the "mystery" and step inside. God is there waiting for you. And he is smiling.

10th - The scripture for today, March 10 (3/10), is **Colossians 3:10** as found in the New Testament of the Bible:

"And have put on the new self, which is being renewed in knowledge in the image of its Creator."

Did you ever make something with your hands and it was your pride and joy? Were you so proud of it that you would stop at nothing to take care of it and make sure that it lasted forever? Yes, you had a few rules about its care. You had a few rules about who could touch it and who couldn't. You have a few rules about whether it should be kept at high or low temperature, should or shouldn't be exposed to water. You were its creator and it was, in a sense, a part of you.

Do you resist knowing the Bible because you think of it as being full of rules from a God who doesn't really like you and is just giving you a hard time so you can't have any fun?

Think again. He made you. You are his pride and joy. He will stop at nothing to make sure you will last forever. He made a few rules for your daily spiritual care.

He is your Creator. He loved you enough to make you, and you are a part of him. Now he wants to take care of you so that you can last forever. Can you love him back ~ your maker and the lover of your soul?

11th - The scripture for today, March 11 (3/11), is **Ecclesiastes 3:11** as found in the Old Testament of the Bible:

"...He has also set eternity in the hearts of men...."

People have always thought about eternity. Everyone wonders sometimes why we are here and what happens when we die. All people hope to live on.

That instinct is God speaking to us saying, "Yes, there is an eternity, and I want to be part of yours."

Indeed, there is a God-shaped emptiness in the heart of man. God wants to fill it. We want him to.

But how bad do we want him to? If we spend each day so busy pursuing things and pleasures and power, it's easy to forget about him. Then our heart aches, and we do not understand why.

It is eternity calling out to you still. It is God calling out to you still. Listen! He's calling you in His Word ~ the Bible. Open it and listen. Shhh. Don't you hear him?

12th - The scripture for today, March 12 (3/12), is Ezekiel 3:12 as found in the Old Testament of the Bible:

"The Spirit lifted me up and I heard behind me a loud rumbling sound ~ May the glory of the Lord be praised in his dwelling place!"

This is quite interesting because, despite some who preach being "slain in the Spirit," the Spirit does not make people fall down. The Spirit lifts people up. The Spirit did this to Ezekiel on several occasions; always, if he was sitting or lying down, the Spirit lifted him up onto his feet.

There are so many things we think we know about the Bible, but when we begin to investigate, it just isn't there.

>What about Joseph dying after Jesus turned 12? When Jesus was rejected after preaching in Nazareth a year before his crucifixion, they mentioned Joseph in the present tense.

>Or the Holy Land always having been desert? The Bible tells of nine forests plus those on mountains.

>Or the prodigal's brother? As the oldest son, he was going to inherit the entire estate, but his insane greed wanted his brother's party too.

>Or David being just a boy when he killed Goliath? He had already killed a lion and bear before that, and big Saul's armor fit him.

>What about "Doubting Thomas"? The other apostles refused to believe before they saw Jesus alive again. More, when Jesus wanted to go to Jerusalem, his apostles said no, but Thomas said, "Let us go to Jerusalem so we may die with him."

>Or everyone going inside the temple to worship? Only priests were allowed inside the building. Commoners worshiped in the courtyard.

>Or Bethlehem being a little town? It was a fortified walled city.

What excitement to read the Bible for yourself and

discover its treasures for yourself. Open it. Read it. Be delighted.

13th- The Scripture for today, March 13 (3/13), Is **Ezra 3:13** as found in the Old Testament of the Bible:

"No one could distinguish the sound of the shouts of joy from the sound of weeping, because the people made so much noise. And the sound was heard far away."

Solomon's great temple had been destroyed and the Jews forced to go to Babylon. Now, 70 years later, they were back and had rebuilt the temple. The older Jews who had seen Solomon's temple wailed in grief because it was not nearly so grand as Solomon's. The younger ones shouted for joy because at least they now had a temple again. So the laughing of the young people and the crying of the old people mingled.

Today, sometimes the laughing and crying around us get too loud and put our lives in confusion. We don't understand what is going on. Sometimes the laughing or crying is our own. Sometimes we need to get away from the loud laughing and crying.

Turn off the television. The radio. The phone. The computer. Don't answer the door. Go into a room where you can be alone in complete silence. Then pick up the Bible and begin to read Luke about the life of Christ, or Philippians about peace, or the Psalms about overcoming adversity, or James about the direction your life is going. Read the whole book in one sitting.

Be still. Hear it now?

It is God's heart calling your heart.

14th - The scripture for today, March 14 (3/14), is **Philippians 3:14**, as found in the New Testament of the Bible:

"I press on toward the goal to win the prize for which God has called me heavenward in Christ Jesus."

Jesus knew that, out of jealousy, the religious leaders were trying to kill him. So for a while he stayed out of Jerusalem where the religious headquarters was. But eventually the time came for him to put himself in their hands. Was it easy for him to do? Definitely not! For he knew his death would be by torture.

"They were on their way up to Jerusalem with Jesus leading the way, and the disciples were astonished while those who followed were afraid" (Mark 10:32).

Jesus pressed on. He did not want to go through the crucifixion. Hebrews 5:7 says that "during the days of Jesus' life on earth, he offered up prayers and petitions with loud cries and tears to the one who could save him from death."

As difficult as it was for him, Jesus pressed on toward the goal to win the prize. But the prize was not for himself; it was for us ~ eternity in heaven instead of hell!

None of us has to go through what he did for our salvation and avoidance of hell. Our little bit of sacrifice is nothing by comparison. Shall we throw away the prize Jesus sacrificed so much for so we can have a little more fun, accumulate a few more things, be a little more important to our friends?

Are you throwing away your prize?

15th - The scripture for today, March 15 (3/15), is **Colossians 3:15** as found in the New Testament of the Bible:

"Let the peace of Christ rule in your hearts, since as members of one body you were called to peace. And be thankful."

Paul was encouraging the Christians at Colossae to get along with each other. After all, they were all members of the one body ~ the one church. In the next verse, he gave them a way to help it along: Sing.

Today, let us sing. Sing to sing to each other. Sing in unison to unify your heart with others. Sing in harmony to harmonize their lives together. Sing to show thanksgiving for your brothers and sisters.

What a wonderful way to mend a rift. Sing. Sing with the person you are not getting along with. Watch the smile on your face drift over to them. Watch the smile on their face rise up out of a heart that really does want to love you.

Let not little things interfere with your love for others. You do not want to cause pain to your heavenly Father when his children do not get along. Let us please each other ~ and sing!

16th - The scripture for today, March 16 (3/16), is **John**

3:16 as found in the New Testament of the Bible:

"For God so loved the world that he gave his one and only Son, that whoever believes in him shall not perish but have eternal life."

Guess what? Many people have heard there is such a scripture as John 3:16, but they do not know what it says. And among those who do know what it says, many have no idea what Jesus dying on the cross has to do with going to heaven.

It is important for us to read the entire Bible so we can understand the isolated scriptures we hear or read. There was a song written several years ago called, No Man Is An Island. No scripture is an island either. Just as every person influences other people in some way, every scripture influences other scriptures.

The meaning of John 3:16? Romans 3:23 says "All have sinned and come short of the glory of God." And Romans 6:23 says, "The wages of sin is [spiritual] death."

There are certain truths that cannot be broken. For example, it is impossible for God to lie. Another truth is that both good and evil exist. It is obvious both are in a battle to win. Satan is the seat of evil. God is the seat of good. God is stronger than Satan. How do we know? Whatever Satan does, God can undo. When Satan causes someone to be sick, God can heal them. When Satan causes someone to sin, God can forgive them. When Satan causes someone to die, God can bring them back to life.

Satan held mankind hostage because we all sin The ransom to free mankind was the death of God. But God was smarter than Satan. God sent his Word down to us in flesh (John 1:1f, 14) ~

Jesus ~ who lived that perfect life that is impossible for us to live. Then, the fleshly-part of God paid the terrible ransom: He died physically and spiritually on the cross.

The ransom was now paid (Matthew 20:28 and I Peter 1:18-21). Then God played a trick on Satan. Only the flesh part of Jesus died. And even then, that body came back to life.

Today, we have a choice: Become a Christian or tell God the way we live is none of his business. Think. Think about this. Deeply. "God so loved the world he gave his only begotten son." Understanding the price he paid to keep us out of hell, how can anyone walk away from him?

17th - The scripture for today, March 17 (3/17), is **Zephaniah 3:17** as found in the Old Testament of the Bible:

> **"The Lord your God is with you,**
> **He is mighty to save.**
> **He will take great delight in you,**
> **He will quiet you with his love,**
> **He will rejoice over you with singing."**

God sings? It's right there in the Bible! God sings! We were created in his image. Everyone has music in their heart. We inherited it from God.

Therefore, today while riding or walking somewhere, or just sitting at home, why not join God and sing? Sing about everything. Sing about springtime or winter snow. Sing about family and friends. Sing about puppies and bullfrogs and trees. Sing about heaven. Sing about that mutual love between you and God.

It will delight him...

...and quiet your soul.

18th - The scripture for today, March 18 (3/18), is **Ephesians 3:18** as found in the New Testament of the Bible:

"...[you] may have power, together with all the saints to grasp how wide and long and high and deep is the love of Christ.'

We can never escape! It's everywhere! The love of Christ! No matter where we go! It follows us! His love is behind us and ahead of us. It is above us and below us. His love will never,

never,

never

let us go!

19th - The scripture for today, March 19 (3/19), is **Habakkuk 3:19** as found in the Old Testament of the Bible:

"The Sovereign Lord is my strength; he makes my feet like the feet of a deer, he enables me to go on the heights."

The little book of Habakkuk was written during a period when the leaders were oppressing the desperate poor. Habakkuk complains to God, "Why do you tolerate wrong?". God answers that he's getting ready to put an end to it. Not satisfied, Habakkuk asks the same question again.

God's answer renews Habakkuk's faith. Perhaps he asked himself, "Why had I worried so much?" "Why had I felt so abandoned?" "Why had I thought God didn't notice?" "Why had I decided God didn't really care?"

Everyone grows impatient when leaders are doing wrong. But we must understand that we see just part of the problem, and that God is waiting until the right time to put an end to it ~ a time when people are so desperate with helplessness that even unbelievers can't help but know God intervened.

So when times come in your own life that everything seems to be going wrong, read the little book of Habakkuk and know that God is still in control, he has not forgotten you, and he has special plans for you.

20th - The scripture for today, March 20 (3/20), is **Revelation 3:20** as found in the New Testament of the Bible:

"Here I am! I stand at the door and knock. If anyone hears my voice and opens the door, I will come in and eat with him, and he with me."

A couple days ago we read how the love of Christ is everywhere.

But he will not force himself on you. He calls to you and knocks on the door of your heart and mind. If you have too much noise going on in your life ~ coming and going to work, coming and going to clubs, coming and going to education and training, athletics and hobbies, you cannot hear him. If the radio and television and phone and movies are blaring all the time with no silence, you cannot hear him.

Stop what you are doing right now. If there is any background noise, turn it off. Sit in silence a moment. Read a scripture about the life of Christ (Matthew, Mark, Luke, or John) if you have a Bible, and let him knock on the door of your heart. In such silence you will be able to hear him.

He's calling you! Do you hear?

21st ~ The scripture for today, March 21 (3/21), is **1st Peter 3:21** as found in the New Testament of the Bible:

"This water symbolizes baptism that now saves you also ~ not the removal of dirt from the body but the answer of a good conscience toward God. It saves you by the resurrection of Jesus Christ."

Jesus' part in saving us was to pay the wages of our sins to Satan through his terrible death. Our part is to believe he did. Then to confess it to others. Then to repent of the sins that he died for. Some people call this process (and it is a process) giving their heart to the Lord.

But many people go through life wondering if they were

sincere enough when they gave their heart to the Lord. What is in one's mind long ago sometimes becomes a fuzzy memory. So they re-give their heart to the Lord all over again periodically throughout their life.

Thank God, he has given us something we can do, an action to prove we were sincere enough, more than a long-ago state of mind. He gave us an action to reassure our conscience toward God ~ "baptism that now saves you", the same baptism wherein you are reborn to live a new life (Romans 6: 4)

22nd - The scripture for today, March 22 (3/22), is **Lamentations 3:22** as found in the Old Testament of the Bible:

"Because of the Lord's great love, we are not consumed, for his compassions never fail."

Jeremiah had spent years warning people of the coming destruction of their country and beloved Jerusalem due to their selfish sinful life and taking advantage of each other. He endured taunts, reprimands, imprisonments and threats to his life. Now it has happened. All hope is gone. Nothing left but ashes.

There were innocent people who suffered as a result. Would they let Satan get his way and destroy their lives, their spirits, their souls too? It is at this point that lamenting Jeremiah utters bravely amidst his own tears, "We are not consumed."

Are there things going on your life that seem to be consuming you? Do you feel utterly hopeless? Do you feel as though life may not worth living anymore? Look up. God is still there. He still loves you.

When you have the love of God, you have the courage to take the next step and the next and the next You have the courage to keep walking and walking and to hold your head high. Nothing and nobody can ever take away the love God has for you. With his love, you can never be consumed.

23rd - The scripture for today, March 23 (3/23), is **Colossians 3:23** as found in the New Testament of the Bible:

"Whatever you do, work at it with all your heart, as working for the Lord, not for men."

Perhaps you are in a job that is unfair ~ you are given too much work, you are underpaid, you are not given enough work, you are given too must responsibility, you aren't given any responsibility, you have been passed over for promotion by someone less qualified than you.

Think not that you are working for the person who supervises you. S/he is only human. You are working for God. You are representing God. If you are being treated unfairly and smile anyway, others will wonder why. Keep smiling and keep working. Others will keep noticing.

Eventually someone will ask you, "How can you keep going?". Then you can tell them how you have God's approval, and that makes you feel like number one. Therefore, nothing anyone can say or do to you can ever make you feel otherwise.

So keep on keeping on. The world notices.

24th - The scripture for today March 24 (3/24), is **1st John 3:24** as found in the New Testament of the Bible:

Those who obey his commands live in him, and he in them. And this is how we know that he lives in us: We know it by the Spirit he gave us."

Some people think we can tell that we are obeying God and he is therefore in us by how we feel, by our emotions. But emotions are fickle. We can feel great one day and sad the next and frustrated after that, then great again. It can be confusing to rely on how we feel as to whether or not God's Spirit lives in us.

Jesus said in John 14:17 that he was going to send us the Counselor, the Spirit of Truth. And in John 17:17 Jesus said God's Word is Truth.

Now that makes more sense! Even in the days before the New Testament was assembled into one book, Christians were given the gift of prophecy by the Spirit of Truth, and sometimes they wrote it and circulated it.

In the meantime, the Apostles went everywhere teaching, and they wrote letters that were circulated (even those we don't know about today). Those letters that were preserved were copied and circulated everywhere.

Finally, these letters were assembled into what we call the

New Testament. So today we can still know by reading the Bible ~ God's Word ~ and following it. God thought of everything. His word is clear, and that is how we know we have obeyed him and he lives in us.

How grateful we are today for his Bible. No guessing.

25th - The scripture for today, March 25 (3/25), is **Lamentations 3:25** as found in the Old Testament of the Bible:

"The Lord is good to those whose hope is in him, to the one who seeks him."

That's all? Just hope? I don't have to have a deep, deep faith for God to be good to me? All I have to do is hope he exists? Hope he loves everyone. Hope he loves me?

Were you raised by atheists or have you attended a university where professors criticize theists (believers in God)? Have you been told deity is just the essence of the universe with no personality? Are you confused by it all? You can still hope there is only the One God who does exist, has personality, knows your name and loves you.

Have you had a major tragedy in your life and can't understand how a good God could allow that bad thing to happen (heaven on earth)? Do you live among people who believe all the gods in the world are the One God, so don't pay special attention to any of them?

Amidst such confusion, is it hard for you to sort it all out and have faith in the One God of the Bible? What is faith anyway? It is the evidence of what you hope for. If you cannot go so far as to say you have a deep faith in the One God, you can still hope! Keep that hope alive. Let the Lord be good to you.

26th – The scripture for today, March 26 (3/26), is **Galatians 3:26f** as found in the New Testament of the Bible:

"You are all sons of God through faith in Christ, because all of you who were baptized into Christ have clothed yourselves with Christ."

The Muslim religion teaches that God is too far above humans to have such a relationship ~ you know, the parent-child kind, a family relationship. They are taught God created humans to have someone to worship him and be his slaves. Oh, how much they are missing. And the rest of the world too.

Our Bible says God created humans to have someone to love. He wants to be more than a distant God; he wants to be our heavenly Father. So, when we come out of the waters of baptism, it is like coming out of a watery womb; Romans 6:4-5 says we are then born into a new spiritual life.

Everyone in the Christian world knows that baptism is in the Bible. Today's scripture explains "...because you who were baptized into Christ have clothed yourselves with Christ" and therefore we have become sons with Christ ~ adopted sons. (See also Ephesians 1:5).

No need to be spiritually blind and poor and naked (Revelation 3:17). You can gain spiritual insight, be rich in grace, and be clothed with Christ.

No need to be spiritually orphaned ~ you can become a child of God. He holds out holy arms to you. He wants to embrace you and hold you close as you finish this life on earth. And then, wonder of wonders, the Creator of the universe wants to bring you home with him.

27th - The scripture for today, March 27 (3/27), is **Proverbs 3:27f** as found in the Old Testament of the Bible:

"Do not withhold good from those who deserve it, when it is in your power to act. Do not say to your neighbor, 'Come back later; I'll give it tomorrow' ~ when you now have it with you."

Christians generally are good people. They stay out of trouble at work and in the neighborhood. They obey the laws. They don't use profanity, they don't lie, they don't cheat, they don't steal, they don't commit adultery, they don't murder. These are bad things Christians don't do ~ sins of commission.

But what about good things Christians do not do? Too busy to stop and look around you for someone needing help? Too busy to drive someone to the doctor, or watch a child when a parent is sick, or fix a meal when a family is bereaved, or send a card for someone's birthday, or call someone who is lonely? Too shy to say something to someone in distress? Too afraid to bring up heaven and hell to a lost one? These are sins! Sins of omission and they are just as serious.

Today, look around you. Who needs you? Not needs your neighbor, or a relative, or someone else at work, or one of the other members of your congregation, but you? You! When do they need you? Not tomorrow or next month or next year, but today!

Get out of your comfort zone. Quit committing sins of omission. Make a point to do something for someone else. When? Today. Too busy? What if God made as much time for you and you do for others?

28th - The scripture for today, March 28 (3/28), is **Mark 3:28f** as found in the New Testament of the Bible:

"I tell you the truth, all the sins and blasphemies of men will be forgiven them. But whoever blasphemes against the Holy Spirit will never be forgiven; he is guilty of an eternal sin."

This is confusing to many because we aren't sure what it means to speak against the Holy Spirit. Jesus clarifies it in John 14:17 where he said he was going to send to us another Comforter, the Spirit of Truth. And in John 17:17 he said God's Word is Truth ~ the Bible.

If we refuse to believe what is in the Bible, then we are going to refuse to believe in a Savior and refuse to repent of sins. These things are unforgivable because we have no belief in Jesus or sin, and no remorse.

Have you ever tried reading the Bible through in a year? If it's too much for you, the Old Testament half was written to the Jews and the New Testament half was written to the Christians; choose one. It will fill you with an amazing amount of knowledge and understanding, all from the Holy Spirit ~ the Spirit that communes with your spirit.

29th - The scripture for today, March 29 (3/29), is **Luke 3:29** as found in the New Testament of the Bible:

"...the son of Joshua, the son of Eliezer, the son of Jorim, the son of Matthat, the son of Levi...."

Who in the world were these five men: Joshua, Eliezer, Jorim, Matthat and Levi? Some were named after famous Jews, but no one in this list was famous himself. In fact, nothing else is said in the Bible about any of these men. They're just a single name in a single but long list.

Who were they that they earned even one brief mention in the Bible?

They were ancestors of Joseph, the human "father" of Jesus. What else? They were born and survived long enough to have sons. Not important at the time? No, but eventually it was.

We read obituaries and sometimes wonder about our own. Our whole life reduced to born, married, had a job, had children, died. That's it. Nothing out of the ordinary. Just another one of billions in the world having come and gone.

Hold on! Maybe not!

Maybe your life, as ordinary as it seems now, will some day serve a greater purpose through a descendant or someone you become friends with. In a later generation ~ maybe ten or twenty generations from now ~ someone may do something extremely important for souls of the world. And it was made possible because of your "unordinary life" way back in the early twenty-first century when you survived one day at a time.

30th - The scripture for today, March 30 (3/30), is **John 3:30** as found in the New Testament of the Bible:

"He must become greater; I must become less."

This is John the Baptist speaking. He had a great following. People "were constantly coming to be baptized" by John (3:23). He had it made! But at the height of his popularity, he said, "I will be stepping down soon."

Can you do this? Are you at the height of your popularity, perhaps at a club, an organization, church? Could you step down if someone more qualified than you came along? Or will you say, "I started this _______, and I was here first, so this is my project!" ?

Look inside. Deep inside. What are your motives for doing good? Selfish ambition or love for others? 1st Corinthians 13:1 says that, even if I offer my body to be burned and do not have love, it benefits me nothing.

Jesus warned, “Be careful not to do your acts of righteousness before men to be seen by them. If you do, you will have no reward from your Father in heaven.”

Think. Think long and hard. Do you have some repenting to do? Father in heaven, help me look at myself the way You do.

31st - The scripture for today, March 31 (3/31), is **Mark 3:31ff** as found in the New Testament of the Bible:

"Then Jesus' mother and brothers arrived. Standing outside, they sent someone in to call him. A crowd was sitting around him and they told him, 'Your mother and brothers are outside looking for you.' 'Who are my mother and my brothers?' he asked. Then he looked at those seated in a circle around him and said, 'Here are my mother and my brothers! Whoever does God's will is my brother and sister and mother.' "

Do we need a mediator between Jesus and ourselves? Jesus said his followers are his brothers, sisters and mother. We do not need anyone to intercede and beg Jesus to give us special attention. He already gives us special attention. After all, we are his family.

1st - The scripture for today, April 1 (4/1), is **Ephesians 4:1** as found in the New Testament of the Bible:

"As a prisoner for the Lord, then, I urge you to live a life worthy of the calling you have received."

Paul, a prisoner for spreading the word about Jesus? Now he wants others to follow his example, even if they end up in prison like him?

Did Paul's incarceration stop the Christians he was writing to? More, did Jesus' crucifixion stop them for fear they would be crucified too?

Did early Christians decide it was too dangerous to tell people the way to escape hell and go to heaven? Never. They loved people so much, they were willing to take insults and persecution and imprisonment and even death in the hopes that their persistent love would eventually lead to people becoming Christians and being saved from eternal hell. They knew their calling as Christians.

How about today? Do you live a life worthy of your calling as a Christian? Do you stand up for Jesus and reach out to the lost, regardless of the cost? Or do you cower and use the excuse, "Once people see my godly life, they will ask me how to be saved"? How many times do the lost really do that?

Rise up! Stand tall as a brave soldier of the Lord. Dare to march into enemy territory and do everything you can to snatch the lost out of the claws of Satan.

No matter what they do to you.

2nd - The scripture for today, April 2 (4/2), is **Exodus 4:2f** as found in the Old Testament of the Bible:

"Then the Lord said to him, 'What is that in your hand?' 'A staff,' he replied."

God had just called Moses to go into Egypt and free his people from their slavery ~ one man against an entire nation. Moses objected that he couldn't do it. Five times In Exodus 3 and 4 he argued with God. "BUT I'm not famous," "BUT they won't believe I come from the God of their ancestors," "BUT they won't believe God sent me, "BUT I'm not a good speaker," "JUST send someone else."

Then God replied, "What is that in your hand?".

Moses had a staff. God showed him how to use it to perform miracles. Today, are you using excuses to claim there is nothing you can do to show the love of God? "What is that in your hand?" It is a steering wheel, a shovel, thread, a computer, a spoon, a wrench, a cookbook, a band aid. Whatever is in your hand, God can use to bless people through you.

God does not take 'no' for an answer. God challenges you.

He wants to stretch you to do what you think you cannot do. You are God's hands and feet. Go ahead. Use them. Today.

3rd - The scripture for today, April 3 (4/3), is **1st Timothy 4:3** as found in the New Testament of the Bible:

"They [false teachers] forbid people to marry and order them to abstain from certain foods, which God created to be received with thanksgiving by those who believe and who know the truth."

Is it hard for you to think that smiling, humble, Bible-quoting, holy-looking church leaders could be false teachers and condemned by the God they claim to represent? Yes, it's hard. We want to think well of everyone; isn't that the way Christians are to be? But sometimes thinking well of someone and thinking well of the truth can clash. Now you have a choice to make ~ a hard choice.

The author, the apostle Paul, warned of false teachers in the church that would come in the future. Indeed it did happen. A time came when certain Christians were ordered not to marry, and not to eat certain foods (for instance, on Friday). Where do church leaders come up with those things? They claim it is a sin to disobey them and don't show you the scriptures they refuse to obey.

Remember, your church leaders are going to be judged by God just like everyone else. Always, as the apostle Peter once warned, "We ought to obey God and not men" (Acts 4:19). Besides, do you think this is one reason people have turned against "organized religion"?

This is why it is important to read the Bible for yourself. Use a concordance to look up all scriptures in the Bible with any keyword and you will learn what is true and not true. Isn't it time for you to sort through everything you have been told? Isn't it time for you to discover pure truth?

4th- The scripture for today, April 4 (4/4), is **Psalm 4:4** as found in the Old Testament of the Bible:

"In your anger do not sin."

You've gotta be kidding! That's impossible! When people get angry, don't we lash out at other people? And yell and call them names? And show our temper? Maybe even throw a few things? After all, that's the only way to get across to the other person that we are really angry.

Hold on. If your child, for instance, you told your child not to do something for their own safety but your child did it anyway, of course you would become angry. Why? Your child put himself in danger because of his action.

You can choose to lash out at your child wildly so that your emotions mask your words. Or you can choose to talk calmly and explain the dangers your child was put in because of that action. Maybe punishment is in order. You can calmly but firmly tell them what their punishment is. You can calmly punish your child without losing your temper.

It is the same way with adults. If you lose your temper and

shoot daggers with your eyes and rant and rave, all your actions distract people from your words. Aren't your words of explanation more important than the emotionalism and yelling? If you were hurt, just say so. If they hurt themselves, just say so.

While we're at it, not all words help. Name calling does not help. Name calling is done when you choose not to explain how you feel. Name calling such as, "You're irresponsible," locks the other person in and sets them up for future failures between you and them. Losing your temper during anger gets you off the issue and into sin.

Next time, try to remain calm and then explain the problem in tones that the person who has angered you ~ whether child or adult ~ can truly listen to and learn from. If you have trouble doing this, practice when you're alone. It will come to you in the right way. It will teach you to remain calm when you're angry.

Anger is not the same thing as sin. What you do with it can be. Choose a calm anger. Thereby, you will have a peace that passes understanding.

5th- The scripture for today, April 5 (4/5), is **Micah 4:5** as found in the Old Testament of the Bible:

"All the nations may walk in the name of their gods; we will walk in the name of the Lord our God forever and ever."

Nations rise and fall. Nations come and go. Nations are founded upon terror and aggression, or peace and democracy. Some nations follow religions which declare that peasants are peasants as punishment for previous lives, so must remain peasants. Some nations follow religions chosen by their national governments and which must be followed upon pain of death. Some nations deny religion completely and destroy anyone who believes anyway.

What kind of nation do you live in? As strong as your nation is, it cannot control your heart, your spirit, your soul. As strong as your nation seems to be, as much power as your government uses to control its citizens, it will not and cannot last forever.

Always remember, there is a forever nation ~ the nation of God, the kingdom of God. No matter what nation you live in, you can have "dual citizenship". And by being a citizen of God's forever kingdom, you will walk in it forever and ever and...

6th - The scripture for today, April 6 (4/6), is **1st Corinthians 4:6** as found in the New Testament of the Bible:

"...learn from us the meaning of the saying, 'Do not go beyond what is written.' Then you will not take pride in one man over against another."

Periodically through the Bible there appears this same warning for us to not "go beyond what is written." 2nd Peter 1:20 says prophecy is scripture. Prophecy was needed before the New Testament was written, but no more after that, for now the prophecy of the apostles had been written down and were being passed around.

It is important to find out if what we are being taught is "beyond what is written." It can be done. How? Simple. Use a concordance. A concordance is the size of a large-city telephone book in fine print and includes every keyword in the Bible and every scripture that contains each word. Many libraries have one. Or you can order one from your local bookstore. There are some concordances on the internet too. Here is one: **http://bibletab.com**

You are an intelligent person. Don't take for granted what others tell you. Check things for yourself. Read the Bible for yourself. Decide for yourself whether any of your church leaders have gone "beyond what is written." You can do it: Find out for sure.

It is liberating. Your heart will soar and your soul will embrace God in a whole new way.

7th- The scripture for today, April 7 (4/7), is **Proverbs 4:7** as found in the Old Testament of the Bible:

"Wisdom is supreme; therefore get wisdom. Though it cost all you have, get understanding."

The verse just before this says, "Do not forsake wisdom, and she will protect you; love her, and she will watch over you." And the verse just after today's says, "Esteem her and she will exalt you; embrace her, and she will honor you."

How do we get wisdom? The Bible is full of it. Proverbs was

written by Solomon, the wisest man in the world. Just reading and applying Proverbs would give a person Wisdom. And the entire Old Testament gives examples of numerous people through the centuries who did or did not do right, and the result of their decisions.

Many religious people neglect the Old Testament. It is not always pleasant reading. But by reading it, we can avoid the mistakes made by many, and perhaps gain courage to imitate the courageous ones who made the right choices.

How about reading the Bible through every year? To read both the Old and New Testament through in a year would take about 20 minutes a day. Some people have read the entire Bible front to back forty or fifty times. Make this a priority and you may be surprised how much is absorbed into your being, your life.

Ah, Wisdom. We love you, Wisdom!

8th- The scripture for today, April 8 (4/8), is **2nd Timothy 4:8** as found in the New Testament of the Bible:

"Now there is in store for me the crown of righteousness which the Lord, the righteous Judge, will award to me on that day ~ and not only to me, but also to all who have longed for his appearing."

The Apostle Paul was somewhere around his seventies at this writing. He'd been converted probably in his thirties. He'd spent the past forty years telling people how to escape a place they didn't believe they were going to and disrupting the religion they already had.

Forty years of tolerating persecution, sometimes hungry and cold and beaten and hated. Forty years of seldom staying in a city longer than a few months, always on the go. Forty years of never being satisfied with the number of people he had reached with the Good News of their escape from Satan, the Good News of a God who actually loved them, Good News of heaven.

Now he was in prison.

"I am already being poured out like a drink offering, and the time has come for my departure. I have fought the good fight, I have finished the race, I have kept the faith."

Oh, that we all could say this at the end of our life.

9th- The scripture for today, April 9 (4/9), is 1st John 4:9f as found in the New Testament of the Bible:

"This is how God showed his love among us: He sent his one and only Son into the world that we might live through him. This is love: Not that we loved God, but that he loved us, and sent his Son as an atoning sacrifice for our sins."

How perplexing. We are stymied. There is no solution. We humans do not have the will to live perfect lives. We give in to sin. We can never get it right. Romans 6:23 says the wages of sin is death. In the Old Testament era, God let people kill an animal in their place whenever they sinned, but it had to be done over and over. But still, every time we sinned, our souls died a little more. Then came our answer, our rescue our solution. But the cost. It was so high. God sent his Son to us for a while with a body so his Son's body could be killed (collecting our wages, the cost of our sins) in our place.

Finally, God invited mankind to bring our souls back to life through him ~ that is, become Christ-ians. How do we become alive through Jesus? Of course, we know about believing Jesus was the Son of God and repenting of our sins. Also, Romans 6:4 says when we are baptized and come forth out of the Spirit's watery womb, our souls are born again and we now have a new life.

But it does not stop there. We must try the best we can to live as Jesus lived, speak as Jesus spoke, love as Jesus loved. With Jesus living in us, we are his mouth, his hands, his feet. It is then that we offer our own bodies as daily sacrifices (Romans 12:1).

Oh, Lord God. I want to do this. Help me do this. Help me.

10th - The scripture for today, April 10 (4/10), is **Zechariah 4:10** as found in the Old Testament of the Bible:

"Who despises the day of small things?"

We tend to admire big things ~ big buildings, big empires, big trees, big causes. Sometimes it is difficult to remember that those things started out small.

Have you been wanting to accomplish something big? All buildings started out with one board or one stone. All empires started out with one person. All big trees started out as one seed.

All big causes started out with one dream.

Perhaps your dream started out small but stayed small. That doesn't mean it will always be small. It may become big years from now, or even in someone else's lifetime. Don't despise what you have now.

Have you been putting off trying to make your dream reality because it won't be big and people will laugh at you and you will get depressed? Do not fear it. Have faith in it. Plant that small seed. Do not despise it. Embrace it. Nourish it.

Make today the day of your new beginning. Launch your dream. Soar with it, even if you're the only one who does.

11th- The scripture for today, April 11 (4/11), is **Exodus 4:11** as found in the Old Testament of the Bible:

"Who gave man his mouth? Who makes him deaf or mute? Who gives him sight or makes him blind? Is it not I, the Lord?"

This is a dynamic verse, for it helps answer the question: "If God is so good, why did he allow me/my relative to become deaf/blind?"

Here is the answer. Satan is the prince of this world. So, God takes countermeasures to defeat him. Everything Satan does God can undo. But he does it in his own way. He does it through us.

God gives each of us an assignment. We all have something God wants us to overcome. Why? Because it makes us spiritually stronger. It is intended to turn us into spiritual giants. Wow!

His assignment may be the family we were born in to, the country we were born in, an earthquake, a flood, an unfair professor, a mean boss. Amidst our tears as we face sometimes unbearable assignments, the challenge is for us to carry on with the smile of faith on our lips.

Paul said in 2nd Corinthians 12:10, "For Christ's sake, I delight in weaknesses....For when I am weak, then I am strong!" If God did not believe you or your relative or friend could handle your affliction, he would not allow you to have it.

It's almost as if the more affliction you have, the more faith God has in you. After all, 2nd Corinthians 6:1 says we are workers together with God.

Has God given you an assignment? What a privilege!

12th - The scripture for today, April 12 (4/12), is **Colossians 4:12** as found in the New Testament of the Bible:

"He is always wrestling in prayer for you."

Do you have fast-food prayers? Drive in, ask for something for yourself, and drive out two minutes later?

How about trying gourmet prayers ~ where you gather many ingredients, not just one? They take longer, but are very special and rewarding.

Your menu is your prayer list. People on your list don't even have to be people you know personally. They can be from the newspaper, teachers at a local school, government officials, your neighbors, your congregation. List people by name. Pray for them by name.

Then tell these people you are praying for them. You may think you'll get some strange looks, but mostly, even from the unreligious, you will get a smile and a whispered thank you. Some will actually reply, "No one before has ever told me they were praying for me." After a while, you will begin receiving word from some of them, "I am praying for you too."

Prayer is wonderful. It is most wonderful when it centers, not on yourself, but on struggling in prayer for others.

One by one you will begin seeing amazing answers in the lives of those you pray for. And that's a promise!

13th - The scripture for today, April 13 (4/13), is **Philippians 4:13** as found in the New Testament of the Bible:

"I can do everything through him who gives me strength."

Life is not easy. Plans are scattered, dreams are shattered, and even predictable every-day things sometimes give way to the unknown and unforeseeable. Maybe you have made bad decisions, or you weren't prepared for emergencies, or you are an innocent victim of someone else's problems.

There is Someone who knows everything that is happening to you and who will walk beside you down whatever path you find yourself. And, as amazing as it sounds, even if you lose faith in Him, He will not lose faith in you.

When you don't feel like it, reach out to God. Pray, even if all you can think of talking about is how terrible things are right now. At least you're talking. And read the Bible, for that is God talking to you. Keep the two-way communication going. Amidst your weeping when you fall, God will give you strength and someday once again lift you up.

14th - The scripture for today, April 14 (4/14), is **Esther 4:14b** as found in the Old Testament of the Bible:

"And who knows but that you have come to the kingdom for such a time as this?"

Today's scripture is about a reluctant young lady who won a beauty contest and was chosen to be queen of Persia. Time has passed, and now a command has just gone out to kill all Jews. Queen Esther was a Jewess but had not told anyone at the royal court. She could continue to hide her nationality and let all her people die, or she could intervene with the king. She was the only Jew the king would have listened to. So she took the chance that she, too, would be killed, and spoke on behalf of her people. They were saved.

There are always situations in life in which you are the only one who can accomplish something very needed. Perhaps you are the only adult standing near a strange child who is about to run out into a busy road. Perhaps you are tall and a short person needs to reach something at the store. Perhaps you know a particular language and others around you need you to explain something to them. Perhaps someone called a wrong number on the telephone and reached you instead.

As we go through life, there are situations in which you are the only one who can handle them. Do you? Do you watch for those situations, or do you walk around in your own little world?

Listen! It's the silent cries of people only you can help. Do you hear them?

15th- The scripture for today, April 15 (4/15), is **1st John 4:15** as found in the New Testament of the Bible:

"And we have seen and testify that the Father has sent his Son to be the Savior of the world."

The New Testament was written by people who walked and talked with Jesus. They saw his miracles, they heard his amazing words. They were eye witnesses.

Several first- and second-century manuscripts still exist that were passed down from some who actually knew the eye witnesses. A few were even written during the late lifetime of the last living apostle, John. The Bible has more existing ancient manuscripts (over 5000) than any historical writing in the world.

Read the New Testament. It was written by inspired men with a passion that would not let them stop talking about this Jesus. He consumed their life when he was on earth, and consumed their spirit after he left.

Through the centuries, men and women have given their lives so that you today may have the writings (New Testament) of those eye witnesses in our own language and read it for yourself. Many were ridiculed and tortured terribly, and then died a long excruciating death so that the apostles' testimony could live on.

Do not take for granted the words of Jesus' eye witnesses. Jesus lived and died for you. Those witnesses, in a sense, also lived and died for you. Read what they testified to. Then, if necessary, live and die for it.

16th - The scripture for today, April 16 (4/16), is **Hebrews 4:16** as found in the New Testament of the Bible:

"Let us then approach the throne of grace with confidence, so that we may receive mercy and find grace to help us in our time of need."

Anyone who has lived very long has committed some sin they hope no one ever finds out about. Some people have committed many such sins. Sometimes because of that one "big" sin or the constant repetition of a particular sin, do you punish yourself by putting words in God's mouth? Do you say, "God could never forgive me for that"? Perhaps you can never forgive yourself, but God is greater than you.

Jesus told Peter we must forgive our brothers 70 times 7. If kept literally, that would mean we'd have to forgive the same sin 490 times. It is figurative for forgiving all the time. 1st Corinthians 13, the "love chapter" of the Bible, says, "Love...keeps no record of wrongs." That means not holding grudges.

In addition to forgiving yourself and others, can you reach out to help people who cannot forgive themselves? Are you strong enough to imitate God? Are you strong enough to find enough mercy and grace in your heart to forgive?

17th - The scripture for today, April 17 (4/17), is Mark 4:17 as found in the New Testament of the Bible:

"But since they have no root, they last only a short time. When trouble or persecution comes because of the Word, they quickly fall away."

We may be mentally prepared for persecution out in the world. But what about persecution among our friends who we attend worship with all the time? They can turn on us too.

Perhaps someone has discovered a new truth and is trying to get members of our congregation to believe it. If members get the feeling someone is trying to prove them wrong and make them look bad, they will turn on that person much like people do a "whistle blower" in the business world.

On whose side will you stand? Your friends' so you can continue to be friends with them, or God's? It's easy to let things slide and pretend that new truth no longer exists so you can keep your friends. How deep are your roots? Who shall you worship? Your friends or your God? What is more important? Your friends or your eternity?

18th - The scripture for today, April 18 (4/18), is 2nd Corinthians 4:18 as found in the New Testament of the Bible:

"So we fix our eyes not on what is seen, but on what is unseen. For what is seen is temporary, but what is unseen is eternal."

In a sense, what is unseen is the true reality. We cannot see love, but we see its influence, and it is stronger than anything in the world that we can see. We cannot see God, but we can see his influence, and he is more real than anything in the world that we can see.

Sometimes we all say we wish we could see God and touch God. But if that were the case, he wouldn't be God, for he couldn't be everywhere at once. He would only be able to hear the prayer of one person at a time, and only able to answer the prayer of one person at a time. By being unseen by human eyes, God can be everywhere.

It's a hidden blessing! Every one of us among the billions of people on earth can feel we are God's special ones. Every one of us can feel his presence, his soul, his love.

19th - The scripture for today, April 19 (4/19), is 1st Corinthians 4:19a as found in the New Testament of the Bible:

"But I will come to you very soon, if the Lord is willing."

God knows each step you take through life. He knows all the roads you take in each phase of your life, and what is awaiting you along the way and at the other end. The road you are on today may lead you to where you do not want to go. But not being able to see the future, you do not always know that.

The writer of the above scripture was telling his friends he was coming to see them soon "if the Lord is willing." Sometimes a decision seems so right. But there may be danger on the way. Or there may be a different road to take leading you to somewhere even better.

Thank God he does not say yes to all of our prayers. Try to remember, when you ask God for things, to add "Your will be done". His will is for you to have the best life possible.

20th- The scripture for today, April 20 (4/20), is **1st John 4:20** as found in the New Testament of the Bible:

"If anyone says, 'I love God,' yet hates his brother, he is a liar. For anyone who does not love his brother, whom he has seen, cannot love God, whom he has not seen."

Jealousy and hatred are very much akin. Are there people you are jealous of? Do they have a position you want, and so you say and do things to undermine their character or work, so you can get their position? Do you have a position you love, and there is a new person who could perform better, so you undermine that person's ability in order to protect your position?

God eliminates jealousy this way: What you accomplish in public isn't as important to him as what you accomplish in private. Jesus said those who receive acclamation by people already have their reward, so will not be acclaimed by God (Matthew 6:1-5, 16-18). As much as it goes against human nature, prefer to do your good deeds in private, and God will reward you openly.

21st - The scripture for today, April 21 (4/21), is **Mark 4:21** as found in the New Testament of the Bible:

"Do you bring in a lamp to put it under a bowl or a bed? Instead, don't you put it on its stand?"

Jesus said something similar in Matthew 5:14f, "You are the light of the world. A city on a hill cannot be hidden. Neither do people light a lamp and put it under a bowl. Instead they put it on its stand, and it gives light to everyone in the house. In the same way, let your light shine before men, that they may see your good deeds and praise your Father in heaven."

Do you spend your energy on yourself and family? That is good. Your family needs your light. But try going further. Do something for someone else. But who? It requires looking around. Looking around your neighborhood, your school, your job, your club, your community.

Someone is in darkness and needs light. Always keep looking around. Keep searching for little nooks and crannies in the lives of others where you can bring the light of a good deed to someone's world.

Dare to spread light over them so they know where they are going. They need your light. Can you find it? Do you know where you left it?

22nd - The scripture for today, April 22 (4/22), is **Proverbs 4:22** as found in the Old Testament of the Bible:

"...for they [my words] are life to those who find them and health to a man's whole body."

Nearly everyone with a Bible picks it up at some time or another and reads something out of it. But random reading is like picking up a novel and randomly reading a few passages now and then. The passage itself may be beautiful, but does not have a lot of meaning without knowing what came before and after that passage in the novel.

Why not read the entire Bible, beginning to end? Perhaps you can read a chapter a day. Or, if you want to read it through in a year, you can count the total number of pages in your Bible, divide by 365, and read that number of pages each day. Or, if you have time, why not sit down and read it in just a few sittings? This way you will know all the things that occurred before and after your favorite scriptures. Then they will take on new meaning for your life.

For help with how the Bible is organized, go here: http://www.churchofchrist-cg-az.com/files/BibleOrganization4.htm

Proverbs even says God's Word adds to your health. Do you suffer from any physical problems caused by anxiety? A lot of physical problems are. This is yet another reason to know the Word of God.

So much comfort. So much information. So much of answering our questions of how and why. So much of filling an empty soul.

23rd- The scripture for today, April 23 (4/23), is **Mark 4:23** as found in the New Testament of the Bible:

"If anyone has ears to hear, let him hear."

Some of us read a passage in the Bible and say, "I know it says that, but it doesn't mean that." We just don't want to hear it.

It's hard to admit we are wrong, isn't it? It's human nature. And in the realm of religion, it is even harder because we're talking about our eternal soul. So reading that we're supposed to be doing or not doing something that we've never followed before is like being on a bridge over a roaring river, and suddenly realizing the bridge is breaking and we are not as safe as we thought we were. Let us take our human egos out of the way.

Let's say, for example, you have a wood or cooking project. If you leave a major step out, it results in your creation not turning out right. You might turn a blind eye to the correct way, give up and throw your creation away so that you never have the joy of whatever you were creating. Or you may go back and check what you have done until you find your mistake, are glad you found the mistake, see it with seeing eyes, correct it, and then have the joy of your creation.

Let us not fight God like spiritual teenagers trying to boss their parents. We are God's creation. He is just trying to help us. Instead of spiritual blindness and deafness, let us have eyes that truly see, and ears that truly hear the Word of God.

24th - The Scripture for today, April 24 (4/24), is **Jeremiah 4:24** as found in the Old Testament of the Bible:

"I looked at the mountains and they were quaking; all the hills were swaying."

I was living in a village near the bottom of Mt. St. Helens when it blew. We had lived there for eight years. We had taken our children up to it and gone sledding, building snow forts, making snow angels, the works.

It was our mountain. Our beautiful mountain. It reminded me of an upside-down ice-cream cone. It was perfect in every way. Everyone knew it was a volcano, but it had formed thousands of years before and would continue like it was for thousands of years in the future. It was our mountain and it belong to us to do with as we pleased.

But it wasn't our mountain. One morning I looked outside. It seemed as though we had been plunged into the interior of a furnace with all its ashes. I stared. It was snowing gray ash. I stared more, wondering what the birds had done. Relieved, I saw them huddled together under bushes.

Of course, the radio and TV had switched to Emergency. We were told to stay indoors because ash is deadly to the lungs. If we did go out, we had to wear surgical masks. If we drove, we were told to put nylons over the air filter and to not go over 10 mph. Even then, the ash flew everywhere. Our freeway entrance and exit were blocked. The most disturbing thing I heard on the radio (yes, everyone kept their radio on) was that we were at the top of the San Andreas Fault. And so, we like the birds, huddled and waited for more unknown.

Not only was our mountain turned inside out, but our world was turned inside out.

We have expressions that something is "as eternal as the mountains" or "as old as the hills". Not true. Nothing on earth is eternal. That also includes things, people, power, position, belongings, even dreams. Eventually they quake and sway and are gone. Only that which is spiritual is forever.

25th - The scripture for today, April 25 (4/25), is **Proverbs 4:25** as found in the Old Testament of the Bible:

"Let your eyes look straight ahead, fix your gaze directly before you. Make level paths for your feet and take only ways that are firm. Do not swerve to the right or the left; keep your foot from evil."

There are a lot of interesting and fun distractions in life, so we have to remind ourselves over and over what is most important to us. We have only so much time in a day and in a lifetime. We can run back and forth from one sideroad to another; one fun thing to another, one power thing to another, one great-looking thing to another.

Before we know it, we have been on that side road a long time. Too long actually. We can barely see the main road we were on before. And God? He is now so far away. How can that be? We were always told God would always be there for us.

But God pretty much treats us the way we treat him. If we don't like being around him, he doesn't much like being around us. If we don't like listening to his word (the Bible), he doesn't much like listening to our word (prayer). If we don't like to spend special time with him, he doesn't much like to spend special time with us. God gives us the same courtesy we give him. God will not force himself on us, for he is a Gentleman.

So what do you have in your sights to do today? Next year? The rest of your life? What road are you on? Where is it leading you? Is that what you really want?

26th- The scripture for today, April 26 (4/26), is **Galatians 4:26** as found in the New Testament of the Bible:

"But the Jerusalem that is above is free, and she is our mother."

There is more confusion on the "new Jerusalem" than you might think. Well, let's ask God.

What is "the Jerusalem that is above"? Revelation 21:2 says, "I saw the Holy City, the New Jerusalem, coming down out of heaven from God, prepared as a bride beautifully dressed for her husband."

Aha! We learn two things. The New Jerusalem already exists. And the New Jerusalem is sometimes called our mother and sometimes the Bride of Christ!

So, what is the Bride of Christ? Ephesians 5:25,27 says, "Husbands, love your wives just as Christ loved the church and gave himself up for her to make her holy...and to present her to himself as a radiant church, without stain or wrinkle or any other blemish, but holy and blameless." How exciting! The New Jerusalem which is the Bride of Christ is the Church – all of us.

What else can we learn about the New Jerusalem? Well, the foundation of the New Jerusalem is the apostles. Revelation says it and Ephesians 2:20 says it.

Hmmm. This is getting more interesting all the time. Okay, let's look at the 12 gates leading into the church. They are the 12 tribes of Israel, Judaism where all the prophecies of Jesus are found.

Always check out the symbolism in the Bible. It deepens your spiritual understanding. Like the Walls of Salvation around the New Jerusalem insurmountably high. The River of Life and Tree of Life are there in the New Jerusalem, the church.

Can you imagine on the final day when the church arrives in heaven and we are all arrayed in sinless white and are rushing into the arms of our groom, our Jesus.

27th - The scripture for today, April 27 (4/27), is **Acts 4:27b** as found in the New Testament of the Bible:

"...your holy servant Jesus, whom you anointed."

In this prayer of early Christians, they acknowledged that God had anointed Jesus. What does anointing mean? In the Old Testament, men were anointed to become the high priest or the king.

Aaron was the very first high priest (Leviticus 6:20,22) and his son [and descendants] who succeeded him as high priest was also anointed. Saul was the very first king of the Jews (I Samuel 15:1) and he and all succeeding kings were anointed. This was a form of coronation.

And so when God anointed Jesus, he made him both high priest and king. Hebrews 4:14 says, "we have a great high priest who has gone through the heavens, Jesus the Son of God." And in Mark 15:2, Jesus acknowledged that he was King.

And so we worship the anointed one.

28th - The scripture for today, April 28 (4/28), is **Mark 4:28** as found in the New Testament of the Bible:

"All by itself the soil produces grain ~ first the stalk, then the head, then the full kernel in the head."

Jesus was explaining that the kingdom of heaven is like a seed planted in the ground. It grows almost miraculously. The church is, indeed, like this. Planted some 2000 years ago, it has survived through every adversity and attack contrived by man. Sometimes the attacks were even from within. But at such times, just when it looked as though it was going to die, just like a seed dying in the earth, it would begin to sprout anew and grow up stronger than ever.

A little seed turning into a stalk is miraculous and amazing. The survival of the church for 2000 years in a hostile world is even more miraculous and amazing.

God is still on his throne, and all is well.

29th - The scripture for today, April 29 (4/29), is **Deuteronomy 4:29** as found in the Old Testament of the Bible:

"But if from there you seek the Lord your God, you will find him if you look for him with all your heart and with all your soul."

Ah, to find God. Who are you, God? What do you do all through my day? What do you have to say to me? Or do you not say anything? Do you even see me, God? Where are you? I cannot find you.

Open your eyes, friend. God is always nearby. There is an old expression, "To know him is to love him." So true. To find God, get to know him. He is talking to you right now in his Bible, explaining what he is like and how he reacts to every possible situation in life. Open your Bible. Look through the mini-books within. God not only gives you examples of right and wrong ways to seek Him, but he gives you beautiful psalms and proverbs for your everyday life. And, wonder of wonders, He tells how He came down to us and walked among us as Jesus. Seek him there. He is talking to you.

Well, don't you have anything to say about this? Of course, you do. The conversation turns the other way when you talk to him in response to what you have read, or what you are trying to apply to your life, or your concern for others.

Yes, seek and you will find. This mutual conversation with God is the with-all-your-heart-and-soul kind. You can do it. He's waiting for you.

And it is good.

30th - The scripture for today, April 30 (4/30), is Ephesians 4:30f as found in the New Testament of the Bible:

"And do not grieve the Holy Spirit of God, with whom you were sealed for the day of redemption. Get rid of all bitterness, rage and anger, brawling and slander, along with every form of malice."

Do you think God has no choice but to let you into his heaven because you do not steal, cheat, or murder? Think again.

There's more to it than that; it's called sins of attitude. Are you bitter about something? Let it go or it will take you to hell. Do you have a problem with rage and anger? Do you enjoy a good mental or physical brawl? Do you slander people who have done you wrong? Do you harbor grudges year after year? Let go of them. Please. They are taking you to hell.

The average person does not have trouble with bad actions. The big problem is with bad attitudes. Let go of them. God will take care of the problems. Let go of people you consider your enemies and wish them well. Do not grieve the Holy Spirit. Do not grieve yourself.

Live in sweet inner peace. Live at peace with God. Make God's Holy Spirit smile.

May

1st- The scripture for today, May 1 (5/1), is **Romans 5:1** as found in the New Testament of the Bible:

"Therefore, since we have been justified through faith, we have peace with God through our Lord Jesus Christ."

Of course, if we do not have faith in Jesus, we will not obey any of his commands. He said in John 15:14, "You are my friends IF you do what I command."

How do we become his friends? By obeying all his commands. But we have all sinned and fallen short of the glory of God (Romans 3:23) and the wages we earn with our sins is body and soul death (Romans 6:23).

That makes it impossible for us to live in heaven. Only the just can enter heaven. Otherwise, heaven wouldn't be heaven. But how do we become just when the fact remains that we sin by actions, attitudes, and good things we leave undone?

Every time we sin, we come in the clutches of Satan, the originator of both body and soul death. He holds us hostage. So, God came to us in flesh, paid our fine, our bail, and bought us out of the death prison of Satan. He got us out and declared us not guilty.

But we have to believe he did that for us. What amazing God we have. We can barely comprehend it. It stretches our mind, our heart, our soul.

Yes, it is a beautiful thing what God did for us. That was his part. Our part is to believe it, accept it, and actively follow it.

That, too, is beautiful.

2nd- The scripture for today, May 2 (5/2), is **Micah 5:2** as found in the Old Testament of the Bible:

"But you, Bethlehem Ephrathah, though you are small among the clans of Judah, out of you will come for me one who will be ruler over Israel, whose origins are from of old, from ancient times."

In today's world completely connected and interconnected universally, people are asking "Who is the Higher Power?". Some say the Muslim Allah is, some say the Hindu Brahman is, some say the Buddhist Nirvana, some say the Jehovah of Christianity is.

This is called the "New Age Movement".

Buddhism (though most people do not realize where it came from) has infiltrated the young American culture by declaring there is no such thing as truth. One thing is true to one person, an opposite thing is truth to another person, so believe what you want.

None of the writings of these religions have been proven true. The Bible is the only religious book in the world with built-in proofs that it is of divine origin. Prophecies of many events in the life of Christ and entire empires flow throughout the Old Testament. No human could have known these hundreds of known facts hundreds of years before they happened. And, if these prophecies were truth, then the rest of the Bible is truth.

Today's amazing scripture prophecies where the "ruler...from ancient times" will be born. It gives the exact city Jesus (who had been in heaven before his human birth) would be born in but was written seven centuries before his birth.

The Word of God in flesh wasn't just a prophet, he wasn't just a good man, he wasn't a fraud. Thank God, He thought of everything to help us believe Jesus was, indeed, the Son of God!

3rd- The scripture for today, May 3 (5/3), is **Psalm 5:3** as found in the Old Testament of the Bible:

"In the morning, O Lord, you hear my voice; in the morning I lay my requests before you and wait in expectation."

Morning. The time of new beginnings. Birth is a morning.

Graduating from a school is a morning. Marriage, a new job, birth of a child ~ these are obvious mornings.

You can create your own morning of life in a spiritual way too. You can stop depending on yourself and begin following and depending on God. You cannot fix all your problems. Sometimes you get yourself into your own problems and don't know how to get yourself out. But God knows.

Lay your requests before God. Then wait. The waiting can create frustration. But wait in peace. God does things in his own timing.

He loves you as his child and knows when the moment is right. Sometimes when you look back, you are most grateful he did not answer a prayer for you; he had something better in mind. And then, it was morning.

God loves to answer prayer. Therefore, wait. Wait in peaceful expectation. Soon will come your morning.

4th- The scripture for today, May 4 (5/4), is **1st Peter 5:4** as found in the New Testament of the Bible:

"And when the Chief Shepherd [Jesus] appears, you will receive the crown of glory that will never fade away."

The world is frustrated with and has left "organized religion" and it is our fault. We brought it on ourselves. We have organized our denominations to death, and the spiritually minded have said, "Enough is enough. I want none of it. I just want Jesus."

Look at all the denominations that appoint someone to be the head of their religion at their world headquarters. He goes by different titles ~ bishop, high priest, father, president. Their headquarters may be a small office or a multi-story building, or an entire complex of buildings.

From here the head meets regularly with others to make decisions for their denomination. They pass regulations on who can hold office, where their contributions must be spent, amendments to their particular creed, and on and on.

Here is a unique thought: Let us set this system aside and replace everything with Jesus as the only head, and let the world headquarters be in heaven! We do not have to rely on the decisions of men, but on the decisions of God the Son who loved us so much that he became human for a while so he could die for us. Maybe we need to sell our big buildings, give the money to mission work and the poor, and return to meeting in unorganized homes.

We don't even need a creed, because if it is less than the Bible it isn't enough, if it is more than the Bible it is too much, and if it is the same as the Bible why have it?

No more "organized religion." No more divisiveness. No more denominationalism. Just one united church of Christ with its divine Founder as our sole leader, and His divine words as our sole creed. This will never fade away.

Jesus is the crown giver. Return Him to His throne and watch the world return to Him.

5th - The scripture for today, May 5 (5/5), is **Micah 5:5a** as found in the Old Testament of the Bible:

"And he will be their peace."

The little book of Micah was written during a time when his country was full of prosperity. But it was also full of abused power. The lower on the social scale, the more the people suffered at the hands of the powerful few.

In the midst of warning the social elite, Micah offers comfort to their victims. You may be going through economic distress such as losing your job or losing your home. You may be going through social distress such as being passed up for a promotion or losing friends because of your moral code.

Seek peace. Deep peace.

Sometimes, it is only possible to reveal powerful abusers by revealing their victims to the world. Sometimes our job is to just survive so that a future generation can find justice and acceptance. Or sometimes we must lose everything so that we can quit worrying about this world and look forward to the next.

Seek peace. Deep peace.

So, when you feel left behind with nothing, look up! God is still on his throne. God still holds out his arms. God still wipes away tears. Possibly it is at such times that you can feel God's love most warmly and God's peace most deeply.

6th - The scripture for today, May 6 (5/6), is Song of Solomon 5:6 as found in the Old Testament of the Bible:

"I opened [the door] for my lover, but my lover had left; he was gone. My heart sank at his departure. I looked for him but did not find him. I called him but he did not answer."

Jesus is the lover of your soul. He opens the door for you, but perhaps you're spending all your time thinking about material things. His heart sinks when you run away from him. Oh, how his heart aches with loneliness for you.

So Jesus goes out looking for you. He looks everywhere you go. He calls you by name. But perhaps your life is so full of the noise of doing and going and accomplishing, that you do not hear him.

Stop! Allow some quietness into your life. Then listen. Do you hear that? Jesus is calling for you....

7th – The scripture for today, May 7 (5/7), is **1st Peter 5:7** as found in the New Testament of the Bible:

"Cast all your anxiety on him because he cares for you."

Oh, how hard life can be sometimes. We wonder why God doesn't stop all the bad things. But, if there were no evil and bad things happening, we would have heaven on earth. Satan is the Prince of this world.

How many times in a week are you anxious about something? Your job, your home, your children, your neighbors, your government, your health? How many times in a day? Are they heavy? Sometimes almost too heavy to bear?

Name them to God. Tell him all about them. Go into as much detail as you like. Then put them all on his shoulders. That's what he wants you to do. He will carry those burdens for you.

Yes, this is not heaven on earth. But Jesus provides a way for us to escape to the other world in heaven. We don't have to escape; he doesn't force us. In the meantime, he calls out, "Come to me, all who are weary and burdened, and I will give you rest" (Matthew 11:28). Why? He cares for you.

8th - The scripture for today, May 8 (5/8), is **Psalm 5:8** as found in the Old Testament of the Bible:

"Lead me, O Lord, in your righteousness, because of my enemies ~ make straight your way before me."

An enemy would like nothing more than to get into a good fight with someone. Do not let that happen. You have better things to do than argue with people.

Set your eyes, not on your enemy, but on the Lord. The path of enemies will take you on all sorts of side trips that lead to dead ends. The path of God rises up before you ~ straight and direct. Never let your attention stray from that path.

Keep on walking on the path of God.

And keep on walking,

and keep walking,

and walking, and walking....

....Until at last you walk right through the gates of heaven.

9th- The scripture for today, May 9 (5/9), is **Matthew 5:9** as found in the Old Testament of the Bible:

"Blessed are the peacemakers, for they will be called the sons of God."

Jesus, the only begotten Son of God (Christians are adopted sons) was a peacemaker. He came to earth to help us make peace with God. After all, "all have sinned and come short of the Glory of God" (Romans 3:23). It only takes one sin to be a sinner. And God cannot dwell with sin. What was the solution?

Romans 6:23 says the wages of sin is death. In Old Testament times, God let people kill a perfect animal in their place and collect their death wage. But they kept having to do it. Finally, Jesus came to earth and lived that perfect life that is impossible for us to live as the perfect Lamb of God. Then he allowed himself to take our punishment for our (not his) sins and collect the death wage in our place.

His was the final sacrifice. Now, by following Jesus, God adopts us and makes us his children. Jesus was a peacemaker between God and man.

You, too, can be a peacemaker. You can help people be at

peace with themselves. You can help them be at peace with each other. And you can help them be at peace with God. Thereby, you can share in what God's begotten Son was ~ a peacemaker.

10th- The scripture for today, May 10 (5/10), is 1st Peter 5:10f as found in the New Testament of the Bible:

"And the God of all grace, who called you to his eternal glory in Christ, after you have suffered a little while, will himself restore you and make you strong and firm and steadfast. To him be the power for ever and ever."

This earth is not meant to be your paradise, to be your eternal home. This earth is just the foyer. God stands at the door to heaven and calls you.

Are you too busy watching over things here to look over at his door? Are you too caught up with temporary things of this world to stop and listen for God?

Is there too much noise in your life? The noise of problems with job, home, family, government, neighbors, health? Remember, you are only in the foyer.

Life is not always easy. Do you have the stamina to not be side tracked? Do you have the fortitude to keep walking toward his door?

God can make you strong and firm and steadfast if you will stop the noise and listen for him. God can make you strong and firm and steadfast if you keep your eyes on his door.

You're not home yet.

11th - The scripture for today, May 11 (5/11), is 1st Peter 5:11 as found in the New Testament of the Bible:

"To him be the power for ever and ever. Amen."

God has the power to do more for you than you ever dreamed. He can take you in new directions in your life; arrange for you to meet wonderful people; provide the ability to overcome not-so-good things in your life.

All you have to do is ask. Perhaps more than once. Perhaps many times. But he wants you to ask. Why?

Parents sometimes tell their children "no" the first time they ask for something. Maybe it's because the child needs to find out for him/herself how badly s/he wants it. It's in the asking that they find out. So, God waits for the request. Sometimes the request never comes. And so, the blessing never comes.

Remember, God has the power. He may have something special in mind for you. So, ask.

12th - The scripture for today, May 12 (5/12), is **1st Kings 5:12** as found in the Old Testament of the Bible:

"The Lord gave Solomon wisdom, just as he had promised him."

God makes a promise of wisdom to Christians today. James 1:5 says, "If any of you lacks wisdom, he should ask God who gives generously to all without finding fault, and it will be given to him."

Amazing! God doesn't sit around and tell certain people, "You really messed up. Your life is full of turmoil. Now you come to me expecting me to fix it for you." No, God does not throw your faults in your face. It's no use dwelling in the past; that is history.

He is ready and willing to provide guidance for the present and future, the now and later. How can you know God's wisdom? He certainly does not make you guess.

He put everything he wants you to know in his Word, the Bible ~ examples of people who did and did not mess up their lives and words of advice. All you have to do is open it and ask God to help you understand it and apply it with wisdom.

God promised. And he keeps his promises.

13th- The scripture for today, May 13 (5/13), is **1st John 5:13f** as found in the New Testament of the Bible:

"I write these things to you who believe in the name of the Son of God so that you may know that you have eternal life. This is the confidence we have in approaching God: That if we ask anything according to his will, he hears us."

What a wonderful and comforting promise: The God of the universe, the Creator, the King of all kings hears you!

But how are you supposed to know God's will? By a feeling deep in your heart? Feelings are fickle. Can there be another way? Of course. It's simple. Just read his very words to you in the Bible.

The Bible is full of examples of people who did right and who did wrong, to help you see the consequences of good and bad decisions. The Bible is also full of God's advice to you. Proverbs is one of the books that is full of such advice along with all the apostolic letters in the New Testament. Read the Bible. You do not have to guess what God's will is.

What about asking God's will on whether you should move to this place or that, whether you marry this person or that, whether you take this job or that? Perhaps all your choices are good. God has also given you free will. Always remember, "ALL things work together for good to those who love the Lord and called according to his purpose" (Romans 8:28).

14th - The scripture for today, May 14 (5/14), is **2nd Corinthians 5:14a** as found in the New Testament of the Bible:

"For Christ's love compels us...."

On a distant hill a very long time ago, something unbelievable happened.

Jesus died both physically and spiritually in our place! (Remember when he said God had forsaken him?) He knew we couldn't come back from either kind of death on our own, so he did it for us. Such terrible things he went through for us!

Love is powerful! It causes us to do things for someone we love that we never wanted to do and never dreamed we could do.

How powerful is your love for Christ? Do you share the love of Christ with others? 1st John 4:18 says, "Perfect love casts out fear."

You must reach out to people who think Jesus will ruin their fun, or has too many rules, or could never forgive them, or wouldn't stop a tragedy from happening to them. If not in person, tell them in a note, a phone call, email, even a song. There are ways. Reach out. You can and you will if Christ's love compels you.

15th - The scripture for today, May 15 (5/15), is **Ecclesiastes 5:15** as found in the Old Testament of the Bible:

"Naked a man comes from his mother's womb, and as he comes, so he departs. He takes nothing from his labor that he can carry in his hand."

As most people enter their senior years, they finally understand this verse. In their youth they struggled to get jobs and status and things. Some accomplished it and some didn't. But in the senior years....

when health is gradually declining....

the world is passing them by....

and they are sitting in their chair most of the time

....the main thing people look back on is what difference they made in their world, and how they did or did not help people important to them.

Often in their senior years when their income goes down and they are....

living only on a small pension, and they are unable to keep their big house, and fancy car, and impressive stuff

....they realize they are still the same person inside regardless of what they own.

Ask a senior what they want for a birthday present. It is not likely to be things. It is likely to be time spent with a loved one or something special given to someone in need.

What about you? How much time are you spending on things?

16th - The scripture for today, May 16 (5/16), is **1st Thessalonians 5:16** (KJV) as found in the New Testament of the Bible:

"Rejoice evermore."

But how can we rejoice when something terrible has happened?

The Apostle Paul who wrote this knew that the Thessalonians were being terribly persecuted (2nd Thessalonians 1:4), but he still said, "Rejoice evermore." How could he say such a calloused thing amidst their suffering? Had he no feeling, no empathy?

Sometimes we have to suffer so the true nature of bad

people pretending to be good can be revealed to the world. Sometimes we have to suffer so we can build our spiritual muscles. Sometimes we have to suffer so we can understand others going through the same thing.

Just remember that, just as God was grieved when his Son suffered on the cross, he is grieved when you suffer. And just as God was able to bring something wonderful out of his Son's suffering, he can bring something wonderful out of yours too.

In the meantime, chin up, shoulders back, stand straight, be brave, and smile. The world will wonder why.

17th - The scripture for today, May 17 (5/17) is **John 5:17** as found in the New Testament of the Bible:

"Jesus said to them, 'My Father is always at his work to this very day, and I, too, am working.' "

Psalm 115:12 says God is thinking about you all the time. When you're walking, riding, talking, doing, coming, going. God is always working for you. A popular song a few years ago was, "He's Got the Whole World In His Hands."

But does he always keep you from harm? He gave you free will, and sometimes you don't make good choices. Others around you have free will, and they sometimes don't make good choices.

If everything was perfect, this would be heaven. But it is not. Heaven is for later after we go through some tests. Regardless of what happens here, God is beside you if you fall, ready to get to work, ready to hold out his hand to lift you up.

How he loves you and cherishes you and cares for you. He always will if you follow him. Then, after you have fulfilled your own work here on earth, you can follow him right into that perfect world ~ heaven.

18th - The scripture for today, May 18 (5/18), is **1st Thessalonians 5:18** as found in the New Testament of the Bible:

"Give thanks in all circumstances, for this is God's will for you in Christ Jesus."

This is one of the most difficult verses in the Bible to follow. How can we rejoice with the loss of a loved one, of health, of a job, of a home, of a position? The Christians at Thessalonica, in Greece, had been suffering a lot of persecution for being Christians. Some had even been killed.

Satan will do all he can to cause bad to happen in your life in order to get you to blame God and forsake him. But the real blame belongs on Satan. It may sometimes seem like the harder you try to follow God, the worse things get in your life.

In that case, apparently Satan is afraid of your strength in the Lord and is trying more than ever to weaken you and get you back on his side. He doesn't have to attack people he already has.

And sometimes God stands back and tells Satan, "Do your best. This person will grow stronger, not weaker." Along with the Christians in Thessalonica, you can "become a model....your faith in God can become known everywhere" (1st Thessalonians 1:7-8).

So rejoice that Satan is so afraid of you. And at the same time, keep your eyes on Jesus who never gave in when Satan caused bad to happen to him. Rejoice that you are counted worthy. Can you do that?

19th - The scripture for today, May 19 (5/19), is **Ephesians 5:19** as found in the New Testament of the Bible:

"Speak to one another with psalms, hymns and spiritual songs. Sing and make music in your heart to the Lord."

What is so interesting about this scripture is how we are to make music to the Lord. In the original Greek the New Testament of the Bible was written in, the term "make music" means to play on strings. But put with the rest of the verse, we see that it means to play on the strings of our heart.

How beautiful! In God's ears, the strings of our heart are far superior to any musical instrument we can contrive. So, why would we want to use them as a substitute? Shall we not please the One we are worshiping? Let us be attuned, not to what we love, but to what God loves.

And so, let us sing! And in the process, let our singing be accompanied by the beautiful strings of our worshiping heart.

20th - The Scripture for today, May 20 (5/20), is **2nd Corinthians 5:20a** as found in the New Testament of the Bible:

"We are therefore Christ's ambassadors, as though God were making his appeal through us."

We all have a special longing. When we are in pain and long for reassurances that God is with us, one of the things we often want is to see God, feel God's touch, look into God's eyes. This is where Christians come in. God says to Christians, "Go to those in pain. Let them see you, feel your touch, look into your eyes."

Someone in your life needs you right now because they need God. They don't know how to reach out to God, but you do. They don't know how to understand God, but you do. Stop whatever you have planned for today that is kind of important. Replace it with the very important. Go see someone or call them or Skype them.

Are you or are you not God's ambassador? Is God doing anything through you? Yesterday? Today? Tomorrow?

21st - The scripture for today, May 21 (5/21), is **2nd Corinthians 5:21** as found in the New Testament of the Bible:

"God made him [Jesus] who had no sin to be sin for us, so that in him we might become the righteousness of God."

A lot of people do not understand what Jesus' death has to do with going to heaven. The key is in Romans 3:23 that says "The wages of sin is death." When Adam and Eve sinned, immediately their souls died, and the bodies gradually died. That was the wages they collected for sinning.

It's been happening to everyone since then. But, during Old Testament times, God allowed people to make a perfect animal take their wage, shed its blood and die in their place when they sinned.

This was only a temporary fix, however. Hebrews says the blood of animals cannot truly take away (take the substitute punishment for) sins; they are remembered again every year (Hebrews 10:3-4).

Finally, John the Baptist announced Jesus was "the Lamb of God" (John 1:29). In order to forever stop all the sacrificial substitute dying, God prepared his own perfect Lamb ~ Jesus, who never sinned. For 33 years, God's Word took human form in Jesus and became one of us. Then he had to shed his blood and die in our place. In so doing, he collected our wages forever.

Jesus did two things impossible for us to do: Live a perfect life without sin, and come back to life after he died ~ both physically and spiritually. Why? So we could do another thing that is impossible for us to do on our own: Enter heaven, the home of the perfect.

Heaven is not for people who do a lot of good works and only sin sometimes so that God will have no choice but to take them into his home. It only takes one sin to be a sinner. God cannot exist with sin.

God invites us to his heaven if we will just follow Jesus. We don't even have to be perfect ~ just forgiven. Jesus was perfect for us. What amazing love.

22nd - The scripture for today, May 22 (5/22), is **Galatians 5:22f** as found in the New Testament of the Bible:

"The fruit of the Spirit is love, joy, peace, patience, kindness, goodness, faithfulness, gentleness and self-control. Against such things there is no law."

There are some people in the world who call people who practice these traits "losers." They distrust people who love everyone, are kind to everyone and are always happy. "People like that are not for real." They believe you have to stick up for yourself and get ahead of the pack or the world will trample you and pass you by.

They are a lot like drivers out on a highway who think they have to pass every car. Once they do, there is usually a brief period when they are ahead of all the others. But soon they catch up with another pack of cars and begin all over again to pass every one, to get ahead of the pack. And so, it happens over and over endlessly. They never relax, for they are never ahead of the others for very long.

Today, relax a little. Exercise patience and self-control. There is no law against slowing down. And in the process find gentleness and find peace.

23rd- The scripture for today, May 23 (5/23), is Exodus 5:23 as found in the Old Testament of the Bible:

"Ever since I went to Pharaoh to speak in your [God's] name, he has brought trouble upon this people, and you have not rescued your people at all."

This is Moses talking to God, and Moses is very angry. Is it a good idea to be mad at God? Deuteronomy 34:10 says there was never a prophet like Moses "whom the Lord knew face to face."

Getting angry [not violent, that's different] sometimes is part of a healthy relationship, as long as we are willing to stick around long enough to understand the other person's point of view. Moses did not desert God. He spoke his mind, then waited to see how God would reply.

It wasn't that God didn't want to rescue his people from slavery in Egypt. God was not quite ready yet. And he probably did not rescue his people in the manner Moses had in mind. But eventually ~ after a little patience on Moses' part ~ it happened: God rescued his people.

Are you angry at God over something? Tell him so. Then stick around and wait for him to express his point of view. It will happen someday. Maybe it won't be your point of view. Probably it will be better.

24th - The scripture for today, May 24 (5/24),

is **Amos 5:24** as found in the Old Testament of the Bible:

"Let justice roll on like a river, righteousness like a never-failing stream."

When individuals of a nation begin taking advantage of each other, the nation loses its standard of justice. Eventually nations fall because of it ~ maybe not right away, but eventually.

Although acting justly may decrease someone's income or status or power, that nation will roll on and on like a river.

Injustice is not impersonal. Injustice begins with you. One person at a time, then eventually an entire nation falls. On the other hand, justice also begins with you. One person at a time, and the nation rolls on and on like a river.

What are you doing for your nation?

25th- The scripture for today, May 25 (5/25), is **Galatians 5:25f** as found in the New Testament of the Bible:

"Since we live by the Spirit, let us keep in step with the Spirit. Let us not become conceited, provoking and envying each other."

When someone is better than you in doing something, do you pick fights with them as punishment, or spread gossip about them in order to get others to quit respecting them?

Perhaps you don't do this all the time. But what about times when there is something you feel you are really good at, but another person not as talented gets the honor? That's when it's hard to "keep in step with the Spirit."

Whenever you envy someone, deep down you consider that person your enemy. Jesus said, "Love your enemies and pray for those who persecute you, that you may be sons of your Father in heaven" (Matthew 5:44-45a).

To many, loving our enemy is the most difficult command in the Bible. Perhaps one way to love your "enemy" is to realize that Jesus loved his enemies. Every time you sin, you become one of his enemies. But Jesus keeps right on loving you, even when you don't want to stop doing whatever you shouldn't.

Jesus demonstrates the love of the Son of God. And here he says, if you love your enemies, you are demonstrating what the children of God do. And that is far more important than honor that goes to those you envy. Leaving behind conceit makes it much easier to love everyone.

26th - The scripture for today, May 26 (5/26), is 1st Thessalonians 5:26 as found in the New Testament of the Bible:

"Brothers, pray for us."

Do you have a prayer list? There are many people we can pray for besides ourselves. Often prayers get bogged down and short because the only person we "remember" in prayer is ourselves. Well, and maybe a relative or two.

There are many people who need your prayers: Your family

is obvious. How about your neighbors? If you don't know their names, pray for them by house or apartment number. What about the newspaper? Every one of those bad-news stories is crying out for prayer. The school near you needs your prayers ~ students, teachers, administrators, janitors. It doesn't matter whether you have a child in that school; pray for them anyway. Who are your local government officials? Not liking them doesn't make any difference, for Jesus said we are to pray for our enemies too. And that leads to the list of your enemies; do you have any at your work place? Include them too. It's pretty hard to resent someone you pray for.

One other thing you might try doing in addition to having a prayer list: Have an answered-prayer list. Write down when you pray for someone, then when it is answered. Keep it as a reminder when you are down and don't think He's ever going to answer your requests. God does care after all.

And speaking of requests, by the time you're done praying for all the other people on your prayer list, you won't have a lot of time to pray for yourself. And that is okay too, for others are praying for you!

27th - The scripture for today, May 27 (5/27), is **Job 5:27** as found in the Old Testament of the Bible:

"We have examined this, and it is true. So hear it and apply it to yourself."

How many times have we gone to worship or listened on TV to a minister/priest/rabbi/imam and believed everything he said because the speaker looked so holy and convincing? Isn't that confusing when so many different holy-looking religious leaders teach different things and conflict with each other?

What is the answer to this dilemma? Examine the Bible for yourself! You're smart! You can do it!

The best way is to get a concordance. It lists every word in the Bible alphabetically, and every scripture that contains that word. If you want to know God's opinion instead of man's, use your concordance and look up every passage your chosen topic appears in. You can buy one (it is the size of an unabridged dictionary but not expensive) or use one on the internet.

Then examine everything God ~ not man ~ has to say about anything. Then there are no doubts. You have examined the facts. Now you know the truth. Now you are ready to apply it to yourself. The truth will set you free.

28th - The scripture for today, May 28 (5/28), is **Luke 5:28** as found in the New Testament of the Bible:

"And Levi got up, left everything and followed him [Jesus]."

This Levi was a tax collector, who, in those days, was allowed to set his own tax rates so he could pocket some of it for himself. Why would such a man follow Jesus, a man who apparently didn't have much money of his own? He had to trust Jesus and believe that he was truly a friend.

And why would Jesus ask him? Jesus was certainly taking a chance, since the uppity leaders of society and their religion openly declared Jesus a bad person for associating with "sinners and tax collectors". Jesus, in turn, had to trust and believe in Levi.

A lot of Christians brag that their only friends are those who worship with them. They don't really trust anyone else, so don't really want to be anyone else's friend. Well, how are they supposed to bring anyone to Jesus? Jesus went out to "seek and save the lost."

And sometimes there is a visitor at worship who isn't dressed right ~ perhaps with uncombed hair, or smell from no shower, or makeup put on too heavy, or clothes not in style, or maybe even dressed too richly. Are we ashamed to be seen with them? Jesus wouldn't have been. He was color blind, style blind, class blind.

Today, reach out and make friends with someone you have been staying away from. Jesus did. And thereby, you will be like him.

29th - The scripture for today, May 29 (5/29), is **Acts 5:29** as found in the New Testament of the Bible:

"Peter and the other apostles replied, 'We must obey God rather than men.' "

There are many countries in the world today where a person is beaten, imprisoned and/or killed for believing in Jesus Christ or owning a Bible. They must stay in the background and try to remain relatively unnoticed in order to survive. But their faith continues unabated, even amidst their fears. The church has survived persecution for 2000 years.

Even if they're not killed, they are by-passed for promotion at work or fired, they are harassed when out shopping, they are threatened in public transportation, they are turned down for a good education, and they must tolerate derision just walking down the street or waiting at a bus stop. But their faith continues unabated, even amidst their fears.

Such events are usually covered up by their governments and news media, and the good people of those countries never know it is happening. There are various newsletters on the internet about the persecuted that you can sign up for. One is at

www.persecution.org that sends news as soon as it happens. Let us daily hold up these brave souls in our prayers ~ those who obey God rather than men.

In eternity, God will deal with the persecutors. In eternity, it will be to God the persecuted will turn to, not men.

30th - The scripture for today, May 30 (5/30), is **John 5:30** as found in the New Testament of the Bible:

"By myself I can do nothing; I judge only as I hear, and my judgment is just, for I seek not to please myself but him who sent me."

It is hard to judge people you know and leave your own ego out. If you are jealous, you may judge them harshly. If you admire the person, you may judge them too leniently. Perhaps if you try to walk in their shoes, it will help you understand and not judge too harshly. And perhaps if you compare an admired person to Jesus, it will help you understand and not judge too loosely.

We're not talking judgmentalism here where you go around sizing other people up all the time so you can feel superior to them. In judging, you judge, then you accept people where they are. Only then can you become their true friend.

If you truly love others, you will not, when judging, seek to please yourself, but to please your Creator who knows your heart and loves you the very best.

31st - The scripture for today, May 31 (5/31), is **Deuteronomy 5:31** as found in the Old Testament of the Bible:

"But you [Moses] may stay here [on the mountain] with me [God] so that I may give you all the commands, decrees, and laws you are to teach them to follow in the land I am giving them to possess."

Many people believe that the "Law of Moses" consisted only of the Ten Commandments. But there was much more. It took Moses 40 days to write them all down. How many? Over 600 "commands, decrees and laws."

Some people today want to dip back into the Law of Moses to get showy types of worship ~ candles, incense, stoning for adultery, instruments of music, choirs, animal sacrifices, separate priesthood, special clothing for priests, and tithing to pay for it all. Jesus nailed the old law to the cross (Colossians 2:14) and created a much simpler New Testament/Covenant!

Other people want to rebuild the temple in Jerusalem. Why? So they can revert to animal sacrifices and thus nullify the sacrifice Jesus made of himself? James said that, if we keep part of the Law, we are obligated to keep it all (James 2:10).

By calling this covenant [testament] 'new' he has made the first one obsolete; and what is obsolete and aging will soon disappear' " (Hebrews 8:13). Not part of it. All of it. Hebrews goes on to say that the Holy of Holies is now in heaven, the curtain in the temple is now Jesus, etc. Rebuilding the temple would mean going backward from grace to legalism.

Thank God we do not have to keep all those 600+ commandments in the Law of Moses. They were controlling and tedious, and some were impossible to keep. Why would God give a law impossible to keep? To help us understand that it is impossible for us to be perfect. Finally, understanding that, he was ready to send his Son to earth to be perfect for us.

June

1st - The scripture for today, June 1 (6/1) , is **Psalm 6:1** as found in the Old Testament of the Bible:

"O Lord, do not rebuke me in your anger or discipline me in your wrath."

This is not only a good request to God, but it is a good request to each other ~ family and friends alike. When you disagree with someone, do you "back it up" with loud yelling or throwing or hitting things? Do you believe that your point cannot be understood and will not be accepted without a "tantrum"?

This scripture indicates that it is indeed possible to rebuke someone without the tantrum. In fact, it is more effective. When you calmly tell someone you disagree with them, it does not raise their blood pressure and put them on the defensive. With tantrums, they may react like you want on the outside, but you drive them farther from you on the inside.

Calm rebuke does not mean you don't mean it; it means you are convinced enough, your point of view does not need reinforcement. In that case, the other person is likely to be convinced too.

Today, practice saying calmly what you normally back up

with a tantrum. Practice in front of the mirror. Practice when driving. Practice when cooking or mowing the lawn or combing your hair. Then, next time you disagree with someone close to you, you will be ready. Ready to not rebuke in your anger.

2nd - The scripture for today, June 2 (6/2), is **Galatians 6:2** as found in the New Testament of the Bible:

"Carry each other's burdens, and in this way you will fulfill the law of Christ."

In case you're thinking people should take care of their own problems, you are right. But the term "burdens" here refers to overloads.

The main reason this is hard to do is that taking on someone else's overloaded burdens upsets our daily routine and our peace of mind. It is inconvenient.

Just remember, it is always inconvenient for those people to have an overload of burdens. They don't want them. Many times they didn't ask for them. But, even if they did ask for them with foolish acts, can we not roll up our sleeves and help them out a little while (not forever)?

We do not have to take on all their problems. But we can give them relief of some of the basic problems so they can concentrate on the more serious ones. If they need a babysitter, find one for them. If they don't have decent clothes to go to work, take them to Goodwill. If they're behind financially, buy them a tank of gas. Wash their dishes for them so they can have a clean kitchen at least until the next day. If they haven't written their parents for a year, sit with them while they write that letter. Take their overburden from them.

What if Jesus had said, "Hey, it's not my problem! Those people on earth mess up their lives all the time. Why should I leave the comforts of heaven to live among sinners and misery?" But he didn't say that. Thank God he didn't say that.

Inconvenient for him to take our overloaded burdens to his cross? Yes. Did he want to do it? No. But he did what was necessary to rescue us. Do we really and truly want to be like Him?

3rd - The scripture for today, June 3 (6/3), is **Romans 6:3f** as found in the New Testament of the Bible:

"Or don't you know that all of us who were baptized into Christ Jesus were baptized into his death? We were therefore buried with him through baptism into death in order that, just as Christ was raised from the dead through the glory of the Father, we too may live a new life....because anyone who has died has been freed from sin."

Oh! Baptism does all that? Some people say no, but God says yes. Indeed, in baptism we obtain a new life ~ are born again. And in baptism we are freed from sin ~ forgiven. Look at it this way: Just as Jesus died carrying our sins on himself, we die to our sinful nature ~ the part of us that sins and doesn't care. Then just as Jesus was buried in his tomb, we are buried in our watery tomb. And just as Jesus came up out of his tomb the Savior, we come up our of our tomb the saved ~ with a "new life" and "freed from sin."

Everything works together beautifully ~ hearing, believing, confessing, dying to sin, being baptized. What an honor and privilege we have been given to imitate what he did for us! 1st Peter 3:21 says it is an answer of a good conscience toward God.

4th- The scripture for today, June 4 (6/4), is **Psalm 6:4** as found in the Old Testament of the Bible:

"Turn, O Lord, and deliver me; save me because of your unfailing love."

Have you ever walked away from God then couldn't figure out how to make a turnaround and get your life back on track? Are you there now? Stop!

Stop whatever you are thinking and feeling and considering. Look behind you. God is a gentleman and will never force himself on you. When you turn away from him, he turns away from you. But, oh, how he misses you. He wants you back so you can feel his love again.

All you have to do is stop everything and call for him to come get you. "Turn, O Lord! Turn! Deliver me!"

Why would God be so good to someone walking away from him? Because he loves you and is always listening for your voice. His love is unfailing.

5th- The scripture for today, June 5 (6/5), is **Deuteronomy 6:5** as found in the Old Testament of the Bible.

"Love the Lord your God with all your heart and with all your soul and with all your strength."

Jesus said this is the greatest of all the commandments (Mark 12:29). He didn't say that any of the Ten Commandments were. He chose one of the over 600 commandments God gave to Moses in the Old Testament. It might have been lost in the crowd, but Jesus called it out and gave it special attention.

Although we no longer keep the Old Testament Law of Moses, we do have the New Testament Law of Jesus. There aren't as any commandments, but there are some. Sometimes Jesus' law repeats something in the Old Law such as the one above. But it was his choice what to carry over, not ours.

Some people don't even know that they're obeying any of the Laws of Moses. Well, then, all we have to do is read that Law and see if we recognize anything we're doing. Some people have ritualized themselves "to death".

On the other hand, do we love the Lord our God enough to keep all of the commandments of Jesus or do we say the church is too modern now to keep certain ones and, besides, we don't believe in any commands at all? We do not tell our parents, "I love you, but you have no right to command me to do anything." We do not tell our government, "I'm going to drive on any side of the road I want because I'm not going to obey any of your commands"

Let us not be like the clay telling the potter what to do (Isaiah 64:8). Let us love the Lord our God with ALL our heart, soul and strength. Jesus said, "If you love me, you will keep my commands" (John 14:15). Commands does not mean someone is trying to hold you down; commands means, "I love you and want you to be safe." Give it a try. Life just might get a little better.

6th- The scripture for today, June 6 (6/6), is **1st Timothy 6:6f** as found in the New Testament of the Bible:

"But godliness with contentment is great gain. For we brought nothing into the world, and we can take nothing out of it."

Still, don't we all do it? Compare what we own with what our neighbor owns? Work and strive to gain more and more?

A long time ago, a man wrote a book called, How to Want What You Have. He emphasized that, to people who are never content with what they have, happiness is always right around the corner. If we could just buy that object, or get that house, or obtain that promotion. But once we get it, we are only satisfied briefly before happiness slips away again, and we decide we would truly be happy if we could buy yet another object, or get yet another house, or obtain yet another promotion. And so we live our lives.

Let us dare to look around us today and tell ourselves, "I have all I need."

7th - The scripture for today, June 7 (6/7), is **Ephesians 6:7** as found in the New Testament of the Bible:

"Serve whole-heartedly, as if you were serving the Lord, not men."

God had just previously said that we were to obey our earthly masters (bosses). But, as hard as you try, sometimes what you may be told to do is very hard to do, especially if your boss is rude, or someone was promoted ahead of you, or you feel like s/he is being a "slave driver."

At times like those, do what is asked of you anyway, knowing that you are really doing it for God. The next verse says, "because you know that the Lord will reward everyone for whatever good he does, whether he is slave or free."

What you do as an employee in a difficult situation does not go unnoticed. God sees and God will reward you.

8th - The scripture for today, June 8 (6/8), is **Romans 6:8** as found in the New Testament of the Bible:

"Now if we died with Christ, we believe that we will also live with him."

We all want to live with Christ, but how do we die with him? Earlier in this same chapter, God inspired the writer to say this: "We died to sin....don't you know that all of us who were baptized into Christ were baptized into his death? We were therefore buried with him through baptism into death in order that, just as Christ was raised from the dead...we too may live a new life" (Romans 6:2-4).

So, just as Christ did a physical action to die for us, we do a physical action to die with him. And just as Christ's physical death overcame spiritual death, so our physical action overcomes our spiritual death. Then we are born again, or as this verse says, we "live a new life"

Some say this is water salvation. But it is no more water salvation than the cross was wood salvation. We live in a physical world and God has us sometimes do physical things in order to obtain a spiritual outcome. Our singing praise songs is a physical thing, but it is no less spiritual in its outcome. Our eating the Lord's Supper is a physical thing, but it is no less spiritual in its outcome.

Have you died with Christ?

9th- The scripture for today, June 9 (6/9), is **Job 6:9-8** found in the Old Testament of the Bible:

"Oh that I might have my request, that God would grant what I hope for, that God would be willing to crush me, to let loose his hand and cut me off!"

Job was suffering terribly. The Bible says he had sores all over his body. There were other symptoms listed elsewhere in Job that indicate he had a form of leprosy. Now he just wanted to die.

When we get into a life problem that seems hopeless, do we

just give up and say, "God, I can't go on like this. Just take my life right now. It's too hard. I can't do it anymore"?

God knows what you are going through. God knows that Satan is attacking you. When things are desperately low, your job is just to hang on. It often takes God time to shift around a lot of other people's lives in order to alleviate your pain.

Remember, God hurts just as much when you suffer as when he watched his own Son suffer on the cross. His Son's suffering accomplished something wonderful for others. So too, someday your suffering will somehow in some way accomplish something good. And ultimately, just by surviving, Satan loses and God wins.

This too will pass. You may not think so, but it will. You may think you will never smile again, never want to go around people again, never sing again. But you will. Just like Job did.

10th - The scripture for today, June 10 (6/10), is **Proverbs 6:10f** as found in the Old Testament of the Bible:

"A little sleep, a little slumber, a little folding of the hands to rest ~ and poverty will come on you like a bandit and scarcity like an armed man."

Oh! This scripture really comes to the point, doesn't it? Perhaps during difficult economic times for some people, this can be a gentle reminder. If you can't work for money, you can work for free. There is always work to do as a volunteer either in an organization or just by yourself. All it takes is for you to look around.

Well, if you're already in the clutches of poverty, what will volunteering do to help the situation? People will notice you. They will notice your work ethic, and your cheerfulness, and your thoughtfulness. They just might tell people looking for someone to hire. And in the process, you are helping others. That in itself can make you feel rich ~ even if you're not.

11th - The scripture for today, June 11 (6/11), is **Job 6:11** as found in the Old Testament of the Bible:

"What strength do I have, that I should still hope? What prospects that I should be patient?"

Many people use the expression, "patience of Job." But he had on-and-off patience, for he was very sick. By descriptions he gave of himself ~ sores, rancid breath, low voice, partial blindness, skin turned hard and black, bloating, nightmares, extreme pain, unrecognized by his closest friends, some believe he had a grotesque form of elephantitis leprosy.

What did he need from his friends? He surely didn't get it, for they spent their time trying to prove that he had sinned and God was right to be punishing him. His reply? "I have heard many things like these; miserable comforters are you all! Will your long-winded speeches never end? What ails you that you keep on arguing?" (Job 16:2f).

So how do we comfort someone who feels utterly hopeless?

We certainly don't put the blame on them, nor do we tell them it's "all in your head' or to "snap out of it". We can share times when we felt hopeless. We can weep with them. We can hold their hand. We can sit with them in silence. We can pray aloud for them. (Some people have never heard their name mentioned in a prayer.)

And we need to let them talk. Sometimes they will say things they don't mean in the long run, but at that brief moment they do. Or sometimes they need to talk through things they are unsure about. They may even say contradictory things.

At one time Job said, "Surely, O God, you have worn me out; you have devastated my entire household....God assails me and tears me in his anger and gnashes his teeth at me" (16:7f). But another time he said, "I know that my Redeemer lives, and that in the end he will stand upon the earth....I myself will see him with my own eyes ~ I and not another. How my heart yearns within me" (19:25f).

Do you have a very sick friend? Let your heart yearn with them.

12th - The scripture for today, June 12 (6/12), is **Luke 6:12** as found in the New Testament of the Bible:

"One of those days Jesus went out to a mountain side to pray, and spent the night praying to God."

How in the world did Jesus think of enough things to say that he could pray all night? Most of us on a good day only manage a 5-minute prayer. The next verse says that the next morning he selected his twelve apostles. He had probably spent at least half an hour each praying for them by name, as well as for others he was considering.

Who do you pray for by name? Do you have a prayer list? How about opening the newspaper and praying for all those people in the news ~ perpetrators, victims, causes, governments, situations? Or everyone you work with? Or everyone your children go to school with? Or all their teachers and administrators? Or the clerks in the stores you go to regularly? Or members of an organization you belong to?

There are always people in need of prayer. And one of the joys of such a prayer life is now and then telling people whom you know that they are in your prayers; or writing a note to someone who was a stranger to you that you pray for them.

Some people have never heard their name in prayer. Some people have never even been told that someone prays for them.

God loves to answer prayer. Do you love prayer?

13th - The scripture for today, June 13 (6/13), is **Judges 6:13f** as found in the Old Testament of the Bible:

" 'But sir,' Gideon replied, 'if the Lord is with us, why has all this happened to us? Where are all his wonders that our fathers told us about? .But now the Lord has abandoned us and put us in the hand of Midian [enemies].' The Lord turned to him and said, 'Go in the strength you have.' "

How dynamic! When you feel trapped, God says, "Go." When you feel paralyzed, God says, "Go." When you feel hopeless, God says, "Go."

Sometimes you spend your time concentrating on your problem rather than a possible solution. Or you try to find someone else to solve your problem for us. Or you feel so helpless, you sit huddled in a dark corner and ask God to take care of your problem for you. When Captain Gideon did this, God replied, "You've still got strengths. Use them."

Yes, you have to wait for God's final solution, but he does not expect you to sit idly by while he does all the work. "But how?" you ask. You are not a rock or tree or grain of sand. You are not an elephant or tiger or worm. You are a human being made in God's image. God breathed life into you and gave you special gifts and talents.

Don't sit idly by while bad things happen around you. Everyone has God-given strength. Look deep within your heart. It's there. Then go forth in the strength you have.

14th- The scripture for today, June 14 (6/14), is **Numbers 6:14** as found in the Old Testament of the Bible:

"There he is to present his offerings to the Lord...a year-old ewe lamb without defect for a sin offering.... "

A lot of people don't understand what Jesus dying on a cross has to do with going to heaven. Romans 6:23 says "the wages of sin is death." ~ both physical and soul death. It is Satan who pays us our wages. In Old Testament times, God intervened and allowed people to kill a perfect animal in their place whenever they sinned. But it was only a temporary fix because it is impossible for us to be perfect.

Finally, God the Word came to earth as a human, and John the Baptist called him the Lamb of God (John 1:29). Jesus was perfect; that is, he never sinned (Hebrews 4:15). Then he took the wages of sin from Satan and died as the perfect Lamb of God in our place ~ both physically (separation from people on earth) and spiritually (separation from God the Father). He even went a step further and miraculously came back to life!

Then God said, If you'll believe and imitate Jesus, I will c and consider your debt paid in full and consider you perfect too (Romans 6). Then I'll bring you back to life in heaven. How amazing!

And, by the way, since he came back to life on Sunday, that's what makes Sunday so special. It's an I'm-sorry-you-had-to-die-for-my-sins Day. It's the "Do-this-in-remembrance-of-me" Lord's Supper Day. It's a Gratitude Day.

15th - The scripture for today, June 15 (6/15), is **1st Timothy 6:15** as found in the New Testament of the Bible:

"...which God will bring about in his own time ~ God, the blessed and only Ruler, the King of kings and Lord of lords!"

But it's hard to know just when God's time is. You may think it is when an opportunity arises, but something happens and it doesn't turn out. So later another opportunity arises, but something happens there too and it still doesn't turn out.

This verse can carry you from hope to hope from discouragement to discouragement. That is because you cannot see what God sees.

Your life is like a line drawn across a piece of paper, and you have to stay on that line. But God looks down and can see the entire line at once, and he can also see everything going on around you. Those other events may not be good for you to become involved in. There may never be a time when events around you will be good for you.

Rather than give up on God and decide he doesn't really love you like he claims, amidst your tears of disappointment, stretch your spirit and praise him anyway. Acknowledge him. Then rest until his own time, whether it be soon or in eternity.

16th- The scripture for today, June 16 (6/16), is **Jeremiah 6:16** as found in the Old Testament of the Bible:

"Stand at the crossroads and look; ask for the ancient paths, ask where the good way is, and walk in it, and you will find rest for your souls."

We need history, not only for an appreciation of what our forefathers did for us, but also to learn which mistakes not to make all over again. This is true with religion also. There are hundreds of denominations and religions out there. This divisiveness hurts us. It seems the more denominations and religions we have, the fewer people are interested in spiritual things. They call it "organized religion".

Within Christianity, think about creeds for a moment. If a creed is less than the Bible, it isn't enough. If it is more than the Bible, it is too much. If it is the same as the Bible, why have it? Let us change our loyalties away from denominationalism and toward the Bible. All this confusion is exhausting!

Human nature has always been the same, and the Bible written long ago applies just as much to human nature today as it did then. Proverbs! The life and speeches of Jesus! The many mistakes made by people in the Old Testament! The advice to Christians in the New Testament!

It's not confusing. And maybe then, we will find rest for our souls.

17th- The scripture for today, June 17 (6/17), is **Matthew 6:17** as found in the New Testament of the Bible:

"But when you fast, put oil on your head and wash your face."

This is interesting because Jesus did not say "If, you fast" but rather "When you fast." It was as though he was teaching us to take for granted that we would fast ~ it would be second-nature to us. In a sense it is, for when most people go through a sudden tragedy such as loss of a loved one, they often cannot eat.

But what about voluntary fasting? The early church sometimes fasted. Acts 13:2 says a congregation in Antioch, Syria, fasted and worshipped, then chose men to go out as missionaries. Queen Esther fasted before going to the king uninvited with a request he might not like (Esther 4:16). Isaiah 58:3 says people fasted in order to humble themselves.

Some people respond, "I'd die if I had to fast." Perhaps that's kind of the idea. We know we would die if we went without food long enough. So perhaps one day of fasting is a way of saying, "God, I would die for you if I had to." Yes, fasting is a humbling experience, and frightening to some people. But perhaps that is the point.

Is something important coming up that you know you will be urgently praying about? Once you skip one meal, you will have conquered your desire to eat. Then, with your brain not having to concentrate on digesting food, it will be able to focus more on that important thing happening in your life. Your prayers will be more focused. You will be more focused with your eyes more clearly on God.

So, take a shower, comb your hair, put on some nice clothes, and look like you have something important to do. Then fast.

18th - The scripture for today, June 18 (6/18), is **2nd Chronicles 6:18a** as found in the Old Testament of the Bible:

"But will God really dwell on earth with men? The heavens, even

the highest heavens, cannot contain you."

Did you ever want to see God, to talk to him face to face? Perhaps something bad had just happened in your life and you had this urge to bawl him out, then let him explain why. Or did you ever want to touch God? Perhaps you were so very lonely that you desperately needed his arms around you, and feel his touch as he brushed away your tears.

But, if you could see him and touch him, it would mean that he could not be with others in the world at that time and could not hear anyone else's prayers at that time except yours. Try to be grateful that you cannot see and touch him for now. He is always available to you, regardless of where you are in this vast world and regardless of how many others are praying to him at that moment.

How he can sort out all our prayers at once is mind-boggling. How he can be everywhere at once is amazing. How he can love each one of us as though we were the only person alive is miraculous and incredible.

19th - The scripture for today, June 19 (6/19) is **1st Corinthians 6:19f** as found in the New Testament of the Bible:

"Do you not know that your body is a temple of the Holy Spirit who is in you whom you have received from God? You are not your own. You were bought with a price. Therefore, honor God with your body."

Your body is pretty valuable. The purchase price was high. Jesus bought you back from Satan with something very expensive ~ his body and the blood within it.

This world's temples are sometimes small and sometimes large. Sometimes plain, sometimes fancy. Sometimes there is complete silence in a temple. And sometimes it echoes with song. Sometimes it has many people, sometimes it stands alone. People can usually figure out that each is a temple whether or not it has a sign.

Can people tell what you are without you having to tell them? When your family and friends need a place of quiet and rest, can they come to you? When people need a place of joy, can they come to you? After you part company with someone, are they glad you're gone, or do they feel good about themselves and look forward to the next time they can be with you?

What kind of building would you describe your body?

20th- The scripture for today, June 20 (6/20), is Matthew 6:20f as found in the New Testament of the Bible:

"But store up for yourselves treasures in heaven, where moth and rust do not destroy, and where thieves do not break in and steal. For where your treasure is, there your heart will be also."

In describing heaven, terms are used like pearls, diamonds, emeralds, gold, and so on. So certainly God is not against riches. Otherwise he would not have described heaven with those terms.

So what is the problem? Ask yourself, "If I lost everything tomorrow, could I face life?". You may say yes, but what about friends? They may not want to associate with someone with nothing. So, it is not only a greed problem, but a social problem. It is a problem of losing both your possessions and your friends.

Some have solved this problem by moving out into the country where possessions and social status don't mean so much. Or you could stay where you are and just change your choice of friends. Your new friends may be truer friends than you ever had before and may need you more.

Lastly, if you lost your job, your car, your home ~ your identity ~ would you be so devastated that you would contemplate suicide as some have done? Or would you be able to look around and see what you can do without having and a job to occupy your time?

There are always things you can do for others. Is that truly where your heart is? In that case, loss of everything would not bring catastrophe. Rather, it would give opportunity to reveal what stuff you are made of deep down inside where your true treasure is ~ in your heart.

21st- The scripture for today, June 21 (6/21), is **Romans 6:21ff** as found in the New Testament of the Bible:

"What benefit did you reap at that time from the things you are now ashamed of? Those things result in death. But now that you have been set free from sin and have become slaves to God, the benefit

you reap leads to holiness, and the result is eternal life. For the wages of sin is death, but the gift of God is eternal life in Christ Jesus our Lord."

Sometimes you do things you are ashamed of, and decide God would be too ashamed of you to accept you as his child. But God can get rid of the shame, for he can forgive so completely that it is as though we never did those things.

Do you bristle at the phrase "slaves to God" or "slaves to Christianity" or even slavery at all? But we're all slaves to something ~ a big car, high position, beauty, a hobby, chasing after the opposite gender, reading, eating, music, sports, etc. What are you a slave to?

From the beginning of time, sin has always been rewarded with death. Death means "separation" , and in the case of sin, it means separation from God. God allowed us in Old Testament times to kill a perfect animal in our place, but we had to keep doing it throughout life. Then Jesus came as our perfect Lamb of God, and allowed himself to be killed in our place.

The wages were collected from Satan by Jesus. Yes, Satan pays mankind our due. He is for justice. God is for forgiveness. Instead of paying us what we deserve, God pays us what is not just. It is his love.

22nd - The scripture for today, June 22 (6/22), is **Ephesians 6:22** as found in the New Testament of the Bible:

"I am sending him to you for this very purpose: That you may know how we are, and that he may encourage you."

Have you sent a letter to anyone in your family lately? How about your elderly parents, your grown children, aunts or uncles, nieces or nephews? Do they love you? If they do, they are going to worry about you until they hear how you are.

I have a letter written by my great grandmother to her daughter (my grandmother) saying (besides the usual chit-chat), "You never write." I have another letter written a generation later by my grandmother to her daughter (my mother) saying, "You never write." And I have a letter from my mother saying to her daughter, "You never write."

Each generation goes through this. We grow up, go out on our own, get busy, and forget to write our loved ones. They spent somewhere around 20 years raising you, taking care of you, making sure you were clean, your clothes decent, you did your homework, you got along with your friends, your scratches were healed, you ate right. How can they devote that much daily time and energy (both physical and emotional) on someone until they are grown, and then just turn it off? Just quit caring? They cannot.

So today, sit down and write a letter to someone who helped raise you. If you think you don't have anything to say, you really do. Tell them what you had for lunch yesterday, what song on the radio you heard, where you went, who you saw. Just chit-chat things. All they want is to know how you are. Then they will feel a lot better. Because they love you.

23rd - The scripture for today, June 23 (6/23), is **2nd Chronicles 6:23** as found in the Old Testament of the Bible:

"Then hear from heaven and act. Judge between your servants, repaying the guilty by bringing down on his own head what he has done. Declare the innocent not guilty and so establish his innocence."

Did you notice here that God brings down on our head what we do to others? It includes how we treat him too. If we don't have time for God, God doesn't have time for us. If we put God last, he puts us last. If we refuse to forgive others, he refuses to forgive us. This is the boomerang effect. Here are several scriptures that reflect God doing to people what they do.

"The nations have fallen into the pit they have dug; their feet are caught in the net they have hidden. The Lord is known by his justice; the wicked are ensnared by the work of their hands." (Psalm 9:15-16)

"In his arrogance the wicked man hunts down the weak, who are caught in the schemes he devises." (Psalm 10:2).

"The wicked draw the sword and bend the bow to bring down the poor and needy, to slay those whose ways are upright. But their swords will pierce their own hearts." (Psalm 37:14-15)

"Let the heads of those who surround me be covered with the trouble their lips have caused." (Psalm 140:9)

"He mocks proud mockers." (Proverbs 3:34)

"Can a man scoop fire into his lap without his clothes being burned?" (Proverbs 6:27)

"If a man digs a pit, he will fall into it; if a man rolls a stone, it will roll back on him." (Proverbs 26:27)

"Woe to you, O destroyer, you have not been destroyed! Woe to you, O traitor, you have not been betrayed. When you stop destroying, you will be destroyed; when you stop betraying, you will be betrayed." (Isaiah 33:1)

"According to what they have done, so will he repay wrath to his enemies and retribution to his foes." (Isaiah 59:18)

"I will judge you according to your conduct and repay you for all your detestable practices." (Ezekiel 7:8)

"As you have done, it will be done to you; your deeds will return upon your own head." (Obadiah 1:15)

In the meantime, we're to leave punishment to God. And, if you are falsely accused of anything, God will declare you innocent. His is the important judgment.

24th- The scripture for today, June 24 (6/24), is **Numbers 6:24f** as found in the Old Testament of the Bible:

"The Lord bless you and keep you; the Lord make his face to shine upon you and be gracious to you; the Lord turn his face toward you and give you peace."

This beautiful blessing from the Bible has been set to music and turned into a spiritual song. Enter this on the internet, and you should be able to hear it sung: **http://bit.ly/1HAztLI**

25th- The scripture for today. June 25 (6/25), is **Matthew 6:25** as found in the New Testament of the Bible.

"Therefore, I tell you, do not worry about your life, what you will eat or drink; or about your body, what you will wear. Is not life more important than food, and the body more important than clothes?"

Do you sometimes wonder how God can allow people to starve with such a promise as this? Try to remember the Big Picture.

Remember the Jews being in slavery in Egypt for 400 years? They must have prayed thousands of times to be freed, but most died still in slavery, believing their prayers never had been answered. God had a greater plan for them ~ a plan to give them time to multiply from the original 70 people who went to Egypt to the over 3 million who left Egypt.

So, too, God has a Master Plan for each person and each nation. It is your assignment to hang on and keep believing in Him and that which you do not understand. That means you may have to sacrifice something important to you for a future generation. It may even mean sacrificing your life for a future generation.

You may not understand, but God always does.

26th - The scripture for today, June 26 (6/26), is **1st Chronicles 6:26ff** as found in the Old Testament of the Bible.

"Elkanah his son, Zophai his son, Nahath his son, Eliab his son, Jeroham his son, Elkanah his son and SAMUEL his son. The sons of Samuel: JOEL the first born and Abijah the second son."

This is a little long, but I think you will enjoy it.

The prophet Samuel came from a musical family who descended from Levi's son Kohath. Samuel's son listed in this scripture was Joel. Verse 33 called the son of Joel and grandson of Samuel "Heman the musician". Just what did Heman the musician do?

David told the Levites to appoint "singers to sing joyful songs, accompanied by musical instruments: lyres, harps and cymbals". Heman was the first one they appointed (I Chronicles 15:16f) and he had two assistants ~ Asaph and Merari (I Chronicles. 6:39, 44). David put them in charge of the music in the house of the Lord and they performed their duties according to the regulations (verses 31f).

So what David appointed was a choir and orchestra. When David first appointed them, Heman had 120 relatives in his clan, and his assistants had 220 and 130 in their clans (I Chronicles. 15:5-7; 19-22; 27-28) so they had a total of 470 musicians. Wow! And these musicians had a full time job!

They were to minister before the Lord "according to each day's requirements" of sacrifices as written in the Law of Moses. Heman and the others were responsible for sounding the trumpets and cymbals and playing the other instruments ~ lyres, harps and cymbals (15:19-21) ~ for sacred song (16:37-42). In addition to playing the prescribed lyres, harps and cymbals, trumpets were to be sounded to announce sacrifices, etc. (16:4-6).

By the time David was old, there were "four thousand...to praise the Lord with the musical instruments" (I Chronicles 23:5)! What an amazing choir and orchestra they had by this time! Remember, they were all male Levites, and were to help Aaron's descendants, the priests, in the temple every day and at special feasts (verse 28, 30f). And what instruments were they still playing? Cymbals, lyres and harps "for the ministry at the house of God" (I Chronicles. 25:1 & 6).

Years later after David died and his son Solomon had completed the grand Temple in Jerusalem (II Chronicles. 5:1), "all the Levites who were musicians...stood on the east side of the altar dressed in fine linen and playing cymbals, harps and lyres, accompanied by 120 priests sounding trumpets. The trumpeters and singers joined in unison as with one voice to give praise and thanks to the Lord. Accompanied by trumpets, cymbals and the other instruments, they raised their voices in praise to the Lord" (verses 12-13).

Can you imagine such an orchestra and choir? The tinkling of the harps and lyres, with cymbals keeping the tempo, and trumpets calling attention to it all? And all those singers! Was God pleased? Indeed he was, for in the form of a cloud "the glory of the Lord filled the temple of God" (verse 14).

All this occurred around 1000 BC. Three centuries later when Hezekiah was king, the same instruments were being played ~ cymbals, harps and lyres (II Chronicles. 29:25f). Why? Because they were prescribed by David, Gad the seer and Nathan the prophet as commanded by God through his prophets. (Acts 2:29-30 says David was a prophet too.)

So we see that during Old Testament times, God commanded that they have full-time musicians to sing and play during daily sacrifices and special feasts and they had to be male Levites and they had to play cymbals, harps and lyres, sometimes accompanied by trumpets.

What a family Samuel had! And I'll bet he was musical himself. How proud he would have been of his descendants.

Interestingly, although God specified every detail of the instruments that had to be played in the Old Testament, nothing like that was specified in the New Testament. Did God forget? Perhaps God took us to a higher plain in the New Testament era. We do know that in I Corinthians 14:15, we are told to both pray and sing with mind and spirit.

And in Ephesians 5:19 we are told to "Speak to one another with psalms, hymns and spiritual songs. Sing and make music in your heart to the Lord." The term "make music" in the original Greek language of the New Testament is to play on strings. Since we are to make music in our hearts, then it looks like we are to play on the instrument of our heart. How beautiful!

About 40 years ago when my father died, the funeral was in a little country church. The music consisted of a small group from the congregation who sang hymns without the accompaniment of an instrument. They were not good performers ~ they twanged a lot and sometimes were a bit off key. But it was some of the most beautiful music I have ever heard. Why? Because their singing was accompanied by their heart. They were telling my family, "We love you," and I really felt that they did.

God looks down at our singing ~ no matter how good or feeble ~ and says, "I can tell you love me." And that's all that matters.

27th- The scripture for today, June 27 (6/27), is **Daniel 6:27** as found in the Old Testament of the Bible:

"He [God] rescues and he saves, he performs signs and wonders in the heavens and on the earth. He has rescued Daniel from the power of the lions."

This was proclaimed by none other than Darius, Emperor of Persia and Babylon. He normally worshipped idols. What made him respect God? It was Daniel's example of being true to God even in the face of death.

Everyone has problems. You can consider them opportunities. People of the world do not see any benefits to Christianity in their everyday life. You can show them the advantage by how you face your own difficulties. They will notice.

A friend of mine was a logger (lumberjack). This big guy got up at 4 AM every day and didn't get home from work and finish eating dinner until about an hour before bed time. So he began reading his Bible out in the forests during his lunch break. The other men made fun of him.

They had to ride a small bus together to get deep into the forest, and the guys would harass him on the bus. One day they harassed and teased him so bad because of his Christianity (he wouldn't cuss and swear with or at them) and Bible reading, that he asked the bus driver to stop. He got out and walked ten miles toward his home.

Some time later one of the men who had teased and harassed my friend went to him in private with a problem. He said, "I teased and harassed you with everyone else, but deep down I admired you." Then he went on to explain his problem to my friend "because you are the only one I know to turn to."

So today, if you are facing a problem, face it together with God. Face it with courage. Face it with the belief that it is for a reason and that reason may be so you can be an example of godly strength to others. Give it a try. You can do it!

28th - The scripture for today, June 28 (6/28), is **Luke 6:28f** as found in the New Testament of the Bible:

"Bless those who curse you, pray for those who mistreat you. Do to others as you would have them do to you."

There was a book published several years ago entitled, Hurt People Hurt People. Have you been hurt? Perhaps by an insult, a neglect, an illness, losing your job? Have you turned bitter? Do you lash out at everyone, or a group of people or a particular someone?

One method of lashing out is when someone tries to console someone who has lost a loved one in death by saying, "I know how you feel." Then the hurt person lashes out at the other person and says, "You DON'T know how I feel! How dare you pretend that you do!"

That is a hurt person trying to hurt someone else. It's as though they are bragging, "My hurt is so amazingly great, any effort on your part to understand is puny and not worthy of the greatness of my hurt."

How do you react to your pain? Do you run people off?

Stop letting that old hurt punish you. Stop putting your life on hold and living in the moment over and over for eternity. Stop being the victim and the aggressor both. You're killing yourself ~ your mind, your spirit, your soul.

It is okay to smile again. Try it in private. Then in public. It is okay to let it go and hand it over to God. It is okay, when you feel cursed, to not curse back. It is a blessing to bless.

29th - The scripture for today, June 29 (6/29), is **John 6:29** as found in the New Testament of the Bible.

"Jesus answered, 'The work of God is this: To believe in the one he has sent.' "

Yes, it is true that the gift of salvation is just that ~ a gift, a free gift. And it is true that you cannot be good enough to earn salvation, because you don't know how to be sinless, and heaven can only accept the perfectly sinless.

But at the same time, James 2:18 says "Show me your faith

without deeds, and I will show you my faith by what I do." In other words, there are things you need to do to obtain salvation. You have to believe there is a gift for us somewhere, walk over to it, reach out, and grasp it.

Repenting is a work. And Jesus himself said believing (faith) is a work.

And how do you go about obtaining faith? By believing what other people tell you to believe? Romans 10:17 says faith comes by hearing/reading the Word of God ~ the Bible. It is going directly to God's Words to find out for yourself. It takes a little bit of work to read through it. But then, you can know that what you believe is really what God said.

30th- The scripture for today, June 30 (6/30), is **1st Kings 6:30** as found in the Old Testament of the Bible:

"He also covered the floors of both the inner and outer rooms of the temple with gold."

About 40 years ago it was figured that Solomon put $3 trillion worth of gold in the temple to line the ceiling, walls and floor. And that figure would probably be around $12 trillion today. Talk about streets of gold in heaven!

There are some people today asking for money to rebuild the temple in Jerusalem. Even if they accomplished it, what would it do for Christians? The book of Hebrews in the New Testament explains to the Hebrew (Jewish) Christians that they no longer need or want the temple. Why? Hebrews 8:13 says, "By calling this covenant (Testament) 'new' he has made the first one [Old Testament] obsolete."

Let's look at the temple in a spiritual sense through the eyes of a Christian ~ and of Jesus himself in Hebrews 9:1. Now the FIRST COVENANT [TESTAMENT had regulations for worship and also an earthly sanctuary. 7 Only the High Priest entered the inner room [Most Holy Place]...and never without blood..... 11 When Christ came as High Priest of the good things that are already here, he went through the **greater and more perfect tabernacle [temple] that is not man-made**. 12. He did not enter by means of the blood of goats and calves, but he entered the Most Holy Place once for all by his own blood [He being the Lamb of God ~ John 1], having obtained eternal redemption. 24. For Christ did not enter a man-made sanctuary that was only a copy of the true one; he entered HEAVEN ITSELF. For this reason, Christ is the mediator of a NEW COVENANT [TESTAMENT].

Why in the world would anyone want an imitation temple and holy of holies made with hands back in Jerusalem again, along with all the animal sacrifices on the altar, and priests who would have to be of the Tribe of Levi, and tithing and all the other over 600 laws of Moses? It makes no sense.

Thank God, we live in a more spiritual age ~ the age of Christ and the temple of heaven itself.

1st - The scripture for today, July 1 (7/1), is **Leviticus 7:1f** as found in the Old Testament of the Bible.

"These are the regulations for the guilt offering, which is most holy. The guilt offering is to be slaughtered in the place where the burnt offering is slaughtered, and its blood is to be sprinkled against the altar on all sides."

Romans 3:23 says the wages of sin is death. The earnings are paid by Satan, the author of death. The earnings for your sins were collected by substitute deaths of substitute perfect animals over and over in the Old Testament. But Jesus nailed the Old Law to the cross (Colossians 2:14), and with his one sacrifice made it so that no more blood sacrifices were necessary (Hebrews 8-9).

In a sense, Jesus, the perfect Lamb of God, laid down on the altar of the world where his blood flowed from all sides of the cross to all sides of the earth. Why would anyone want to rebuild the temple in Jerusalem and nullify that horribleness Jesus went through in our place?

Jesus collected your wages from Satan for your sins in your place. We can never, ever thank him enough. Instead of temple ceremonies, he asked you to commemorate his death with the

Lord's Supper, the Holy Communion each week. Do you? On Sundays, the day he came back to life, do you?

2nd - The scripture for today, July 2 (7/2), is **Proverbs 7:2ff** as found in the Old Testament of the Bible.

"Keep my commands and you will live; guard my teachings as the apple of your eye. Bind them on your fingers; write them on the tablet of your heart. Say to wisdom, 'You are my sister,' and call understanding your kinsman."

It is popular today for people to reject Christianity because they don't like rules. That is not logical. Everything in life has rules ~ getting tired and having to sleep is a rule, eating to stay alive is a rule, not running your car into someone else's car is a rule. True Christianity has the same kind of logical rules.

But it seems, everywhere we turn, we are given differing religious rules, and way too many. They cannot all be true, yet people who give them seems to be so good. They all pray and do good deeds, and never lie, cheat or steal.

How can they all be right when they contradict each other? Preachers and creeds and elders and dogmas. No wonder people are turned off by all the man-made rules. When it comes down to it, only God's opinion counts.

So how do we get God's opinion? We look up everything in the Bible using the key word we are concerned about. We look it up for ourselves and decide for ourselves. We do not let other people decide for us.

Well, how do we find all those verses? By using a concordance which is like a large dictionary listing all the words in the Bible and what verses carry those words. It is the size of a large-city telephone book. You can also get it on the internet free here: **http://bibletab.com/**

So today look up something about Christianity you have always been curious about. It will open up a whole new world for you. Then you'll have wisdom, understanding, and God's opinion.

3rd- The scripture for today, July 3 (7/3), is **Acts 7:3** as found in the New Testament of the Bible:

" 'Leave your country and your people,' God said, 'and go to the land I will show you.' "

This is part of a speech by Christian Stephen soon after the church began. He was reminding the Jewish leaders how God told their ancestor Abraham to leave his religion, home and family, and move to where God had something special for him ~ to begin the Jewish nation and religion.

But when Stephen got to the part where now God wanted his audience to leave the Jewish religion and move on to a still better one ~ the Christian religion ~ they were outraged. They were not like Abraham; they did not want to change. So, not liking the message, they killed the messenger. These religious leaders stoned Stephen to death.

It is hard to change. It takes a great big "leap of faith." But when God does the recommending, we can know he has something special in mind for us. So, gear up and take that leap!

4th- The scripture for today, July 4 (7/4) is **Romans 7:4** as found in the New Testament of the Bible:

"So, my brothers, you also died to the law through the body of Christ, that you might belong to another, to him who was raised from the dead, in order that we might bear fruit to God."

This is not talking about just any law. It is talking about the law, a specific law ~ the Law of Moses.

Have you ever tried wading through Leviticus, the third book of the Bible? It's full of all those laws in the Law of Moses (over 600 of them). Thank God Jesus nailed them to the cross and we are no longer bound by killing animals, stoning people for adultery, tithing, having priests, burning incense, going to the temple three times a year, only traveling 1/3 of a mile on the Sabbath, paying for traveling mercies, and on and on.

How did "we" in today's scripture die to the law? He said in the previous chapter (6:4) "we were therefore buried with him through baptism into death" and in Colossians 2:14 where Christ "having canceled the written code with its regulations that was against us and that stood opposed to us; he took it away, nailing it to the cross" and in Hebrews 9:13, 10:1 "By calling this covenant 'new' he has made the first one obsolete; and what is obsolete and aging will soon disappear.... The law was only a shadow of the good things that are coming."

God now freely gives us His gifts through Jesus Christ our Lord. How amazing. How blessed.

5th - The scripture for today, July 5 (7/5), is 2nd Corinthians 7:5ff as found in the New Testament of the Bible.

"For when we came into Macedonia, this body of ours had no rest, but we were harassed at every turn ~ conflicts on the outside, fears within. But God, who comforts the downcast, comforted us by the coming of Titus, and not only by his coming but also by the comfort you had given him. He told us about your longing for me, your deep sorrow, your ardent concern for me, so that my joy was greater than ever."

Oh how much we need each other.

Sometimes in life we go into our own Macedonia where we have no rest and are full of fear. Our Macedonia may be religious or political or medical; or it may be at work, out on the street, or at home.

At such times we need a Titus to help us, to encourage us. Our Titus may be a relative, a neighbor, a friend, or even a stranger.

Have you been a Titus to anyone lately? Look around. Be a Titus to someone today. You are so very needed.

6th - The scripture for today, July 6 (7/6), is **Mark 7:6f** as found in the New Testament of the Bible.

"He [Jesus] replied, 'Isaiah was right when he prophesied about you hypocrites; as it is written: "These people honor me with their lips, but their hearts are far from me. They worship me in vain; their teachings are but rules taught by men.' "

It is the trend today to say that all religions ~ even those who teach opposing things ~ are right and all are good. But Jesus did not say this. Well, then, how do we know which religious things we are taught and do today are from God and which from men?

You are smart. Don't be lazy. Read the holy books of all major world religions for yourself. Who knows? What you have been told all your life may be wrong. Do the other holy books have built-in proofs they really originated from God? Perhaps scientific, archaeological, ancient inscriptions, prophecies fulfilled? Here is a website with those holy books on it: **http://www.sacred-texts.com** Here is a website with nearly 400 proofs the Bible is from God: **www.churchofchrist-cg-az.com/Bible**

If you conclude the Bible is true, use a concordance and do a study of everything the Bible says about any topic. That way you will have God's opinion, not men's.

Here is a website with an online Bible concordance and it's easy to use: **http://bibletab.com**

You can find out for yourself,~ you can KNOW ~ whether

what you were told to believe by family, friends, and leaders is what God told you to believe~

7th- The scripture for today, July 7 (7/7), is **Matthew 7:7** as found in the New Testament of the Bible:

"Ask and it will be given to you, seek and you will find; knock and the door will be opened to you."

How beautiful. The Creator of the universe pays attention to each and every one of us. How does he do it? How does he even sort us all out when thousands of us are praying to him at the same time?

Sometimes you may think he is not listening to our prayers. But it takes time to answer some of them. If I am praying to meet my future husband or wife, God may have to move him or her from the other side of the country, get a new job for him or her, and arrange for us to "accidentally" bump into each other. This is just one example.

Also, when Jesus said whatever we seek will be given to us, he had already explained that we must "seek first his kingdom and his righteousness" (Matthew 6:33). So only within that context, God will give us our heart's desire.

Maybe today you can do a little bit of extra seeking and extra knocking.

8th- The scripture for today, July 8 (7/8), is **Ecclesiastes 7:8** as found in the Old Testament of the Bible:

"The end of a matter is better than its beginning, and patience is better than pride."

Years ago there was a little boy who belonged to the Pee-Wee Baseball League. A lot of teams played in different parts of a very large ball field. He would get in line to wait his turn to bat the ball. But he'd become impatient, feeling that he should be able to bat as often as he wanted.

So he'd take off across the field and get in the line of another team, hoping his turn at bat would come sooner. When he didn't go to bat as soon as he thought he should, he'd take off across the field in yet another direction and get in line of yet another team, hoping his turn at bat would come sooner.

After doing all that, he'd finally give up and come back to his own team. By that time, if he had just stayed in line with his own team, he could have come up to bat two or three times. His pride got in the way, his impatience got in the way, and he ended up losing all his turns.

What you hope and dream for may happen today, a year from now, a decade from now. Learn to wait for your turn.

9th- The scripture for today, July 9 (7/9), is **Deuteronomy 7:9** as found in the Old Testament of the Bible:

"Know therefore that the Lord your God is God; he is the faithful God, keeping his covenant of love to a thousand generations of those who love him and keep his commands."

Our amazing God! He loved our great great grandparents and He will love our great great grandchildren. The average age of having children is 30. Therefore, if we took this literally, 1000 generations would be 30,000 years. In that case, we've only just begun.

If taken figuratively, 10 to the Jews meant all inclusiveness, and 1000 is 10 x 10 x 10 or all inclusiveness times all inclusiveness times all inclusiveness. This means God will love us all inclusive years, times all inclusive years, times all inclusive years ~ for eternity!

And God gives everything we ask of him if it is good for us. All he asks in return is for us to give the little bit that he asks of us ~ faithfulness and keeping his few commandments. Then he will help us escape this world for his world. What a small price for us to pay and what grand arrangement!

10th - The scripture for today, July 10 (7/10), is **Psalm 7:10** as found in the Old Testament of the Bible:

"My shield is God Most High, who saves the upright in heart."

You wouldn't need a shield if everything on earth was good. God gave you free will to love him or not, to follow him or not. He did not want robots to love and follow him, for that is not true love or true commitment.

And so you have your assignment in life: To be strong in the Lord when others want to tear you away from him. Be an example of those who choose to follow Jesus in order to escape from this world into his world.

So, when sometimes things get too difficult for you, God stands ready to shield you while you rest.

11th- The scripture for today, July 11 (7/11), is **Matthew 7:11** as found in the New Testament of the Bible.

"If you, then, though you are 'evil', know how to give good gifts to your children, how much more will your Father in heaven give good gifts to those who ask him!"

Yes, we are evil. Evil and sin mean the same thing. If we are sinful, then we are evil. Hard to think of ourselves that way. Could we do nice things to someone who did bad things to us every day? God can. God does.

The Creator of the Universe our Father? The master-mind behind the intricacies of our bodies our Father? The One who can be everywhere at once our Father?

How unworthy we are. All we can do is fall at his feet and whisper, "You are so great. I am so small. I am overwhelmed by your love."

12th - The scripture for today, July 12 (7/12), is **Revelation 7:12** in the New Testament of the Bible:

"Amen! Praise and glory and wisdom and thanks and honor and power and strength be to our God for ever and ever. Amen!"

How often do we praise God? Praise is more than thanking Him. Praise refers to God's attributes. Let's see what these words mean in the original Greek language of the New Testament:

Glory: magnificently beautiful
Wisdom: great understanding
Thanks: bestowed favor
Honor: great weight and power

God deserves all this from us. Some people think God is ugly, He doesn't understand them, He is against them, and is for weaklings. Some even hate God and are even repulsed at the idea of worshipping him. They just don't know God. Today, will you help someone know God?

13th - The scripture for today, July 13 (7/13), is in **Job 7:13ff** in the Old Testament of the Bible:

"When I think my bed will comfort me and my couch will ease my complaint, even then you frighten me with dreams and terrify me with

visions, so that I prefer strangling and death, rather than this body of mine. I despise my life; I would not live forever. Let me alone; my days have no meaning."

Job was extremely depressed. It happens to everyone sometimes. His depression was certainly valid ~ he had lost all his income and all his children in a recent storm. Now he had what the Bible translated as "boils" but the symptoms indicate he had a form of leprosy. This particular form leads to nightmares in addition to the physical problems. Job had every right to be depressed. So depressed was he, that he no longer wanted to live, for his life no longer had meaning.

But, as miserable as Job was, he hung on. Patiently he hung on during the bad times. Sometimes during our bad times, the greatest thing we can do is "hang on" ~ be patient.

Romans 8:28 says all things work together for good to those who love the Lord. Job loved the Lord. Even in his misery and desire to die, he continued to love God and trust Him.

And although at such times you may believe your misery will never end, you may believe you will never even smile again, it will happen. The misery comes to an end. It did for Job. He got his health and wealth back and more children to comfort him. God will see you through too.

14th - The scripture for today, July 14 (7/14), is **2nd Chronicles 7:14** as found in the Old Testament of the Bible:

"If my people, who are called by my name, will humble themselves and pray and seek my face and turn from their wicked ways, then will I hear from heaven and will forgive their sin and will heal their land."

There is always a little bit of turmoil in all nations of the world. Of course, there is more in some. The average person cannot make their own nation call on God. But the average person can do this: "I urge, then, first of all, that requests, prayers, intercession and thanksgiving be made for everyone ~ for kings and all those in authority" (I Timothy 2:1-2). Further, we should pray for them by name.

Even if you think some people in authority in your nation are against you, you must pray for them anyway. Then wait quietly for God to work things out. It may take Him a year, a decade or a lifetime to bring about your heart's desire for your nation. But keep praying.

Your job, in the meantime, is to follow God's ways yourself. Romans 13:1,3-4 says, "Everyone must submit himself to the governing authorities, for there is no authority except that which God has established...For rulers hold no terror for those who do right....For he is God's servant to do you good."

God is aware of the suffering going on around you. He will not leave you or forsake you.

15th- The scripture for today, July 15 (7/15), is **Matthew 7:15** as found in the New Testament of the Bible.

"Watch out for false prophets. They come to you in sheep's clothing, but inwardly they are ferocious wolves."

Jesus said this. Maybe sometimes the "false prophet" is within yourself. You have a pet theory you want very much for God to agree with you on. So you read through the Scriptures trying to prove your point correct. Of course, taking a verse here and a verse there, you can "prove" anything you want.

So how do you find out if you are being your own "false prophet"? When you see a verse that contradicts your pet theory, look for other scriptures similar to this one. Use a concordance ~ a book that lists alphabetically every word in the Bible and every verse it appears in.

Or, if you believe in a different holy book of a different world religion, you can read it, then honestly search for built-in proofs it is truly from a mind that knows things humans do not such as prophecies of the future that were fulfilled. Thereby you can decide if you've been listening to a false prophet.

And as you honestly struggle, pray about it.

Yes, it is humiliating to believe you just might have been wrong, and then actually admit you were wrong. But it is also liberating.

Many people have already gone through this and can testify that changing from our viewpoint to God's viewpoint is not only liberating, but ultimately brings peace.

16th- The scripture for today, July 16 (7/16), is **Genesis**

7:16 as found in the Old Testament of the Bible:

"The animals going in were male and female of every living thing, as God had commanded Noah. Then the Lord shut him in."

Does your life sometimes feel like a downpour of unending bad events or a flood of tragedies? Whenever that happens, why not just enter an ark of safety and let God shut the door? When God shuts the door on something, try to recognize it, accept his decision, and take advantage of its peace and quiet.

Your ark of safety is in your mind, your heart, your soul. Your ark of safety is quietness in Jesus.

"My heart is not proud, O Lord....I have stilled and quieted my soul" (Psalm 131:1f)

"In quietness and trust is your strength" (Isaiah 30:15b)

"The fruit of righteousness will be peace; the effect of righteousness will be quietness and confidence forever" (Isaiah 32:17).

Today, instead of being angry at God for a closed door, stop, take a deep breath, and rest in the ark of his arms.

17th - The scripture for today, July 17 (7/17), is **1st Corinthians 7:17** as found in the New Testament of the Bible:

"Nevertheless, each one should retain the place in life that the Lord assigned to him and to which God has called him."

In some situations in life, this scripture is hard to accept. Sometimes life gets very, very hard. Sometimes it is difficult to keep smiling, even to keep breathing. When will it end? Will it ever end?

But can it be that this is where God wants you? Can it be that the difficulties in your life right now are your assignments from God? God fights Evil from heaven and it is our place to fight Evil from earth. It is an ongoing battle. "For our struggle is not against flesh and blood, but against the rulers, against the authorities, against the powers of this dark world and against the spiritual forces of evil in the heavenly realms" (Ephesians 6:12).

For some reason that cannot be understood right now, you are where God wants you to be. This is your assignment from God. Remember, we are "ambassadors for Christ" (II Corinthians 5:20). We must show the world that "all things work together for good to those who love the Lord" (Romans 8:28).

As a soldier for Christ, be brave. Think with a clear head. Stand firm of faith, strong in spirit, pure of heart.

18th - The scripture for today, July 18 (7/18), is Acts 7:18 as found in the New Testament of the Bible:

"Then another king, who knew nothing about Joseph, became ruler of Egypt."

Does God really answer prayers? When the Jews first arrived in Egypt, they received "royal treatment" because they were relatives of "Prime Minister" Joseph. Then he died, but his Jewish relatives stayed. Eventually they were resented, then feared, then made slaves of the Egyptians.

For the following 400 years, the Jews prayed for God to release them from their slavery. Generation after generation died believing that God does not answer prayers.

But God saw the big picture. He saw that the 70 relatives of Joseph who originally went to Egypt would become more than three million over the next four centuries. Then and only then would they be large enough to begin a new nation ~ the Jewish nation. In Egypt during those centuries, they were in a form of "protective custody".

Are you frustrated and confused because God is seemingly not answering some very important prayers? Perhaps you are part of a bigger picture that God only knows about. Perhaps your job is to stay where you are and just keep hanging on. Are you up to the task God has assigned to you?

19th - The scripture for today, July 19 (7/19), is found in **Romans** 7:19 as found in the New Testament of the Bible.

"For what I do is not the good I want to do; no, the evil I do not want to do ~ this I keep on doing."

Doesn't this pretty much describe all of us in some area of our life? It may be eating too much, breaking the law by going over the speed limit, laughing at dirty jokes, habitual lying, stealing "little things" at work, cheating on tests, jealousy, impatience, temper ~ any number of things.

Sins of habit and attitude are hard to break. So we go to God over and over asking him to forgive that which, deep down, we know we're going to do again.

Perhaps this emphasizes the importance of us forgiving others who habitually do wrong to us. We do not know their struggles any more than they know our struggles.

Jesus said, "If you forgive men when they sin against you, your heavenly Father will also forgive you." (Matthew 6:14).

Satan wants us to quit trying to do better. And he wants us to quit forgiving each other. Let us not give in to Satan. Let us give in to God. God's way leads to ultimate forgiveness by him.

20th - The scripture for today, July 20 (7/20), is **Ecclesiastes 7:20** as found in the Old Testament of the Bible:

"There is not a righteous man on earth who does what is right and never sins."

Many people believe if we don't murder or steal, and if we help people poorer than ourselves, and aren't mean to our family, God will have no choice but to let us into heaven. But it only takes one sin to be a sinner.

God ~ who is Perfect Goodness ~ cannot dwell with sin. But mankind has never figured out a way to be perfectly good.

God said in the Garden of Eden that the moment we sin,

our soul dies. Satan holds us for ransom. I Peter 1:18-19 says, "...knowing that you were not ransomed with perishable things like silver or gold from your futile way of life inherited from your forefathers, but with precious blood, as of a lamb unblemished and spotless, the blood of Christ."

Jesus became that perfectly good person (Hebrews 4:15) ~ that perfect Lamb of God (John 1:29). Then he paid the terrible ransom to free us from Satan. But, it does no good if we do not believe he did this. We cannot despise Jesus and say he is too demanding. Our part is the easy part.

All he asks is that we love him, thank him, worship him, follow his examples and his all commands (there aren't many). Then Satan can no longer hold us hostage. God the Father will consider us perfect too. Then we will be accepted into heaven.

21st- Our scripture for today, July 21 (7/21), is **Matthew 7:21ff** as found in the New Testament of the Bible:

"Not everyone who says to me 'Lord, Lord' will enter the kingdom of heaven, but only he who does the will of my Father who is in heaven. Many will say to me on that day, 'Lord, Lord, did we not prophesy in your name, and in your name drive out demons and perform many miracles?' Then I will tell them plainly, 'I never knew you. Away from me, you evildoers!' "

There are hundreds of denominations/sects out there all contradicting each other. It's impossible for them all to be right. We cannot all be on different roads going to the same place. We cannot all be pleasing God if we decide opposing things please him.

We can never rely on what someone else says just because they look and act holy and say all the right holy words and phrases and pray such holy-sounding prayers. We must never rely on our religious leaders to tell us what to believe. Shall we take their opinion or God's opinion?

Romans 10:1 in the Bible mentions some people who had a lot of zeal for God, but were lost because it was not according to the proper knowledge.

Well, how do you get God's opinion? Read the Bible for yourself! Use a concordance (lists every word in the Bible and every scripture with that word) and look up your chosen subject. Then, having found the truth, why not go back to the religious leaders in love and try to teach your teachers? Some just might listen to you.

22nd - The scripture for today, July 22 (7/22), is **2nd Samuel 7:22** as found in the Old Testament of the Bible.

"How great you are, O Sovereign Lord! There is no one like you, and there is no God but you, as we have heard with our own ears."

How do you know there is no God but the God of the Bible that we read about and "hear with our own ears" (when scriptures are read aloud)? How do you know our God is the only true God, and our Bible his only true words?

Investigating the numerous built-in proofs is how we know. Prophecies fulfilled of people and entire nations as given in the Bible and verified in secular encyclopedias. Scientific facts not known in early centuries. Over 300 archaeological facts. Here is a colorful website showing most of them:

bit.ly/BibleKingdomProphecies

Therefore, you can KNOW what God is like, what he wants and how he views you, for you have heard with your own ears and seen with your own eyes. How lucky you are. How blessed.

23rd – The scripture for today, July 23 (7/23), is **1st Corinthians 7:23** in the New Testament of the Bible.

"You were bought at a price; do not become slaves of men."

Who were you bought from? Satan. God told Adam and Eve the day they sinned their soul would die. Satan is the source of death. When we sin, he holds us hostage. I Timothy 2:6 says Jesus paid the ransom to free us from Satan. "For He rescued us from the domain of darkness and transferred us to the kingdom of His beloved Son, in whom we have redemption, the forgiveness of sins" (Colossians 1:13-14).

God loved you so much, he put his words in a human body. Why? Hebrews 2:14 says, "Since the children have flesh and blood, he too shared in their humanity so that by his death he might break the power of him who holds the power of death—that is, the devil."

Then God told the world through his Bible that, if you will believe this really happened and follow his will for you, he will consider you perfect through the blood of Jesus and eligible to enter his perfect home ~ heaven.

But it is not automatic. Romans 6 speaks a lot of who we are slaves to and how to break those chains and come under the umbrella of what Jesus did for mankind.

You were bought a great price ~ the blood of Jesus Christ. On Sundays ~ the day he came back to life and overcame that terrible soul and body death for you ~ where are you? Who do you worship?

24th - The scripture for today, July 24 (7/24), is **Matthew 7:24** as found in the New Testament of the Bible:

"Therefore everyone who hears these words of mine and puts them into practice is like a wise man who built his house on the rock."

The problem we have with putting into practice the Words of God is that we sometimes read blindly. We don't see the significance of something. We may read it over and over for years and never see its significance.

Take, for example, the story of Jesus' birth. We sometimes see pictures of baby Jesus in a stable with the shepherds and three wise men all gathered around him. But Matthew 2:11 says by the time the wise men arrived, Jesus and his parents were living in a house. Further, the Bible does not say how many wise men there were; it just says they gave three kinds of gifts ~ gold, incense and myrrh. And, Jesus' age was close to two by then.

How about 1st Timothy 3:2? "Now the overseer must be above reproach, the husband of but one wife, temperate, self-controlled, respectable, hospitable, able to teach." This word "overseer" is sometimes translated bishop, sometimes elder, and sometimes pastor. It's all the same office. We might think at first glance that we believe all this. But do we glaze over the fact that he must have a wife? Hmmm....

Here's another one. At funerals we often quote Psalm 23:4, "Even though I walk through the valley of the shadow of death, I will fear no evil, for you are with me, your rod and your staff they comfort me." But for the Christian, there are no shadows in the valley of death. Jesus was born "to shine on those living in darkness and in the shadow of death to guide our feet into the path of peace" (Luke 1:79).

Did you know the word "baptism" is never translated in most Bibles? It is a Greek word meaning immersion. Did you know the word "unknown" never appears next to tongues in the Bible? Did you know the word "tongues" is translated most places as languages?

Oh, so many things we over look ~ meaningful things. Let us continue to study God's Word daily with our mind and heart open to new things our religious leaders never told us so that we can build the house of our lives "on the rock."

25th- The scripture for today, July 25 (7/25), is Hebrews

7:25 as found in the New Testament of the Bible:

"Therefore he is able to save completely those who come to God through him [Jesus], because he always lives to intercede for them."

Indeed, ALL of mankind is invited to come to God through Jesus. There are scriptures in the Bible about being chosen by God. But when you check the original Greek, it means you are being invited by God. A company puts out a newspaper ad inviting people to be interviewed for hiring. Then they find a qualified person. Still, the qualified person is not in the company until the company invites him and they accept the invitation. So being chosen is not a passive thing.

Then there are people who live for themselves ~ never reading God's word, going on outings on Sunday morning, praying only in emergencies. They consider "religion" weakness. But, as long as they don't murder, steal big things, and only swear a little bit, God will suddenly let them into his home, heaven, when they die. If they could care less about God in this life, they would be miserable in heaven.

There are even those who do worship on Sunday morning but forget why Sunday worship is different from worship the other days of the week. According to Acts 20:7, the early Christians met on Sunday to (for the purpose of) break bread (the Lord's Supper). Jesus said hours before his agony to do this. But we disobey him and tell ourselves it's okay to spend our worship time in performing and other things.

Remember what happened on Sunday? He broke the

chains of hell for us on Sunday. He broke the power of death for us on Sunday. He came back to life for us on Sunday. But football and outings are more important, and me showing off how good I can perform is more important.

Oh, Jesus, help me bury my selfishness. You gave up so much for me. Help me remember what you sacrificed for me. Help me live for you. Help me live with you.

26th - The scripture for today, July 26 (7/26), is **John 7:26** as found in the New Testament of the Bible:

"Here he [Jesus] is speaking publicly [in the temple], and they are not saying a word to him. Have the authorities really concluded that he is the Christ? But we know where this man is from; when the Christ comes, no one will know where he is from."

These people standing around the temple refused to believe in Jesus because they chose to disregard a scripture that all Jews knew about. They said no one would know where the Christ (the Messiah) would come from. But they did know. It was in their own scriptures ~ Micah 5:2

"But you, Bethlehem...out of you will come for me the one who will be ruler over Israel."

Are you sometimes like all those people standing around in the temple? Do you sometimes make up your mind about something religious; and even if the Bible says something different, you refuse to acknowledge it? Does your ego sometimes get in the way? Or are you afraid of pressure from your friends?

As you read the Word of God, open wide your heart and mind. Walk the beautiful path that God has created for you ~ a path that leads you deep into the mind of your God.

27th - The scripture for today, July 27 (7/27), is Luke 7:27 as found in the New Testament of the Bible:

"This is the one about whom it is written: 'I will send my messenger ahead of you, who will prepare your way before you.' "

"The way" could also be considered "the path" or "the road". To prepare "the way" would be to straighten out the curves temporarily leading in the wrong direction, or clear out the stumbling rocks, or fill in the jarring ruts made when it rains.

You can prepare "the way" ahead of crises for your loved ones by example, by being a true friend, by prayer, by sharing the Word of God. You can also prepare "the way" for yourself. We all have our ups and downs. You know yourself better than anyone. You know best what you need to hear when you are down in order to lift you back up. Write yourself a letter. Tell yourself what you need to hear. Then put your letter away in preparation for one of your down times.

Life is hard. Are you always preparing "the way" for people you know? Have you prepared the way for yourself?

Today, sit down and write yourself that letter. Then think of someone else for whom you can begin to prepare "the way".

28th - The scripture for today, July 28 (7/28), is **2nd Samuel 7:28** as found in the Old Testament of the Bible:

"O Sovereign Lord, you are God! Your words are trustworthy, and you have promised these good things to your servant."

What a beautiful praise. Praising God is different from thanking him. It is acknowledging him for His traits ~ not for what He does, but what He is.

He is trustworthy!
He is able to hear all our prayers at once!
He is everywhere and all knowing!
He is perfect love!
He is anxious to forgive!
He considers us his children!

Sometimes in life, we come to a point when there is no one to trust about a certain thing. What a lonely feeling. But, if we have God, we have someone we can always trust.

29th -The scripture for today, July 29 (7/29), is **Ecclesiastes 7:29** as found in the Old Testament of the Bible:

"This only have I found: God made mankind upright, but men have gone in search of many schemes."

You begin your life upright ~ sinless. But as you grow out of innocent childhood, you begin to want recognition, money, and to make your surroundings beautiful.

True, God does not want to deprive you if you can obtain these things. But Solomon (who wrote this), was the richest man in the world with all his worldwide fame, wealth, and beauty. Yet, he still felt empty.

Today, you can even read the Bible and go to worship and still feel empty. Why? Because you need to add good works to your faith (James 2) ~ helping others with the same enthusiasm with which you pursue recognition, money and beauty – yes, and worship.

Sometimes, to fill your emptiness, you need to just return to your early childhood when you saw life through innocent eyes. Through simple eyes. Through eyes that believe so easily in God, and so easily love him.

Sometimes as you progress through life, why not return to that more innocent way of life?

30th - The scripture for today, July 30 (7/30), is **John 7:30** as found in the New Testament of the Bible:

"At this they tried to seize him, but no one laid a hand on him, because his time had not yet come."

Even though during the last two years of his life, many people wanted to kill Jesus out of jealousy or fear or pure meanness, he was never afraid to keep teaching. Why? Because he knew his life was ultimately in the hands of the heavenly Father.

Do we feel fear sometimes because of things going on around us? Do we fear failure, or ruin, or false rumors, or even imprisonment or our life? Remember, each life is in the heavenly Father's hands.

So do not fear. Keep on keeping on. Hold fast. Stand firm. Do the right thing. Stand up for Jesus. And, if some day, your time does come, know that God has everything under control. And God will never, ever, ever stop loving you.

31st - The scripture for today, July 31 (7/31), is **1st Corinthians 7:31b** as found in the New Testament of the Bible:

"For this world in its present form is passing away."

How easily that which we have slaved for over a period of years can pass away. It can happen as the result of fire, flood, storm, war, economic crisis. Every day something in this world "is passing away."

What are we working for day to day? That which can so easily pass away? Or that which is eternal and will never pass away? What are your plans for today? Think about it.

1st - The scripture for today, August 1 (8/1), is **Romans 8:1** as found in the New Testament of the Bible:

"Therefore, there is now no condemnation for those who are in Christ Jesus."

There are a lot of religious groups out there in the world who control their people with fear. If you don't do such and such, it proves you aren't spiritual enough. If you do such and such one second before you die, you're going to hell.

They put burdens on you that just are not in the New Testament. By making you feel guilty, they make you depend on them for your salvation and that boosts their ego. The Apostle Paul wrote to the congregations in Galatia (today's Turkey) and warned them with tears:

"I am astonished that you are so quickly deserting the one who called you by the grace of Christ and are turning to a different gospel ~ which is really no gospel at all. Evidently some people are throwing you into confusion and are trying to pervert the gospel of Christ. But even if we or an angel from heaven should preach a gospel other than the one we preached [past tense] to you, let him be eternally condemned! As we have already said, so now I say again:

If anybody is preaching to you a gospel other than what you accepted, let him be eternally condemned! Am I now trying to win the approval of men or of God? Or am I trying to please men? " (Galatians 1:6-10).

Are you sure you are IN Christ Jesus? Do your church leaders dance around scriptures they wish weren't in the Bible and tell you they don't really mean what they say? Or add things that the scriptures say nothing about? Are you sure they aren't people pleasers instead of God pleasers? What do they do with Romans 6:3-4 and Galatians 3:27? Look it up and compare.

Oh to be sure we are indeed IN Christ Jesus and can someday live in his world. This is our longing. Our hope. Our reason for being.

2nd- The scripture for today, August 2 (8/2), is **Matthew 8:2** as found in the New Testament of the Bible:

"A man with leprosy came and knelt before him and said, 'Lord, if you are willing, you can make me clean.' Jesus reached out his hand and touched the man. 'I am willing,' he said. 'Be clean!' Immediately he was cured of his leprosy.' "

People in Jesus' day who had leprosy had to live outside of town in what we would call a leper colony. And if someone without leprosy started getting close to them, they were required to call out, "Unclean! Unclean!"

But here was a man who apparently pushed his way through a crowd where he didn't belong. He didn't ask Jesus if he could heal him; he asked if he was willing to. After all, he was "unclean". Remarkably, Jesus said yes.

Then Jesus did another remarkable thing: He touched the man. He touched the leprosy. Not only was he willing to be seen with an unclean man, he was willing to touch him.

Jesus still does this today. When we come to him with a diseased heart wondering if we are good enough, Jesus reaches out across the centuries and touches us. And his voice echoes across the centuries and says, "I am willing."

No matter how much sin mars your life, Jesus still today wants to say, "Be clean."

3rd - The scripture for today, August 3 (8/3), is **1st Corinthians 8:3** as found in the New Testament of the Bible.

"But the man who loves God is known by God."

How can God know us all individually? Just how does God do it? There are multiplied millions of us. All praying with our own set of problems, sometimes thousands of us at once. All singing our various hymns. All trying to do right in the name of God.

This Creator of the entire universe, the Maker of stars and sunflowers and little puppies and unfathomable oceans, knows each person who loves him. Not "knows about", but KNOWS! With all that is going on in the world, yea even in the universe, he still knows which ones of us love him, and he takes the time to fix things in our lives, hold our hands, bless us with just what we need. All tens of thousands of us at once. How does he do that?

How large he is. How small we are.

Utter amazement!

And so we worship him.

4th - The scripture for today, August 4 (8/4), is **Acts 8:4** as found in the New Testament of the Bible:

"Those who had been scattered preached the word wherever they went."

Sometimes our plans get scattered, our dreams shattered. We lose our home, our job, our chance at an education, our savings, our family.

Satan loves to discourage you. He's good at it. But Romans 8:28 says that God can make something good come out of all things ~ good or bad.

Do you use your circumstance in life as an excuse not to share the Good News that people can be saved from hell and go to heaven instead?

What if, for instance, you lose your home or job and go to another one? You would be the same person you were at the old home or job. If your old excuses were not valid any longer, would you then share the Good News? What is the likelihood you will be any different when your life is "scattered"?

Do not let Satan put excuses in your mind. Rise up! Rise up and do as our Lord Jesus did. Seek and save the lost wherever you go.

5th - The scripture for today, August 5 (8/5), is **Romans 8:5** as found in the New Testament of the Bible:

"Those who live according to the sinful nature have their minds set on what that nature desires, but those who live in accordance with the Spirit have their minds set on what the Spirit desires."

That makes sense to a Christian. But how are you supposed to know what the Spirit desires? Certainly, God doesn't leave you to guessing.

Jesus said in John 14:17 that he was going to send the Comforter ~ the Spirit of Truth. And in John 17:17, talking to the same people, he said, God's Word is Truth. Amazingly simple.

If you want to know what the Spirit desires, then find out what the Word desires. God has given you the Bible full of examples of every possible circumstance and experience of life ~ what works and what doesn't work.

Someone says, "Well, I shall let the Spirit move my heart." However, by researching all verses in the Bible where someone's heart was moved, it was always by God the Father, not God the Spirit. Isn't that interesting? Not what most of us have been told.

Some people pray and pray about a major decision believing Romans 8:28 says "all things work together for the best..."

It does not say that. It says "for good". In other words, whatever decision you make, God will turn it into some kind of good. So, go ahead and make your decision. Whatever it is, God will make it work out for you.

You can always rely on what the Bible says, which is exactly what the Spirit says.

6th - The scripture for today, August 6 (8/6), is **1st Corinthians 8:6f** as found in the New Testament of the Bible:

"Yet for us there is but one God, the Father, from whom all things came and for whom we live; and there is but one Lord [Word], Jesus Christ, through whom all things came [by a Word] and through whom we live [by the Word]. But not everyone knows this. Some people are still so accustomed to idols."

We all believe in Jesus, so we think we're not involved with idols. But we all sometimes idolize something when we should be idolizing Someone. With advertising of things all around us, we are tempted to trade God for things. Having once turned things into our idol, we set Jesus aside.

Oh, we may still worship at least once a week. And pray every morning. We may even read a chapter of the Bible every day. But what do we spend the rest of the day thinking about and doing? Yes, when we're on the job, we must think about giving our employers an honest day's work for an honest day's wage. And we have families we must love and attend to.

But after that........
Then what?

7th- The scripture for today, August 7 (8/7), is **Hosea 8:7** as found in the Old Testament of the Bible:

"They sow the wind and reap the whirlwind."

This is the boomerang effect. We throw a boomerang into the air and no matter how we throw it, it always comes back to us. In the same way, God treats us the same way we treat him.

If we draw near to God, God draws near to us (James 4:8). If we don't have time for God, God doesn't have time for us. If we don't want to do what he says, God doesn't want to do what we say. If we reject God, God rejects us:

Psalm 9:15-16; Psalm 10:2; Psalm 37:14-15; Psalm 140:9; Proverbs 3:34; Proverbs 6:27; Proverbs 26:27; Isaiah 33:1; Isaiah 59:18; Ezekiel 7:8; Obadiah 1:15.

Another viewpoint is that there may be people out there mistreating us. Someday their mistreatment will boomerang right onto themselves. In the meantime, our assignment is to remain true to God with patience and calm. God will take care of the boomerang.

8th- The scripture for today, August 8 (8/8), is **Zechariah 8:8** as found in the Old Testament of the Bible:

"I will bring them back to live in Jerusalem; they will be my people, and I will be faithful and righteous to them as their God."

The Jews had done terrible things against God. They had worshiped terrible idols that required ghastly things be done in their honor such as setting up brothels with so-called "priestesses" and sacrificing their children on an altar of fire. They had nailed the doors of the Temple closed. They had broken every one of God's rules. They had sworn at him, rejected him, hated him.

So God punished them with 70 years of exile in Babylon. What a light punishment for what they had done! Still, it was the boomerang effect. They had rejected God, so God rejected them.

But it was not permanent. God is love and has no choice but to love and give people a second chance. Isn't He amazing? The God of Second Chances?

9th - The scripture for today, August 9 (8/9), is **2nd Corinthians 8:9** as found in the New Testament of the Bible:

"For you know the grace of our Lord Jesus Christ, that though he was rich, yet for your sakes he became poor, so that you through his poverty might become rich."

Such love! Jesus gave up streets of gold for streets full of trash. Gave up a heavenly mansion for a barn. Gave up the ability to be everywhere at once, to being confined to a body. Gave up eternal bliss for 33 years of struggle. Gave up adoring angels for crowds that hated him. And finally he gave up sinlessness to take the blame for our sins and allow himself to take our punishment.

What have you given up for him lately?

10th - The scripture for today, August 10 (8/10), is **Nehemiah 8:10b** as found in the Old Testament of the Bible:

"This day is sacred to our Lord. Do not grieve, for the joy of the Lord is your strength."

After exile for 70 years for forsaking God, the Jews were led by Ezra and Nehemiah back to Jerusalem. On a special day, Ezra read the Law of Moses to all the people. And they wept. They were so embarrassed and so sorry they had betrayed God. The above scripture quotation is from that occasion.

But many people find it too humiliating to admit to others that they were wrong. Others find it easy to repent, but never regroup and pull themselves up so they can try again. Still others say, "What I've done is so bad, God could never forgive me."

God can perform miracles. That means he can forgive the greatest sinner. So grieve. Ask for forgiveness. Then start over fresh ~ innocent in the eyes of God.

Remember, the joy of the Lord is always your strength.

11th - The scripture for today, August 11 (8/11),

is **Romans 8:11** as found in the New Testament of the Bible:

"And if the Spirit of him who raised Jesus from the dead is living in you, he who raised Christ from the dead will also give life to your mortal bodies through his Spirit, who lives in you."

Death literally means separation. Physical death means separation from this body on earth. Spiritual death means separation of our soul from God who is Life. Whenever we sin, our soul dies. It happened to Adam and Eve who didn't think God meant it when he said, "In the day you eat of the fruit, you will die." They could no longer walk and talk with God in the garden because they were now separated from him, spiritually dead. With that eventually also came physical death.

There are certain spiritual laws that cannot be broken. For example, it is impossible for God to lie. It is also impossible for God to sin. Therefore, God cannot co-exist with sin. We sin. Another law is that sin demands death. For centuries, Satan allowed mankind to sacrifice an animal in their place to take their death punishment. But it was just a temporary fix.

Finally, God sent the Son in bodily form to be sacrificed in our place and take our death punishment. Now, all we have to do is be "in Jesus" which is accomplished by baptism: Galatians 3:26 says this.

What is the role of our spirit? When we die, we say our spirit has left our body. So, as long as we are alive, it means our spirit is still in us. We are not conscious of our spirit being in us; we just know it is because we are still alive.

In the same way, when we become Christians by believing, repenting, confessing and being baptized, God's Holy Spirit enters us; Acts 2:38 says so. This is when we become spiritually alive; Romans 6:3-4 says so. We are not overtly conscious of God's Spirit being in us, but we know it is true because our soul is now alive.

12th- The scripture for today, August 12 (8/12), is **John 8:12** as found in the New Testament of the Bible:

"When Jesus spoke again to the people, he said, 'I am the light of the world. Whoever follows me will never walk in darkness, but will have the light of life.' "

Jesus had only about six months left to live. He knew the religious leaders were after his life out of jealousy. Before going to Jerusalem, he told his brothers, "The world cannot hate you, but it hates me" (John 7:7). Knowing people were wanting to execute him, he slipped into Jerusalem after everyone else got there (John 7:10, 14). Then suddenly he appeared in the middle of the Temple complex ~ the size of many football fields. He knew he was safe as long as there was a crowd.

Jesus answered some private questions, and then "he cried out, 'You know me! You know where I am from!' " (John 7:28).

Every day of this feast, a priest would ceremonially pour out some water to represent the water that poured out of the rock when the Jews wandered in the wilderness. But on the last day, the priest did not do this, for it represented their ancestors finally arriving in the Promised Land. It was on this last day of the feast that Jesus "stood and said in a loud voice... 'If anyone is thirsty, let him come to me and drink! Whoever believes in me, as the Scripture has said, streams of living water will flow from within him!' " (John 7:38f)

First thing the next morning at dawn he returned to the Temple court. Maybe it was a beautiful sunrise. When the sun was up and the crowds returned, he shouted something else to everyone, "I am the light of the world!" (John 8:12).

He had compared himself to the water ceremony of the day before, and now he was comparing himself to the new dawn. There he was. God the Son crying out to humanity. "Come to me! I am doing everything I can to help you! Won't you come? Please listen to me! Please come! I can save you!"

Such stubborn love.

13th- The scripture for today, August 13 (8/13), is **Isaiah 8:13f** as found in the Old Testament of the Bible:

"The Lord Almighty is the one you are to regard as holy, he is the one you are to fear, he is the one you are to dread, and he will be a sanctuary."

"Holy" in both the Hebrew and Greek means someone or something set apart as very special. Who or what do you daily set apart as someone or something special? Do you in a sense "worship" that person or thing? Whoever or whatever you worship, you become a slave to. Are you a "slave" to anything in your life? Is there something you cannot control because it controls you? Are you a slave to attention or food or money or power or clothes or houses or cars or etc?

Then, when there is a tragedy in your life, can you rely on those things to get you through? Who or what will be your sanctuary in times of trouble? Will you be able to say, "The Lord Almighty...he will be my sanctuary" even though he is not a sanctuary to people who have put him at the bottom of their list? Where is the Lord Almighty in your list of gods?

14th - The scripture for today, August 14 (8/14), is **Romans 8:14** as found in the New Testament of the Bible.

"Those who are led by the Spirit of God are sons of God."

Well, how are you supposed to know the Spirit is leading you? Is it guess work? Does it depend on your emotions and how you are feeling that day? It doesn't seem fair of God to leave you guessing.

But God does not make you guess. Jesus said in John 14:16,17, "And I will ask the Father, and he will give you another Counselor to be with you forever ~ the Spirit of Truth." And in John 17:17, praying to God the Father, Jesus said, "Sanctify them by the Truth; your Word is Truth."

Jesus said you are sanctified by God's Spirit, God's Truth, God's Word. How? Not by feelings. Not because someone else said so. Not by touching it or carrying it around in your pocket. But by reading it and following it. Romans 10:17 says, "Faith comes by hearing, and hearing by the Word of God". That is how the Spirit leads you.

You don't have to guess. Just follow it. Even if you are feeling rotten today, as long as you are following the Spirit of Truth, you are a child of God ~ not a slave, but His child.

15th - The scripture for today, August 15 (8/15), is **Romans 8:15** as found in the New Testament of the Bible:

"For you did not receive a spirit that makes you a slave again to fear, but you received the Spirit of sonship."

I knew someone a long time ago who went through a period of being afraid of everything, something she just could not control. Then she found this scripture and applied it to all her fears. She had read it many times before, but this time was able to apply it to her constant fear. She thought to herself, "Stop being afraid! You are a child of God! He is right there with you. Be brave now. And rest in God."

Are there times in your life when you are a slave to fear? Perhaps it is fear of the dark. Or fear of losing health. Or fear of strangers. Or of a certain nationality. Or of losing a job or home. Or of losing a loved one.

Stop being afraid! Children of God are not afraid. God is right there with you. Be brave. And rest in God.

16th - The scripture for today, August 16 (8/16), is **Romans 8:16** as found in the New Testament of the Bible:

"The Spirit himself testifies with our spirit that we are God's children."

This is so similar to the scripture of a few days ago on how to know if the Spirit is living in you. You can use the same approach to determine how the Spirit teaches you that you are God's child."

Once again, John 14:17 says the Comforter Jesus sent us was the Spirit of Truth. And Jesus said in John 17:17, God's Word is Truth. So it is through God's Word that you are taught how to become God's child. You do not have to guess!

This is what is so wonderful about Christianity. The Hindu, Buddhist, Shinto, Shamanist and many other religions leave the followers to guess because their "god" has given them no instructions. Ninety-nine percent of them believe they are not children of God. They also believe there are not saved because they can't be perfect, so have to be reincarnated thousands of times to try to be perfect. The Muslim religion says followers are slaves, and they won't know until the Day of Judgment if their good deeds outweigh their bad deeds.

In all other world religions, followers never know if they are children of God and saved. As hard as you try, you cannot be perfect. But Jesus came and was perfect for you. All the good works in the world will not get a sinner into God's home ~ heaven~

because we are still sinners. Jesus collected the wages for your sin, thus making Satan's threats of hell ineffective. If you believe this and follow what he says in the Bible, you can become God's child and live with Him forever after you go through the happy door of death.

Praise God! He has given you The Map, the Way ~ the Holy Bible, God's Word in written form. Such solace. Such comfort. Such reassurance.

17th - The scripture for today, August 17 (8/17), is **Romans 8:17** as found in the New Testament of the Bible:

"Now if we are children, then we are heirs ~ heirs of God and co-heirs with Christ, if indeed we share in his sufferings in order that we may also share in his glory." (see also Galatians 3:16)

I Peter 4:12-14 says we should not be surprised when persecution happens, "as though something strange were happening to you." If we are insulted because of Jesus, we are blessed.

Notice, we are co-heirs with Christ IF we share in his suffering. Have you shared in Jesus' sufferings lately? Have you ever in your entire life shared in Jesus' sufferings? If not, you haven't told very many people about Jesus loving them, or stood up for Jesus when people around you were making fun of him or using his name as a swear word.

Are you sinning by omission? Do you huddle with your church friends all the time and brag that all the friends you have are

Christians? Jesus didn't. Jesus went out to "seek and save the lost." Are you seeking?

Sometime today, say something to someone about Jesus ~ someone in a store, at work, a neighbor, a fellow passenger on a bus. They probably won't insult you. This may be exactly what they've been looking for. But if they do insult you, accept it graciously. Then go on your way feeling honored to be a "co-heir with Christ" by "sharing in his suffering."

Try it. You will be glad you did.

18th – The scripture for today, August 18 (8/18), is **Mark 8:18f** as found in the New Testament of the Bible:

"Do you have eyes but fail to see, and ears but fail to hear? And don't you remember when I broke [in pieces] the five loaves for the five thousand [hungry people]? How many basketfuls of pieces did you pick up?"

Economic and political times are uncertain and unstable right now for a lot of people. How much do you worry about it? Planning is good. But worrying?

Instead of spending your time worrying and tearing down your mental and physical health, do what you can, then look around. Is there someone else you can help? Visit someone who is sick and clean up their kitchen for them? Tell a story to a little child? Sing a song to an elderly person and invite them to sing along with you? Write a letter to your parents or a ground child? Read to someone with poor eye sight?

While you're busy helping others, take Jesus' advice and remember your past. Ask yourself, "Has God forsaken me in the past?

Sit down and make a list of every time you made it through a bad period of time in your life. How did God get you through it then? This is your proof.

Remember your proof.

19th- The scripture for today, August 19 (8/19), is **Isaiah 8:19f** as found in the Old Testament of the Bible:

"When men tell you to consult mediums and spiritists who whisper and mutter, should not a people inquire of their God? Why consult the dead on behalf of the living? To the law and to the testimony! If they do not speak according to this word, they have no light of dawn."

It has always been a popular thing to do among some people to try to reach into the spirit world, the world of demons and the dead. They may be very religious people. They may pray a lot and go to worship a lot and read the Bible a lot. But God's word is not enough for them, so they delve into the other world. God says "they have no light of dawn."

Do you want to talk to someone in the other world? Pray. God is in the other world. Do you want someone in the other world to talk to you? Read the Bible. That is God talking to you from the other world. What more could you ask?!

Whisperings and mutterings? Don't need them. God has given you all you need. And we love him for it.

20th - The scripture for today, August 20 (8/20), is **Proverbs 8:20** as found in the Old Testament of the Bible.

"I walk in the way of righteousness, along the paths of justice."

Interestingly, the original Hebrew of "way" is customary **path**, and the original Hebrew of "paths" is customary **road**.

If you had a house out in the country, it would have paths leading to and from it. These paths would be taken in your day-to-day life without much thought. In the same way, we live out our principles and moral standards pretty much the same every day on such paths.

But eventually these paths can merge into major roads. Now we have to make major decisions. Our life decisions on such roads must be based on justice.

It is sometimes hard to make right judgments because we can get emotionally involved and start wishing for an outcome that cannot possibly occur. In those cases, we must stand back and consider, "What would be the just thing to do if someone else had to make this decision?".

We could also ask ourselves, "What would Jesus do?". After all, Jesus said, "I am the Way, the Truth, the Life" (John 14:6).

21st - The scripture for today, August 21 (8/21), is **Ezra 8:21a** as found in the Old Testament of the Bible:

"There, by the Ahava Canal [from the Euphrates R.], I proclaimed a fast, so that we might humble ourselves before our God."

In our modern society, does anyone fast anymore? Not drinking our food (juice) for a day and calling that a fast, but a true fast where we drink only water to stay hydrated, but that's all. And we turn off all computers, phones, radios and televisions for the day.

Jesus said in his sermon on the mount, "When you fast...." (Matthew 6:16). He didn't say, "If you fast...." No, he assumed his followers would fast. Do we?

If we do, do we do it as a group? Does anyone else know about it? They shouldn't know, unless they are the reason for our fast. Fasting is an act of self-restraint. It belongs to the sphere of humble self-discipline. It is strictly a personal and private matter.

All moral and bodily restraint, all humbleness of body and spirit are represented by fasting, and it is a complete failure of self-restraint to want to show the world our self-restraint. An unknown author wrote this:

Let us keep our fast within,
Till heaven and we are quite alone;
Then let the grief, the shame, the sin,

Before the mercy-seat be thrown.

Fasting is a way of starving ourselves temporarily, a way of saying, "God, I would do this and more for you; I would die for you." Or, "God, I would trade lives with this person I am fasting for to give them rest if it were possible. I would even die for this person." It is a deep expression to God that goes beyond words.

Also, when we fast, our minds are freed from trying to digest food, so we can think clearer and deeper. And we can face ourselves more honestly. Just what are we deep down? Do we truly love God as much as we claim? Do we truly love our families as much as we claim? Our neighbors? Our fellow Christians? Our enemies? It is a time of self-reflection and self-honesty. When we humble ourselves this much, we can grow closer to God.

22nd - The scripture for today, August 22 (8/22), is **Jeremiah 8:22** as found in the Old Testament of the Bible:

"Is there no balm in Gilead? Is there no physician there? Why then is there no healing for the wound of my people?"

There is a very beautiful African-American spiritual of unknown origin that many of us have sung. You may be able to hear it sung a cappella here: **http://bit.ly/1PfHxrJ** Here are the words to that spiritual:

There is a balm in Gilead

To make the wounded whole;
There is a balm in Gilead
To heal the sin sick soul.

Sometimes I feel discouraged,
And think my work's in vain,
But then the Holy Spirit
Revives my soul again.

If you can't preach like Peter,
If you can't pray like Paul,
Just tell the love of Jesus,
And say He died for all.

Have a blessed day.

23rd - The scripture for today, August 23 (8/23), is **2nd Kings 8:23** as found in the Old Testament of the Bible:

"As for the other events of Jehoram's reign, and all he did, are they not written in the book of the annals of the kings of Judah?"

All the years of this great king's life were reduced to a few pages in a book. When you die, what will there be to write about? Will people list only the date and place of your birth, marriage and death ~ your statistics? What will you be remembered for? What will be in your obituary?

Better still, what is God writing about you in his books? "And I saw the dead, great and small, standing before the throne and books were opened. Another book was opened which is the book of life. The dead were judged according to what they had done as recorded in the books" (Revelation 12).

Will your book be thin with not a lot worth writing about? Will it be thick and full of all you've accomplished for good and God in this life? What will be in your book?

24th - The scripture for today, August 24 (8/24), is **Romans 8:24f** as found in the New Testament of the Bible:

"For in this hope we were saved. But hope that is seen is no hope at all. Who hopes for what he already has? But if we hope for what we do not yet have, we wait for it patiently."

Sometimes you go through a period of your life in which it is difficult to have faith that God exists; or even if he does exist, that he cares what happens to you. During those times, you may not be able to have faith.

But you can HOPE. You can hope that God exists, you can hope he cares what happens to you. Even the weakest person can hope. Hope holds you until you are strong enough to, once again, have faith.

So the next time your faith wavers (and it happens to everyone at some time in their life), remember, you can still hope.

25th- The scripture for today, August 25 (8/25), is **John 8:25** as found in the New Testament of the Bible:

" 'Who are you?' they asked. 'Just what I have been claiming all long,' Jesus replied."

They knew who Jesus was. He had made people's arms and legs grow back, he had fed multiple-thousands on a plate of food, stopped storms and brought lifeless people back to life. They knew! But they kept asking because they wanted a different answer than the obvious one.

Jesus and his apostles tell you certain things in the Bible. Sometimes, you read them over and over, and still don't get the point. Perhaps you have been blinded by well-meaning religious leaders or family or friends who tell you over and over, "It doesn't mean what it says." Are you wanting a different answer than the obvious one?

Dare to read the teachings of Jesus and his apostles with open eyes and open heart. When you read something, just accept it. Your soul is at stake. These are the words of the God of the universe. Do you prefer that God fit your mold, or you fit God's amazing mold?

26th - The scripture for today, August 26 (8/26), is **Romans 8:26** as found in the New Testament of the Bible:

"In the same way, the Spirit helps us in our weakness. We do not

know what we ought to pray for, but the Spirit himself intercedes for us with groans that words cannot express."

The Holy Spirit in the New Testament is always linked with communication between God and Man. Even the miracles, made possible by the Holy Spirit, were a guarantee that the words and teachings accompanying the miracles were from God. This was needed before the New Testament was written. But the Holy Spirit does more than this.

God speaks to us in his Word, the Bible. Then we speak to him in return in prayer. But sometimes all we can do is bow our head in silence and know that God understands ~ His Spirit communes with our spirit.

In the Beginning, God the Mind decided to make the universe, God the Word spoke the words to make the universe, and God the Spirit made it happen and brought life to the universe. When humans die, we say their spirit left their body. Therefore, God's Spirit brings life to our Spirit when we are born again.

So, we see God's Spirit brings life to our spirit and keeps it alive by communing with our lowly spirit. Unfathomable yearning. Inescapable love.

27th - The scripture for today, August 27 (8/27), is **Mark 8:27** as found in the New Testament of the Bible:

"Jesus and his disciples went on to the villages around Caesarea Philippi. On the way he asked them, 'Who do people say I am?' "

Do we ask our family, our neighbors, our friends how they feel about God? Who do people say God is? We don't know unless we ask. A lot of people are just waiting for someone to ask. Otherwise, they don't know how or when to bring it up.

Whenever I meet someone who has gone through a tragedy, I ask them "How's your faith?". Now this person may not have darkened the door of a church building for 20 years, but s/he always knows what I mean. Since I am sympathizing with them at the time, they are always honest and reply, "Not very good," usually meaning their faith is nearly gone if not all the way gone.

Then I tell them, "You know, Satan causes bad to happen to people, not Jesus." They always stare at me a moment, and then breathe a sigh of relief. They hadn't wanted to blame God for their tragedy, but they had a need to blame someone. They'd forgotten Satan exists, and were grateful they could now put the blame where it belonged.

There are many other people today who believe in a "Higher Power" but have no idea who that "Higher Power" is. Many, even in America today, have never read the Bible and are curious about it. Ask people you know, "Who is the High Power", and listen to them. Then offer to show them how the Bible is divided up and how to read it (especially Genesis, then the New Testament).

We must continually be on the watch for people who need help in understanding their relationship with God. Be brave. Go ahead and ask. You'll be surprised at how many WANT to talk about it. Be delighted as you open up a whole new world to them and watch them become awed.

28th - The scripture for today, August 28 (8//28), is **Romans 8:28** as found in the New Testament of the Bible:

"And we know that in all things God works for the good of those who love him, who have been called according to his purpose."

This is a favorite verse of many people. Notice, God can make all things work together for good. ALL things. That means bad things, disappointing things, unfulfilled things. But, it doesn't say God will make them all work together for the best. What is says is that he will bring some kind of good out of them, no matter how terrible they are.

What has been your most recent disappointment, tragedy, heartbreak ~ something that just did not go the way it should have? At such times, it is easy to blame God instead of Satan. You're playing into Satan's hands when you blame God and forsake him. Try to remember that, with every disappointment and tragedy, God gives you a promise: Someday you will smile again.

Are you are living according to his purpose? The promise is only to those who are. If, indeed you are, believe God will take your heartbreak and turn it in to some kind of good especially for you. Will you let him?

29th - The scripture for today, August 29 (8/29),

is **Matthew 8:29** as found in the New Testament of the Bible:

" 'What do you want with us, Son of God?' they shouted. 'Have you come here to torture us before the appointed time?' "

If you are not familiar with this passage, these are the words of a demon. If you have ever studied demons in the Bible, you will find that they never tried to spook or scare people. They never made dishes rattle or lamps fall over.

All they did was cause physical problems during the lifetime of Jesus and his apostles. There is no evidence of demons doing this in the Old Testament before Jesus, nor after his apostles died, either in the Bible or in the writings of the apostolic fathers. It is as though the demons were loosed for a season so Jesus could show his power over them also ~ Ephesians 1:20-21.

Notice, demons never said bad things. If they talked at all, it was out of fear and honesty. James 2:19 says all demons believe in Jesus. In the book of Matthew they knew who Jesus was. They called him the Son of God.

Jesus told them to be quiet. Why? He didn't want evil beings telling people who he was; he wanted goodness to tell people who he was. And Jesus never did incantations or any begging to lure demons out. He demanded them to leave and immediately they obeyed him.

The movies have warped our understanding of demons. Let us search the scriptures to find out their true nature. Then we no longer have to guess. We can know.

30th- The scripture for today, August 30 (8/30), is **Acts 8:30** as found in the New Testament of the Bible:

"Then Philip ran up to the chariot and heard the man reading Isaiah the prophet. 'Do you understand what you are reading?' Philip asked."

Our friends, family and neighbors will continue riding their chariots and understanding little of the Bible unless someone asks, "Do you understand?".

"Do you understand why you are here?" "Do you understand why Jesus had to die?" "Do you understand that Satan holds mankind hostage and Jesus paid our ransom with his blood?" "Do you understand the Bible can be proven true?" "Do you understand how much God loves you?" "Do you understand how the Bible is divided up and which parts give the life of Christ?"

People are afraid to ask us questions because they think we will make fun of their ignorance. We'll probably never know what they don't understand unless we do the asking. Let us go up to their chariots and offer to help them so that they, too, can understand.

31st- The scripture for today, August 31 (8/31), is **John 8:31f** as found in the New Testament of the Bible:

"To the Jews who had believed him, Jesus said, 'If you hold to my

teachings, you are really my disciples. Then you will know the truth, then the truth will set you free.' "

Myriads of people call themselves believers in or disciples of Christ; in other words, Christians. What is Jesus' definition of a believer or disciple? He explained, IF we hold to his TEACHINGS, then we are his disciples.

It's not automatic? So being born into a Christian family doesn't automatically make us a Christian? Being born in a Christian nation doesn't automatically make us a Christian? Owning a Bible doesn't automatically make us a Christian? Believing Jesus is the Son of God doesn't automatically make us a Christian? (Demons believe that and aren't Christians.)

"But, Jesus," we might say, "I really feel like I'm a Christian." And Jesus replies, "Hold to my teachings, then you are really my disciple."

So if we learn Jesus' teachings and hold to them, THEN the truth will set us FREE.

September

1st - The scripture for today, September 1 (9/1), is **Psalm 9:1** as found in the Old Testament of the Bible:

"I will praise you, O Lord, with all my heart; I will tell of all your wonders."

I knew a lady many years ago who talked to God all day as though he was sitting or standing beside her, whether she was cleaning floors, washing dishes, going shopping, or just received a telephone call. She talked to God about everything she was doing. God was her constant companion.

What opportunities you miss to talk to God during the day. Every time you do, you are praising Him. How? By acknowledging His concern with everything you do, and in the process acknowledging His omnipresence. And what a wonder His omnipresence is!

Does this include times when everything in your life is going wrong? You bet! On some days, the wonders of God are about the only positive things you can find in our life.

Praising God for his wonders amidst your frustrations, tears, fears and helplessness can lift you out of the mire. It can remind you that you are not alone; for God sees what is happening to you, and in his own way he will perform a wonder for you.

2nd - The scripture for today, September 2 (9/2), is **Job 9:2** as found in the Old Testament of the Bible:

"Though one wishes to dispute with Him [God], he could not answer Him one time out of a thousand."

There are so-called sophisticated intellectuals in the world who want to come up with all the answers about God. Many even make God in their image instead of we being made in God's image. They try to reduce God to complete human understanding.

That cannot be! If we could understand everything about God, He would not be God! Let us rejoice that there are things about God we do not understand. Let us rejoice that there are events in our life that we do not understand ~ the good, the bad, the ugly. Let us rejoice that such a God loves us in our finiteness.

3rd - The scripture for today, September 3 (9/3), is **1st Kings 9:3** as found in the Old Testament of the Bible:

"The Lord said to him, 'I have heard the prayer and plea you have made before me; I have consecrated this temple, which you have built, by putting my Name there forever. My eyes and my heart will always be there.' "

The New Testament builds spiritual concepts on the basic material patterns of the Old Testament. For example, "Don't you know that you yourselves are God's temple and that God's Spirit lives in you?" (1st Corinthians 3:16). This is the temple God wants now, not the old material temple of the Old Testament.

Just as there was just one material temple of God in the Old Testament, God looks upon each Christian as though we are the only temple; for he is with us constantly and hears our every word, our every song, our every prayer.

Is your heart troubled today? Is your heart joyful today? Are you at peace with everything around you? Do you see conflicts that you do not know how to solve?

As God's temple, God's eyes and heart are with you. God sees and watches out for you in everything you do. He knows your cares, your heart's desires, your joys, your worries. God's eyes and heart are forever with you, for you are God's temple!

4th- The scripture for today, September 4 (9/4), is **Daniel 9:4** as found in the Old Testament of the Bible:

"I prayed to the Lord my God and confessed: 'O Lord, the great and awesome God, who keeps his covenant of love with all who love him and obey his commands....' "

A lot of people in the world think God should feel obligated to take them to heaven. After all, they are fairly good, and better than some. God couldn't possibly in all good conscience turn them away.

Yet, their entire life they resent God. They don't like his few commands; they don't want anyone telling them what to do or not do. Or they claim to love God, but create their own commands that just aren't in the Bible, making themselves God. What confusion!

Ultimately, heaven is God's home, not ours. He is not obligated to invite anyone into His home. Besides, only perfection can live with God who is perfect. It only takes one sin to make us an imperfect sinner.

So how do we become perfect? That's where God's awesomeness is demonstrated. By following Jesus who was perfect and never sinned, and obeying Jesus' few commands, God considers us perfect by proxy.

But it's like a boomerang. God treats us the way we treat him. If we don't take time for God, he doesn't take time for us. If we don't like to spend time praising him, he doesn't spend time praising us. Actually, if we don't really like anything about God, we would be miserable in heaven.

God never forces himself on anyone. But he keeps on calling. Shhh. Listen. Do you hear him?

5th - The scripture for today, September 5 (9/5), is **Nehemiah 9:5a** as found in the Old Testament of the Bible:

"And the Levites ~ Jeshua, Kadmiel, Bani, Hashabneiah, Sherabiah, Hodiah, Shebaniah and Pethahiah ~ said 'Stand up

and praise the Lord your God, who is from everlasting to everlasting.' "

Who in the world are these eight men? We know nothing about them before this event, and nothing about them after this event. But they are forever memorialized in the Bible because, on this one day, within this one hour, in this one moment in time they "stood on the steps of the temple...and called with a loud voice" (Nehemiah 9:4) for the people to "stand up and praise the Lord".

Can we do that? Can we stand and shout to people around us, "Stand up and praise the Lord your God"? Yes, we can. We can write letters to the editor, we can encourage other students of the Bible, we can start Bible studies in our home or even the internet for adults or children, we can take scripture tray favors to a hospital or nursing home.

In what way can you tell people around you to "stand up and praise the Lord your God"? Write down some ideas. Then act.

6th - The scripture for today, September 6 (9/6), is **Isaiah 9:6** as found in the Old Testament of the Bible.

"For to us a child is born! To us a son is given! And the government will be on his shoulders. And he will be called Wonderful Counselor, Mighty God, Everlasting Father, Prince of Peace!"

This is one of the most amazing scriptures in the entire Bible explaining how God is One and self-existent. It is as astounding as

John 1:1,14 that says, "In the beginning was the Word. The Word was with God and the Word was God...The Word became flesh and dwelt among us."

This child predicted to be born unto us was both Father and Son and God. He created Himself. He was self-existent.

He is the image of the invisible God. "For in him all the fullness of God was pleased to dwell" (Colossians 1:15, 19; cf. 2 Corinthians 4:4). The men who saw Jesus Christ saw God (John 12:45, 14:9). God's blood (God's Word in flesh) was shed on the cross (Acts 20:28).

In America, we sometimes say about a son, "he is the spitting image of his father." Jesus said, "If you want to look at the Father, look at me." God is a Spirit but created us in a material world. So, sometimes God materialized in the Old Testament. In the New Testament he materialized as Jesus.

This is so amazing. And we have been so blest beyond full comprehension.

7th - The scripture for today, September 7 (9/7), is **2nd Corinthians 9:7** as found in the New Testament of the Bible:

"Each man should give what he has decided in his heart to give, not reluctantly or under compulsion, for God loves a cheerful giver."

There are many religious leaders who insist that Christians tithe. But that was part of the Law of Moses, which we no longer keep. If we pick one item, we have to pick them all including stoning people.

Let's look at Law-of-Moses tithing:

Actually, the Jews were required to give more than a tenth. (1) Deuteronomy 26:12 said the Jews had to give an extra tithe every three years for their welfare program. So, if someone tithed $900 a year, s/he would have to tithe an average of $300 more per year for the welfare program, equaling $1,200 year. If the yearly income was $9000, this would take it up to 13.3% a year.

(2) Also, according to Leviticus 27, they had to pay for their vows, which in many cases were really special prayer requests. (3) They also had to buy animals for sacrifices for intentional sins, unintentional sins and sins requiring restitution.

(4) If they wanted to thank God for anything, they had to buy grain for a sacrifice (Leviticus 1-5). If they didn't have to buy the animals or grain, they had to take them out of their own supply, thus depleting their own "pay check."

(5) And every time one of their flocks or herds had a first-born, they had to sacrifice it ~ another depleting of the "pay check."

So the good Jew under the Law of Moses did not just tithe. He ended up giving about one third of his income. Galatians 5:3 says that, if we keep one part of the Law, we have to keep all of it. There were over 600 burdensome commandments in the Law of Moses!

In today's scripture, Christians are being released from this burden. Instead, they are being told to decide in their own heart. Christians are released from serving and giving through obligation, and set free to serve and give out of love.

8th - The scripture for today, September 8 (9/9), is **Daniel 9:8** as found in the Old Testament of the Bible:

"O Lord, we and our kings, our princes and our fathers are covered with shame because we have sinned against you."

Have you prayed for your government lately? I Timothy 2:1 & 2 says "I urge, then, first of all, that requests, prayers, intercession and thanksgiving be made for everyone ~ for kings and all those in authority."

At the time of this writing, Nero Caesar. First-century historian Tacitus said this about Nero in his Annals 15:44: "But all human efforts, all the lavish gifts of the emperor, and the propitiations of the gods, did not banish the sinister belief that the conflagration was the result of an order. Consequently, to get rid of the report, Nero fastened the guilt and inflicted the most exquisite tortures on a class hated for their abominations, called "Christians" by the populace.

Christus, from whom the name had its origin, suffered the extreme penalty during the reign of Tiberius at the hands of one of our procurators, Pontius Pilate, and a most mischievous superstition, thus checked for the moment, again broke out not only in Judaea, the first source of the evil, but even in Rome, where all things hideous and shameful from every part of the world find their center and become popular.

"Accordingly, an arrest was first made of all who pleaded guilty; then, upon their information, an immense multitude was convicted, not so much of the crime of firing the city, as of hatred against mankind. Mockery of every sort was added to their deaths. Covered with the skins of beasts, they were torn by dogs and perished, or were nailed to crosses, or were doomed to the flames and burnt, to serve as a nightly illumination, when daylight had expired."

If the Apostle Paul could pray for such a government leader, can't you follow his instructions? Why don't you stop and pray for your own government right now?

9th - The scripture for today, September 9 (9/9), is **Zechariah 9:9** as found in the Old Testament of the Bible:

"Rejoice greatly, O Daughter of Zion! Shout, Daughter of Jerusalem! See, your King comes to you righteous and having salvation, gentle and riding on a donkey, on a colt, the foal of a donkey."

Most people think Jesus riding on a donkey made him humble. Not at all. Donkeys and mules were rides of kings.

Judges 5:9-10 says, "My heart is with Israel's princes....you who ride on white donkeys." Supreme Judge Jair led Israel 22 years, and had 30 sons who rode 30 donkeys (Judges 10:3-4). Supreme Judge Abdon, who ruled Israel 8 years, had 70 sons and grandsons who rode on 70 donkeys (Judges 12:14).

II Samuel 18:9 says Absalom, King David's son, rode on a mule. In I Kings 1:33,38,44, David ordained that his son, Solomon, ride on his own mule through the street as one proof that he chose Solomon to be the next king.

The people of Jerusalem knew Jesus was not only riding the ride of kings when he entered their capitol city, but he was also at last fulfilling the centuries-old prophecy they all knew so well (today's scripture).

This is the humility that Jesus did exhibit: He rode on the colt of a donkey.

Do we blindly follow whatever our religious leaders tell us? Do we know the scriptures as well as we think we do?

Let us glory in learning new things about our King of Glory.

10th - The scripture for today, September 10 (9/10), is **Psalm 9:10** as found in the Old Testament of the Bible:

"Those who know your name will trust in you, for you, Lord, have never forsaken those who seek you."

What if we had a friend who we never called by name? It was always "Hey, you". Our friendship wouldn't last long because the other person would feel like we weren't friends after all. Makes sense.

So, what does "Lord" mean in the original Hebrew language of the Old Testament? It is Yahweh, translated in the Greek as Adonai.

In Exodus 3:15b God told Moses what his name was: " 'The LORD, the God of your fathers...This is my name forever, the name by which I am to be remembered from generation to generation.' "

And what does Yahweh mean? Exodus 3:14 explained, "God said to Moses, 'I AM WHO I AM. This is what you are to say to the Israelites; 'I AM has sent me to you.' " God is the great I AM.

Today's verse does not say the Great I Am will keep you from all harm. What it says is that he will go with you into that harm and stay with you the whole way, giving you strength and courage.

And so, in peace or war, in comfort or pain, in well-being or devastation, he will be right there with you. He will never forsake you. Therefore, never forsake him. Keep on worshipping ~ the Lord our God, the Great I AM.

11th - The scripture for today, September 11 (9/11), is **Matthew 9:11** as found in the New Testament of the Bible:

"When the Pharisees saw this, they asked his disciples, 'Why does your teacher eat with tax collectors and "sinners"?' "

Jesus did not make friends with people who could lift him up. He made friends with people that he could lift up. We are not divine, so we need both. It is true that our closest friends should be Christians. However, many brag that those are our only friends. That isolates and insulates them.

We must make some friends among the lost in order to show them God's love, and try to lift them up. They can be people at work, in a club, in your neighborhood, someone we sit next to waiting for a bus, or even someone we meet by accident while waiting in line at a store.

We must always be on the watch. Always prepared to become more than just casual acquaintances. Always be prepared to get "up close and personal" with some of our friends. Most people have questions about the Bible. If you don't know the answer, look it up in a Bible Concordance and pass it on to them. You will be delighted and they will be fascinated.

Jesus did it. He was our example.

12th - The scripture for today, September 12 (9/12), is found in **Genesis 9:12f** in the Old Testament of the Bible:

"And God said, 'This is the sign of the covenant I am making between me and you and every living creature with you, a covenant for all generations to come. I have set my rainbow in the clouds, and it will be the sign of the covenant between me and the earth."

On the technical side, how can it be that there was never a rainbow before Noah's time? Genesis 2:5b-6 explains, "The Lord God had not sent rain on the earth, and there was no man to work the ground, but streams came up from the earth and watered the whole surface of the ground."

Up until the time of Noah, people lived to be several hundred years old. Christian scientists have said that, before the flood, the earth had a constant cloud covering with a thick ozone layer that created the greenhouse effect of vapors, and protected man from the aging process. It was much like Venus.

So rainbows were not possible when the sun could never break through the ever-present clouds. It was because of a terrible world-wide cataclysm that the beauty of the rainbow was made possible.

On the faith side of this story, we see a man who had such faith in God that, although he probably had never seen rain, believed it would happen. Such amazing faith! Later, through the pain of losing his stubborn father and probably other extended family, he was blessed with the lives of his direct family members. Then God gave him one more reward ~ the rainbow ~ that he could not only enjoy in his generation, but generations even today.

Out of disaster came beauty.

13th - The scripture for today, September 13 (9/13), is **Psalm 9:13f** as found in the Old Testament of the Bible:

"O Lord, see how my enemies persecute me! Have mercy and lift me up from the gates of death, that I may declare your praises...and there rejoice in your salvation."

We all experience difficult things in our life ~ some minor, some major. Do you let them define your entire life? Or do you cling to them, never getting over them, never letting them go, and reliving them over and over in your mind?

You cannot be "more than conqueror" (Romans 8:37) unless you have something to conquer. You cannot have "victory in Jesus" unless you have something to be victorious over.

God said that he can make "all things work together for good" to those who love the Lord (Romans 8:28). Today, with the courage of God in your heart, the love of God in your soul, and the might of God in your very being, rise up! Rejoice! Thank God for your problems. It is only when you have problems that you can experience victories.

14th - The scripture for today, September 14 (9/14), is **Hebrews 9:14f** as found in the New Testament of the Bible.

"How much more then will the blood of Christ, who through the eternal Spirit offered himself unblemished to God, cleanse our consciences from acts [sins] that lead to death so that we may serve the living God! For this reason, Christ is the mediator of a new covenant [testament] that those who are called may receive the promised eternal inheritance ~ now that he has died as a ransom to set them free from the sins committed under the first covenant [testament]."

This is a very interesting passage. Just previous to this, the author was talking about the blood of bulls and goats being sacrificed for sins under the old Law of Moses [Testament]. But now that the Son of God, the Lamb of God, had been sacrificed for our sins, we no longer need any more blood sacrifices.

Further, Jesus' sacrifice was retroactive! It reached back to the faithful who lived under the first/old covenant [Testament] and set them free from their sins too.

Aren't you glad God did away with the old Law of Moses with all its 600+ rules and regulations, and its requirement for animal blood sacrifices, and brought us a law of grace? What a God! What a Savior! Jesus did all this to save us from hell.

Have a day of deep gratitude.

15th- The scripture for today, September 15 (9/15), is **2nd Corinthians 9:15** as found in the New Testament of the Bible:

"Thanks be to God for his indescribable gift!"

Can you imagine dying in the place of someone else? We occasionally hear stories from the battlefield of a man falling on a grenade so he is the only one killed, thus saving his buddies.

But closer to home, if you saw a child in the path of a car, would you run out and throw the child out of the way knowing there will be no time for you to escape death?

What if you were hiking or sailing with a friend and got lost? Would you split the food and water evenly, or would you give it all to your friend? What would you do if you were lost with someone who hated everyone? Would you give them all the food and water knowing you would die and the hateful person live on?

What if you were with a friend and were arrested for a crime the friend did? Would you take the blame and the punishment of twenty years in prison so your friend could go free? What if that person was a habitual criminal, you happened to cross paths at the wrong time, and you were both arrested for his heinous crime? Would you take the blame and his punishment (execution) for him?

Now try to imagine making your child die in the place of your enemy ~ your sinless, innocent child.

It is indescribable.

It is unimaginable.

It is unthinkable.

But God did exactly that.

How can we thank Him for his indescribable gift of Jesus redeeming us from Satan? We fall silently at His feet and worship.

16th- The scripture for today, September 16 (9/16), is **1st Corinthians 9:16** as found in the New Testament of the Bible:

"Yet when I preach the gospel, I cannot boast, for I am compelled to preach. Woe to me if I do not preach the gospel!"

The Apostle Paul said this. An Old Testament prophet, Jeremiah, said almost the same thing in 20:9: "If I say, 'I will not mention him or speak any more in his name,' his word is in my heart like a fire, a fire shut up in my bones. I am weary of holding it in! Indeed, I cannot!"

Are you so full of the Word of God that you have to share it? Do you work it into your daily conversations?

I knew a lady once who took several church bulletins with her every Sunday. Then during the week, if she heard a conversation at a bus stop, she'd interrupt them and say, "I couldn't help but hear what you were saying. Perhaps God in your life would help." Then she'd hand them a bulletin. She'd do the same thing at a fast-food place like McDonalds, or in the waiting room of a doctor. She could not hold it in. She had to share, even if it was with strangers.

There is a man in Afghanistan who is a partially secret Christian. When he thinks he can trust someone, he tells them the gospel. He has run for his life three time in the last eight years. He tells me, "I will not stop until they kill me."

What about you? Is the Word of God overflowing in you so much you cannot keep it in? Tell someone today that God loves them. Watch them smile with a gleam in their eye that says, "I'd like to know more".

17th - The scripture for today, September 17 (9/17), is **Nehemiah 9:17** as found in the Old Testament of the Bible:

"They refused to listen and failed to remember the miracles you performed among them. They became stiff-necked and in their rebellion appointed a leader in order to return to their slavery. But you are a forgiving God, gracious and compassionate, slow to anger and abounding in love. Therefore, you did not desert them."

Such love! Do you rebel against God (who is only trying to save you) over and over because you don't want anyone telling you what to do? God forgives you over and over. First Peter 3:9 says "The Lord...is patient with you, not wanting anyone to perish, but everyone to come to repentance."

God could turn you into a robot and force you to love and obey him. But that wouldn't be real love. God is Love, and he cannot go against his own nature.

And so God follows you around and pleads over and over, "Follow my Son to safety!"

How he hurts when you do not; how he smiles when you do.

18th - The scripture for today, September 18 (9/18), is Leviticus 9:18ff as found in the Old Testament of the Bible:

"He slaughtered the ox and the ram as the fellowship offering for the people. His sons handed him the blood, and he sprinkled it against the altar on all sides. But the fat portions of the ox and the ram ~ the fat tail, the layer of fat, the kidneys and the covering of the liver ~ these they laid on the breasts, and then Aaron burned the fat on the altar. Aaron waved the breasts and the right thigh before the Lord as a wave offering, as Moses commanded."

The Law of Moses did not have just Ten Commandments. It had over 600! They were intricate commands that had to be kept exactly. The above is just a small portion of what they were supposed to do for a particular sacrifice.

Thank God, Jesus nailed the Old Law of Moses to the cross (Colossians 2:14). Yet some religious leaders continue to dip back into the Old Law to copy showy types of worship ~ robes, candles, choirs, harps, incense ~ many things, and all commanded. But if they do that, they must keep all of the Law of Moses ~ stoning for adultery, giving 1/3 of their income (not just 1/10), not working on Saturday (even cooking), going to Jerusalem three times a year.

They can't just pick and choose which ones they like. The Apostle Paul said in Galatians 5:17 "Again I declare to every man who lets himself be circumcised [just one command in the Old Law of Moses] that he is obligated to obey the whole law."

James said in 2:10, "For whoever keeps the whole law and yet stumbles at just one point is guilty of breaking all of it." Old Testament worship was showy, elaborate, and demanding to the nth degree. New Testament worship is just the opposite.

Mark 14:26 says that after Jesus instituted the Lord's Supper/Communion, "When they had sung a [single] hymn, they went out..."

Acts 2:41-42 says, "Those who accepted his message were baptized, and about three thousand were added to their number that day. They devoted themselves to the apostles' teaching and to the fellowship, to the breaking of bread and to prayer."

Acts 20:7 says, "On the first day of the week, we came together to break bread. Paul spoke to the people..."

I Timothy 4:13 says, "Devote yourself to the public reading of Scripture, to preaching and to teaching."

Nothing complicated about it. Just simple worship. Worship the way Jesus and his apostles worshiped. Worship the way God likes it. He said so himself.

19th – The scripture for today, September 19 (9/19), is **Acts 9:19f** as found in the New Testament of the Bible:

"He got up and was baptized, and after taking some food he regained his strength."

This is the story of Saul, as he was known to the Jews and to us as Paul, who became an apostle. Notice the order he did this: He was hungry, but that wasn't important. He had to do what was important first. He was baptized.

Why was Paul baptized? In Acts 22:16 Paul recalls that day when he was told, "Get up: be baptized and wash your sins away, calling on his name."

Further, notice who baptized him. Was he part of the clergy, someone with an ordained title in the church? Acts 9:10 says, "In Damascus there was a disciple named Ananias. The Lord called to him...Go to the house of Judas on Straight Street and ask for a man from Tarsus named Saul." What title did Ananias have? None. He was just another disciple. Disciple simply meaning follower.

Little did this otherwise unknown disciple realize that day, that the person he baptized would end up writing much of the New Testament.

Do you feel ordinary like you are an "unknown disciple" to followers of Jesus around you? Find something to do, and God will make it great. And remember, do the important thing first.

20th - The scripture for today, September 20 (9/20), is **Luke 9:20** as found in the New Testament of the Bible:

" 'But what about you?' he asked. 'Who do you say I am?' "

Jesus is still asking that question today. Who do you say Jesus is? Some people in the world say Jesus was the savior of the Christians, the same person as Moses to the Jews, and Mohammed to the Moslems, and Buddha to the Buddhists. In the name of being fair to everyone, they claim these are all saviors of different religions going by different names but of the same God.

Let us not be caught in the web of the New Age Movement that claims all saviors are the same savior and all gods are the same God.

This is an impossibility. These religions contradict each other. Read their holy books and you will discover this. So, which one is right?

The Bible is the only religious book in the world that can be proven to be divine with fulfilled prophecies of entire kingdoms. It says regarding our Jesus, "Salvation is found in no one else, for there is no other name under heaven given to men by which we must be saved" (Acts 4:12).

Investigate. Read. Compare. Then stand up for Jesus, THE Savior! Stand up and be counted!

21st - The scripture for today, September 21 (9/21), is Hebrews 9:21f as found in the New Testament of the Bible:

"In the same way, he [Moses] sprinkled with the blood both the tabernacle and everything used in its ceremonies. In fact, the law requires that nearly everything be cleansed with blood, and without the shedding of blood, there is no forgiveness."

The wages of sin is death (Romans 6:23). Death means separation. In a physical sense, we are separated from people living on earth. In a spiritual sense, we are separated from God in heaven. God is life, and cannot dwell with death. It is not in his nature.

But he loves us dearly. So he sent a final blood sacrifice for us ~ his own Son, the perfect Lamb of God ~ to shed his blood in our place, to collect the terrible wages of our sin for us ~ so mankind could be forgiven of our sins.

What a God we have! Let us fall at his feet and worship.

22nd - The scripture for today, September 22 (9/22) is Luke 9:22 as found in the New Testament of the Bible:

"And he [Jesus] said, 'The Son of Man[kind] must suffer many things and be rejected by the elders, chief priests and teachers of the law, and he must be killed and on the third day be raised to life."

Jesus did not look forward to his death. Hebrews 5:7 says,

"During the days of Jesus' life on earth, he offered up prayers and petitions with loud cries and tears to the one who could save him from death...." Loud cries!

Yet, in today's scripture, shortly after he announced to his apostles that he would be killed in Jerusalem, over in verse 51 it says, "As the time approached for him to be taken up to heaven, Jesus resolutely set out for Jerusalem."

Jesus had to use every bit of self-determination he could muster up to face that terrible death he had to suffer for us. What kept him to his goal? He knew only he could save us from hell by taking the death wages from Satan (Romans 6:23). Then his work would be done ~ all would be fulfilled ~ and he could return to heaven.

Is it difficult for you to get up on Sunday morning to go to church? Is it difficult for you to read the Bible every day? Is it difficult for you to invite a friend to church with you? Do you love Jesus as resolutely as he loves you?

23rd - The scripture for today, September 23 (9/23), is **Luke 9:23** as found in the New Testament of the Bible:

"Then he said to them all: 'If anyone would come after me, he must deny himself and take up his cross daily and follow me.' "

There is another verse similar to this: II Timothy 3:12 ~ "Everyone who wants to live a godly life in Christ Jesus will be persecuted."

Have you been playing it safe? Have you been associating

only with other Christians and thereby sheltering yourself from persecution? Have you been withholding the gospel from people who might be persecuted if they believe, even if they will be saved by following it?

I know a Christian convert in Afghanistan who keeps telling his Muslim friends about Jesus and his life has been threatened three times now over a period of six years. He says, "I will not stop until they kill me." I know a Christian convert in Iraq whose wife's relatives beat up because he became a Christian. I know a Christian convert in another part of Iraq whose mother-in-law locked her in a room and beat her every day, trying to get her to return to Islam.

Jesus came to seek and save the lost (Luke 19:10). To do that, you must seek out the lost and try to save them, even when they do not think they are lost. It will end in persecution sometimes ~ you, them, or both. That's a fact.

Dare to not play it safe all the time. Jesus didn't.

24th - The scripture for today, September 24 (9/24), is **Luke 9:24** as found in the New Testament of the Bible:

"For whoever wants to save his life will lose it, but whoever loses his life for me will save it."

Romans 6 explains this phenomenon best. We are to put our old self to death ~ to crucify that part of us that sins and doesn't care, that part of us that puts ourselves first (verse 7) ~ in imitation of

Jesus dying. Once we decide to put that part of ourselves to death, we are buried, just like Jesus was buried (verse 3 & 4a).

And then, "just as Christ was raised from the dead as the savior, we rise from the dead as the saved. Why? "If we have been united with him like this in his death, we will certainly also be united with him in his resurrection" (verse 5). Having been "brought from death to life" (verse 13) through baptism, we have been born again!

This is a spiritual death, of course. There is another spiritual death called the second death in Revelation 21:8. If we go through the first spiritual death at baptism, we will not have to go through the second spiritual death in hell. We will have lost our life of sin and in the process saved our souls.

It's all there. Study it. Absorb it. Mull it. And be amazed.

25th- The scripture for today, September 25 (9/25), is **1st Corinthians 9:25f** as found in the New Testament of the Bible:

"Everyone who competes in the games goes into strict training. They do it to get a crown that will not last; but we do it to get a crown that will last forever. Therefore, I do not run like a man running aimlessly...."

Every few years there are world-wide Olympic Games with many races. The racers must eat properly, rest sufficiently, and exercise daily.

The Bible has been called the Bread of Life. As a Christian, you need to eat your spiritual meal every day to stay fit.

You cannot keep up your strength without it. Your time of rest is prayer. You enter a room alone and talk to God every day. You need your rest. You cannot keep up your strength without it.

I Timothy 4:8 says, "For physical training is of some value, but godliness has value for all things, holding promise for both the present life and the life to come." You exercise your godliness by being out in the world and being a good example in the face of temptation. You exercise your spiritual muscles daily.

The race is your Christian life. You run every day. How is your race going?

26th - The scripture for today, September 26 (9/26), is **Hebrews 9:26f** as found in the New Testament of the Bible:

"Then Christ would have had to suffer many times since the creation of the world. But now he has appeared once for all at the end of the ages to do away with sin by the sacrifice of himself. Just as man is destined to die once, and after that to face the judgment."

According to the Old Law of Moses, sacrifices of perfect animals had to be made to temporarily pay the ransom of death for people's sins. But it wasn't enough because what Satan really wanted was the death of God so he could take over.

Finally, Jesus became the perfect Lamb of God and gave Satan what he wanted (Matthew 20:28). In a sense he laid down on the altar of the world. He paid the ransom Satan demanded to release our sinful souls from his clutches.

Then Jesus fooled Satan. Satan thought he got what he wanted ~ God in the body of Jesus died. But three days later he played a trick on Satan: He came back to life! The ransom had been paid and our souls released both in one fell swoop.

And so, just as Jesus died once, we too die once. Then our judgment. No second chances. No reincarnations. No going back and trying to be perfect again and failing again. No trying for yet another 1000 years because supposedly Jesus didn't get it right the first time.

Jesus released us from all of our failures at being perfect. Thank God, he was perfect for us. And now, after dying once, when he returns, his followers will meet him in the air among the clouds (I Thessalonians 4:17). The rest will face judgment.

How amazing God's plan for us!

27th - The scripture for today, September 27 (9/27), is Nehemiah 9:27 as found in the Old Testament of the Bible:

"So you handed them over to their enemies who oppressed them. But when they were oppressed, they cried out to you. From heaven you heard them, and in your great compassion you gave them deliverers, who rescued them from the hand of their enemies."

What was going on here? The Jews had started worshipping false gods, putting some of their altars in the temple of God, and even offering their children as sacrifices to the fire god. God let their enemies take them captive until they stopped their horrible practices and started praying only to the one true God. Then he rescued them those enemies.

Do you know anyone who could care less about God? The only exception is when they feel oppressed by something or someone in their life? More than likely, they blame God because Satan has convinced them he does not exist and therefore did not cause their problems.

Wait! Don't be so hard on them. That can be a good thing. Perhaps they hadn't given God a second thought since their last calamity. But now they're thinking about him. They may be angry at God, but at least they're thinking about him. Now is your chance to approach a broken, desperate, but softened spirit.

Let us thank God for times of oppression. Sometimes that is what it takes for God to get their attention. Then perhaps God can show them he wants to be their friend.

28th - The scripture for today, September 28 (9/28), is **Hebrews 9:28** as found in the New Testament of the Bible:

"So Christ was sacrificed once to take away the sins of many people; and he will appear a second time, not to bear sin, but to bring salvation to those who are waiting for him."

Waiting is hard to do. We wait for relatives to arrive at our house for a visit. We wait for our next promotion. We wait for babies to be born. We wait for enough money to buy new clothes.

But what about waiting for something that we have never seen? Waiting for something we believe in by faith? Waiting an entire lifetime?

All the more reason to keep your eyes on the Word,your activities in good works, and your heart on your Creator and Savior. It's a long spiritual walk. But just keep walking, and keep walking, and keep walking until some day in the distant future you walk right through the gates of heaven.

Then, when you look back from eternity, you will say, "The wait wasn't so long after all."

29th - The scripture for today, September 29 (9/29), is **Matthew 9:29** as found in the New Testament of the Bible:

"Then he touched their eyes and said, 'According to your faith will it be done to you.' "

Sometimes when we pray for healing during sickness, a well-meaning friend will say, "Well, you haven't been healed because you didn't have enough faith." But Jesus did not heal everyone according to their faith.

The boy in Nain he brought back to life (Luke 7:14-15) did not have any faith at all. The girl in Capernaum he brought back to life (Luke 8:51-56) did not have any faith at all. When Jesus turned water into wine at the wedding feast in Cana (John 2:1-9) the hosts did not have any faith at all.

This is encouraging, because often we pray for the healing

of non-religious friends. It would be futile to ask God to bring them back to health if it depended on their faith all the time.

He is not a God of futility. He is a God of hope.

30th - The scripture for today, September 30 (9/30), is **Luke 9:30f** as found in the New Testament of the Bible:

"Two men, Moses and Elijah, appeared in glorious splendor, talking with Jesus. They spoke about his departure, which he was about to bring to fulfillment at Jerusalem."

Hebrews 5:7 says something very startling to most people. "During the days of Jesus' life on earth, he offered up prayers and petitions with loud cries and tears to the one who could save him from death."

Jesus did not look forward to going to the cross, even though many thousands of others had died that way. Why was it different for him? Because he had to take on all our sins as though he had committed them himself ~ every lie we've told, every gain from cheating, every insult, every slander campaign against another, every adultery, every murder ~ everything ~ all our sins! How could he bear it?

Not only that, but he had to experience both physical and spiritual death. Spiritual death means being separated from, being forsaken by God. What a terror to experience!

And so, a few weeks before his crucifixion, as he prayed on the mountain, Moses and Elijah appeared to him and they spoke about his death. They surely gave him courage to do what had to be done to save you and me who deserve hell.

The crowning glory of this conversation with Moses and Elijah is that the Father reassured him by announcing, "THIS IS MY SON! WHOM I HAVE CHOSEN! LISTEN TO HIM!"

Jesus was to nail the Old Law of Moses to the cross (Colossians 2:14). He had promised people, "Do not think that I have come to abolish the Law and the Prophets: I have not come to abolish them but to fulfill them" (Matthew 5:17).

On the cross, he said, "It is fulfilled." Indeed, by the time Jesus returned to heaven, he had lived the Old Law introduced by Moses perfectly ~ something no man had ever been able to do. And by the time he returned to heaven, he had fulfilled every prophecy about his birth, life, and death, the first such full-time prophet being Elijah.

Oh the things Jesus went through for us. We fall at his feet and worship him.

October

1st - The scripture for today, October 1 (10/1), is Romans 10:1f as found in the New Testament of the Bible:

"Brothers, my heart's desire and prayer to God for ______ is that they may be saved. For I can testify about them that they are zealous for God, but their zeal is not based on knowledge."

Being "religious" isn't enough. There are lots of religions. Feeling "spiritual" isn't enough. There are lots of differing religions that induce a "spiritual" feeling. Confidence of salvation isn't enough. There are lots of differing religions that create questionable confidence of salvation. Dedication to prayer isn't enough. There are lots of differing religions that require much prayer.

Sincere Christian leaders today may want us to rely on feelings and inducements and confidence and dedication, but they can be sincerely wrong. If we base our salvation on feelings and inducements and confidence and dedication only, we have zeal, but our zeal is not based on knowledge. Some may defensively call "knowledge" legalism.

God gave us his Word ~ the Bible ~ for a reason. He wanted us to reason. Hebrews 11:1 says faith is accepting the evidence ~ not wishful thinking. Romans 10:17 says faith comes from hearing/reading the Word of God for ourselves ~ not someone's sermon. Let us search the scriptures daily for ourselves. And, let us not be afraid to approach our religious leaders and try teaching the teachers. Then their zeal as well as ours can be based on knowledge

2nd – The scripture for today, October 2 (10/2), is Daniel 10:2ff as found in the Old Testament of the Bible:

"At that time I, Daniel, mourned for three weeks...On the twenty-fourth day of the first month...I looked up and there before me was a man dressed in linen with a belt of the finest gold around his waist. His body was like chrysolite, his face like lightning, his eyes like flaming torches, his arms and legs like the gleam of burnished bronze, and his voice like the sound of a multitude....Then he continued, 'Do not be afraid, Daniel. Since the first day that you set your mind to gain understanding and to humble yourself before your God, your words were heard, and I have come in response to them. But the prince of the Persian kingdom resisted me twenty-one days. Then Michael, one of the chief princes, came to help me because I was detained there with the king of Persia.' "

The description of the speaker indicates he is an angel, possibly Gabriel. Michael is another known angel. In Daniel 12:1 he is called "Michael, the great prince who protects your people." Jude 9 refers to Michael as an archangel who disputed with Satan over the body of Moses.

Revelation 12:7-9 says, "And there was war in heaven,

Michael and his angels fought against the dragon, and the dragon and his angels fought back. But he was not strong enough and they lost their place in heaven. The great dragon was hurled down ~ that ancient serpent called the devil or Satan, who leads the whole world astray. He was hurled to the earth and his angels with him."

Now, let us look back at Daniel 10. Daniel prayed for 21 days. The un-named angel (Gabriel?) appeared to him on the 24th day and said Daniel's prayers had been heard the first day, but God's angel could not break away to help because of fighting Satan's angels.

Now look at Ephesians 6:12, "For our struggle is not against flesh and blood, but against the rulers, against the authorities, against the powers of this dark world and against the spiritual forces of evil in the heavenly realms."

Does our persistence in prayer give strength to the angels? Something to think about....

3rd - The scripture for today, October 3 (10/3), is **John 10:3ff** as found in the New Testament of the Bible:

"The watchman opens the gate for him, and the sheep listen to his voice. He calls his own sheep by name and leads them out....I am the gate for the sheep. All who ever came before me were thieves and robbers, but the sheep did not listen to them. I am the gate; whoever enters through me will be saved."

First of all, we use the term saved/salvation so loosely, we tend to think we are saved to heaven. But we are not saved to something; we are saved from something. We even tend to forget what we are being saved from. We are being saved from hell! This is not a minuscule matter.

Second, how do we avoid hell? Through Jesus! This is the only way.

How many of us have been to funerals where the deceased was preached into heaven? So many people believe they are "good enough" or "not too bad" and so God would be horrible to not let them into heaven. Such people will climb in through windows so to speak into heaven as the "thieves and robbers" Jesus referred to.

But heaven is God's home, not ours. He has a gate into it, just like we have doors on our house. Just like we are not obligated to open the gate or door into our home to just anyone, God is not obligated to open his gate to just anyone. Our door and God's gate are there for a reason. Let us enter heaven through the gate ~ Jesus. Then God will smile and say, "Welcome home."

4th- The scripture for today, October 4 (10/4), is **Romans 10:4** as found in the New Testament of the Bible:

"Christ is the end of the law so that there may be righteousness for everyone who believes."

When Jesus nailed the Law of Moses to the cross (Colossians 2:14) it came to an end. Thank God. There were over 600 commandments in the Law of Moses, not just the "ten commandments." They were tedious. Try reading Leviticus and see if you can keep every commandment in it.

Jesus was the only one who ever kept the Law perfectly (Hebrews 4:15). Once that occurred, he could be the Perfect Lamb of God without blemish, and he could be sacrificed on the altar of the world (the cross) in our place ~ take the blame and punishment for our sins.

And with his death came the introduction of a New Law covered in the New Testament. (The book of Hebrews explains it all.). Read the New Testament in its entirety. It is not tedious. It is beautiful. Let us not try to dip back into the Old Law and bring back showy worship practices done back them. He put it to death and gave us a new and wonderful and simple law of grace and love.

5th - The scripture for today, October 5, (10/5) is **2nd Corinthians 10:5f** as found in the New Testament of the Bible:

"Nevertheless, God was not pleased with most of them; their bodies were scattered over the desert. Now these things occurred as examples to keep us from setting our hearts on evil things as they did."

This is about the 40 years the Jews wandered in the wilderness between leaving their slavery in Egypt and beginning a nation for themselves. They had the mindsets of slaves. They did not know how to make decisions for themselves. One of those decisions was to leave the gods of Egypt and worship only the one true God.

It was easier to fall in line with what they were raised to believe. They took the easy way out rather than follow the God who had proved the Egyptian gods were not gods at all. They would rather die than change. So they did. They died.

Do you take the easy way out? Do you stick with things you were raised to believe even though you have learned more of the Bible and see those old beliefs are not what God said?

The early Jews did not listen to God, so God did not listen to them. He is calling out to you even now. "Come to me. I want to save you. Please come."

6th - The scripture for today, October 6 (10/6), is **Jeremiah 10:6** as found in the Old Testament of the Bible:

"No one is like you, O Lord; you are great, and your name is mighty in power."

You are the glorious God of the universe and beyond. You are also the God of the minute and dwell in such small specs, no one can even imagine you are there. Mostly you are the God of my heart. I adore you. You forgive me for the same things over and over. How can you? Because you are Love and to be less would be beyond your very nature. I am so small and unworthy, but you see me anyway. You even think about me all the time. I am never out of your thoughts. The magnitude of your heart transcends worlds and all that exists.

Thank you, God, for pouring your heart out to the world in your Bible. Now we can know you and have no doubts. How many in this world are willing to pour out their heart to others as you did?

I praise and adore you, God of all heaven and earth. God of existence. You are greater than death, for you are the life giver. You will be there when I die, welcoming me into a realm of joy and beauty and peace that I cannot even begin to imagine. Life here is like living in a cave compared with heaven. How I long to be in your world and before your throne. I think when I get there, I shall try to sing to you louder than anyone else. Would that be a sin, Lord?

What a mighty God you are. You speak and your words roar and echo through the universe. You sing and your song echoes from star to star. You whisper and the wind swirls and makes the clouds bump lazily into each other. You sigh and I feel your Spirit within my soul. Mighty and tender and a wonder to behold. (Excerpt 365 Prayers to Draw Closer to God)

7th- The scripture for today, October 7 (10/7), is **Joshua 10:7f** as found in the Old Testament of the Bible:

"So Joshua marched up from Gilgal with his entire army, including all the best fighting men. The Lord said to Joshua, 'Do not be afraid of them; I have given them into your hand. Not one of them will be able to withstand you.' "

We today cannot imagine a good God condoning violence,

let alone promoting it. But think back. Mankind was quite barbaric in the centuries and millenniums before Christ. For example, when Alexander the Great got offended at what a friend said to him, he cut off his nose and ears and put him in a cage the rest of his life.

God never runs very far ahead of mankind, or else mankind would not understand and would not even try to follow God. By the time Jesus came, God was saying, "No more violence."

In this scripture for today, God was telling Joshua to attack people in the Promised Land ~ Canaan. This brings up another question: Why would a good God allow one group of people to kill off another group of people? God told Abraham centuries earlier, "In the fourth generation your descendants will come back here, for the sin of the Amorites has not yet reached its full measure" (Genesis 15:16). By this time they were sacrificing children to their gods.

In Leviticus 18:24, 28, God warned the Jews through Moses, "Do not defile yourselves in any of these ways because this is how the nations that I am going to drive out before you became defiled....And if you defile the land, it will vomit you out as it vomited out the nations that were before you." So God warned the Jews that, if they got as bad as the previous people in Canaan, he would drive them out too. (Eventually they did, so God did.)

Further, in Old Testament times, God often punished people immediately. Why punish them? Partly to get them away from the good people. And God used armies of believers to do the punishing for him.

Today God does not expect us to do the punishing. Romans 12:19 says, "Do not take revenge, my friends, but leave room for God's wrath, for it is written, 'It is mine to avenge; I will repay' says the Lord. On the contrary, If your enemy is hungry feed him....Do not be overcome by evil, but overcome evil with good."

Thank God, he has taken the terrible task of vengeance away from us. We can just forgive our enemies and hand things over to God to take whatever steps need to be taken. In the meantime, we can read the Old Testament and learn that God takes notice when people are doing bad things to us. God does take care of us. God does love his children.

8th- The scripture for today, October 8 (10/8), is **Romans 10:8f** as found in the New Testament of the Bible:

"But what does it say? 'The word is near you; it is in your mouth and in your heart,' that is, the word of faith we are proclaiming: That if you confess with your mouth, 'Jesus is Lord' and believe in your heart that God raised him from the dead, you will be saved."

The word is in your mouth through confession of your faith in Jesus, and in your heart for truly believing it and not just saying it.

Some say you are not saved by works, and it is true in the sense that you cannot go around doing so many good works that God will feel obligated to take you into his home. You can never be good enough because you sin and those sins need to be washed away (Acts 22:16).

In the sense that you do not have to do anything to be saved, it is not true. After all, Jesus himself said faith is a work: "Jesus answered, 'The work of God is this: To believe in the one he has sent' " (John 6:29).

To many faithful Christians there are times in their life that faith is indeed hard work. Are you sometimes beset with so many problems you begin to wonder if Jesus really cares like he claimed?

Continue to work at your faith. You will have your ups and our downs. Sometimes your faith will be strong and sometimes weak. But remember, even when you doubt God, God never doubts you.

9th – The scripture for today, October 9 (10/9), is **Job 10:9** as found in the Old Testament of the Bible:

"Remember that you molded me like clay. Will you now turn me to dust again?"

Job was sick, his so-called friends came to him to say God was punishing him, and Job was frustrated. He could not reason with his friends, so he tried to reason with God. It was a lovers' quarrel.

By verse 18, he was so upset with God that he said, "Why then did you bring me out of the womb? I wish I had died before any eye saw me." Job's body was broken, and even more his spirit was broken. Satan was doing everything he could to get Job to deny God. But, even though Job argued with God and perhaps came close to denying him, he always acknowledged the good God did along with the bad. He just didn't understand the bad.

We don't understand the bad in our lives. But remember, it is Satan that causes the bad to happen. God may step back and let Satan give it a try, but we are not their toys. We are soldiers in the army of God. When Satan throws darts at us, we hold up the shield of faith.

Sometimes, the bad happening in your life is God's assignment for you. You are part of the war between God and Satan. As a good and loyal soldier, you take your assignments and stand firm. You may complain, but you still stand firm. You may trip sometimes, but still you stand firm. Being a soldier in the army of God is not easy. But the battle will be won. Some day. So stand firm!

10th - The scripture for today, October 10 (10/10), is **Proverbs 10:10** as found in the Old Testament of the Bible:

"He who winks maliciously causes grief, and a chattering fool comes to ruin."

How can eye winking be malicious? Let's look further at Proverbs 6:12-14 ~ "A scoundrel and villain, who goes about with a corrupt mouth, who winks with his eye, signals with his feet and motions with his fingers, who plans evil with deceit in his heart ~ he always stirs up dissension."

Have you ever said something to someone, but turned to someone else in the room and winked as though to let the second person know you didn't really mean what you just said? That made your words a lie.

You might have pre-arranged signals before a meeting, such as crossing your feet as a signal you do or don't like what is being said. Or you may run your fingers over your hair, or tap three times on a table as a pre-arranged signal to someone else in the room. If you are saying one thing but signaling something else to your partner, then your words are lies.

Perhaps you think it is purely innocent and claim that everyone does it. But Revelation 21 says "...all liars ~ their place will be in the fiery lake."

So, from now on, be truthful in everything you say in word and deed. It can be done. And it is liberating.

11th - The scripture for today, October 11 (10/11), is **Psalm 10:11** as found in the Old Testament of the Bible:

"He says to himself, 'God has forgotten; he covers his face and never sees.' "

You believe in God in some form. And you believe that God knows what you do. But do you sometimes bury your beliefs in your subconscious mind so you can go around doing things you know are wrong? Do you believe you won't get caught, and you can slide into heaven doing whatever you want?

In other words, do you justify your favorite sins? Do you justify your sins of attitude such as jealousy, impatience, pride, short temper under the guise of an unhappy childhood or getting what you deserve? Do you justify your sins of omission ~ good things you should be doing, but are not ~ under the excuse that you don't have time to do good works? Do you justify questionable things you do by saying they're "not so bad" or God is so good, he will forgive anything you do as long as you say you're sorry every time you do it?

Do you do as children do who cover their eyes so they cannot see anyone and think that, therefore, no one can see them?

God loves you more than you can ever imagine. He never forgets you. He sees and hears everything you do. The only things he does not approve of are things that will ultimately hurt you and which he calls sin.

Here's a jewel for you. Polish it, shine it up and put it on display: Pleasing God is the ultimate form of pleasing yourself.

12th- The scripture for today, October 12 (10/12), is **2nd Corinthians 10:12** as found in the New Testament of the Bible:

"We do not dare to classify or compare ourselves with some who commend themselves. When they measure themselves by themselves and compare themselves with themselves, they are not wise."

But that is how most of the Christian world is run. You go to a church and do what they do to get their approval. Or you go one step above what the others do to get a little more approval. Or you go one step below what the others do, and say you're "not so bad" because, at least, you go to church all the time.

What you do must be compared with what Jesus (God materialized on earth) did. Jesus went everywhere doing whatever was necessary to spread the Good News. Instead of saying, "Well, our congregation never did such-and-such before, so it must be wrong," you must say, "Jesus did it, so I will too." Instead of saying, "Well, brother or sister so-and-so in our congregation is worse than me, so why object to me?" you must say, "Jesus did not do those things, so I will not either."

Who are you comparing yourself with? Your works, your fancy doctrine, your faith? Dear, dear friend. Jesus gave up heaven and daily associating with angels to become one of us on an earth full of grime and selfish. He gave up being able to be everywhere at once to being confined in a body. Why? For us.

To show us how it is done ~ constantly on the go to find people who need God's love and attention. He was so busy and so holy.

Never compare with others; always compare with Jesus. Keep your eyes on Jesus.

13th- The Scripture for today, October 13 (10/13), is **1st Corinthians 10:13** as found in the New Testament of the Bible:

"No temptation has seized you except what is common to man. And

God is faithful: He will not let you be tempted beyond what you can bear. But when you are tempted, he will also provide a way out so that you can stand up under it."

What are you tempted to do or not do on a regular basis in your everyday life? Then look at the source of your everyday temptations ~ Satan. Do you really want to be Satan's slave?

Romans 6:16 explains it this way: "Don't you know that when you offer yourselves to someone to obey him as slaves, you are slaves to the one whom you obey ~ whether you are slaves to sin, which leads to death, or to obedience, which leads to righteousness?"

Take a long hard look at your everyday temptations and remind yourself of the source. Then, with courage in your soul and boldness in your heart, stand up and say, "No more! I am not your slave, Satan. I will win over you. God and I are stronger than you. Satan, get used to it: You will lose.

14th - The scripture for today, October 14 (10/14), is **John 10:14** as found in the New Testament of the Bible:

"I am the good shepherd; I know my sheep and my sheep know me ~ just as the Father knows me and I know the Father ~ and I lay down my life for the sheep."

How amazing that Jesus is willing to follow you when you do not follow him, and bring you back to his protective fold. He died while doing just that.

Yet we continue to leave him and his instructions that would keep us safe, and we wander into thistles, near cliffs, down into pits. This requires more work for Jesus. Yet we do it anyway. Catch me if you can! We may laugh, but he weeps because he knows the danger we are headed for.

How much grief do we give our spiritual Father, our spiritual Big Brother, our spiritual family? If they are not laughing over what we're doing, perhaps we should not be either.

God, forgive me when I wander from You.

15th - The scripture for today, October 15 (10/15), is **Deuteronomy 10:15** as found in the Old Testament of the Bible:

"Yet the Lord set his affection on your forefathers [Abraham, Isaac, Jacob] and loved them, and he chose you, their descendants [Jews], above all the nations, as it is today."

Mankind has spent millenniums trying to figure out how to be perfect so we can deserve heaven.

God gave us that opportunity the first several thousand years of mankind. Some people of the world he left alone to figure out on their own how to be perfect. They created many kinds of religions. But to the Jews he sent the Law of Moses containing over 600 intricate laws which, if kept perfectly, would make them perfect. In both cases, no one could be perfect.

Then, when mankind was willing to admit we cannot be perfect, the Word of God materialized and came to us to live that perfect life that is impossible for us to live. Now, all you have to do is follow Jesus and be IN Jesus (Galatians 3:27) for the forgiveness of your sins, and God will consider you perfect too.

God sets his affections on you. He will not force you, but he runs after you begging you to come to him for safety. Oh, how he loves you.

16th - The scripture for today, October 16 (10/16), is **Acts 10:16** as found in the New Testament of the Bible:

"This happened three times, and immediately the sheet was taken back to heaven."

This is about a vision where God let down a sheet full of animals that were "unclean" or not allowed to be eaten according to the Law of Moses. (See Leviticus 11:1-8.) God told Peter he could now eat them.

Peter already knew that Jesus nailed the Old Law of Moses to the Cross (Colossians 2:14). But it just hadn't sunk in yet. As many times as Jesus told his apostles about his Sonship of God and proved it with astounding miracles, it wasn't until just before his death that Jesus told them, "You believe at last!" (John 16:31).

Similarly, sometimes you read the same scripture over and over and it goes right over your head. You are not seeing what God wants you to see. You assume that what you've always been doing will always be right. You assume that others in church do things a certain way, so it has to be right.

Do this: Search everything in the scriptures on topics that you assume you know all about, and get everything God has to say about it. Then compare scripture to practice.

It IS possible to get God's opinion on things, and that is who, in the end, you are trying to please. He will judge you, not your friends. He alone can save you.

17th - The scripture for today, October 17 (10/17), is **Romans 10:17** as found in the New Testament of the Bible:

"Consequently, faith comes from hearing the message, and the message is heard through the word of Christ."

The King James version reads "Therefore, faith comes by hearing, and hearing by the Word of God."

Faith is not just a feeling or responding to what a friend tells us. It is not responding to a religious book or to a spiritual movement. Faith is the result of hearing/reading the Word of Christ, the gospel ~ for ourselves ~ all of it!

Faith is based on knowledge; zeal is not enough (Romans 10:1). Faith is based on considering the evidence; a feeling in one's heart is not enough (Hebrews 11:1).

You who study the Bible for yourself are doing the right thing. Do not rely on anything but what you have read for yourself.

All other religious people are going to be judged by God just like you are. When compared to God's Word, their word is not important. We are trying to please God, not people. We are worshiping God, not people. Let us rely only on what He says, and know for sure.

18th- The scripture for today, October 18 (10/18), is **2nd Corinthians 10:18** as found in the New Testament of the Bible:

"For it is not the one who commends himself who is approved, but the one whom the Lord commends."

Do you look at your life and decide some of your bad habits are not so bad, considering what some other people you know are doing? Do you look at your life and decide your lukewarmness in good works and spreading the gospel is not so bad, considering what most others around you are doing?

Jesus said you will receive only one reward, and we must choose it: (1) Being commended by each other, or (2) being commended by God. You can't have both (Matthew 6:5; 18).

And that brings up how you judge other people. You may decide certain Christians you know are not pulling their share of the load in your congregation, not doing their part. That may be a wrong judgment.

A lot of Christians you know may be doing good works you will never learn about. "Your Father, who sees what is done in secret, will reward [them]" (Matthew 6:18a). Who knows? That time someone mowed your lawn while you were in the hospital may have been one of those "do-nothings". I wonder how many stars they have in their crown.

19th - The scripture for today, October 19 (10/19), is **Hebrews 10:19** as found in the New Testament of the Bible:

"Therefore, brothers, since we have confidence to enter the Most Holy Place by the blood of Jesus...."

The entire book of Hebrews explains in detail how the Jewish Old Testament Law of Moses with its 600 laws was replaced by the New Testament law of Jesus' Grace, not just for Jews, but for every nation on earth.

Only Levites (male descendants of the Jewish tribe of Levi) were allowed to enter the Holy Place ~ first room in the temple. Only the high priest, (a Levite descendant of Aaron, Moses' brother) was allowed to enter the Most Holy Place, and even then only once a year on the Day of Atonement. Leviticus 16 explains that on that Day, the high priest was to kill a goat and sprinkle its blood inside the Most Holy Place for the atonement (forgiveness) of the people.

The Jewish temple was destroyed about the time the book of Hebrews was written. This book explains that we no longer need an earthly high priest and an earthly Most Holy Place. Jesus is our high priest (Hebrews 7:24-26) The Most Holy Place is heaven and open to all Christians throughout the world (Hebrews 9:24-

26).

Hebrews 9:12-14 explains, "He did not enter by means of the blood of goats and calves; but he entered the Most Holy Place once for all by his own blood, having obtained eternal redemption. The blood of goats and bulls and the ashes of a heifer sprinkled on those who are ceremonially unclean sanctify them so they are outwardly clean. How much more, then, will the blood of Christ ~ who through the eternal Spirit offered himself unblemished to God ~ cleanse our consciences from acts that lead to death, so that we may serve the living God!"

God created the pattern in the Old Testament, and the spiritual reality in the New Testament.

Some people are collecting money and breeding red heifers to rebuild the temple and begin blood sacrifices again. Why in the world would they do that? Do they really want to annul Jesus' New Last Will and Testament and return to stoning adulterers, paying 1/3 of their income (not just 1/10) to the temple, requiring all males to go to the temple three times a year, etc.? And where are they going to find a direct descendant of Aaron, Moses' brother to be the high priest? James said that, if you keep part of the Law, you must keep all of it (James 2:10).

Read the book of Hebrews for yourself. It is fascinating and renewing.

20th - The scripture for today, October 20 (10/20), is **Deuteronomy 10:20** as found in the Old Testament of the Bible:

"Fear the Lord your God and serve him. Hold fast to him."

I praise you, Jehovah, Creator of everything I observe and more. You are too large to see but a speck of you. You are too small to perceive, too much to fathom, too wise to comprehend. You are my monarch, my sovereign, my emperor, my king. You reign over my heart, my mind, my spirit, my soul.

Lord God, you are crowned with the sun. Your scepter is tipped with the moon. Your robe spreads across the Milky Way. Your throne is the dome of the cosmos encircled with a thousand rainbows. Your eyes sparkle like stars, your laughter is like the thunder, your tears like raindrops, your touch like billowy clouds gliding across the sky. Oh, my Lord. I love you, adore you, worship you.

In the Hebrew, "fear" is *yirah*. It means to revere. Psalm 111:9 (KJV) says, "Holy and reverend is His name," not somebody else's name. Some preachers say, "Well, I'm honoring God when I add 'Reverend' to my name." 6Really?

We are told to hold fast to God. Hold fast to Reverend God, and he will hold fast to you.

21st - The scripture for today, October 21 (10/21), is **Proverbs 10:21** as found in the Old Testament of the Bible:

"The lips of the righteous nourish many, but fools die for lack of judgment."

What do you talk about during the day? What kind of judgment do you use? Do you nourish others by what you say to them?

Are you a complainer or complementor? Are you rude or patient? Do you glare or smile? Do you criticize the wrong a person does, or praise the right that person does? Do you sing of your love of God on Sunday and use swear words the rest of the week?

Today, go out of your way to nourish everyone you talk to. Start a new habit. They will see God in you.

22nd - The scripture for today, October 22 (10/22), is **Hebrews 10:22** as found in the New Testament of the Bible:

"Let us draw near to God with a sincere heart in full assurance of faith, having our hearts sprinkled to cleanse us from a guilty conscience and having our bodies washed with pure water."

The previous verse said that Jesus is the great (high) priest over the house of God (the church). Therefore, the sprinkling refers to the sprinkling of blood the high priests did on the Day of Atonement once a year. (See Leviticus 16 in the Old Testament.) Today your heart (which we cannot see or touch) is sprinkled with the blood of Jesus.

And how are you to be cleansed from that guilty conscience with our body (which we can see and touch) being washed? I Peter 3:21 says, "Even so does baptism now save us, not the putting away of the filth of the flesh but the answer of a good conscience toward God."

You do not have to guess whether you were sincere enough when you gave your heart to the Lord. Your conscience never has to wonder if you did it right. For God gave you something you can actually do to give you a good and clear conscience toward him.

From hence forth, you can draw near to God in full assurance. Full! Not partial. Not wondering. Not with ups and downs of faith. But full! God thinks of everything!

23rd - The scripture for today, October 23 (10/23), is **Jeremiah 10:23** as found in the Old Testament of the Bible:

"I know, O Lord, that a man's life is not his own; it is not for man to direct his steps."

Just how are we supposed to know what steps God has directed us to take? Do we have to guess, rely on a feeling, depend on the movement of our heart, a vision? Actually, we have a guide, a road map.

Jesus said in John 14:16-17 that after he left, the Father would send another Counselor ~ the Spirit of Truth. In John 16:13 Jesus said The Spirit of Truth will guide us into all truth." In John 17:17, Jesus said, "Your Word is truth."

Yes, the Holy Spirit, the Spirit of Truth, guides us through the Word of God, the Bible.

We don't have to guess! We don't have to wonder! We don't have to get discouraged! God has given us his Word to direct our steps. All we have to do is open his Word and read the map.

24th- The scripture for today, October 24 (10/24), is **1st Corinthians 10:24** as found in the New Testament of the Bible:

"Nobody should seek his own good, but the good of others."

The context of this verse is that some of the members of the church in Corinth were expressing opinions or doing things that were offensive to some of the other members. They hurt the consciences of some of the weaker members.

Today, do you do anything during the public worship that is offensive to some people? Do you do them as an example of how "holy" you are? Do you even try to get God on your side and say that any Christian could do those things if they had as much faith as you do? Can you control your ego in this?

What about committee meetings? Do you suggest something that the others just aren't excited about? Do you allow your ego to eventually seep in and begin to feel slighted or challenged because your idea wasn't accepted? Do you even try to get God on your side and say he will be more glorified if the other committee members accept your plan? Can you control your ego in this?

One way to look at things objectively is to ask yourself, "Would my congregation survive without me?" What if I were killed in an auto accident and suddenly taken from them tomorrow? Would they continue to worship? Would they continue to do good works? Would they continue to meet as a congregation? Ninety-nine percent of the time your congregation would survive without you.

So, try (struggle, if necessary) to lay aside your ego that gets hurt or feels challenged, and seek the comfort, welfare and good of your fellow members. Jesus was King, but he laid aside his ego. And he triumphed!

25th - The scripture for today, October 25 (10/25), is **Hebrews 10:25** as found in the New Testament of the Bible:

"Let us not give up meeting together, as some are in the habit of doing, but let us encourage one another ~ and all the more as you see the Day approaching."

Do you declare, "I can walk through nature ~ the temple of God ~ and feel God is closer there than in a church building"? Well, do you really do it? How often? The purpose of the church meeting is not so much to encourage yourself as to encourage your fellow Christian and visitors along with worshiping God.

Look at the context. Verse 23 says "Let us hold unswervingly to the hope we profess" and verse 24 says, "Let us consider how we may spur one another on toward love and good deeds." How do you do these things? A lot of it is done during your congregation's worship and encouragement service.

And what comes after our verse for today? Verse 26 says, "If we deliberately keep on sinning after we have received the knowledge of the truth, no sacrifice for sins is left." Meeting together with other congregational members is one of the major experiences that keeps you and your friends from falling and missing heaven. Or does worshipping all the time in heaven sound boring too?

Should you meet once a week? This scripture says to meet "all the more as you see the Day [of Judgment] approaching.' Do you say, "But that's too inconvenient"?

It was inconvenient for Jesus to leave a perfect heaven for an imperfect earth. It was inconvenient for him to leave the company of angels for the company of sinners. It was inconvenient for him to do this for 33 long years. Inconvenient to take the blame for your sins, and then take your punishment. Inconvenient to experience agonizing spiritual death when God left him alone on the cross I your place, and then that agonizing physical death in your place.

Do you really know inconvenience? Do you love Jesus or not? Do you love your fellow Christian or not?

26th- The scripture for today, October 26 (10//26), is **1st Corinthians 10:26** as found in the New Testament of the Bible:

"For 'The earth is the Lord's, and everything in it.' "

This is a thanksgiving scripture.

The beautiful part of God's creation is that he left a lot of it undone for us to finish. After all, we are created in his likeness.

He left the stones and clay in the ground so that we could

dig it up and build cities. He left the wool on the sheep so we could shear it and make warm garments. He left the trees growing tall so we could hew them and build barns and houses. He left the gravel in the ground so we could harvest it and build roads.

He left the ore in the ground so we could mine it and make sky scrapers, airplanes, ships, trains, automobiles. He left the water in the lakes and seas so we could capture it and create power and transportation ways. He left the beautiful stones unseen so we could dig them up, shape them, polish them, and make beautiful decorations.

Yes, we were created in the likeness of our Creator. He loved to create. So do we. So, whenever we make something good from his creation, we honor him.

27th - The scripture for today, October 27 (10/27), is **Mark 10:27** as found in the New Testament of the Bible:

"Jesus looked at them and said, 'With man this is impossible, but not with God: All things are possible with God.' "

Can we be perfect? God let mankind try for many centuries to be perfect.

To one group of people he gave over 600 laws and said, "If you keep these, you will be perfect." But, as hard as the Jews tried, no one could keep the Law of Moses perfectly.

To the rest of the world he basically said, "Try to figure out for yourselves how to be perfect." So they tried all kinds of religions, but with all of them, they could not be perfect.

Finally, mankind was ready for Jesus. He came to earth and lived that perfect life that is impossible for us to live. He became the perfect Lamb of God, and became our sacrifice for our sins, for Romans 6:23 says "the wages of sin is death." He collected the wage of death from Satan for us.

So now, according to Romans 6:3-4, just as Jesus died on the cross, we too can die to our sinful nature ~ the part of us that sins and doesn't care. Then, just as Jesus was buried in his tomb, we too can be buried in a watery tomb of baptism. And finally, just as Jesus was raised up out of his tomb the Savior, we rise up out of our watery tomb the saved.

Then God considers us perfect too. God cannot associate with sinners in his heaven. He can only have perfect people in his heavenly home. Impossible for us to live there with him some day? Yes. But, God sent Jesus to fix that problem. With God, nothing is impossible.

28th - The scripture for today, October 28 (10/28), is **Matthew 10:28f** as found in the New Testament of the Bible:

"Do not be afraid of those who kill the body but cannot kill the soul. Rather, be afraid of the One who can destroy both soul and body in hell. Are not two sparrows sold for a penny? Yet not one of them will fall to the ground apart from the will of your Father."

This scripture indicates that sometimes God's allows you

to "fall to the ground" ~ your body suffers, or you are killed. How can that be? After all, God is so loving. Surely a good God would not allow any harm to come to someone if he truly loves them.

But we all have our assignment from God in this war between Good and Evil. Just as Job in the Old Testament lost his entire family and entire wealth and then his health, he refused to blame God. He even said, "Shall we accept good from God and not trouble?" (Job 2:10).

Satan causes bad to happen to you. Why? In order to get you to blame God for it. Your assignment is to refuse to deny God. That way, Satan loses one more battle, and God wins one more.

There is an old Christian song called "Victory in Jesus." How can you have victory in Jesus if you do not have something to be victorious over? Romans 8:37 says we are more than conquerors. How can you be a conqueror if you have nothing to conquer?

Stand strong and say with James (1:2) that you consider it pure joy whenever you face trials. Hard to say? Of course, it is. But it could turn your life around.

29th - The scripture for today, October 29 (10/29), is **John 10:29** as found in the New Testament of the Bible:

"My Father, who has given them to me, is greater than all; no one can snatch them out of my Father's hand."

No other person can take your salvation away from you. They may badger you, belittle you, torture you, kill you, but they cannot take your salvation away from you. The only one who can do that is you.

The Apostle Peter said, "Therefore, my brothers, be all the more eager to make your calling and election sure. For if you do these things, you will never fall....Be on your guard so that you may not be carried away by the error of lawless men and fall from your secure position" (II Peter 1:10; 3:17).

Hebrews 2:1 says, "We must pay more careful attention, therefore, to what we have heard, so that we do not drift away."

Jesus himself said, "All men will hate you because of me, but he who stands firm to the end will be saved" (Matthew 10:22).

Determine now to read the scriptures for yourself (God speaking directly to you) and praying (you speaking directly to God) and meet with other Christians to encourage each other and be better able to stand firm. You cannot do it alone. We need each other.

30th - The scripture for today, October 30 (10/30), is **Hebrews 10:30** as found in the New Testament of the Bible:

"For we know him who said, 'It is mine to avenge; I will repay' and again, 'The Lord will judge his people.' "

In the Law of Moses, people were expected to avenge those who did not follow the law. The vengeance was to be carried out by the person who had been hurt. Some things were even punishable by death.

But Jesus told you to forgive people so that God in turn will forgive you (Matthew 6:14).

What is forgiveness? It is not condoning the bad someone did. Forgiveness is letting go and letting God do any punishing that may be required. Forgiveness is wishing the other person well. You may not trust the other person to not do the bad thing again, and you may forever fear that person. But you can always hope and pray that their lives and hearts will change for the better someday. No one is so bad that you cannot wish them well and pray for them. That's forgiveness.

Vengeance only prolongs the pain; vengeance is hard on you. So, as the old saying goes, "Let go, and let God." God will do his part ~ the hard part. He has left the easy part for you.

31st - The scripture for today, October 31 (10/31), is **1st Corinthians 10:31** as found in the New Testament of the Bible:

"So whether you eat or drink or whatever you do, do it all for the glory of God."

How is your everyday life while around other people? What kind of employment do you have? Secretary, engineer, manual labor, going to school, teaching school, keeping your home, watching your children?

Some jobs are exciting, some are boring. Some require decisions, some require none. Some can involve a little bit of misrepresenting the truth. Some may be under a boss who is mean. Some may be among fellow-employees who shirk their duties and try to get by with doing as little as possible. Some may be among people who steal from the company.

Always remember that, wherever you are, that is God's assignment for you in this universal battle between Good and Bad. You must do whatever you do in your daily life as good and honestly as possible. Will others notice? You bet they will! Will they resent you? Maybe. Will they blame God for the way you act? Deep down the resenters probably will. But at least it will make them think about God.

Then someday when they have a problem they are desperate to work through but cannot, who will they turn to? You. And God.

So, be strong. Hold Fast. Stand firm. Do the right thing. And ultimately God will be glorified.

November

1st - The scripture for today, November 1 (11/1), is **Hebrews 11:1** as found in the New Testament of the Bible;

"Now faith is the substance of things hoped for, the evidence of things not seen" (KJV).

Notice, faith is not based on a feeling. It is full of substance, for it is based on evidence. What evidence?

First, faith is complete confidence that the Bible is divine. You can know this in large part because the prophecies about large nations and empires during Bible times came true after the lifetime of the prophets. Today, most people never heard of many of those large nations and empires because their destruction was so complete. But an investigation of encyclopedias shows that, in Bible times, they did exist.

Second, faith is complete confidence that Jesus on earth was divine. You can know this in large part because numerous prophecies about his birth, ministry and death came true centuries after the prophecies were made. No one man could have contrived and forced all those prophecies to be fulfilled in his lifetime.

Finally, faith is complete confidence that the account of Jesus' life was written accurately by witnesses who saw him and talked with him. These witnesses afterwards traveled the world telling people about him, suffering hardships, and often torture and death. They would not have gone through all this for a lie. Further, we have manuscripts that date back to less than a century of the actual events, something no other ancient writing can do.

Yes, faith has substance because it is based on evidence. And in the Bible, you can have all you need.

2nd - The scripture for today, November 2 (11/2), is **Proverbs 11:2** as found in the Old Testament of the Bible:

"When pride comes, then comes disgrace, but with humility comes wisdom."

The word "disgrace" comes from Hebrew qalon meaning **confusion**. It is also translated **dishonor** and **reproach.**

Pride is so hard to control. With the church or clubs or other organizations, do you think your ideas, your points of view, your ways of doing things are the right ideas, views, and ways? Do you accuse others of not cooperating if it is your ideas, views and ways they don't go along with? Is it hard to give up your ideas views and ways for the sake of peace?

Even in doing daily business, does your pride show up? Do you become impatient with clerks in stores who do not help you, with other drivers on the road who are too slow for you, with people delivering things to your home who do not deliver them right to your door, with kids throwing rocks at things that belong to you, people who try to cut in line ahead of you, fellow workers who take credit for your work, and on and on?

Is it hard to sit by and let others be praised when you do better work than they do, or you work harder than they do, or they get the promotion you deserve?

How do you control your pride? Perhaps by comparing yourself, not with others around you, but with Jesus? In the same circumstance, what did he do?

3rd - The scripture for today, November 3 (11/3), is **Luke**

11:3 as found in the New Testament of the Bible:

"Give us each day our daily bread."

This is part of the ideal prayer that Jesus taught his followers to say. We claim to agree with it. But do we completely?

Do you feel like it is your hard-earned money that bought that bread? Do you claim it is our ability to cook that created that bread? Do you claim it was the hard work of the farmers and their equipment that brought us the grain from whence the bread is made? Or the mills that ground it into flour? Or the stores that brought the flour to the consumers?

Ultimately you must look past all of this to that which is beyond your control. It is God who makes the sun shine down upon the seed. It is God who makes the rain to come down to water it. It is God who places life in the buried wheat germ for it to reproduce with a flourish.

Many activities of man bring you your daily bread. But ultimately it is God the Creator who makes it all possible. He not only makes it possible for good people, he brings bread also to the bad. He loves everyone.

4th- The scripture for today, November 4 (11/4), is **Psalm 11:4a** as found in the Old Testament of the Bible:

"The Lord is in his holy temple; the Lord is on his heavenly throne."

No matter what happens in our life, in our town, in our nation, God is still on his throne. No matter how confusing things become, God is still on his throne. No matter how discouraging, God is still on his throne.

Therefore, no matter what, we will worship him

(This has been set to music. Listen to it here: **https://www.youtube.com/watch?v=Ma3lJwa1tbk**)

5th - The scripture for today, November 5 (11/5), is **Ecclesiastes 11:5** as found in the Old Testament of the Bible:

"As you do not know the path of the wind, or how the body is formed in a mother's womb, so you cannot understand the work of God, the Maker of all things."

Are you ever frustrated because you cannot touch God or see God? In times of deep unbearable distress, probably a lot of people feel that need. But, if you could touch or see him, he could not be everywhere at once; he could not be omnipresent. That means, if he was with you where you could see and touch him, the rest of the world would have to wait for him to get done with you and go to the next person.

Are you ever frustrated because you cannot figure out God? In times of great challenges to faith, probably a lot of people feel that need. But, if you could figure out God, He would not be superior to you. It means that either he would not be God, or you would be God also.

Be grateful that you cannot touch or see God. Be grateful you cannot fully understand God. Be grateful that, despite all his greatness, he dearly loves you ~ you, a mere speck in the cosmos. He even knows your name. Ah, what a God ~ the lover of your soul.

6th - The scripture for today, November 6 (11/6), is **Nehemiah 11:6** as found in the Old Testament of the Bible:

"The descendants of Perez who lived in Jerusalem totaled 468 able men."

Just who was Perez, and why was this even mentioned in the Bible? Perez was a descendant of Judah, and an ancestor of Jesus (Matthew 1:3).

Why was living in Jerusalem a big deal at that time? Because Jerusalem had been attacked and destroyed. It was nothing but rubble and ashes. Earlier, other Jews had returned to Jerusalem and rebuilt the temple. Now it was time to rebuild the walls.

These 468 brave people had to agree to move into a burned-out city and rebuild on the ashes of previous homes. In the process of moving building stones out of the way to reuse in the city wall, they surely found skeletons of those who had been slaughtered in the attack decades before.

At first, the Jews had blamed the Babylonians for destroying their city and temple. But eventually they began re-

reading the prophets who had warned them about their own sins. Finally they turned inward and placed the blame where it really belonged: Themselves. Their own pride had destroyed their temple and their city.

Following repentance, they acted. Was it easy rebuilding a broken city? Not any easier than rebuilding a broken home, a broken congregation, a broken life. You must look at your own part in your own destruction and begin building anew.

It took grit. What is yours like? Have you rebuilt anything important lately?

7th - The scripture for today, November 7 (11/7), is **Psalm 11:7** as found in the Old Testament of the Bible:

"For the Lord is righteous, he loves justice; upright men will see his face."

The face of God! How all who believe in God long to see his face. With human perceptions you cannot comprehend it. But you can comprehend this.....

God's eyes ~ "The eyes of the Lord are everywhere, keeping watch on the wicked and the good" (Proverbs 15:1).

God's mouth ~ "I have put my words in your mouth" (Isaiah 51:16).

God's nose ~ "The Lord smelled the pleasing aroma....The smoke of the incense together with the prayers of the saints went up before God" (Genesis 8:21; Revelation 8:4).

God's ears ~ "The eyes of the Lord are on the righteous and his ears are attentive to their cry."

Perhaps when you continually watch both good and bad people around you with the same kind of care that God does, perhaps when you speak the words that come out of the mouth of God, perhaps when you send your prayers like sweet incense to God, perhaps when you are attentive to the silent cry of those around you ~ just perhaps, in some way, you are seeing the face of God. Just perhaps.

8th- The scripture for today, November 8 (11/8), is **Proverbs 11:8** as found in the Old Testament of the Bible:

"The righteous man is rescued from trouble, and it comes on the wicked instead."

We know that God does not always rescue us from trouble here on this temporary earth. He certainly didn't rescue Jesus from all his troubles.

Sometimes God has an assignment for you just as he did for Jesus. He may want you to be in the midst of trouble ~ war, an enemy at work, an obnoxious neighbor, death of a loved one caused by a reckless driver, a government worker demanding a bribe ~ so you can demonstrate to the world the contrast: God's ways vs. Satan's ways.

Eventually, the boomerang effect will take place on those following Satan. What they inflict on you will be inflicted on them.

And eventually, if you have followed God's ways even in times of trouble, he will indeed rescue you. He will welcome you into his home ~ heaven ~ safe for all eternity.

9th - The scripture for today, November 9 (11/9), is **Luke 11:9** as found in the New Testament of the Bible:

" 'So I say to you: Ask and it will be given to you; seek and you will find; knock and the door will be opened to you.' "

Does this mean that, if you ask for your favorite team to win, they will win? Does this mean that, if you ask for a particular job, you will get that job? Or, if you have your eyes on a particular young man or young woman, you will marry that person?

In the context that Jesus said this, he had just taught his disciples what many call the Lord's prayer. In that prayer, Jesus instructed us to ask for a little bit of the physical and a whole lot of the spiritual.

You might say, "Well, that doesn't leave me much to pray for." Oh, yes it does. Shift your focus from yourself. It leaves the rest of the world to pray for. What about their little bit of physical and their whole lot of spiritual? How many people do you pray for? Not as a group, but by name? Not occasionally, but every day?

Well then, will God give you every one of the souls you pray for? God gives everyone free will. He does not force people to follow him. God provides opportunities for people you pray for, and he even moves their hearts. But he does not force them. You must still, keep on praying, even when you feel like someone is hopeless. Maybe they are hopeless during your lifetime. But sometimes someone's soul is saved after your death.

So, pray for others and never tire of it ~ a little bit of the physical and whole lot of the spiritual. Seek and you will find. God will answer in his own way. And that's a promise.

10th - The scripture for today, November 10 (11/10), is **Acts 11:10** as found in the New Testament of the Bible:

"This happened three times and then it was all pulled up to heaven again."

Acts 11 is about God telling Peter that his new heavenly kingdom was for the whole world, not just the Jews. What was pulled up to heaven was a "sheet" holding all the unclean animals which the Old Law of Moses commanded not to eat. Now God was saying, "Eat it. The Old Law of Moses isn't in effect anymore."

This was hard to grasp. So hard that, even though it was God telling Peter directly a new spiritual concept, Peter refused it. So hard for him to believe it, that God had to tell him three times!

Is this the way you are? You read something in the Bible that you never believed before. You read it and re-read it and re-read it, and it never sinks in. After all, you never believed that before. None of your religious friends or leaders believe it. No one on Christian radio/TV or in Christian magazines or the internet believes it.

But God's Word remains what it says. So, over the weeks and months and years you pass through that scripture and read it and re-read it. Over the weeks and months and years its meaning for your life goes right over your head.

Then one day, the light goes on! Viola! You see it! You get it! You are blessed!

11th - The scripture for today, November 11 (11/11), is **Romans 11:11a** as found in the New Testament of the Bible:

"Again I ask: Did they stumble so as to fall beyond recovery? Not at all!"

Weak humans may decide to live for God. But you are still a weak human. Satan has lost you and wants you back. He will try hard to make that happen. Often, the new Christian is the one he attacks the hardest.

Still, Satan never lets up and periodically causes bad things to happen to you so you'll blame God, just as he tried to do with Job. He will tempt you with more things than before you became a Christian in his attempts to get you back. So sometimes you stumble and fall.

God knows what is happening. He stands with you. He is so proud of you when you stand up to Satan and say, "Never! I will not blame or forsake my Lord." He sees how your spiritual muscles are growing.

But, if you sometimes fall, you are not beyond hope. Never,

never believe you are beyond hope! That is a lie! God never leaves you. He continues to stand next to you, holding out his hands and saying, "Take them. I will lift you back up. You will be okay again."

So, you do. And so, he does.

He is amazingly patient with us. He loves you so very much.

12th - The scripture for today, November 12 (11/12), is **Leviticus 11:12** as found in the Old Testament of the Bible:

"Anything living in the water that does not have fins and scales is to be detestable to you."

Is the Law of Moses still in effect, including its requirement for tithing? The scripture above is just one of the over 600 laws in the Law of Moses. They were intricate laws governing both their worship and their everyday life. This one chapter in Leviticus says in part they could not eat camels or coneys or rabbits or pigs. They could not eat eagles, vultures, kites, ravens, owls, gulls, hawks, osprey, storks, herons, hoopoes or bats. But they could eat locusts, katydids, crickets and grasshoppers. And this is just part of chapter 11!

Why did God give so many intricate laws to the Jews? To give them a chance to keep them all perfectly so they could be perfect. In the meantime, God did not give any laws to the Gentiles; He let them try whatever means they could on their own to become perfect. But during the same time period, both the Jews and Gentiles proved to themselves that it was impossible to keep their religions perfectly and thus be perfect themselves.

Now Jesus was ready to come. He lived the Jewish law perfectly, then nailed it to the cross (Colossians 2:14) and established a new last will and Testament (Hebrews 8-9). Now you live under a law of grace, and his commandments revolve around loving God and loving each other.

God cannot co-exist with imperfection. But he loves you and wants you to be his child. Through Jesus he accomplished it; he set you free. He has released you from having to be perfect under the Law, and sees you now through the blood of Jesus and his holy eyes as perfect.

13th - The scripture for today, November 13 (11/13), is **Zechariah 11:13** as found in the Old Testament of the Bible:

"And the Lord said to me, 'Throw it to the potter' ~ the handsome price at which they paid me! So I took the thirty pieces of silver and threw them into the house of the Lord to the potter."

The book of Zechariah is full of prophecies about Jesus, especially circumstances surrounding his death. Compare the above scripture with this written five centuries later when Jesus was betrayed and crucified::

"Then one of the Twelve ~ the one called Judas Iscariot ~ went to the chief priests and asked, 'What are you willing to give me if I hand him [Jesus] over to you?' So they counted out for him thirty silver coins" (Matthew 26:15).

and....

"When Judas, who had betrayed him, saw that Jesus was condemned, he was seized with remorse and returned the thirty silver coins to the chief priests....So Judas threw the money into the temple and left. Then he went away and hanged himself....So they [chief priests] decided to use the money to buy the potter's field as a burial place for foreigners" (Matthew 27:3, 6-7).

The prophet Zechariah wrote this prophecy some five centuries before Jesus. The prophet had been long dead before it was fulfilled. This could not possibly have been contrived to fit such a distant future ~ the exact sum Judas was paid, the money being thrown into the temple and then given to the potters.

This is only one of many proofs. The Bible is the only religious book in the world with built-in proofs it is of divine origin.

Why not keep a collection of the prophecies so you will be prepared when a friend says "The Bible is full of myths"?

14th - The scripture for today, November 14 (11/14), is **Job 11:14f** as found in the Old Testament of the Bible:

"If you put away the sin that is in your hand and allow no evil to dwell in your tent, then you will lift up your face without shame; you will stand firm and without fear."

Job's misguided friend, Zophar, was advising Job that, if he would become perfect ("allow no evil"), he would stand firm before God.

Oh, Zophar! Hadn't he caught on yet? Hadn't he yet realized that no one can be perfect? At the end of this ancient book, God told Zophar and his friends to repent of their accusations toward Job.

Throughout the Old Testament, the Jews tried unsuccessfully to be perfect with the help of the Law of Moses, but they couldn't do it. In the meantime, the nations that had not received the Law were left to try with their own methods to be perfect, and they couldn't do it either.

The only thing that ever has allowed mankind to be perfect has been the blood of Jesus. He was the perfect Lamb of God. It has been eons since Zophar insisted that, if Job became perfect, he wouldn't be sick anymore. As of 2000 years ago, everyone who follows Jesus is able to stand firm, because Jesus can make you perfect, washing away your sins (John 1:29; Acts 22:16).

What treasures we miss when we misinterpret God.

15th - The Scripture for today, November 15 (11/15), is **Revelation 11:15** as found in the New Testament of the Bible:

"The seventh angel sounded his trumpet, and there were loud voices in heaven which said: 'The kingdom of the world has become the kingdom of our Lord and of his Christ, and he will reign for ever and ever!' "

You belong to a kingdom/nation in this world. It is not perfect. Its leaders can sometimes do very bad things. And you wonder how you can stand some of the terrible things that sometimes happen within a government.

But your worldly kingdom/nation is not the only one you can live in. Colossians 1:13 says Jesus "has rescued us from the dominion of darkness and brought us into the kingdom of the Son he loves, in whom we have redemption, the forgiveness of sins."

Rescued! Brought you! Past tense! The kingdom isn't something in the future. It is here now. And it goes by yet another name. Verse 18 says, "And he [Jesus] is the head of the body, the church."

So, when you sometimes become discouraged about your kingdom/nation in this world that you live in, take hope. You can have dual citizenship! For there is another kingdom here, a spiritual one. The king of that kingdom will love you. Forever love you.

16th - The scripture for today, November 16 (11/16), is **John 11:16** as found in the New Testament of the Bible:

"Then Thomas...said to the rest of the disciples, 'Let us also go that we may die with him.' "

This apostle is most often called "Doubting Thomas." We've all heard the story about Thomas being absent when Jesus appeared to the other apostles, then later said he wouldn't believe Jesus was alive again unless he could touch him. Well, the other apostles hadn't believed until they saw him either.

After returning to life, Jesus first appeared to the women. Then, "when they came back from the tomb, they told all these things to the Eleven and to all the others...But they did not believe the women because their words seemed to them like nonsense" (Luke 24:9-11).

Now let's look at our scripture for today. In the months before Jesus' death, he had been traveling everywhere except to Judea where Jerusalem and the religious leaders were. Those leaders had plans to kill Jesus, and everyone knew it. Then Lazarus got sick just six miles from Jerusalem and his sisters begged Jesus to come heal him. It was dangerous for Jesus to go there. He didn't go and Lazarus died.

John 11:7-8 says, "Then he [Jesus] said to his disciples, 'Let us go back to Judea.' 'But Rabbi,' they said, 'a short while ago the Jews tried to stone you, and yet you are going back there?' "

After explaining that he needed to get to Lazarus, it was Thomas who bravely spoke up and said, "Let us also go that we may die with him!"

Later, when Thomas did finally see Jesus, he called him "My Lord and my God (John 20:28).

Doubting Thomas? Far from it! Brave Thomas. Devoted Thomas. Thomas who was willing to follow his Lord to the death. Thomas who was the first to call him God. That was the real Thomas.

17th- The scripture for today, November 17 (11/17), is **1st Chronicles 11:17f** as found in the Old Testament of the Bible:

"David longed for water and said, 'Oh, that someone would get me a drink of water from the well near the gate of Bethlehem.' So the Three broke through the Philistine lines, drew water from the well near the gate of Bethlehem and carried it back to David."

The people who followed David admired him because he knew how to be a good leader. So, many were willing to do anything to make "Captain David" happy. David had been born and raised in Bethlehem. Now he was grown and had a following of those evading power-hungry King Saul, many of whom were brave soldiers. They had traveled throughout the country either evading or defending themselves against this and other enemies.

Their travels took them back to David's home town which was being held by enemy Philistines. For old-time's sake, he longed for a drink from the well he had drunk from many times in his youth. Three of his strongest men risked their lives to bring their captain, David, that drink of water.

How much do you admire the Captain of your Salvation, Jesus? How much are you willing to sacrifice for him? Do you say, "I'm too busy to do anything for Jesus and his kingdom today"? Do you say, "I'm afraid if I say something about Jesus to so-and-so, s/he will insult me"? Do you say, "Someone at church offended me, so I'm not going to worship Jesus anymore?" Do you admire Jesus enough to put yourself in the slightest danger just to do the smallest thing for him?

Ah, Lord Jesus, you put yourself in danger for me. Help me have that same kind of love for you.

18th - The scripture for today, November 18 (11/18), is **Deuteronomy 11:18f** as found in the Old Testament of the Bible:

"Then the Lord's anger will burn against you, and he will shut the heavens so that it will not rain and the ground will yield no produce, and you will soon perish from the good land the Lord is giving you. Fix these words of mine in your hearts and minds; tie them as symbols on your hands and bind them on your foreheads."

Sometimes the country you live in goes through very bad times. You pray for the bad times to end, but they do not. What is going on? The above warning was to the Israelites just before they entered their promised land. God had just said through Moses, don't worship idols.

Perhaps your country is going through bad times because of idol worship. Probably not like the hand-made idols of ancient times, but idols of money and power and lack of morality and ethics.

You may feel all alone in trying to get the people you know to do better. They may laugh at you, scorn you, fire you from you're your job. There have been times in the Bible when a good man prayed, "God, I am the only one left who worships you." God would reply there were a few others trying to do right too. But he never replied he was going to stop the punishing. The country hadn't turned back to God yet.

Therefore, when you are suffering unjustly for what a majority of your countrymen have been doing, you must do it bravely. And while you wait it out, continue to remind yourself, your family, your neighbors, your countrymen of the righteous ways they should be acting.

In bad times, this is your assignment. Be brave and spread

the news. Keep reminding and being as patient with them as God is with you. Perhaps someday, they will listen.

19th - The scripture for today, November 19 (11/19), is **Ezekiel 11:19** as found in the Old Testament of the Bible:

"I will give them an undivided heart and put a new spirit in them; I will remove from them their heart of stone and give them a heart of flesh. Then they will follow my decrees and be careful to keep my laws. They will be my people, and I will be their God."

Although the 600+ commandments in the Old Testament /Covenant Law of Moses were nailed to the cross (Colossians 2:14; Hebrews 8:10-13), God has always had laws to keep us safe. In the New Testament/Covenant era he does not have a lot of laws, but he still has them.

What is our worship like? Is it full of things God never asked us to do? Does our worship elevate God or ourselves? When we're done worshiping, do we say, "We were so great!" or "God is so great!"?

We add all kinds of things to our worship that were commanded only under the Old Testament/Covenant Law of Moses, or things we think would "add to the effectiveness" of our worship. If, for example, it's okay to add things to our singing and praying because then they would sound better, then it is okay to add lemon pie to the Lord's Supper because then it would taste better.

Again, the question: Who are we worshiping and trying to please? God or ourselves? Do we deep down have a heart of stone, but put on our halo and say, "Surely not me"?

20th - The scripture for today, November 20 (11/20), is **Hebrews 11:20ff** as found in the New Testament of the Bible:

"By faith Isaac blessed Jacob and Esau in regard to their future. By faith Jacob when he was dying, blessed each of Joseph's sons....By faith Joseph, when his end was near, spoke about the exodus of the Israelites from Egypt and gave instructions about his bones."

Do you have children that were loving and good when they were young, but when they became older, they changed? Do you sometimes wonder, "How could I have gone so wrong with my children?" True, they have free will. But do you feel like a failure because your children did not turn out the way you had hoped and prayed?

Have faith ~ the faith of Isaac, Jacob, and Joseph. Isaac blessed his sons with his land, even though he did not yet own the land. Jacob blessed his sons with power, even though they did yet not have power. Joseph blessed his sons and his brothers' sons with the land, yet they no longer lived there.

Isaac, Jacob, and Joseph all blessed their children with something they believed would happen someday, even though the evidence was not there. Why? Because they had faith in their children? Actually, it was mostly because they had faith in God. They had faith in what God would do for their children.

Don't give up. Keep trusting God. Never stop having faith in what God (even after we die) will (not can, but will) do for your children.

21st - The scripture for today, November 21 (11/21), is **Acts 11:21** as found in the New Testament of the Bible:

"The Lord's hand was with them, and a great number of people believed and turned to the Lord."

What had just happened? Some Christians in Phoenecia (today's Lebanon), Cyprus (the Mediterranean Island) and Cyrene (in today's North Africa), went to Antioch, a city in Northern Syria near the southern border of today's Turkey. There they established a congregation.

This little congregation ended up being the home congregation of Paul and Barnabas for many years. It started small; we don't know the size it grew to. Regardless of the size, it had foresight and eventually did great things.

Perhaps you live in a town full of churches, but you've compared them with the New Testament, and none of them follows that pattern. Perhaps you have even given up going to church because of this problem. What is stopping you from beginning a little congregation after the New Testament pattern in your home?

New Testament churches were simple ~ not elaborate like those mega-churches out there. And those simple churches have always been dynamic in their simplicity. Who knows but that your new little congregation will someday produce a Paul o a Barnabas....

22nd - The scripture for today, November 22 (11/22), is **Genesis 11:22** as found in the Old Testament of the Bible:

"When Serug had lived 30 years, he became the father of Nahor. And after he became the father of Nahor, Serug lived 200 years and had other sons and daughters."

How can it be that people could live so long in the early centuries of the world? Isn't that stretching things a bit? Isn't it just folklore? Here's more.

Noah had his first son at age 502 (Genesis 5:32, 11:10). Noah lived a total of **950** years (Genesis 9:29). Noah's son, Shem, had his first son at age 100, and lived a total of **600** years (Genesis 11:10-11). Now we have Serug, the 7th-generation grandson of Noah, who had his first son at age 30 and lived a total of **230** years (see above).

Do you see the trend downward of ages after the flood? Most of Noah's life was lived before the flood. Some of Shem's life was lived before, but most of it was after the flood. All of Serug's life was after the flood.

Many scientists believe that the earth originally had a

constant cloud covering like the planet Venus does. Genesis 2:5-6 says it had not rained yet, but a mist rose to water everything. The King James Version of the Bible regarding the flood in Genesis 7:11 says the windows of heaven were opened. Genesis 8:2 says the windows of heaven were stopped.

Notice, it did not say the windows of heaven were closed; they were just stopped, meaning it could rain again periodically after that. If, indeed, Earth did have a constant thick cloud covering before the flood, then humans would have been protected from radiation from the sun, and therefore could live longer. After the change in Earth's atmosphere after the flood, humans being exposed to more radiation, would have lived shorter lives.

Something to think about.... And, one more thought ~ rainbows wouldn't be possible with a constant cloud covering. The flood brought us rainbows! (Genesis 9:13).

23rd - The scripture for today, November 23 (11/23), is **1st Corinthians 11:23ff** as found in the New Testament of the Bible:

"For I received from the Lord what I also passed on to you: The Lord Jesus on the night he was betrayed, took bread, and when he had given thanks, he broke it and said, 'This is my body, which is for you; do this in remembrance of me.' In the same way, after supper he took the cup, saying, 'This cup is the new covenant in my blood; do this whenever you drink it, in remembrance of me.' "

How the hearts of Jesus and his closest friends must have been breaking that night. How the apostles must have struggled to hold back the tears. They all knew the religious leaders in Jerusalem were plotting to execute Jesus. They knew he was taking his life in his hands to be in the city ~ their lives too. How could they part with the one they now knew was the Son of God but also the Son of Mankind ~ their dearest friend?

When we take the communion every Sunday, where are our thoughts? What we're going to do after church? What someone sitting near us is wearing? How the person in front of us is blocking our view?

How many of us during the communion weep as Jesus' apostles must have wept ~ and probably even as Jesus himself wept?

Oh, Jesus, it was my sins that caused you to go through that horrible death! My punishment! How could you love me that much? I fall at your feet. I am so sorry.

24th - The scripture for today, November 24 (11/24), is **Ezekiel 11:24** as found in the Old Testament of the Bible:

"The Spirit lifted me up and brought me to the exiles in Babylonia in the vision given by the Spirit of God."

How did the Holy Spirit move people? Not by making them fall down, but by lifting them up. Ezekiel was the prophet who experienced this most often, and the Spirit never made Ezekiel swoon and fall down. It always lifted him up.

Jesus said in John 14:17 that he would send the Comforter, the Spirit of Truth. And in John 17:17 he said, "Your [God's] Word is Truth."

The Word of God does throw some people off emotionally but not physically, and that's because they don't like everything it says. So, they in turn throw the Bible down in a symbolic sense.

Even today, the Word of God lifts up the soft-hearted and receptive. If we let it, the Word of God can turn our lives around (in a symbolic sense ~ we don't physically turn around) and our souls can soar to the throne of God (in a symbolic sense, not literally).

Be careful when reading something in the Bible that is symbolic to not turn it into something literal. Symbolism is there to convey a greater understanding of God that cannot be put into human words. Keep on reading the Word of God and let the Holy Spirit continue to lift you up.

25th - The scripture for today, November 25 (11/25), is John 11:25 as found in the New Testament of the Bible:

"Jesus said to her, 'I am the resurrection and the life. He who believes in me will live, even though he dies.' "

This has always been puzzling to me: People who have been Christians all their lives find out from their doctor that they are going to die, and they weep and beg God to keep them alive. Why? Heaven is your final destination, not earth. You claim you want to go to heaven, but you do not want to do what is necessary to get there. Death is the door to heaven. Death is not the end, but the beginning! Why would anyone want to cling to this life in this world with all its problems? Why would anyone who claims to be a Christian wail and cry? Is it because living here is like living in a dark cave and we cannot imagine life with light and color and warmth? Where is all that faith you claimed to have?

Be willing to look death in the eye and say, "Jesus has conquered you! I will close my eyes here and open them again to behold my Creator and my Savior!"

26th - The scripture for today, November 26 (11/26), is **John 11:26** as found in the New Testament of the Bible:

" ' And whoever lives and believes in me will never die. Do you believe this?' "

Jesus was talking to the sister of his close friend, Lazarus, who had just died. Of course we understand he was talking about spiritual death ~ the death of our souls. And death in the original Greek means separation; so in the case of our souls, it would be separation from God.

Revelation 20:6 & 14 refer to the second death which is the lake of fire. So what is the first death of our souls?

In John 3:3 Jesus said we must be born again of water and the spirit. Romans 6:4 says "we were therefore buried with him through baptism into death [of that sinful life] in order that, just as

Christ was raised from the dead through the glory of the Father, we too may live a NEW LIFE."

Someone has said "Born once [physically], die twice. Born twice [physically & spiritually], die once." If we emerge from the waters of our mother's womb, that is the first birth of our souls. If we emerge from the waters of baptism, that is our second birth."

Ah, the thought of living on inside the walls of salvation in heaven where Satan can never touch us again. The thought of walking and talking with God and never growing tired of it. The thought of singing with God with pleasure unending.

How reassuring to us when Jesus said believers' souls would never die. Oh, glorious thought.

27th - The scripture for today, November 27 (11/27), is **Mark 11:27f** as found in the New Testament of the Bible:

"...the chief priests, the teachers of the law and the elders came to him [Jesus]. 'By what authority are you doing those things?' they asked. 'And who gave you authority to do this?' "

Of course, the answer to their question is that no one needs authority to teach God's Word. You do not have to be "ordained" by someone else who is a teacher. Actually, you do not have to be "ordained" by another preacher to preach although elderships sometimes laid their hands on people to send them out as missionaries. But that is all. Now, what about you as a teacher?

As you learn more of the Bible, consider teaching your

community's Bible leaders and teachers. Have the courage to speak up and quote something in the Bible which that church may not be following? Then, when your religious teachers and leaders go to you wanting to know by what authority you teach something new, be ready for them with the scriptures.

Periodically tell them about this newly-discovered truth in private ~ gently and respectfully ~ again and again.

Just remember that leaders often take longer to accept a new teaching. It may take them months or years to accept it. Keep on keeping on. And be patient with them.

Pray for your community religious teachers and leaders. Ask God to touch their hearts. He will not go against their natural nature, but if they have honest hearts, it will work. Plant the seed, and God will give the increase (1st Corinthians 3:16). God said, "My Word will not return to me void" (Isaiah 55:11).

28th - The scripture for today, November 28 (11/28), is 1st Corinthians 11:28,31 as found in the New Testament of the Bible:

"A man ought to examine himself before he eats of the bread and drinks of the cup [of the Lord's Supper]....If we judged ourselves, we would not come under judgment."

"When they met on THE first day of the week to break bread" (Acts 20:7), these first-century Christians were meeting to keep the Lord's Supper, for the word ("met") in the original Greek of the New Testament means a religious meeting. Interestingly, the word "the" in the original Greek means each and every without exception perpetually.

Even if we did not know the Greek, look how the Jews (and we) interpreted "Remember THE Sabbath Day to keep it holy". They did not remember the Sabbath day monthly, quarterly or yearly, but weekly. Therefore, , the first-century Christians realized that "When they met on THE first day of the week to break bread" (Acts 20:7), it meant every Sunday.

We can sing, pray, teach and read the Bible any day of the week. What makes Sunday special is that's the day Jesus came back to life, the day Jesus ascended back to heaven, and the day the church was established. Today, on the special first day we are to meet to take the Lord's Supper, the Communion ~ the bread representing his body dying in our place, the wine representing his blood dripped out of his body in our place.

During the Communion, we consider Jesus' terrible sacrifice in order to save us from hell. And we consider our sins that made his sacrifice necessary to save us from hell. Today's scripture tells us that. During our weekly partaking of the Communion, we should be examining ourselves, comparing ourselves to Jesus. It is kind of like taking weekly exams so we will be ready for the big final exam on the Day of Judgment.

God thought of everything ~ weekly remembering the sacrifice of our Lord so that we never take him for granted, and weekly remembering our sins. And, in the process, our souls fall at his feet and whisper "Thank you."

29th - The scripture for today, November 29 (11/29), is **Matthew 11:29f** as found in the New Testament of the Bible:

"Come to me, all you who are weary and burdened, and I will give you rest. Take my yoke upon you and learn from me, for I am gentle and humble in heart, and you will find rest for your souls. For my yoke is easy and my burden is light."

Ah, Lord Jesus. I am so weary worn. It seems everything that could ever go wrong in my life is happening right now. Just when I think I have one problem at least partly under control, another raises its ugly head. Or should I say Satan raises his ugly head? Satan, why are you doing this to me? It is you who is causing all the diseases and problems at work, and the car wreck and progressive blindness. Was it you who set me up in that posh job which you knew was never popular in the company and would only cause me grief? Was this new house I bought with my pay raise worth it after all?

I am so tired. Help me, God. I don't know which way is up anymore. God? I'm calling for you. God? Don't you even care?

"Let's trade, my child. I'll take your burdens and you take mine."

But, Lord, I do not understand. What could your burdens possibly be? You're all comfortable in heaven.

"My child, my burden is to reach out to everyone and tell them how much I love them. My burden is to take their burdens on my shoulders. You can do it too. You can write encouraging notes or emails to them every day. You can open up the newspaper and pray for everyone in it by name. You can call someone who is depressed like you and sing them a sweet song."

But when, Lord? When would I find time?

"Use your brooding time, your crying time, your anger time. Let loose of them so I can brood, cry, and be angry for you. Remember, it's a trade."

Friends, will you continue to carry your burdens and let them weigh you down so you cannot move? Or will you let go of them and smile as Jesus smiled, reach out to others as Jesus reached out, teach God's love as Jesus did?

Jesus would not have asked you to do the impossible. It is your choice. Today let go and let God.

30th - The scripture for today, November 30 (11/30), is **Proverbs 11:30** as found in the Old Testament of the Bible:

"The fruit of the righteous is a tree of life, and he who wins souls is wise."

Remember back in the Garden of Eden? Going by the age of their three sons, Adam and Eve were in the Garden close to one hundred years. Instead of centering on what they did wrong, look at what they did right. They were sinless for nearly a century! Hardly any of us can accomplish in 100 minutes.

Just think. Walking through a garden lush with the beauty of holiness. Walking through a garden with the water of life to drink. Walking through a garden with God (materialized) himself.

How many times did Satan, upright like a king's scepter and perhaps with a crown of gold and ruby on his head, make his way gracefully through the garden, laughing and enjoying the company of newly made humans? How many times did he coil up his tail like a maelstrom spiraling through heavens full of light and beauty as he watched the couple enjoy the fruit of the garden? How many times did this magnificent creature sway back and forth, back and forth as cobras do as he spoke hypnotic words to make them feel like gods?

"Oh, look at the fruit on that tree over there? God told you never to touch it, but God is wrong. Go ahead. Touch it. That's right. Did anything bad happen to you? Of course not, because God is wrong. How about touching it with your lips? That's right. You're not really eating it. You're just touching it. Smell it too. Have you ever smelled anything so wonderful? God doesn't want you to have it. He knows you will learn what evil is and then be as smart at him. God is jealous of you. Go ahead. Take a tiny bite. It won't hurt you. See there? Are you dead like he said you would be? No. You are still alive. God is a liar. I am the only one who tells you the truth. I am on your side. God hates you. Sure, go ahead and take another bite, and Adam might like some too. It's harmless. Do not believe anything God says. He hates you. I am the only one who loves you."

That was a long time ago. Now the Tree of Life, which God withheld from Adam and Eve, is in heaven. Today, our assignment is to warn the world of the wiles of Satan and save their souls from him. But be careful, he is still out there, still beautiful, still successful, and still lying his way into people's lives.

December

1st - The scripture for today, December 1 (12/1), is **Jeremiah 12:1ff** as found in the Old Testament of the Bible:

"Lord, you always give me justice when I bring a case before you to decide. Now let me bring you this complaint: Why are the wicked so prosperous? Why are evil men so happy? You plant them. They take root and their business grows. Their profits multiply, and they are rich. They say, 'Thank God!' But in their hearts they give no credit to you. But as for me ~ Lord, you know my heart ~ you know how much it longs for you. And I am poor, O Lord!"

Now compare this with Job 15:20-24:

"All his days the wicked man suffers torment, the ruthless through all the years stored up for him. Terrifying sounds fill his ears....He despairs of escaping the darkness; he is marked for the sword. He wanders about ~ food for vultures; he knows the day of darkness is at hand. Distress and anguish fill him with terror."

These two passages contradict each other. So what is the problem? The words spoken in Job were by Eliphaz, one of Job's well-meaning friends who took it upon himself to help Job figure out why he had lost all his wealth, all his children, and all his health. Was Eliphaz right?

At the end of the book of Job, is this: "The Lord...said to

Eliphaz the Temanite, "I am angry with you and your two friends because you have not spoken of me what is right." Then God ordered Eliphaz and his friends to sacrifice seven bulls and rams (not small sacrifices), then ask Job to pray for them so God "will not deal with you according to your folly."

When we read scripture, let us be careful to investigate its context and ALL other scriptures on the same subject. Only then can we have the whole picture. Only then can we avoid religious folly.

2nd - The scripture for today, December 2 (12/2), is **Hebrews 12:2** as found in the New Testament of the Bible:

"Let us fix our eyes on Jesus, the author and perfecter of our faith, who for the joy set before him endured the cross, scorning its shame, and set down at the right hand of the throne of God. Consider him who endured such opposition from sinful men, so that you will not grow weary and lose heart."

Yes, life gets pretty rough sometimes. And the harder we try to act like Christians among non-Christians, the more difficult it can become. Did such difficulties stop Jesus? No. He was determined to save as many souls as possible. And he was determined to do the job God gave him before returning to heaven.

What is your assignment? God gives everyone an assignment and you can often tell by what is going wrong in your life. Some bad things are our own doing. But Satan never rests, especially among Christians; and the stronger the Christian is, the harder he pushes them. He does this, according to Job, to get us to blame God.

Those with the old excuse, "If God is so good, why does he allow evil?" is still with us long after Job. Satan makes people forget he exists, thus leaving only one being to blame. He is a liar.

First, bad exists because Satan exists. Second, God gave us free will whether to follow him or not and Christians are subject to those who choose to tear down God and all he represents. Third, God is preparing us for something and is testing us to develop our spiritual muscles here on earth. It may have something to do with the servants Jesus mentioned to whom the Master gave cities to rule over Luke 19:11-27). There are an estimated 400 billion galaxies out there.

Where is your determination? Jesus is preparing a crown for you (James 1:12; Revelation 3:11) so you can reign with him (II Timothy 2:12). Keep your eyes fixed on Jesus. Do not "grow weary and lose heart." Jesus has a crown for you. He has a throne for you. He has a job for you. Will you listen to Satan's lies that God hates everyone and is using them as pawns, or will you listen to the God of the Universe?

3rd - The scripture for today, December 3 (12/3), is **Romans 12:3** as found in the New Testament of the Bible:

"For by the grace given me I say to every one of you: Do not think of yourself more highly than you ought, but rather think of

yourself with sober judgment in accordance with the measure of faith God has given you."

The context of this verse is members of a congregation getting along with each other. He explains that each person is given certain gifts such as serving, teaching, encouraging, contributing and so on (12:6-8).

Within congregations, many disagreements come about because one person has an idea about a good work, and someone else has a different idea about it, and still someone else says some other good work should be done. All sincerely believe their way is the best form of outreach and want a committee to be formed to carry it out. Then egos tend to get involved. The egos tend to get involved.

Perhaps the best way to judge whether you are thinking of yourself more highly than you ought, is to ask yourself this: If I moved away or if I died, would this congregation survive without me? Of course it would. Keep praying, Lord, help me see myself as others do.

It does not matter if you can get a committee formed to help you. If your heart is set on a certain good work, you can always do it alone. You do not need a committee. If your heart is truly set, stop waiting for others whose hearts may be on something else. If your heart is truly set, get out and do it.

Perhaps others will see your results and want to join you later. Perhaps not. Just keep following your heart. Be true to your heart. Be true to the souls that will be helped because you got out there and just did it.

4th- The scripture for today, December 4 (12/4), is **Isaiah 12:4** as found in the Old Testament of the Bible:

"In that day you will say: 'Give thanks to the Lord, call on his name; make known among the nations what he has done, and proclaim that his name is exalted.' "

Do you make known to your part of your nation what God has done for you? When a friend tells you of a difficulty, do you share what you went through that was similar, and that God helped get you through it? Are you ready with an easy-to-remember scripture to prove God cares and God helps? When someone is sick or bereaved, do you let them know that God hurts just as much when they suffer as when he watched his own Son suffer on the cross?

You may live in a country where most people are living immoral and unethical lives. You may live in a country where Christianity is illegal. You can still call on Jesus privately to help a friend in distress. Do not under-estimate the power of "word-of-mouth". He can build great things out of ashes.

Look back over your life. Make a list of some difficult times you and God made it through. Find an applicable verse and memorize it. Find out what is going on in the lives of your friends, co-workers, neighbors. Then be ready to share your story and what God has done for you. It's up to each one of us to do this. Thereby God's name can be exalted throughout the world. Even angels will notice.

5th- The scripture for today, December 5 (12/5), is **Psalm 12:5** as found in the Old Testament of the Bible:

" 'Because of the oppression of the weak and the groaning of the needy, I will now arise,' says the Lord. 'I will protect them from those who malign them.' "

Notice, in this scripture the Lord says, "I will now arise." Sometimes God needs you to endure difficulties so that bad people who cause such problems can be exposed for what they are, and ultimately so Satan can be exposed for what he is. Sometimes that difficulty will last months or years ~ sometimes even a lifetime.

First Corinthians 3:9 in the New Testament says you are a worker together with God. Ephesians 6:12 says "Our struggle is not against flesh and blood, but against rulers, against authorities, against the powers of this dark world and against the spiritual forces of evil in the heavenly [spiritual] realms."

You are where God wants you to be. This is your assignment. Are you up to it? Sometimes your job is just to hang on and not give up on God. That's what Satan is always trying to get you to do, just as he did Job in the Old Testament. God won't leave you in a situation that is impossible for you to endure. I Corinthians 10:13 says, "God is faithful; he will not let you be tempted beyond what you can bear."

So, go ahead and groan in your weakness, beg in your frustration, and cry in your frailty, but hang on. Never let go of

God. That's your part.

As soon as the evil around you is exposed for what it is, you have proven good cannot be conquered by evil, and you have grown spiritually as a result of your experience, Then God will arise. That's God's part.

6th - The scripture for today, December 6 (12/6), is **1st Corinthians 12:6** as found in the New Testament of the Bible:

"There are different kinds of working, but the same God works all of them in all men."

Later in this chapter, Paul explains, "The eye cannot say to the hand, 'I don't need you!' And the head cannot say to the feet, 'I don't need you.' On the contrary, those parts of the body that seem to be weaker are indispensable" (12:21f). He further explains, "For we were all baptized by one Spirit into one body...." (12:13).

For ambitious people in the church who "fight" for position, this is hard to take. Standing in front with a microphone are the most sought-after positions in the church. Such positions have the potential of making you famous. Sorry, folks. Not to God. To God you are dispensable. The church could easily survive without you. God could easily get along without you. So, get control of your ego. Huh?

Do you really and truly believe this? Those who do the seemingly menial works (the "weaker") are indispensable to God ~

you who take food to the bereaved, who read the Bible to the sick, who clean the bathrooms, who daily pray for members and the lost, who give a tract to a friend, who share a bulletin with a neighbor, who send a thinking-of-you card to a lonely person, who mow the church building lawn, who pray with someone who has just told you of a problem, who watch the nursery, who periodically quote a Bible verse to a friend in distress ~ such works that are in the background ~ the ones that don't make it into the "schedule of worship," the bulletin, the newspaper, the church periodicals, the billboards are the ones who are indispensable.

To you who are jealous of people who get to have a more public position in the church and stand in front of the congregation and" lead" don't be. Take heart. God is working more in you then them. Further, public approval by people is their reward. Your reward is from God himself.

You may seem weaker to the others, but to God you are strong. You are mighty. You are God's pride and joy.

7th - The scripture for today, December 7 (12/7), is **Luke 12:7** as found in the New Testament of the Bible:

"Indeed, the very hairs of your head are all numbered. Don't be afraid; you are worth more than many sparrows."

Jesus had just said that God knows every sparrow individually. Amazing! This God of ours, this Creator of ours knows everything that is going on in his world, and knows everyone in his world, regardless of where we are in the world.

Not only does He know everyone, but He knows our name, our likes, our dislikes, our struggles, our joys, if we bump into a door, how much we paid for groceries this week ~ everything. He is with us where ever we go. There is no place we can go that he is not there. We are never alone.

8th - The scripture for today, December 8 (12/8), is **Ecclesiastes 12:8** as found in the Old Testament of the Bible:

" 'Meaningless! Meaningless!' says the teacher. 'Everything is meaningless!' "

About thirty-five years ago some Christians in England did a sidewalk survey in the downtown of a major city. One of their inquiries was: "What question about your life do you ask the most?". The answer almost always was, "Why am I here? What is life all about?".

The entire book of Ecclesiastes is about all the things that the richest and most powerful man in the world did in order to have an enjoyable and fulfilling life: He built palaces and grand temples, he cultivated great gardens, he imported tons of gold and precious stones and fabrics from around the globe, he had numerous wives and mistresses, he built the largest army and navy in the world, he studied every possible subject. At the end, he said it was all meaningless.

The meaning of our life is that we were born to die. This life is temporary. It is our proving ground. This life is the foyer of the life we will have eternally ~ a life in heaven or hell. We were not put here just to have fun, but rather to save as many people as possible from the stronghold of Satan, and take as many people with us to the home of God, our Maker, the Lover of our soul. That is the meaning of life.

9th - The scripture for today, December 9 (12/9), is **2nd Corinthians 12:9** as found in the New Testament of the Bible:

"But he said to me, 'My grace is sufficient for you, for my power is made perfect in weakness.' Therefore, I will boast all the more gladly about my weaknesses, so that Christ's power may rest on me."

Oh, how much we need to be reminded of this scripture. We all have weaknesses. Do you lament the hand you were dealt? Do you lament the country you were born in, the family you were born into, the physical limitations you were born with, the mental, emotional or physical deficiencies you ended up with?

This is your chance! Those weaknesses! Go around others with the same weakness you have with joy in your heart, gladness on your lips and a continual gleam in your eyes! Let God's strength shine in your weakness!

When people begin to sympathize with you, interrupt them and tell them how much God loves you, and how much God loves them! Encourage your "encouragers." Let them go away from you with a new understanding of the blessings of weakness! And perhaps be a little more thankful for their own weaknesses.

Lucky you! You are one of the chosen! God will be glorified in you. He is so proud of you!

10th - The scripture for today, December 10 (12/10), is Job 12:10 as found in the Old Testament of the Bible:

"Is not wisdom found among the aged? Does not long life bring understanding?"

Let's talk a moment about teenagers. Many adults joke that their teen is 16 going on 60. What know-it-alls they've become! Let's look at the situation this way. They may have bodies that have grown to that of an adult. But minds grow much slower, and they must give their minds a chance to catch up.

As adults, it is our responsibility to help their minds catch up. Know enough about the Bible that you can apply scriptures to their activities and interests and friends. You may wish to make a list of your teenager's activities, interests and friends, and then list a scripture next to each. Proverbs is an excellent book to start with. Then when the occasion arises, be ready (even if you have to sneak into the other room a minute to consult your list) to instill some wisdom.

This way, it is not you speaking, but God speaking. God said, "My word will not return to me void" (Isaiah 55:11). And God is older and wiser than all of us.

11th - The scripture for today, December 11 (12/11), is **Romans 12:11** as found in the New Testament of the Bible:

"Never be lacking in zeal, but keep your spiritual fervor, serving the Lord."

Sometimes we get physically tired and our spiritual zeal wanes along with it. We just want to rest. Well, while we rest, we can always become prayer warriors.

When you see friends, ask them, "How was your week/day/month?" Don't ask them how they are, for they will probably reply, "Fine." But if you ask how their week has been, that gives them something to talk about. They'll tell you of things they have been doing. Regardless of what they say, reply, "May I pray for your success in...." or "I'd like to pray for your...."

What the world needs is prayer. Many people have never in their entire life heard someone tell them, "I am praying for you." Be the first. Open up their lives to the love of God.

Prayer is powerful, especially when you are not praying for yourself all the time, but rather are praying for others. Do you have a prayer list? How many are on it besides yourself? Ten? Fifty? A hundred? Five hundred? Is that too many to cover? Not at all. How long does it take to read 500 names in earnest, sincere prayer?

You may say, "But just mentioning a name is so meaningless; it's too simple. God expects me to explain all I know about this person's problem and then do some begging." No he doesn't; not with everyone. Prayer is so very, very powerful, that just mentioning a person's name will bring this person before the very throne of God.

Then, even when you are tired and lack physical zeal, your soul can rise up with spiritual fervor to heaven itself.

12th - The scripture for today, December 12 (12/12), is **2nd Corinthians 12:12** as found in the New Testament of the Bible:

"The things that mark an Apostle ~ signs, wonders and miracles ~ were done among you with great perseverance."

This is so interesting. These are not things that mark Christians in general, but the Apostles.

Jesus told his Apostles that, when they taught the world about Jesus and baptized them, miracles and signs would accompany the believers (Mark 16:17). The miracles and signs followed conversions of believers by the Apostles to whom he was speaking.

Acts 3:6f and 9:40f involved healing by the Apostle Peter, and Acts 20:9f involved healing by the Apostle Paul which they performed to prove their words were the Words of God.

In Acts 6:5-6, the Apostles laid their hands on seven men to serve the church in a special way. Of those men, Stephen performed miracles (6:8) and Philip performed miracles (8:5-7), both to prove their words were the Words of God.

In Romans 1:1,11, the Apostle Paul said he wanted to visit the Christians in Rome so he could impart some spiritual gift. In 1st Corinthians 1:6-7 the Apostle Paul said he imparted spiritual gifts to Christians in Corinth.

We have no examples in the New Testament of anyone other than an Apostle passing on the power to perform miracles. Even the writings of the "Apostolic Fathers" in the late 1st and early 2nd century say things like "Even down to those times there were a few miracles being performed including raising the dead."

Yes, the reason for the miracles was to prove the words of the miracle performer were the Words of God (which had not yet been written down). It was this way with Jesus, and this way with his Apostles. Now that we have the New Testament (Jesus' and his Apostles' teachings in written form) we no longer need the miracles.

They were "marks of an Apostle." The miracles including, healing, renewing the maimed (making limbs grow back), and bringing people back to life. All of them.

Interesting, isn't it?

13th - The scripture for today, December 13 (12/13), is **Ecclesiastes 12:13** as found in the Old Testament of the Bible:

"Now all has been heard; here is the conclusion of the matter: Fear God and keep his commandments, for this is the whole duty of man."

When the King James Version was published in the early 1600s, they italicized all words that were not in the original language of the Bible. The word "duty" above was not in the original. Translators inserted it to help us understand the original. But perhaps in this case it did not help. Fearing God is the whole of man ~ not our duty, but our essence.

Fearing the Lord is a gift. Isaiah 11:2 predicted regarding Jesus: "The Spirit of the Lord will rest on him ~

"...the Spirit of wisdom and of understanding,"

"...the Spirit of counsel and of power,"

"...the Spirit of knowledge and of the fear of the Lord." Solomon had tried everything to find happiness, as he explained in his book of Ecclesiastes ~ Pleasure (ch. 2), hard work (ch. 3), advancement (ch. 4), riches (ch. 5). None brought him true happiness. Eventually, he concluded that only one thing can bring that happiness deep down inside where no one and no situation in life can touch it ~ God. God is the whole of man ~ if we let Him be.

Why? Ecclesiastes 3:11 explains it richly: "He has also set eternity in the hearts of men." Another way to view this is "There is a God-shaped emptiness in everyone's heart." Fill your mind with the Word of God. Then God will fill your heart and being, and make you feel complete.

14th- The scripture for today, December 14 (12/14), is **1st Samuel 12:14** as found in the Old Testament of the Bible:

"If you fear the Lord and serve and obey him and do not rebel against his commands, and if both you and the king who reigns over you follow the Lord your God ~ good!"

The Jews had just insisted on having a king rule over them instead of a supreme judge. Samuel replied and said two IFs. IF they serve and obey the Lord, and IF they both (people and king) follow the Lord, then it is good.

Today as then, some people live in a nation where the king/government does not follow the Lord. What to do? Galatians 5:22 tells us to be loving, joyful, peaceful, patient, kind, good, faithful, gentle, and self-controlled, for "against such things there is no law".

Is it hard to do this when crooked officials are getting all the advantages and you are being cheated and even threatened if you do not cooperate? Indeed, it is. It may seem they are on top of everything. In reality, they are at the bottom. Never ever let others drag you down to their level. It is not worth it. Keep your eyes on God!

Hold fast!

Stand firm!

Do the right thing!

In the end, they will lose. You and God will win. And that is good!

15th - The scripture for today, December 15 (12/15), is **Hebrews 12:15** as found in the New Testament of the Bible:

"See to it that no one misses the grace of God and that no bitter root grows up to cause trouble and defile many."

Really? Bitterness can cause us to miss the grace of God? Bitterness only causes trouble for yourself and others, and defiles you. Bitterness comes from you thinking of yourself more highly than you ought (Romans 12:3), and forgetting that all have sinned and come short of the glory of God (Romans 3:23). Bitterness leads to either bullying or shunning, and ends in broken relationships and a cancer of the heart. It can cost us our eternal salvation.

The opposite of bitterness is forgiveness. Forgiveness does not mean you condone what someone else has done. It means you let go of it and let God handle it. It means you wish the best for the offending person or situation. You can wish even the most hardened criminal will someday turn to God and turn his life around. How many times in your lifetime have you asked God to forgive you for the same things over and over? God forgives you as you forgive others.

Forgiveness lifts weights off of you until you feel as though you could soar. Forgiveness takes the clouds away and brings back the sunshine. Forgiveness makes sure you do not miss the grace of God.

16th - The scripture for today, December 16 (12/16), is **Romans 12:16** as found in the New Testament of the Bible:

"Live in harmony with one another. Do not be proud, but be willing to associate with people of low position. Do not be conceited."

Who do you associate with? Just people who are like you?

Do you consider people richer than you as greedy, uncaring and uppity? And people poorer than you as lazy, users and lowlifes?

Do you consider people smarter than you as impractical with their heads in the clouds? And people duller than you as incapable of understanding anything important?

Do you consider people stronger than you as egotistical show-offs? And people weaker than you as not worthy of notice?

How this hurts your Savior who died for everyone. We are all sinners. We all need the same saving grace.

Live in harmony with all. Make everyone ~ both those "above" you and "below" you ~ feel the love of God through you. Feel the harmony.

17th - The scripture for today, December 17 (12/17), is **Revelation 12:17** as found in the New Testament of the Bible:

"Then the dragon was enraged at the woman and went off to make war against the rest of her offspring ~ those who obey God's commandments and hold to the testimony of Jesus."

Verse 9 says the dragon is also the serpent which is also Satan.

Whose side are you on? Do have a hard time coming to terms with your own personality and drives? Are you one of those people who seem to be enraged all the time? You may have long ago given up on being able to change. But you can direct your anger. If you want to be enraged at someone, be angry at Satan. Go to war with Satan. Rage at everything he is doing. Lash out at everything he stands for.

Are you angry at the church or at God? Keep that energy and switch sides. Be a spiritual warrior, a Christian soldier of the Lord.

Have you tried and just cannot get rid of anger in your life? You may mellow in your old age, but that mellowness is a long way off. You have never experienced rage until you have understood Satan. He is enraged at you. He is enraged at anyone who loves God or good people. Go ahead. Get on God's side, enroll in the army of the Lord, and use your anger against Satan.

Does it work? Paul said in 1st Timothy 1:13, "I was a violent man." Yet, he converted thousands of people all over southern Europe, as he "fought the good fight".

18th - The scripture for today, December 18 (12/18), is **Hebrews 12:18ff** as found in the New Testament of the Bible:

"You have not come to a mountain [Sinai] that can be touched and that is burning with fire; to darkness, gloom and storms; to a trumpet blast.... The sight was so terrifying that Moses said, 'I am trembling with fear.' "

"But you have come to Mount Zion, to the heavenly Jerusalem, the city of the living God. You have come to thousands upon thousands of angels in joyful assembly, to the church of the first-born, whose names are written in heaven. You have come to God the judge of all men, to the spirits of righteous men made perfect, to Jesus the mediator of a NEW COVENANT...."

The first paragraph refers to Mount Sinai in Arabia on which Moses received what was called the Law of Moses ~ not just 10 commandments, but over 600 ~ over a 40-day period. It was a terrifying experience for everyone. The second paragraph refers to Mount Zion where the temple was built in Jerusalem by the Jews.

Next, the writer of Hebrews shows that Jesus took mankind higher than either physical mountain through his new agreement with us. He took us from the Old Agreement of the Law of Moses to the New Agreement of the Law of Grace. He took us from the physical to the spiritual. The Christian Jerusalem is in heaven where angels and the living God dwell (Revelation 21).

Why would anyone want to dip into the old Law of Moses to get justification to do showy things in worship when Christian worship is so much more simple and spiritual? Why would anyone want to rebuild the Jewish temple when the temple is in the heavenly Jerusalem? Let us climb down off that old mountain of the Law and physical temple and soar with the angels to the spiritual, the heavenly.

19th - The Scripture for today, December 19 (12/19), is **Romans 12:19** as found in the New Testament of the Bible:

"Do not take revenge, my friends, but leave room for God's wrath, for it is written: 'It is mine to avenge; I will repay,' says the Lord."

Thank God, he took away the old Law of Moses and gave you the new Law of Jesus instead. Under the Law of Moses, you had to take revenge yourself. You had to stone adulterers and children who were disrespectful to you as their parent. If someone killed a relative, you were obligated to go out and kill the killer. If someone knocked out the eye or tooth of a relative, you were required to go out and take that person's eye or tooth.

Now God says to forgive and do good to your enemy (verse 20-21). That's what God did for you who once was his enemy as a sinner. As you are merciful to others, he is merciful to you.

Forgiveness is not condoning evil, but wishing a better life for whoever did something bad to you. You may forever be afraid of that person, but you must forgive. Hard to do? Indeed! But, with God, anything is possible. So, let go of it. Let go of them. Let God take care of it. He has released you of that burden. Released you to "overcome evil with good".

20th - The scripture for today, December 20 (12/20), is **2nd Corinthians 12:20b** as found in the New Testament of the

Bible:

"....I fear that there may be quarreling, jealousy, outbursts of anger, factions, slander, gossip, arrogance and disorder."

It can happen among well-meaning people trying to accomplish the same good work but from different angles. Do you insist your way is the best way, and people will be lost if the committee or congregation doesn't do things your way? Do you then get hurt and think (or say) everyone else doesn't love the lost like you do? Then are you tempted to switch congregations or just drop out of the church completely?

A good test when personalities clash is to ask yourself, "Would this congregation survive without me?" Of course, it would. It did before you came and will after.

A good solution: If your heart is set on a certain good work, but no one else's heart is, do what you can alone. You don't need a committee to follow your heart.

Let us prefer one another, honor one another, and love one another. We are family ~ God's family.

21st - The scripture for today, December 21 (12/21), is **Matthew 12:21** as found in the New Testament of the Bible:

"In his name the nations will put their hope."

Ah, this is the stuff dreams are made of ~ the dreams of Christians, that is. Revelation 21:2, 9, & 26 says regarding the New Jerusalem which is the Bride of Christ which is the Church: "The glory and honor of the nations will be brought into it."

The nation you live in may not be in good hands right now, or it may be thriving with high morals, or it may be diving into poverty. But your nation can hope ~ hope in Jesus.

Never lose hope. You are just one person, but there is great power in one. Jesus came to provide that hope. In your own way, in your own life, use your power of one. Show your nation how it can hope, how it can have glory and how it can have honor.

22nd - The scripture for today, December 22 (12/22), is **1st Samuel 12:22** as found in the Old Testament of the Bible:

"For the sake of his great name, the Lord will not reject his people, because the Lord was pleased to make you his own."

Among all the pretend gods that people have worshiped, there has never been one who made people because he wanted people to love and wanted them to be his children. Islam, for example, teaches Allah made man to have someone to worship him. Allah has 99 names, but none of them is love. It is the same with other purported gods. So sad.

Oh, how much mankind misses by not opening up to the one and only true God. He wants you to be his child! He wants to lavish you with his love.

God made you because God is Love. Love must have

someone to love. That's you, dear friend. That's you!

Amazing love of God. It pleases him to make you his own. It pleases him! You the lowly. You the weak. You the inconsistent. You the sinner.

Let your soul be elevated by the God of Love. Let your heart be warmed. Let your spirit be touched with eternity. Then lift up your voice and shout, "My soul is overwhelmed with joy!"

23rd - The scripture for today, December 23 (12/23), is **1st Samuel 12:23** as found in the Old Testament of the Bible:

"As for me, far be it from me that I should sin against the Lord by failing to pray for you. And I will teach you the way that is good and right."

It's actually a sin not to pray for others!

Do your prayers get bogged down in the mire of me and mine? Do you wonder why you can't pray for more than a couple minutes ~ five on a good day? Satan gets you to do this; he is the enemy of prayer because he knows how powerful it is.

Who is on your prayer list? Pray for people by name. Your neighbors. People you work with. Your government officials ~ both good and bad. People in nursing homes. People in your congregation. People in the military. People being persecuted, imprisoned and even killed because they are Christians. Missionaries. Children in an orphan home. Salespeople at the store. Local school teachers. People in your newspaper.

Pray for 15 minutes a day. Half an hour each day. An hour every day. It's oh so easy when you stop praying only for you and yours and pray for others.

Pray for them by name. And tell them that you do. Some people have never been told, "I am praying for you". God loves to answer prayer.

Do not sin by praying only for yourself and your family. Take the time to take others soaring with you when you pray. Then stand back and watch God respond to your prayers with power that will astound you.

24th - The scripture for today, December 24 (12/24), is **Luke 12:24** as found in the New Testament of the Bible:

"Consider the ravens: They do not sow or reap, they have no storeroom or barn; yet God feeds them. And how much more valuable you are than birds!"

In many nations right now, things are financially strained. Luxuries? No. To be able to live until tomorrow? Yes.

Which is more valuable? To impress men or impress God? A life dedicated to things impresses men. A life dedicated to doing good things impresses God.

I know of a group of believers in Jesus recently in an African country who had to flee soldiers who were after Christians. They had to run immediately upon sight of the soldiers. No time to pack anything. Just run. Escape. Run. Escape.

To get to true safety, they had to walk a hundred miles. What did they eat? Grass. Leaves from bushes. Tree roots. But they made it. They made it to safety and the loving, protective arms of other Christians.

Today, instead of a luxury, can you send the money to people in parts of the world who are struggling to stay alive? Struggling to stay safe because they are Christians?

Consider the ravens.

PS ~ Those of you with children, and you cannot get them much for Christmas: Write IOU's to them and put each one in a box. Wrap each with typing paper if you don't have Christmas paper. And with a red or green crayon, draw a ribbon on top. What's on the IOU's? "One hour of coloring with you." "One hour of playing ball with you." "Three hours of hiking with you." "Two hours of baking cookies with you." Give yourself for Christmas!

25th - The scripture for today, December 25 (12/25), is **Proverbs 12:25** as found in the Old Testament of the Bible:

"An anxious heart weighs a man down, but a kind word cheers him up."

Yesterday, did you see anyone sitting alone looking downcast? Go back there today. S/he may not be there, but someone else may be. It may be a gathering place for the lonely, the discouraged. Smile at them and whisper, "Jesus loves you." Have a lengthy conversation with them and show them they are worthy of your time. Listen to them. Share with them.

Do you periodically see "beggars" at a certain location? They may squander donations or use them to buy food. Either way, being a beggar isn't people's life's goal. You do not know their story. Everyone has a story. Their hearts are anxious about something.

Give them a little change, maybe wrap it in a verse from the Bible. Ask them if they have family and if their family would accept them back. If so, encourage them to "go home." Perhaps pay for a bus ticket back home. If they say they can't go home, try anyway. Tell them you will pray for them. Smile at them, and whisper, "Jesus loves you."

Today, do you know of a place where travelers usually stay or gather? Sometimes at truck stops there are drivers who could not get home. Go to one of these places prepared to give each of them something special, or even invite them to your home for a Christmas feast.

Jesus encouraged and helped the downhearted. Is it uncomfortable being in their world? Yes. Dare to disturb your happiness to enter their world and show Jesus to the downhearted. Dare to be a star shining on them in their darkness.

26th - The scripture for today, December 26 (12/26), is John 12:26 as found in the New Testament of the Bible:

"Whoever serves me must follow me; and where I am, my servant also

will be. My Father will honor the one who serves me."

Ah, Lord Jesus. We claim we understand how humble you were, then build great cathedrals which we claim are to your glory but which are really to our glory. We organize great musical performances which we claim are to your glory, but which are really to our glory.

Just where was Jesus when he was on earth saying this? In a posh hotel in Jerusalem? Did he have great musicians performing in the background? Did he stand on a podium and declare this to multitudes? Who are you fooling when you declare you are his servant.

Who or what are you really a servant to? Power in a work place, club, congregation, neighborhood? Prestige in a community, an occupation, an organization? Self-indulgence of money, music, entertainment?

While you are pursuing things in life, is Jesus there with you? Are you doing what he would be busy doing? Are you where he was when he said this?

Dare to be a servant to the power of Jesus' love, prestige in the eyes of God, self-indulgence in the joy of worshiping Him. In this only is there true and enduring honor.

27th- The scripture for today, December 27 (12/27), is **1st Kings 12:27** as found in the Old Testament of the Bible:

"If these people go up to offer sacrifices at the temple of the Lord

in Jerusalem [not some other capital city], they will again give their allegiance to their lord, Rehoboam king of Judah."

For centuries and millenniums, kings selected a patron god for their nation, a god they most revered to protect them. The patron god was selected by the king. Nations were always ruled by either a high priest or king. Some nations even had priest-kings.

So, when Constantine conquered much of Europe and set up his empire, he needed a patron god. One day during a battle, he looked up and saw a cloud formation that reminded him of things he'd heard about Jesus. So he made Jesus his patron God, and Christianity his empire's required religion. He even rode his army through rivers, then declared them baptized. He ordered conquered peoples to be baptized or killed. Headquarters was Rome.

Luther was friends of the Duke [king] of Germany, so when he broke off from Rome, the official state religion became Lutheranism. John Calvin was in the government of Switzerland, so when it broke off from Rome, the official state religion became Calvinism. When the king of England broke off from Rome, he became head of the Church of England (and Prince Charles is head of the Church there today). John Knox was influential with the parliament of Scotland, so his Presbyterianism became the official religion of Scotland.

In each instance, the king or parliament could force its citizens to follow the chosen religion of that nation. If people didn't, they could legally put them in prison, torture them, and execute them at will. And, in earlier centuries, they did just that.

Eventually, the idea of separating religion from the state government became popular in the Western World. And that is where many nations are today. But it does not mean people in government cannot express religion. It just means they cannot force citizens to be a particular government-selected religion or be in danger of punishment. That is true "separation of church and state".

28th - The scripture for today, December 28 (12/28), is **Hebrews 12:28** as found in the New Testament of the Bible:

"Therefore, since we are receiving a kingdom that cannot be shaken, let us be thankful and so worship God acceptably with reverence and awe."

Notice this is in present tense. The kingdom is not something in the future, but is now.

Jesus said in Luke 9:27 that some listening to him would still be alive when the kingdom came. Colossians 1:13 says God HAS (not will) rescued us from the dominion of darkness and BROUGHT (not will) us into the kingdom.

In fact, at the end, Jesus will not come back to earth to set up a kingdom. Instead, he will at that time hand the already-existing kingdom over to the Father (I Corinthians 15:24).

So what does this mean to us? Revelation 1:5-6 says that all who have been freed from our sins by the blood of Jesus have become a kingdom of priests. And as such, we daily offer our bodies as living sacrifices in the service to our king (Romans 12:1).

Christians have dual citizenship. Christians are citizens of the earthly nation they live in, and citizens of the kingdom of heaven. What glory God has already bestowed upon us.

So let us be thankful, and worship Him with reverence and awe.

29th - The scripture for today, December 29 (12/29), **is Deuteronomy 12:29** as found in the Old Testament of the Bible:

"The Lord your God will cut off before you the nations you are about to invade and dispossess."

Why would a good God drive people (the Amorite nations) from their own land so that other people (the Jews) could live there? Way back in Genesis 15, God promised Abraham that his descendants would possess the land he lived in as a wanderer, but first they would be enslaved in a foreign country some 400 years. During that time, they would multiply. Indeed, they did grow from 70 of Abraham's grandchildren to over three million.

Then it would be time for his descendants to possess the land. Why so long in the future? Verse 16 explains it: "For the sin of the Amorites has not yet reached its full measure." God always gives people plenty of time to repent and change.

The Jews did finally possess the Promised Land, but God warned them, "If you defile the land, it will vomit you out as it vomited out the nations that were before you" (Leviticus 18:28). Indeed, they did eventually defile the land with their own sins, so several centuries later, they were dispossessed and forced to go to Assyria and Babylon by their conquerors. Yes, God keeps his promises ~ to both good and bad.

Today, regardless of the condition of the nation you live in on earth, look ahead to that even better promise of an even better land ~ that spiritual Promised Land ~ heaven. And it will be forever good.

30th - The Scripture for today, December 30 (12/30), is **Matthew 12:30**, as found in the New Testament of the Bible:

"He who is not with me is against me, and he who does not gather with me scatters."

What? You can't just drift along just showing up at church services and that is all? You must gather people to him?. Are you sure? Oh, I don' know enough; besides, I'm too busy.

Deep down inside, do you fear that, if you bring Jesus into a conversation, people will do you great harm and become dangerous enemies? Although in some countries of the world this is true, in most it is not. Still, do you quake at the thought of bringing up Jesus to your friends, and even to strangers?

That is Satan's lie. He has gotten into your head and you are believing him. Most people will appreciate a little discussion about Jesus because most people do not attend worship anywhere and know little about the Bible.

Instead of listening to Satan, perhaps you should quake that some of your friends are headed to hell. Satan puts fear in your heart. Do not give in to Satan. "Perfect love casts out fear" (1st John 4:18). Do as Jesus did: "Seek and save the lost" (Luke 9:10).

Help your friends who do not know they need help. Overcome your fear for yourself and give in to the fear for their souls. It can be done. Stop watching so much television or playing endless games. Give it a try. If it were your soul, would you want someone to at least try to save you? Rise up! Defy Satan! Dare to be a gatherer of souls staring today.

31st - The scripture for today, December 31 (12/31), is **Luke 12:31** as found in the New Testament of the Bible:

"But seek his kingdom and these things will be given to you as well."

The kingdom is already here (Luke 9:27; Colossians 1:13), but heaven is not. That is the final destination of the kingdom. Do you actively seek God's kingdom? Or do you drift and think God should feel obligated to take you into his heaven? Do you feel like you're "not so bad", so God would be bad to not take you into his heaven?

Heaven is God's home, not yours. God has a door into his home, just like you have a door into your home. God is not required to open his door to just anyone, just like you are not required to open your door to just anyone. You cannot just show up at the door and smile and assume he will let you in, any more than people who knock on our door and smile can assume you will let them in.

You let people into your home who you have gotten to know and whose motives you trust. Have you given God a chance to get to know you and trust your motives? Are your daily motives to enter heaven, God's home? Do you even like God?

This life you live on earth is not your permanent life or residence. This is the testing place to see how you handle problems and to see how much your spiritual muscles will grow. God has plans for Christians in heaven we do not know about. What we do know is that he is not a God of idleness. Do you live like the earth is all there is? Do you fear hell? Do you prefer heaven where people will worship all the time? Does that sound boring to you?

You are about to enter a brand-new year. Today, decide to start over fresh and set your new goal: To enter God's home his way and live with him. Forever.

Thank You

Thanks for reading my book! I'm so honored that you chose to spend your precious time with my inspirational thoughts. You are appreciated. I'm an independent author who relies on my readers to help spread the word about stories you enjoy. Would you take a few minutes to let your friends know on Facebook, Pinterest... wherever you hang out online?

Also, each honest review at online retailers means a lot to me and helps other readers know if this is a book they might enjoy. I welcome contact from readers. At my website (below), you can do so. You can also sign up for my newsletter (below) to be notified of new releases, giveaways, gift certificates, and more!

Buy Your Next Book Now

Non-Fiction

CHURCH HISTORY,
CHRISTIAN LIFE &
TOPICS OF THE BIBLE
http://bit.ly/BibleTopics

Workbooks

BIBLE WORKBOOKS TEENS & ADULTS
http://bit.ly/BibleWorkbooks

Historical Novels

THEY MET JESUS Series of 8
http://bit.ly/TheyMetJesus

INTREPID MEN OF GOD Ongoing Series
http://bit.ly/IntrepidMen

Children's Books

A CHILD'S LIFE OF CHRIST - 8-book series
http://bit.ly/ChildsLifeOfChristSet
A CHILD'S BIBLE HEROES - 10-book series
http://bit.ly/Bible-Heroes
A CHILD'S BIBLE KIDS - 8-book series
http://bit.ly/bible-kids

All Ages

PUZZLES & SONGS
http://bit.ly/BibleFun

About the Author

Katheryn Maddox Haddad has a bachelor's degree in English, Bible and social science from Harding University and part of a master's degree in Bible, including Greek, from the Harding Graduate School of Theology, she also has a master's degree in management and human relations from Abilene University.

Having grown up freezing in the northern United States, she now lives in Arizona where she doesn't have to shovel sunshine. She basks in 100-degree weather, palm trees, cacti, and a computer with most of the letters worn off.

The author of over sixty-five books, both non-fiction and fiction, she sees no letup in the future. For many years, she has been sending out every morning a daily scripture and short inspirational thought to some 30,000 people around the world.

Half of her day she spends writing, and the other half teaching English over the internet worldwide using the Bible as textbook. She has taught over 6000 Muslims through World English Institute. Students she has converted to Christianity are in hiding in Afghanistan, Iran, Iraq, Yemen, Uzbekistan, Somalia, Jordan, Pakistan, Palestine, and Tajikistan. "They are my heroes," she declares.

When writing her biblical historical novels, she spends an average of 300 hours researching ancient historians such as Josephus, archaeological digs for the layout of cities, their language, culture and politics.

She is a member of American Christian Fiction Writers, Christian Writers of the West, and Phoenix Screenwriters Association.

Connect With Katheryn

Website: **https://inspirationsbykatheryn.com**
Facebook: **http://bit.ly/Katheryn-Facebook**
Linkedin: **http://bit.ly/KatherynLinkedin**
Pinterest: **http://bit.ly/KatherynsStoryBoard**
Youtube: **http://bit.ly/KatherynBookTrailers**

Bible House carries all my paperbacks at discounts
http://bit.ly/biblehousediscounts

Get A Free Book

Sign up for Katheryn's monthly newsletter with free reads for adults and children, and insider tips on what's coming next. **http://bit.ly/katheryn**

Join My Dream Team

Members get the first peak at my newest book and have fun offering me advice sometimes. I have a point system of rewards for helping me get the word out. Check it out here: **http://bit.ly/KatherynsDreamTeam**

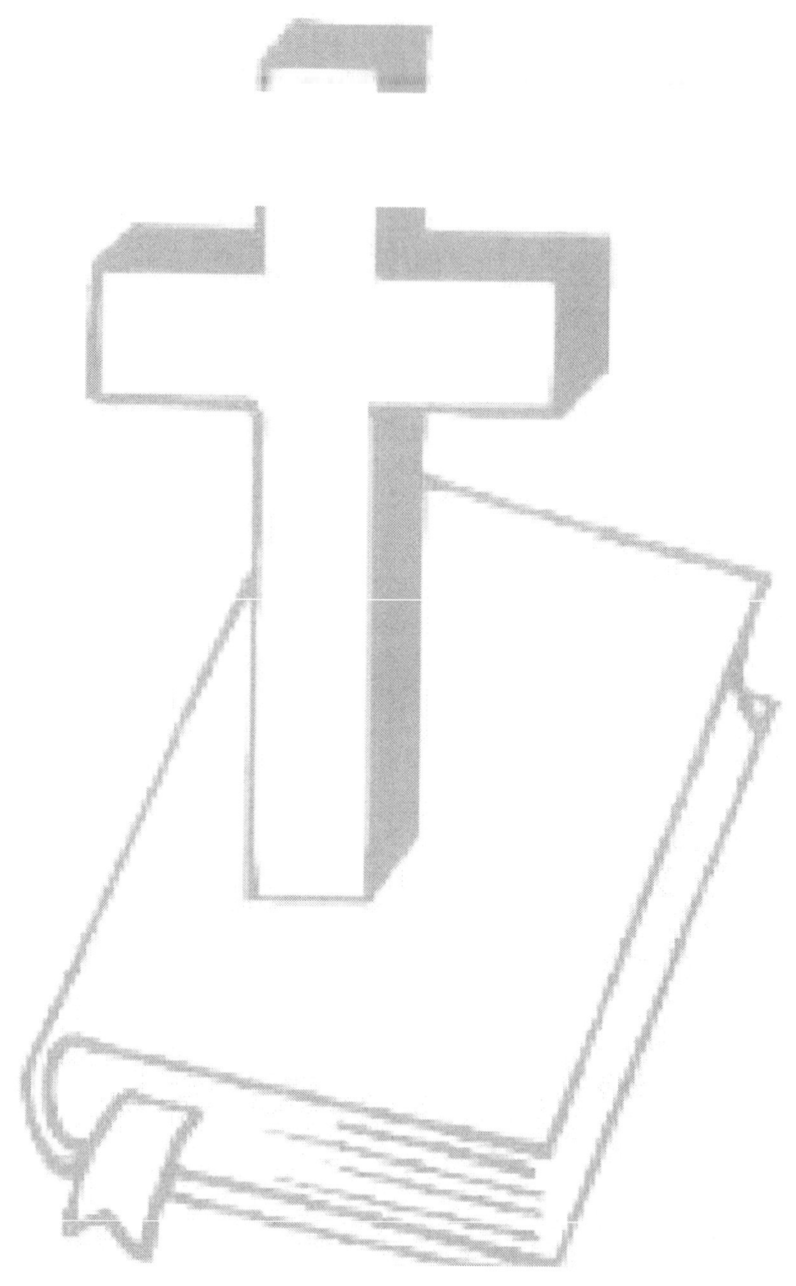